Such As Us

SUCH AS US

SOUTHERN VOICES of the THIRTIES

Edited by

Tom E. Terrill
Jerrold Hirsch

Do you reckon that folks sure enough want to read about such as us?
—Farm woman, Saluda, North Carolina, 1939

W · W · NORTON & COMPANY · New York · London

First published as a Norton paperback 1979 by arrangement with the
University of North Carolina Press.

Books That Live
The Norton imprint on a book means that in the publisher's estimation
it is a book not for a single season but for the years.
W. W. Norton & Company, Inc.

Library of Congress Cataloging in Publication Data
Main entry under title:

Such as us: Southern voices of the thirties
Bibliography: p.
Includes index.
1. Southern States—Social conditions—Case studies.
I. Terrill, Tom E.   II. Hirsch, Jerrold 1948–
HN79.A13S87   1979   309.1'75   79-1135
ISBN 0-393-00927-0 pbk.

1 2 3 4 5 6 7 8 9 0

Contents

Acknowledgments / ix

Introduction / xi

Talking Is My Life / *James Aswell* / 3

The Civil War: Victory and Defeat

  Like a Shadow That Declineth / *Ruth Clark, James Aswell* / 11

  I'se Still Traveling 'Cause I Got Faith in God /
    Geneva Tonsill / 18

  No Stick-Leg / *Bernice Kelly Harris* / 29

Farms and Farmers

  Horse Trader / *Harry H. Fain* / 45

  Ain't Got No Screens / *Walter Rowland* / 54

  Jim Jeffcoat / *William O. Foster* / 58

  The Landlord Has His Troubles / *Bernice Kelly Harris* / 64

  Jackson Bullitt, a Small Landlord / *Bernice Kelly Harris* / 72

  In Abraham's Bosom / *F. Donald Atwell* / 79

  Aaron and Mary Matthews / *Bernice Kelly Harris* / 86

  'Backer Barning / *Mary A. Hicks, Edwin Massingill* / 94

  Tobacco's in My Blood / *Mary A. Hicks* / 99

  A Day on the Farm / *Attributed to Gertha Couric* / 103

  Just a Plain Two-Horse Farm / *Bernice Kelly Harris* / 108

Towns, Mills, and Scattered Places

From the Mountains Faring /
  Dean Newman, Jennette Edwards, James Aswell / 121

Green Fields Far Away / *N. S. McDonald* / 128

A Day on Factory Hill / *Ida L. Moore* / 144

A Retired Mill Worker / *Sadie B. Hornsby* / 147

There's Always a Judas / *Ida L. Moore* / 157

When a Man Believes / *Ida L. Moore* / 170

No Union for Me / *Ida L. Moore* / 188

The Rig-Builder / *Attributed to Ned T. DeWitt* / 190

A Woman's Like a Dumb Animal / *Jack Kytle* / 205

My WPA Man / *Robert McKinney* / 219

Chimney Sweeper's Holiday / *Robert McKinney* / 227

White Over Black: Anxious Times . . . an Uncertain Future

Yes, Lord, I'se Done Tried to Serve You Faithful /
  Grace McCune, Sarah H. Hall, John N. Booth / 243

Tech 'Er Off, Charlie / *Author unknown* / 254

Roger T. Stevenson, Justice of the Peace /
  Bernice Kelly Harris / 260

Sam Sets It Down / *Bernice Kelly Harris* / 270

Appendixes / 283

Bibliographical Essay / 289

Index / 297

Credits for Photographs / 303

Acknowledgments

This is a book about the South as told by anonymous Southerners. While we were enthusiastic about the idea, it was not entirely our own. Thirty-nine years ago The University of North Carolina Press published *These Are Our Lives*. The idea for the book came from W. T. Couch, who was then director of the Press and Southeast Regional Director of the Federal Writers' Project. Couch planned a sequel to *These Are Our Lives*, but because of circumstances beyond his control, he was unable to publish it. The present book exists because of W. T. Couch's past efforts. We also wish to thank him for the personal encouragement he has given us. And we are happy that *Such As Us* is being published by the press that he did so much to establish. We also want to thank both the employees of the Writers' Project who went out and interviewed the people speaking in this book and the people who willingly told their stories. Together we have examined and discussed the materials in this volume and the format in which these stories are arranged. We shared equally the work that went into this volume and we accept equal responsibility for the final results.

Various institutions and their staffs were helpful to us. Without the financial support we received from the National Endowment for the Humanities, and the Committee for Scholarly Research and Productive Scholarship and Provost Keith E. Davis of the University of South Carolina, it would have been difficult for us to have completed this project. The staffs of the Southern Historical Collection, The University of North Carolina Library, Chapel Hill, and of the University of South Carolina Library, Columbia, aided and supported us in our work. We are particularly indebted to Carolyn A. Wallace, director of the Southern Historical Collection, Ellen B. Neal, Richard A. Shrader, and Allen H. Stokes, Jr. Matthew Hodgson, director of The University of North Carolina Press, and his colleagues encouraged our efforts while providing helpful criticism.

Our colleagues at The University of North Carolina and the University of South Carolina listened to us discuss these materials, asked thoughtful questions, and made useful suggestions. Most remarkably, they did not grow tired, visibly at least, either of our enthusiasm for these materials or of us. The following read and commented on various aspects of the manuscript: Jacquelyn D. Hall, John F. Kasson, Frank S. Kessler, John H. Roper, John S. Reed, Marcia Synnott, and Robert M. Weir. They did not always approve of our ideas or how we stated them, but always their comments were valuable. Susan D. Collins, Elizabeth Gourlay, Preshema Y. Harris, Connie Malone, and Carol Wilburn patiently typed the manuscript.

In addition to reading parts of the manuscript, the following individuals played crucial and supportive roles at various stages of this project: Charles W. Eagles, Joseph A. Herzenberg, George B. Tindall, and Sarah N. Terrill and Karen N. Hirsch.

Introduction

The people speaking in this book may at first seem quaint, like curios from a past time and a different world. They lived in a rural, impoverished, and segregated region. For many of them time was measured less by calendar and clock than by season and task—planting, harvesting, and laying by. They worked on farms, in mills, oil fields, coal mines, and other people's homes. They were all adults before 1930. Most were poor before the Great Depression; then things got worse. Their life histories provide a view of the world they saw, experienced, and helped create. They tell about growing up, getting married, having children, prospering (or not), getting old. They describe how major events—the Civil War, Emancipation, World War I, the New Deal—affected them. They talk about race relations, family life, sex roles, and religious beliefs.

Fellow Southerners, employed by the Federal Writers' Project, a New Deal program, collected these life histories. Of the more than one thousand stories collected, only thirty–five were published in the critically acclaimed work *These Are Our Lives* (1939). Plans to issue more volumes were abandoned when rising anti–New Deal sentiment forced the Writers' Project to curtail its most innovative undertakings.

Events elsewhere refocused national attention from domestic disorder to world conflict. World War II forced concentration on a new threat to survival. The war also brought unprecedented prosperity to the South as well as to the rest of the nation. Buoyed by high, sustained levels of government spending, especially for national defense, the prosperity continued for more than twenty years. Thus World War II marks a transition in American life that makes those events immediately preceding it seem part of another world. Our affluence has transformed the landscape of our lives into freeways, suburbs, and shopping centers, a world that appears far removed from cotton fields at picking time and other aspects of our traditional image of the South. During this same period a momentous change occurred in race relations. The civil rights movement, the end of legal segregation, and the enfranchisement of black voters have made the South's traditional racial caste system seem part of a remote and unimaginable past, especially to those outside the South and to those who are young.

Yet the distance between their world and ours is not as great as it first appears. Despite industrialization and urbanization, Southerners are still poorer than other Americans. In 1970 Southern per capita income was $3,185, more than $750 below the national average. In 1976 the Southern industrial worker earned $170 a week, $50 less than his counterpart elsewhere in the nation. A third of the nation's poor live in the South, a region with only a fourth of the nation's population. The worst poverty in the South today can be found in an area coinciding roughly with the old Cotton Belt. Moreover, despite economic, social, and legal change, many Southern values and behavior patterns persist. The mass media and other agencies of mass society must compete with family, church, and community in shaping action and opinion.[1]

An awareness of the distance between the world described in these life histories and contemporary American realities has shaped the selection and organization of the stories presented here. Brief introductions precede each section of the book and are designed to give the reader pertinent background information. These introductions also reflect our awareness that present-day perspectives differ from those of the people who originally collected these life histories and selected and edited some of them for *These Are Our Lives*. Only two of the life histories included here have been published before.[2] Thus, *Such As Us* is a new and distinctive addition to the literature on the Southern past. Taken together, these stories offer a picture of Southern history from the bottom up and a view of part of the world from which ours has evolved.

Such As Us begins with the story of three lives shaped by slavery, the Civil War, and Emancipation: a record of the differing perspectives from which white and black Southerners viewed the past and the conflicting memories they had. In the South of the 1930s these were living memories; such memories permeate the life histories.

The Civil War had ended slavery, but it had not prevented the development of a new racial caste system in the Southern states. The Southern economic system helped maintain a well-defined social and racial hierarchy. More than most Americans, Southerners remained heavily dependent upon farming for a living. In 1930 less than a third of the South's inhabitants resided in cities while over half the rest of the nation did. Southerners also earned less than their fellow citizens in other parts of the country. In 1932 farm income fell to 39 percent of the 1929 level, general incomes to 58 percent. Small renters, sharecroppers, and day laborers earned annually (cash and supplies) between $180 and $400. One of every two Southern farmers did not own the land he farmed. Often farmers paid for the use of the land with a share of the crops they raised. Since they had little money, they had to obtain their supplies at high interest rates. They did well if at the end of the year they broke even. As poor as many white farmers were, black farmers were generally even poorer and more likely to be landless.

In the second section of *Such As Us*, Southerners who lived on the farm tell their story. Much of what they say illuminates the region's agricultural history and reflects the predominance of farming in the South. The evolution of a one-crop agriculture and tenant farming need to be understood as a problem in regional economic development, as a labor system, and as a form of social control. But these accounts also offer the reader a chance to experience vicariously the world these people lived in: to know the landlord who argued that "the sharecropper is the landlord's child," and the wife of a tenant farmer, looking back at a life of hard work, who commented, "We seem to move around in circles like the mule that pulls the syrup mill. We are never still, but we never get anywhere. For twenty-three long years we have begun each year with nothing and when we settled in November we had the same." Through these stories the impact of facts, trends, and forces can be felt as well as understood, felt as they were felt by those whose lives they helped to shape.

Economic realities forced many Southerners to leave agriculture and go to mills, towns, and scattered places. Many of these people went to work in the cotton mills, one of the few alternatives to the farm for whites in the Southeast. But here, too, income and status were low and reinforced each other. Mill workers were called "lintheads" or "mill people," labels that indicated their social place in Southern society as well as in the isolated life of mill villages. They were white—the labor policies of the mills dictated hiring whites only. Most bought from mill stores, sent their children to mill schools, and worshiped in mill churches. Mill workers found steady, low but increasing wages until the Southern textile boom subsided in the 1920s. This slump prompted management to cut wages and to press labor to produce more in less time, stimulating the dramatic outburst of unionization efforts among mill workers which began in 1929 and lasted through the 1930s. These drives to organize labor were crushed by the mill owners. The paternalism of some mill owners was real, but the benefits of paternalism often were limited. Textile manufacturers who called the workers "our people" meant it, yet textile manufacturing in the South persisted as a low-skill, low-pay, non-union industry, and it remains so today.

The unionization drive of the 1930s temporarily focused national attention on mill workers and produced a rash of articles and books. But seldom were the workers permitted to speak for themselves, especially about their daily lives and how they saw their lives. In these life histories, these people become known, not just for their positions on unions, but in aspects of their daily lives, work and play, worship and laughter, victories and defeats.

Mill workers were part of the migration from the farm that rose in successive waves after the Civil War to tidal proportions from the 1890s through the 1920s. This migration reversed itself when job opportunities shrank during the Great Depression.

The New Deal eased the impact of economic decline for many of these people. Relief programs of the New Deal provided some assistance and social security for poor black and white Southerners: "Lord Bless that Old Age! Patey and me don't have to burden our children." Receiving an income outside the existing local economic and social structure gave a new element of independence. Those in distress often viewed New Deal relief workers as allies; a black sharecropper recalled that a relief worker criticized local landlords:

"She [the relief worker] knowed right well I wuz tellin' de Gawd's truth, an' her eyes kinda flash lak, an' she sez: 'Damn em, dey wucks de po' niggers an' white buckra* mos' to death in de spring an' summer, and fall, an' den loads em on us after stealin' dere share de crop! An' den dey got de nerve to cuss de relief! Why *dey's* de ones meckin' money offen de guvment! Damn em!'"

The benefits were immediate and concrete: a job with the Civilian Conservation Corps instead of no job at all; a housekeeper sent by the Works Progress Administration to help an elderly couple; a chance to utilize one's skills on a WPA job, instead of watching them deteriorate in idleness; an adult education course. A tenant

*A term of African derivation used to describe white men.

farmer took pride in these developments: "There ain't no other nation in the world that would have had sense enough to think of WPA and all the other A's."[3]

The New Deal helped these people, but it did not transform their society. It did not even end the Depression—though New Deal reforms did alter the economic system in an effort to make it more just and efficient. Until World War II, when massive government spending became necessary, federal programs were too limited to stimulate complete economic recovery.

Ironically, some New Deal programs intensified the plight of the poor. An unintended consequence of the New Deal farm program was to drive the tenants off the land. They and their children and, in some instances, their children's children, have become an unskilled, chronically unemployed, urban underclass. Moreover, local racial mores were not challenged seriously by New Deal reforms. The strength of the Southern racial caste system made bold actions politically dangerous. Then, too, those New Dealers who believed in racial equality—and not all of them did—assumed that with increased economic and educational opportunity blacks would eventually overcome legal and social prejudice. They seriously underestimated how much of the problem rested with white racism rather than limited black achievement.

Yet, whatever the limitations of the New Deal, black Americans perceived it, the national Democratic party, and Franklin and Eleanor Roosevelt as symbols of hope. Those symbols may have encouraged grass-roots challenges to the Southern racial system in the 1930s. As the last section of the book indicates, those challenges came twenty years before *Brown* v. *Board of Education* and thirty years before the Civil Rights activism of the 1960s.

The last section of *Such As Us* focuses directly on race relations— a constant, if not always fully articulated theme throughout these life histories. The opening section of this volume reflects the sharp contrasts between white and black views of the past, and the closing section reveals the conflicts inherent in their differing hopes and fears for the future. The incidental remarks of blacks and whites show how the caste system molded human relations in the South. The nuances and pervasive assumptions governing race relations are revealed more often in chance remarks than in studied comments. As they talk they place race relations within the context of their lives, their pasts, and their aspirations for themselves and their own.

These life histories show the impact of public events on private lives, the effect of time and change, not on a grand scale, but within the framework of individual biography. The freeing of the slaves was the climactic event in an old black man's life. The journey after World War I from the mountains of Tennesse to Knoxville marked a major turning point for another family, and the rise of the cotton mills meant a job for an orphaned young man.

History is not an abstraction to the people in these stories. Rather, as the folklorist B. A. Botkin observed, "the identification of the individual with a long line of kinfolks and their achievements gives a sense of personal participation in history and tradition."[4] People explain who and what they are partly in terms of their family history. And such knowledge of family history extends in some cases back to the old South. An elderly minister recalls, "My grandpappy Perry come over from Virginny and he settled at Como. . . . And he brought twenty-five slaves, and they helped build old Union Church." Family life helps these people understand the past, organize the present, and prepare for the future.

The family was also a way of maintaining a household, defining the relations between a man and a woman, and raising children. A widower and his son decide that with the limited resources of their small farm they can't both afford to marry. The father agrees that the son is the one who should marry: "Just so we had a woman in the house, it didn't make so much difference whose wife she was." So well defined are the basic elements of the family and male and female roles that in the eyes of one interviewer the most noteworthy fact about two elderly sisters managing a farm is that they have done it without the help of a man.

In some cases, regardless of the division of labor, husband and wife share the decision making. For some men, however, denigration and mistreatment of women is an assertion of their independence and masculinity, a compensation for the frustrations and humiliations in their own lives: "He keeps his jug of liquor in the kitchen and drinks when he pleases. If he wants to beat me or the children, he does, and that's all there is to it. He ain't got no mercy on nothing but mules and dogs." Many men and women had to be satisfied with what were patently unsatisfactory situations. Divorce, as a justice of the peace explains, is too expensive for many couples: "So they just make up their minds to put up with each other as best they can. I'd untie plenty of 'em if I could. . . . More divorces is what the country needs."

Couples for the most part stayed together. And together they faced the task of raising a new generation. Most often children came whether they were wanted or not: "I reckin that was the Lord's will. Anyhow, they came along and I didn't know no way of helpin' it." Day-to-day struggles shaped parents' treatment of their children. On Ransome Carson's tobacco farm those children who are old enough to help do, while their younger brothers and sisters are neglected: "I left . . . [my baby] in the yard once but it eat sand, chicken manure, and strings, so I decided to leave her in the house and take a chance on her eating buttons. If I left the backer every hour or two . . . Ransome would raise the devil."

These individuals in their roles as parents often express contradictory emotions toward their children: "Course sometimes 'for dey got here I felt like I didn't want to own no more, but when dey come dey was welcome." When they considered their hopes for their children, they were forced to contemplate the frustrations and limitations of their own lives. Many parents perceived their own and their children's place in the world as settled. Aaron Montgomery, a black tenant farmer, knew his children wouldn't receive any more education than he had: "Soon as one gits old enough he's put in de field. Dey ain't no time to go to school. . . . Like dese chil'en now, I had to go when the crop was housed and quit when work started." And though some parents hoped they could ensure that their children lived the lives they wished they themselves could have lived, they learned that children intent on leading their own lives frequently betray their parents' fondest wishes: "Me and Calvin wasn't only thinking about easy going for our ownselves when we come to Knoxville. We knowed Cap would have better chance at schooling here. And do you know what? That boy ain't sixteen yet and here he wants to quit school and go to work." While some parents wanted their children to have a different life from theirs, others wanted the self-affirmation of having children who followed in their path: "I sorta wish that my oldest boy was interested in tobacco, but he ain't. . . . He said that working in tobacco was filthy work." Tradition and change, past and future, are all embodied in these family relationships.

Aspects of these life histories transcend the local and particular. These are people like people everywhere—they hope, they struggle, they persevere. But it is not all a record of human triumph. Poor health and lack of education stifled aspiration and limited achievement. And yet not all the problems these individuals faced could have been rectified by social and political reform. Perhaps no one realized better than an ex-slave that life is both joy and tragedy. He remembered rejoicing when the slaves gained their freedom, but he also remembered that "'midst all that joy and shouting, men were digging graves and others were putting in the bodies, just piling three or four in one grave, like dogs, one on top of the other. . . . Chile, it was sad, sad!'"

These life histories allow individuals to reach across time and share their lives with us.

Almost as interesting as the life histories themselves is the story of how they came to be collected. The Federal Writers' Project was a government experiment in work relief and sponsorship of the arts. It was the product of the needs and hopes of a specific time. As part of the Works Progress Administration, the Writers' Project tried to offer meaningful work to unemployed writers. And, in keeping with WPA philosophy, it had to be work which had social usefulness. The Writers' Project centered its efforts on the production of a series of multiauthored state guides. Equally significant were such programs as the recording of ex-slave narratives, published as *Lay My Burden Down* in 1945, and the Southern life history project from which *These Are Our Lives* was taken.

W. T. Couch, regional director of the Writers' Project in the Southeast and director of The University of North Carolina Press, supervised an extensive program for collecting the life histories of common Southerners. He thought and worked in a cultural context in which the South had become an important symbol of the nation's economic problems. He reacted to Southern intellectual developments such as Regionalism and Agrarianism, and to Northern views of Southern problems.

Couch had made The University of North Carolina Press into an organization designed to serve Southern needs. He shared with Howard Odum and Rupert Vance, sociologists who pioneered in the regional approach to Southern problems, the idea that the South could clarify and solve its problems. Couch was concerned that knowledge and discussion of these problems not be confined to experts. From the moment he joined the Writers' Project he began to consider ways in which that program could promote a greater understanding of Southern problems. Couch's vision of the work the Writers' Project could undertake grew out of his reaction to these contemporary currents of thought.

The sudden end of a seemingly endless prosperity brought new attitudes and programs to the forefront of national affairs. The dominant criticism of American life in the 1920s had focused on the shallowness of middle-class life, the excesses of prosperity, and what was considered the cultural backwardness of large segments of the population. The South, along with Sinclair Lewis's *Main Street* and Sherwood Anderson's *Winesburg, Ohio*, provided critics with the symbols of much that was wrong in American life. In the 1930s the South continued to be a symbol of the nation's problems. As one historian observed, "the Bible Belt seemed less absurd as a haven for fundamentalism, more challenging as a plague spot of race prejudice, poor schools and hospitals, sharecropping and wasted resources."[5]

Much of the writing that made the South in the 1930s a symbol of the depression focused on the plight of the Southern tenant farmer. More than any other book, Erskine Caldwell's *Tobacco Road* (1932) inaugurated the new interest in Southern tenant farmers. The world he portrayed was inhabited by degenerate, stunted, and starving people. Couch found little to admire in Caldwell's *Tobacco Road* or in his volume of impassioned reporting, *You Have Seen Their Faces* (1937). Caldwell's plea for collective action on the part of tenant farmers and for governmental control of cotton farming failed to impress Couch, who remarked:

If Southern tenant farmers are at all like the Jeeter Lesters and Ty Ty Waldens with whom Mr. Caldwell has peopled his South, I cannot help wondering what good could come out of their collective action. Nor can much good be expected from government control if the persons controlled are of the type that Mr. Caldwell has led us to believe now populate the South.[6]

The Nashville Agrarians were equally dismayed by Caldwell's portrayal of the South. The burden of the Agrarian manifesto, *I'll Take My Stand: The South and the Agrarian Tradition* (1930), had been a rejection of industrialism and an idealization of a simpler agrarian economy. Couch, however, differed with the Agrarians in thinking that "the South must recognize that evils of the kind Mr. Caldwell describes actually exist in this region, and must do what it can to correct them." He pointed out that instead the Agrarians merely "assert that virtue is derived from the soil, but see no virtue in the Negro and the poor white who are closest to the soil."[7]

More liberal than the Agrarians and yet no less critical of Caldwell's work, Couch developed an idea of his own for examining Southern conditions. He wanted to give Southerners at all levels of society a chance to speak for themselves. In his opinion collecting life histories was one way of doing this. He thought project workers could be used in an effort to provide a more accurate picture of Southern life than had either Caldwell or the Agrarians.

Couch was convinced of the advantages of using life histories as opposed to more conventional methods. He thought that if Southerners spoke for themselves it would demonstrate that Southern life was more complex than earlier, easy generalizations had led people to think. In discussion with other Writers' Project officials, he argued against "the possible objection that only sociologists can get case histories that are worth getting. The fact is that when sociologists get such material, they generally treat their subjects as abstractions." He thought fiction was equally inadequate because of its "composite or imaginary character."[8]

Only by permitting individuals to tell their own stories from their own points of view, Couch thought, could the statistical and sociological evidence already gathered be given meaning and context. What can we learn, he wondered, from knowing that the average sharecropper moved frequently unless we understand what it meant to him in the context of his own life? Underlying Couch's emphasis on the worth of material "written *from the standpoint of the individual himself*" was a strong commitment to democratic values.[9] There had been, he argued, numerous "books about the South . . . written from other books, from census reports, from conferences with influential people." And on the rare occasions "when the people have been consulted they have been approached with questionnaires in hand and with reference to particular problems of one kind or another."[10] This he thought was unsatisfactory: "With all our talk about democracy it seems not inappropriate to let the people speak for themselves."[11]

The democratic impetus of the life-history program was reflected not only in the voices of people who had seldom been heard before, but also in the way the material was gathered. Field workers far removed from the decision making about the life-history program collected the actual materials. In such areas as the Southeast where there were few unemployed writers, the Writers' Project employed literate middle-class individuals who were out of work.

Themselves the victims of the depression, they were not far removed from the people they wrote about. Most had been born and reared in the South, and some, like Bernice Kelly Harris, wrote life histories of people they had known all their lives.[12] Interviewers approached those they did not know in a casual and random manner. Ida Moore remembers choosing "the people to be interviewed more or less by instinct . . . saying I'd like very much to stop by for a few minutes and talk with them."[13] This friendliness, this sharing of a few minutes as between neighbors, perhaps explains why, unlike much similar material, these life histories do not seem to have been cajoled from beleaguered and defenseless individuals, unsure of how to cope with people who wished to study them.

The life histories obtained by the interviewers often had to be edited—subject to the interviewers' approval—by the more competent writers engaged in the project. Some interviewers, however, possessed qualities that compensated for their lack of writing skill. William McDaniel, the director of the Tennessee Writers' Project, remarked of one interviewer, "Her greatest attribute is that she is one of the people. She shares their views, religion, and mode of living, and through that gets into her stories the essence of their community life."[14] This closeness, this sense of community between interviewer and interviewed, accounts for the sympathetic tone that permeates the life histories.

Couch selected the life histories published in *These Are Our Lives* with the aim of capturing the life of a community composed of individuals "who are of different status, perform different functions, and in general have widely different experiences and attitudes —so different, indeed, as to be almost unimaginable."[15] Couch was also interested in emphasizing the strength and dignity of hard-working Southerners. While he had accumulated enough material for a volume that he thought "would make [Erskine] Caldwell's degenerates look like fine upstanding citizens," he had "scruples about publishing such stuff." Although convinced it ought to be published, he was unsure "how it can be handled and not make a bad situation worse." He had long rejected the by now popular idea that the mass of poor white and black Southerners were hopeless misfits, and he had no desire to contribute to the "merriment over psychopaths" to which he attributed Caldwell's success.[16]

Many Southern critics praised *These Are Our Lives* because they thought it provided refutation to *Tobacco Road*. In a review entitled "Realities on Tobacco Road," Virginius Dabney wrote, "One thing which appeals to me . . . is the absence of . . . degenerates. After all, degenerates are the exception, rather than the rule, both North and South."[17]

For Couch and others of his generation *These Are Our Lives* reflected contemporary experience. It was current events. The book soon found its place within a debate over the causes of Southern poverty. That debate has not influenced our editorial judgments in putting together *Such As Us*. We have, however, been influenced by the praise *These Are Our Lives* received in local Southern papers. The reviewers saw in *These Are Our Lives* "our neighbors and the folk who crowd the streets . . . some we see for the first time." Equally, they lauded the book as an illustration of Southern life that defied stereotypes and statistics. "We in the South have been called an economic problem. That is not true. We are millions of problems! We are millions of individuals."[18] The editors hope that readers of *Such As Us* will discover similar qualities in this volume.

There were over a thousand life histories to choose from in editing this volume. The great majority of them are stored in the Southern Historical Collection at The University of North Carolina Library at Chapel Hill. Some are in the Library of Congress, and there are scattered life histories in repositories throughout the South. Project writers collected life histories in Oklahoma and in every state of the old Confederacy except Mississippi and Texas.

In selecting and editing the life histories in this volume, we looked for stories that did more than represent a type and convey facts. We looked for an individual perspective on events. There were more life histories that met this criterion than we could include in a single volume.

Many of the life histories reminded us that the South is not composed solely of native white and black Americans. Life histories of Greek restaurant owners, Chinese laundrymen, Jewish shopkeepers, and Cuban and Italian cigar makers were fascinating. To be effective, however, they would need to be grouped together. Singly, they would appear exotic and peripheral. Therefore, because of limitations of space, we have chosen to limit our selection to the statistically more common aspects of Southern life.

A significant number of life histories were of tenant farmers and mill workers. They were a large element of the Southern population, they were important to the economy of the region, and they were the subject of much contemporary interest.

Few life histories of members of the middle class were revealing. Despite repeated encouragement, project workers found it difficult to obtain life histories of middle-class individuals. Couch wondered "whether it was possible to get cultivated people to talk—I mean really talk and tell about themselves and their feelings about people and things."[19]

Our selection reflects the major strengths of these unpublished materials. The life histories in this volume were not chosen to be representative of the life histories collected, or of the various Southern states, or of the project workers who conducted the interviews. Some aspects of the collection are unrepresented, some states are unrepresented, and we have a disproportionate number of interviews by several project workers. We concentrated on those areas where the material was clearly evocative as well as informative.

We have made few changes in the interviewers' attempts to record dialect, although not all these attempts were skillfully done and some seem stereotyped.[20] The modern reader, unfamiliar with older dialects, might argue that the editors should have modernized the spelling. Nevertheless, we left the dialect unchanged for several reasons. People are not all the same, and it is a false liberalism that insists that they are. The dialect in these stories demands that the reader recognize that the speaker is different from himself and that he have the patience and desire to deal with that fact. A people's speech—its style and rhythm, choice of words, and word order—is also one signifiant record of their history; it is their most important literary creation. Seen from this perspective, the interviewers' attempts to record the dialect of the speakers, even when awkwardly done, is too important to alter.

In our editing of the life histories we have on several occasions deleted material that we thought added little to the story. For the most part this consisted of editorial comments and descriptive materials inserted by the interviewer. All deletions are noted by ellipses. We have, however, corrected obvious typographical errors without noting it. But we have not tried to make the interviews fit our notions of a standard format. The varying format of the life histories may add an element of discontinuity, but, this, too, is an inherent part of the story. These life histories were gathered by numerous relief workers under widely varying circumstances and with little supervision. To totally eliminate the elements that contribute to this sense of variety would falsify the nature of the interview, and would deprive the reader of any way of judging the interviewer's attitude and approach.

We changed the names of all the people (except public figures) mentioned in the life histories to protect their privacy, but left the names of the original interviewers in order to give them their due. Where two or more names are given, the names after the first one are the editors.

How accurate a picture of their subjects do these life histories provide? What factors may have led to distortions? None of the life histories contradicts known facts. The content and tone of the material is supported by historical, sociological, and fictional writings on the South. Yet questions remain. Because they did not have tape recorders, interviewers probably did not write a verbatim account, but a reconstruction from memory and rough notes. While many of the interviewers had little writing experience, many hoped to become writers. This, too, could add a false note. Field workers, however, used detailed guidelines (see appendix) for collecting and writing life histories.

All of the life histories in this volume were recorded by white interviewers. Sometimes they already knew their subjects, sometimes not. The tensions surrounding race relations and the etiquette governing relations between the races may have affected the content of the interview. Couch found that white project workers were often reluctant to interview blacks. Many of the interviewers had to be reminded that "we must have life histories that reveal the way people in the South live, and Negroes and members of other racial groups are people just as well as whites."[21] Class and sex differences between the interviewer and subject could also affect the interview. So the interviews between whites and blacks present problems that differ in degree, not in nature, from interviews where both participants were members of the same race.

Couch thought the best answer to the question of authenticity was "to ask the reader to read carefully a few of the stories. If he does, I am convinced he will agree that real people here are speaking"[22]—real people with their own perspective on their world and themselves, each his own historian, with things to share and things to hide from us and sometimes from himself. Some of these accounts are limited by the interviewer's lack of imagination. In the most engaging of these life histories, one finds oneself posing one's own questions and imagining the answers. The reader, along with the subject and interviewer, becomes a participant in an act of historical recreation.

In the best of these life histories, understanding as well as information about the past can be gained, "knowledge carried to the heart," in the words of the Southern poet Allen Tate. Life as it was experienced by particular individuals, in a unique time, and in a special place is recreated for the reader. Some of those interviewed produced, in collaboration with the interviewer, a work of art out of their lives. Like us, they were engaged in evolving a version of their lives that could help them understand their past, cope with the present, and face the future. Developing a sense of self is each person's greatest creative endeavor. But even in those stories where the individual seems to reveal little of himself and to concentrate primarily on external facts, the reader learns what those facts mean from the standpoint of the individual himself. Representatives of social types and classes, they were nevertheless unique individuals—a paradoxical truth which these life histories affirm.

June 1976   *Jerrold Hirsch*
                                                                               Tom E. Terrill

NOTES

1. This is the central thesis of John Shelton Reed's *The Enduring South: Cultural Persistence in Mass Society* (Lexington, Mass.: D. C. Heath & Co., 1972).

2. "My WPA Man" and "Chimney Sweeper's Holiday," products of the Louisiana Federal Writers' Project, were published in Lyle Saxon, Edward Dreyer, and Robert Tallant, comps., *Gumbo Ya-Ya: A Collection of Louisiana Folk Tales* (Boston: Houghton Mifflin Co., 1945). The former story appeared there as "A Good Man is Hard to Find." There are manuscript versions of these stories in the Federal Writers' Project, Papers of the Regional Director, William Terry Couch (hereafter cited as FWP-Couch Papers), Southern Historical Collection, University of North Carolina Library, Chapel Hill, N.C.

3. Federal Writers' Project, *These Are Our Lives* (Chapel Hill: University of North Carolina Press, 1939), p. 16.

4. B. A. Botkin, ed., *A Treasury of Southern Folklore* (New York: Crown Publishers, 1949), p. 3.

5. Dixon Wecter, *The Age of the Great Depression, 1929–1941* (New York: Macmillan Co., 1948), pp. 159–60.

6. W. T. Couch, "Landlord and Tenant," *Virginia Quarterly Review* 14 (1938): 309–12.

7. Ibid., p. 312; W. T. Couch, "The Agrarian Romance," *South Atlantic Quarterly* 36 (1937): 429.

8. [Couch] to [?], "Memorandum Concerning Proposed Plans for Work of the Federal Writers' Project in the South," 11 July 1938, FWP-Couch Papers.

9. Federal Writers' Project, *These Are Our Lives*, p. x.

10. Couch to Douglas Southall Freeman, 25 March 1939, FWP-Couch Papers.

11. Federal Writers' Project, *These Are Our Lives*, pp. x–xi.

12. Bernice Kelly Harris, *Southern Savory* (Chapel Hill: University of North Carolina Press, 1964), pp. 181–205, offers an informative account of one project worker's experience and what it meant to her.

13. Mrs. Ida Cooley (formerly Ida Moore) to Jerrold Hirsch, no date.

14. McDaniel to Couch, 20 January 1939, FWP-Couch Papers.

15. Federal Writers' Project, *These Are Our Lives*, p. x.

16. Couch to Mrs. Howard Mumford Jones, 21 June 1939, University of North Carolina Press Papers (hereafter cited as Press Papers), Southern Historical Collection, University of North Carolina Library, Chapel Hill, N.C.

17. Virginius Dabney, "Realities on Tobacco Road," *Saturday Review of Literature*, 27 May 1939, p. 5.

18. Robert Register, "Book Delves into History of People," *Greensboro Daily News*, 21 May 1939. This is representative of numerous reviews in Southern newspapers such as the *Raleigh News and Observer*, the *Winston-Salem Journal*, the *Little Rock Gazette*, and the *Birmingham Age-Herald*. Clippings in the Press Papers.

19. Couch to Bernice Kelly Harris, 30 January 1939, FWP-Couch Papers.

20. We have tried not to improve on the interviewers' attempts to render dialect. If the word "dey" is used in one line and "they" in the next, we have made it "dey" throughout that life history. We have not, however, tried to impose a *false* consistency throughout the volume. Some writers, for example, wrote "I's" for "I is" or "I was," others wrote "I'se." We have made the dialect internally consistent within each interview. There is no universal agreement on how to render dialect, as these life histories reveal. These documents are a form of historical evidence. We have been conservative in our handling of the evidence.

21. Couch to State Directors, "Memorandum Concerning Federal Writers' Project: Answers to Frequent Queries on Life Histories," no date, FWP-Couch Papers.

22. Federal Writers' Project, *These Are Our Lives*, p. xii.

Such As Us

Talking Is My Life

BIG IVY, TENNESSEE, 1938 OR 1939

"Nothing on this living earth I'd rather do than get out and hoe a patch of cotton in good weather. These days I ain't got that patch and no hoe to work it with if I did have. Here I set, day in and day out, looking after my poor man Patey and hoping somebody will come by that I can pass a chat with.

"Talking is just about my life these days.

"Now, I know that some folks back through here in Big Ivy will say Aunt Tobe McKinney is a gossip. Law ha' mercy, a gossip is a sharp-tongue woman and I'm not that. I never say a harm word of nobody unless I hear they've done meanness of some kind. Well, I do scatter the news when news is to scatter. Somebody's got to do that or how is people going to know what's going on?

"I reckon I'm as well set to spread the word as anybody. Sixty-six years I've lived here in this community, saving the spell I lived in Texas. My pap and his pappy before him lived in Big Ivy. Both my grandsirs come here from North Carolina back in eighteen hundred and something. Most of the people around here, their grandsirs was the Tarheel kind. I don't know why and when they started calling the community Big Ivy, but they started. They cleared away the hazelnut bushes, they cut the post oaks and elms, and they raised their cabins and begun farming. And that's the way it's been ever since. Only it is downhill now mostly.

"It's pretty hard to tell just where Big Ivy starts and where it leaves off. On one end it's mixed in with Oak Springs. On the other it's tangled with Sand Hill. The only way you can tell where them end families belongs is by the school they send their children to and where they vote. If the children go to Big Ivy school and the menfolks vote at Joe Fulghum's store, why then the family belongs to Big Ivy.

"Cotton is the most thing they raise around here. Generally always farmers will put in a field of corn and a vegetable patch and some raise a few hogs and chickens, but cows is pretty few and milk and beef meat is scarce. Cotton's the standby and always will be, seems like. Now, every place I ever heard of before, cotton and niggers just naturally grow together. It's that way around Zama and Kilburn. But not here, not in Big Ivy. No niggers at all live here, not one. Old Squire Irby Bennett's pappy used t⌐ ⌐wn three or four niggers back before the Confederate War, but the Klux ran them all out. Never been back since then.

"Why, let a nigger start from Oak Springs to Sand Hill. He will cut around through the crosstimbers or go away over to Zama and circle back before he'll pass through Big Ivy. One time Bailus Hardy needed help in his cotton. He couldn't get nobody here to hire to him. So he had to haul in niggers from Zama. And, bless God, them niggers sure did make Bailus get them out of here by good dark, too. The funny thing, though, is nobody would touch a kink on a nigger's head if he was to come in here. The niggers just remember what the Klux done back in them days and they shy wide around Big Ivy. It's their doing, not ours. I've heard more than one man say he wished to his soul he could lay hands on nigger help to crop on the shares or hire on the place. But no—you can't get them to come in noways at all.

"Most of us back through here is Republican Party and own our own land, such as it is. Us people here in Big Ivy holds to the good old ways that's the best ways, when all is said and done. Take this TV and A, this electricity stuff, they talk about these days. It would come in through here if we'd vote it in. Everybody studied it over. But you take this electricity, them wires—why, they's power in them wires. Power to kill a body. Wires will come down then it's mourning for somebody. Yes, we're afraid of that stuff. They's things the good Lord never meant mankind to fuddle with. So we turned the TV and A down.

"They's just two peculiar men in Big Ivy when it comes to religion. One don't believe in nothing and the other one he's a Jehovah Witness man. The rest of us is Baptist, Missionary and Primitive Hard-Shell Baptist. Missionaries go to Shady Grove Church and the ·Hard-Shells to Pilgrim Glory. In my young days they used to have all-day meetings and big singings at laying-by time, and all manner of frolicsome doings like house raisings and play parties. Law me, nothing much like that now. Folks don't even have time to lay by most generally. Just keep humping the year round to make a living.

"Take the young folks now—why, they's not a good dozen of

what you could really call young folks in Big Ivy. Plenty of children, plenty of old people like me and Patey, but where is the young folks? Gone to Poplin because they want to be at the county seat where things is stirring. Gone everywhere and anywhere to get away from farming life. Young folks this day and generation can't seem to abide the hard scuffling ways you have to do to get by on a farm, even with the government paying good money to help out.

"With most of the young hot blood gone, they's mighty little trouble with the law. In olden times many grudges and feud fights happened around here. Even now once in so often a hardness comes up between some of us—one on my own front doorstep right now, my graveyard trouble*—but it scarcely comes down to the point of where blood's spilt these days.

"I reckon you could say it's nothing much out of the way goes on here any more. We just keep to ourselves. Have to in rainy times when you can't find the bottom of these muddy roads with a ten-foot pole, and in dry weather, too, because we're used to it. Oh, sometimes we go over to Zama or maybe to Kilburn on First Monday market days. If they's a big court trial at Poplin and the work's slack, Squire Hardy or the Carmackeses get their cars out and drive eighteen miles in. Squire takes the paper and so does young Earl Henderson, and that's how we hear of the wars in the world.

"But mostly we just work and live our days here in Big Ivy. When we get old and broke down, like me and Patey is, we find some old shackle of a cabin and set back and the Old Age sends us a check every month. Lord bless that Old Age! Patey and me don't have nothing, but we don't starve, we don't have to be a burden on our children. That's a wonderful thing for old folks like me and Patey."

James Aswell

*Two families were quarreling about burial sites. For more information, see James Aswell and Ruth Clark, "Our Times and Seasons," FWP–Couch Papers, Southern Historical Collection, University of North Carolina Library, Chapel Hill.

THE CIVIL WAR: VICTORY AND DEFEAT

When we were growing up, our
Southern country and all of our older
people were still grieving.
—Ben Robertson,
Red Hills and Cotton, 1942

Everybody went wild. We all felt like
heroes. . . . We was free. Just like
that, we was free.
—Ex-slave in B. A. Botkin,
Lay My Burden Down, 1938

The War [has] its inexhaustible
and sibylline significance. Sig-
nificances, rather, for it is an
image of life, and as such is a con-
densation of many kinds of
meanings.
—Robert Penn Warren,
The Legacy of the Civil War, 1963

The old South and its demise in a bloody civil war was living memory in the South of the 1930s. Ex-slaves and Confederate veterans still constituted an unbroken link with the past. Their experiences became memories, and these memories were passed down, and they became, as much as the events themselves, molders of the future.

The experiences of whites and blacks who lived in the old South and fought in the Civil War entered into the life and history of their families and communities. At least two pasts lived in the South of the 1930s. In the white version of the Southern past the black was a presence, not a participant, an object, not an actor. Thus it was understood, without being stated, that a *Southerner* meant a white Southerner, never a black man, no matter how long he and his ancestors had lived in the region. The black man was merely an object for which a glorious army had fought and lost. But from the black perspective, the destruction of the Confederacy was a victory, not a defeat. Yet the largely unwritten black version remained confined to oral tradition. And in reality this was also true for the ordinary white. Life in the old South was viewed from the planter's perspective, not the slave's or the small white farmer's. The romantic image of life in the old South, and the emphasis on the Civil War as the Lost Cause, obscured the actual history of ordinary Southerners. Dashing heroes, endlessly glorified, revealed nothing of the War as experienced by the majority of blacks and whites.

In these life histories a white minister and two ex-slaves become their own historians. They answer questions about life in the old South from the viewpoint of the common soldier of the Confederacy and the black house slave. Perhaps nowhere else in this collection of life histories is the relation between public events and private lives more explicit. Slavery, war, defeat or emancipation, are more than events that touch one's life; they are, like childhood, marriage, and the birth of a child, formative in one's development.

These life histories cannot tell us whether slavery was profitable or whether the Civil War was inevitable, but they can educate our sensibilities. As we read these life histories, the facts acquire meaning, become known, because they are felt.

Like a Shadow
That Declineth

They was a rabbit and a red heifer calf
come through that cornfield, hard as they could tear.

Parson Bill sat in his rocker by the south window where the winter sunlight was warm. His worn brown hat was canted on the back of his head because, "I might git a draft and that makes my head roar now that I'm ninety of age." His cane, a stout polished hickory stick, was at his side and his Bible lay open in his lap. There were straight-backed chairs in the room and an unmade bed. On the walls were pictures of the large Holmes family in its several branches and a highly colored Cardui calendar.*

"I set here the livelong day," said Parson Bill, "meditating *on* the will of the Lord." He spoke in the singsong way of country preachers, stressing words here and there, nodding his head and patting his foot in a kind of ragged rhythm.

"I set here and I do think of all the years I've been *in* the vineyard, the vineyard of the Lord. Oh, you must *know* they's a Gospel train—yes, a train of living Truth which is the Word. Yes, and Christ *is* the engineer on-a that train and no corpse can ride that sweet train. But when he is raised *up* from death's corruption —oh, when that great day comes!—the elect *will* walk in the new-

---

*A widely circulated calendar advertising Cardui, a patent medicine to stimulate the appetite and especially for women during menstruation. Nineteen percent of Cardui is alcohol.

ness of life. God bless your soul, he will git *on* that-a train! All creation cannot stop him! No, when he *is* quickened by the spirit no harm can come him anigh, amen."

The parson sank back in the rocker. He looked over his silver-rimmed spectacles and said more quietly, "My heart ain't set on the comforts of this earth. Heaven, sweet heaven, is my home and—oh—I'm beginning *to* git homesick. I set here and think of all the saints that *is* already gone over yonder. I think how soon I'll jine that heavenly host. I won't bother about who's there and who ain't, but I will rejoice *with* them that is.

"I was born over here in about a mile of old Union, that good old Primitive Baptist church. My grandpappy Perry come over from Virginny and he settled at Como. He built the first store at Como."

The old man had dropped his scriptural manner. He ran knotted age-speckled fingers along the smoothness of his cane. "Yes, grandpappy he brought my mammy and her one sister from over there. And he brought twenty-five slaves, and they helped build old Union Church.

"My grandpappy Holmes come from North Carolina. Him and ten other families, all in one slew. They settled close to where Cottage Grove now is on Walnut Fork. My pappy was jist a shirttail boy then, jist ten of age. He helped my grandpappy Holmes clear their land, for he was a dutiful son.

"Mammy and Pappy was married a hundred years ago. The Lord didn't bless them with increase. Jist me—I was the onliest child, and it takes three children to make for increase. After I was born they moved over in the edge of Obion County. And Mammy did pass away from the consumption. 'Multiply *and* replenish the earth,' so Pappy married again.

"We got along pretty well. I didn't never go to school much. We jist hunted and fished and trafficked around when we wasn't busy in the crop. I like to fish better than anything else. Folks lived at home in them days. Made their own wine and drunk it. The young folks had play parties and dances, but I did not fancy them much. So I reached my manhood stage here in the West Tennessee country.

"I was eighteen and more when the war broke out. 'Thou shalt bring down the noise of strangers as the heat in a *dry* place, even the heat with the shadow of a cloud.' I jined the army then, and so is the sons of men snared in an evil time when it falleth suddenly upon them.

"Yes, I went into the Confederate Army. Remember it like it *was* yesterday. Yes, I was setting in my tent, jist a soldier boy, before the fight at Chattanooga. I was reading my Bible *and* thinking if the Lord see fit to call me in that day's battle, I'd be lost. I did not *have* the hope, the blessed sweet hope, that passeth all understanding. I tried *to* pray *but* I could not pray. No, I hadn't never prayed.

"My dear old uncle that *was* a Primitive Baptist preacher was *in* that Confederate Army. He sought me out *in* my tent there before the battle begun. He see me studying my Bible and he did ask me about my soul.

"I *did* hang my head, I had to say, 'I have no hope, I cannot pray.'

"Well, that good old man looked sad and said, 'Oh, boy, I'm sorry *to* hear that. The Lord *will* call a many a one before this trouble's over. I never see you drinking, Bill. I never see you gamble. I never *see* you do a thing ungodly, Bill, so I thought you had hope, that blessed hope.' He jist turned on his heel and went out and left me.

"But what will be will be, *and* the Yankee balls *jist* buzzed me past *and* done me no harm at all. Oh, it was intended for me to come through that fighting without brack *nor* flaw. Never a bullet made *in* the northern lands could touch Bill Holmes then.

"The battles I fought in, they's so many and mixed together in my head I can't remember but two. The one at Chattanooga and the time the hosts did meet at Shiloh ground. It was a Saturday morning when our regiment was ordered *to* go towards Shiloh. We marched all day and night."

Parson Bill again dropped his sermon style in the excitement of things he recalled. "We fought in a trance all day Sunday. It was Monday before we got a thing to eat. I got around behind the corner of a church, I'd load and fire, then I'd jump back to load again. Bullets was flying thick and fast. A six-pound cannon ball hit Ben Roberts right in the breast. He was as close to me as you are now.

"That morning early my pardner, Burl Duke, said he knowed he'd be dead before night. The firing got hot, so I fell down in a corn middle, flat on my belly. I looked and see Burl coming, falling as he come. Oh, his heart was shot all to pieces. I see my company retreating, so I run and got behind a rail fence and peeped through a crack a while. They was a rabbit and a red heifer calf come through that cornfield, hard as they could tear. I laugh every time I think of them. That battle lasted all day. In the night I went to my tent. Captain Lacy was wounded in my tent, so I made me a bed out of three oak poles and slept next to a wounded Yankee. Maybe I oughten to done it but I stole a good knife out of his pocket.

"The Yankees they caught me and I got in prison at Bowling Green* and stayed three days. They was an agreement on both sides that all prisoners would be paroled and sent home. I jist stayed three days till they paroled me. I was jist broke down sick and wore out. They was a widow woman named Tissel and her daughter taken me in and kept me till I was well. I walked from Bowling Green to Union City.† Wasn't no trouble to git food and a place to sleep. Anybody through that country'd help a Rebel out.

"I wasn't at home but two or three weeks until General Forrest‡ ordered all paroled men back. I stayed then till the war was over. We was fighting to keep the slaves. But it's a good thing they's freed. Still, they sure would have hit the nail square on the head if they'd colonized them niggers. It ain't best to have two races of God's children mixed. One is going to boss the other every time that happens.

"My first wife, Emma, see me two years before I see her. I always thought that was funny. I was with General Forrest. We was after Berry and his clan of bushwackers.§ They had committed several outrages around old Shady Grove Church and in that neighborhood. We rode up to the church. Meeting was a-going on but we didn't disturb. We jist stopped to rest. A lady was at a window. I was setting on my hoss. She beaconed with her hand this a-way, for me to come there. I rode up to the window. She see by the uniform I was a Confederate soldier.

"She says, 'Who are you and what are you doing?'

"I told her we's after Berry and his clan. She says, 'Well, I hope you git him.' She was a teacher and taught right there in that church. I talked on a few minutes. Emma, my first wife, was a-setting right across the aisle and heard every word I said. When the war was over I come home, I was riding to church one day and overtaken her. She was on hossback, too. I taken one good look at her. Her eyes was *as* the eyes of the doves by the rivers of water. Yes, and her face is as Lebanon, excellent as the cedars and her mouth like lilies. So I says, 'You will be my wife.'

"She jist laughed and said, 'Oh, I reckon not.'

"I says, 'I'm a-coming to see you.'

"She says, 'All right.'

---

*Kentucky.
†Tennessee.
‡General Nathan Bedford Forrest.
§The interviewer apparently erred here. The interviewee probably referred to "Tinker Dave" Beatty, a Union guerilla leader who operated in eastern Tennessee.

"So next Sunday I hitched my hoss at her front gate. Wasn't long till we was engaged. I told her I wanted to make one crop before we was married.

"And she says, 'And I want to make some quilts and things.'

"We went to work and got us a little start. Then we was married."

With his chin on his chest, Parson Bill sat laughing to himself. "Such a way to git married! Did ye ever hear of such a courting in your life?"

"There's Emma's picture on the wall, as pretty as a pink. She was as good a woman as God ever let live."

He stared out the window for a while working his lips soundlessly. When he spoke once more, it was in his nasal preacher's chant. "It was after we's married that I found that salvation *which* God give us to work out. You can't work it out until He gives it to you, no more than you can work *out* a garden when you ain't got no garden. By grace are ye saved—by grace through faith *lest* any *man* should boast!

"Oh, whoso boasteth hisself of a false gift *is* like clouds and wind without rain. Oh, I'd be afraid to boast in the sight of God, amen. I'd be afraid to boast for fear I'd be like the forty and two children *that* was eat by the she-bear. Oh, but that blessed sweet hope is a great thing!

"Yes, I was a-hoeing tobacco one day and a-meditating on the sweet word of God. I begin to look around for some place to hide—to hide from man. God bless your soul, they's no hiding from God. Him of the all-seeing eye! No, I wasn't a-wanting to hide *from* Him. Black and vile sinner, worm of the dust as I was, I wanted *to* seek the Lord. I went-a to a thicket of sumacs. Yes, down-a on my knees there I found God. I jist lost myself. I don't know what I said *or* what I done. I shouted praises unto *his* name. I sung songs, I done everything but hoe. Wasn't long till night. I didn't say nothing to Emma till I laid *aside* my garments and sought sweet repose for the night.

"I was a-laying in the bed *and* I begin to laugh. Emma was setting by the fire knitting. She said, 'Bill, what is wrong with you?' I hadn't never acted that silly before.

"I told her that the Lord had blessed my soul and that I was one *of* God's elect. I told her that heaven was my eternal home.

"She said, 'Why, Bill, this evening about *four* o'clock, this very evening, I knelt under a big oak tree and God come to me.'

"I'm telling you we had a sweet hour! On wings of glory and sweet salvation! For the Lord *had* come to us both the same day.

"We jined the church and was baptized. I was twenty-two then. I was twenty-eight when I felt the call to preach. It kept going through my mind, 'Go ye into *all* the world and preach the gospel to every creature, and lo! I *am* with you even to the end.' That jist went through my mind *and* through my mind *till* I couldn't rest nor find no peace.

"I told one of the brethren I'd felt a call to preach. So next conference he got up. He announced that Brother Holmes *had* a gift. One of the brethern says, 'I want Brother Holmes to preach over at my house this very night.' That was the beginning. I *was* of a poor stambling tongue but I knowed it was ordained from my mother's womb, and if I'd stay *in* communion *with* God He'd give me-a utterance.

"Yes, I preached the Word and the Truth *for* fifty and six years. They jist ain't no telling *how* many thousand miles I've gone over. Oh, I've preached in pretty nigh every Old Baptist Association in West Tennessee.

"If you ain't an Old Baptist they's one thing you don't believe. You don't believe you are old *as* God is. For listen. 'Father, I *will* that they also *whom* thou hast given me, be with me where I am that they may behold my glory, which thou *hast* given me! For thou lovedst me *before* the foundation of the world.'

"The Old Baptist believes in a general resurrection and that the whole law was give to Adam. He could do as he wanted but he must not eat *of* the fruit of the tree of knowledge. Satan was a-standing by and laughed to hisself and says, 'I'll tear that up!' So he tackled Eve. He tempted her *and* she did eat and we through Adam all become sinners. All must die, but while we was yet sinners Christ died *for* us. The Lord says, 'Mine elect have I called.' In *the* words of Peter the second we must make that *calling* sure. We know we're saved if we love the brethren. Bless your sweet life, I can clasp the hand of any man *who* has been redeemed *by* that precious blood and call him brother, be he black or white, Jew or Gentile. Children of God know each other. A tree *is* known by his fruits."

Parson Bill talked doctrine for a time. Then he said, "So for many a year did I labor in the vineyard. Three times I married and they *was* all fine women. Sons and daughters and grandsons *and* granddaughters of my seed gladdened my days. 'But though thou shouldst make thy *nest* as high as the eagle, I shall bring thee down from thence.'

"My son Lawson mocked the Lord. Yes, he departed from the

ways *of* righteousness and become as the ravening beast. Oh, he was a masterless man and his hand turned against *his* brethren. He lived in outlaw ways and fought and gambled *and* seeked the flesh-pots.

"So it come to pass that my boy was shot down, shot to death in a drinking brawl and they bringed him home. At first my faith it wasn't strong. I felt hard towards the boy that shot my Lawson. But now I know, bless you, that the boy couldn't noways help it. It was set from the beginning *of* this world for him to shoot Lawson. God raised *him* for that purpose and he couldn't help it."

Parson Bill was tired. His voice had grown more and more uncertain and his chin kept dropping on his chest. "My days is swifter than a weaver's shuttle," he said. "Like the shadow that declineth . . . they's none abiding . . . and that rabbit and the heifer come running through the field . . . so she beaconed me with her hand . . . I suppose. . . . "

Parson Bill was asleep in the warm sun.

Ruth Clark
James Aswell

I'se Still Traveling
'Cause I Got Faith in God

ATLANTA, GEORGIA, 1939

Chile, I could always see things. God Almighty fixed me.

"When the war come on my master took me with him and carried me to the war in Danville, Virginia. My home was in Troup
County, ten miles from LaGrange, Georgia. Luke Weston was my
master. I know'd all of the people around there. I wasn't a soldier
in the war, for they were fighting for us, but my master took me
with him to wait on him.

"When they were fighting I had to stay at the tent, do all the
personal things for my master, and watch him on the battlefield. If
he got hurt I was to go to him, even if they killed me in trying to
bring him in.

"One day I was standing beside the tent and had my hand
resting on the tent. There was fighting all around me, cannons and
guns roaring everywhere, bang, booom, bang, bang, ZZZZZZZ.
Bless God, just like hell itself had opened up. I stood there with my
mind on my master, praying for him to come back safe, although
he and the rest were fighting to keep me under bondage. I loved
him just the same. He was kind to me and I was praying for his
safety. Boom, bang, bang, boom, roared this cannon and that gun
and just as quick as a flash, before I could blink an eye, zip went a
bullet right pass my face and struck my hand. Bless God, I fell
down on my knees and you never saw a nigger pray as I prayed.
They carried me in the tent. A man came and poured a little stuff

on my hand. . . . Boom, bang, boom, the cannon belched fire and smoke, like it was a human being know'd where to strike its deadly blow. Boom, bang, boom, a soldier fell, the ball from a cannon had struck him in the neck, just above the shoulder and so terrific was the force of the ball, his head was cut from his shoulders and rolled every bit of ten or more yards from the body. I saw all of that and I wished I had stayed at home. Boom, boom, bang, bang, on went the guns into the night, seemingly never to end. When I got ready to leave home with my master to go to war, my ole mother told me and him, standing there in that cotton patch, that there was nothing to depend on but God, and I depended on Him, too.

"One day as I stood there at the tent, watching and praying for my master, I saw a big white flag going up toward the skies, like a big white-robed angel, going to heaven. I was too startled at first to grasp what it meant or what it was but, as I got back my senses, I saw it was surrender, surrender, surrender. When the flag went up, surrender, surrender, surrender, Daniel, another slave there to wait on his master, asked, 'Brother Ben, what is that?' I told him, 'We is free, we is free, they have surrendered, they have surrendered.' He said, 'For God's sake, do it say that, do it say that?' We were so full we couldn't talk. Tears ran down his black cheeks and mine and we stood there looking up to heaven, thanking God.

"He couldn't read. He didn't know what the flag said. White folks didn't allow us to learn to read and write. I was with the white boys because I had to wait on my white folks. I learned to read and write. White folks said it would run the niggers away if they learned reading and writing.

"I stood there after I come to myself and shouted, clapped my hands for joy and shouted and shouted, as if the Holy Spirit was coming down. White folks set their guns down and shouted, 'I'm glad of it, I'm glad of it!' And right there midst all that joy and shouting, men were digging graves and others were putting in the bodies, just piling three or four in one grave, like dogs, one on top of the other. There were other men cutting sticks and marking them so that they'd know who was in that grave. Chile, it was sad, sad!

"Them Yankees were running our white men through fields, wheat, corn, and barley, making them prisoners. Them Yankees put our masters in jails. They told us slaves, 'You all is free, free. You work for the people you have been living with if you want to or you go wherever you want to go. They must pay you wages if you stay with them. You are your own bosses now and what you work for is yours.' Chile, that was what we had prayed for and God had heard our prayers.

"There was a lot of us slaves there in camp to wait on our masters. We joined hands, formed a ring and shouted and my hand stopped hurting. I forgot I had been shot.

"I got home before my master 'cause he had to stay in the hospital until he was well. His leg had been shot off in the battle. When I got home the wimmin folks saw me come up, and another such hollering and shouting you never heard. I stood up on a bench and tole them, 'We is free, we is free.'

"Mis' Betsy, my mistress, heard the noise and came to the door to find out who was out there. The cook tole her it was Ben. She asked, 'Where is your master?' When I tole her he was not there, he hadn't come, she was quite sad. She knew he was shot, though. She seemed to feel that I should have brought him and not left him in the hospital. She seemed to say, 'You was to protect him.' She know'd I loved him and would have treated him as a baby.

"Everyone was shouting and happy; even the white wimmin and girls were joining in for they were glad their fathers, sons, husbands, and sweethearts were coming back, some of them. Some of them were sad for they know'd their loved ones would never return. Well, they were shaking my hand and some hugged me and I was afraid, for I was not used to all this 'tention, for they never let me get near them and I didn't want to, for I know'd my place.

"There were about seventy-five slaves on that plantation and when I came up Sara, the ole trusted slave, blow'd a horn and they poured out of their little shanties like bees from a hive to find out what was wrong, for that horn never blow'd less it was calling the slaves for something 'portant. Little 'uns, big 'uns and all, some with children in their arms, some with rags on their heads, some barefooted and every way.

"When they got around me I tole them about we were free and when I got through they shouted and sang:

> The slavery chain done broke and gone,
> Done broke and gone, done broke and gone,
> The slavery chain done broke and gone,
> Done broke and gone, done broke and gone.
> I'se gwine to praise God 'til I die.

"The wimmin went in the smokehouse and got down meat.

They cut hams and the best side meat. We'd never been 'lowed to eat anything but fat meat and we sho' et that day. They cooked biscuits and we had a feast. We'd never had anything but shorts. They never let us eat the flour they et. They cooked everything we hadn't been 'lowed to eat, for the white folks saved it for themselves. We stuffed our stomachs and sang:

> The slavery chain done broke and gone,
> Done broke and gone, done broke and gone,
> The slavery chain done broke and gone,
> Done broke and gone, broke and gone.
> I'se gwine to praise God 'til I die.

"Oh, we were eating ham. Lord God Almighty had unbuttoned the gates and let us out. He heard our calls.

"I sho'ly know'd how to pray when I left the war. Honey, when you needs something call upon God. I'se always done it and I'se still traveling 'cause I got faith in God. He said you may be sick or something the matter but if you call on Him He will heal you. But if He wants you to come to Him, He will say to His angel, 'Go down yonder and bring John, give him anything he may want.' They raised his head trying to keep him here, but the angel of God know'd it wasn't no need to do that for he was taking John away from here. No matter what you do or say, when God gets ready for you, you is gwine away from here. Chile, if you didn't get ready here you can't get ready up yonder. Everybody is traveling, I'se traveling too, I'se depending on the Lord. I got faith in Him that He is gwine to let me travel a long ways. That is why I'se ninety-six years old. God has spared me here. A many one has come and gone, but I'se still here. I thank God too. My mother's gone. She tole me to meet her in Heaven and by the grace of God, I'se gwine to meet her there too. My father's gone, my brother's gone. I'se still traveling, bless God. Honey, I'se still traveling.

"My mother was a good woman. She was a slave and didn't have much to say but she tole us to pray. She couldn't read but she would steal away and let me read the Bible to her, 'cause we weren't 'lowed to read but I stayed round the white folks all the time and learned. I was with the white children a lots but my mother said I was just smart anyway. I learned a lots of things that was taught the white children, I'd read to her. She always encouraged me to try to learn and be somebody, even if I was a slave and I did all I could to do what she wanted.

"We had a hard time. I think of it now and I get so full. We waded in water, deep water, but we kept praying for the Lord to cut them chains.

"Chile, when the slaves wasn't able to pick cotton or do as much work as was set aside for them they'd get lashings. If they said pick 10, 150, or 250 pounds, they expected that to be done, for they had estimated just how much work each one could and was able to do and that had to be done. I didn't do much picking for I had to drive my master round in his fine buggy. I have seen the overseer take girls in, one at the time and lash them. When they carry the girls in, a woman was there to whip them. They'd tie their dresses above their waists and give 15 or 20 lashes. I was the leader, for they thought I know'd mor'n the rest and they listened to me 'cause I stayed round the white folks most of the time. I got the boys together. I was lying down in the cotton patch. Lord Almighty gave me this knowledge.

"I said, 'Let us all get a big rock and let the girls pick cotton, put in the basket so much cotton and then put in the rock, finish filling the basket with the cotton. This was to make the cotton weigh more and keep the white folks from whipping the girls. We boys went to work. Chile, us slaves stood together then. The white folks never learned what we did. When the wimmin got scared and cried 'cause they'd get whipped 'cause they didn't have the amount they were to pick for the day, we'd put a rock in. Then the baskets were taken to the scales. Lizzi know'd she didn't have her 150 pounds and had been crying 'cause she didn't. We had put a rock in Lizzie's cotton and hers was the first to be weighed. The weigher put hers on the scales and there she had hers and one pound over. Fetched Laura's up and put on the scales. Up went the scales. She had 102 pounds, two more than she was to pick. 'Oh,' said the overseer, 'we wont get to whip them tonight.' We'd have to empty the baskets and always the one who emptied the basket know'd about the rock and he'd throw it away. We'd even get up early in the morning before day to throw them rocks away if we didn't have the chance that past evening. My mother know'd I thought it up and she would ask me how I thought it up. I'd tell her, 'Nothing but the Lord showed me what to do.'

"I'd think of how the man's head went off. He was there fighting to keep me under slavery. God Almighty intended that his fighting would not keep us.

"Chile, I could always see things. God Almighty fixed me so I could. No, chile, I didn't study no books to learn, that is a gift just handed down from my forefathers. You know even before we was brought here from Africa by the white folks, and heathens as they say we was, there was that gift shown in many ways. I'se still traveling 'cause I got faith in God. I know you may read of it, but, honey, in them days and it was so in slavery, the more the witch doctor could do, the better he was thought of and he was counted high up. I could do and see things too, even when I was very small. Stand up and let me look at you. Babe, she is a fine girl, ain't she? You can look at her and tell. She knows how to keep that tongue of hers. I could do a lots for you too if you'd believe in me and do what I tell you. And not talk. You see all those folks that come by here and spoke to me. They saw you in here and didn't come in. They know what I can do. They come by to let me do something for them but seeing you they just spoke and went on, but I know'd what they wanted. A lots of them come by to tell me, 'Uncle Ben, what you did for me come out just as you told me.'

"Would I mind telling you what it is I do for them? Uh, wait, let me look at you. Yes, you keep your tongue, I can see it. Oh, look, you are scared. I wont hurt you. I wont do nothing to you. I could help you, though. I'd make life much easier for you if you'd let me fix you up. Anything you'd want would come to you. You could get anything you wanted. I am able to put husband and wife together. Lots of women see men they want and they come to me to fix them up and I do. They come back to tell me it came out just as they wanted. A lots of them come for me to fix them up to be lucky with the the the 'bug' and I do. They always come back to say they won. I could do it for you, too, but I can see you're scared of me. You don't believe what I say is true, I can see it. If you'd believe in me I sho'ly could do it for you and I can see you are scared, so unless you had faith in me I couldn't do much. You got to believe in me.

"Tell you just what I do? You've always wanted to know just what was done? Chile, I couldn't tell you that but if a person wants me to fix them for anything, they always comes by in the day to tell me and the next day they come back. Well, at night I fix up the stuff for them and have it ready for the next day. No, you don't under-stand, you don't believe in it. What do I do with the mixture? I'll tell you this but, mind you, you must keep your mouth and not talk about it. Oh, I know you wont tell. I know you will keep that little red thing in your mouth still. I rub it on them and put some of it in each shoe. Chile, it goes wherever they go and do them good too. Do I charge? No, chile, I just let them give me what they want. Sometime they give a quarter or fifteen cents. I don't say no certain amount. No, chile, I can't tell you more. God give me that power because I trusted in Him. If you believed in it, I'd do a lots for you, too. I see it. I can see plum through you. You're a good woman and works hard for a living. I could help you a lots, too, bless God.*

"When I come here I joined Friendship Baptist Church. Honey, where Friendship is now there was a little road and trees all around. I helped to put in the cornerstone. That was before the present pastor's time and he has been there over sixty years now.

"Daughter, when I come here to this place, you know where the old car shed on the Georgia road is, I helped to put up the wall over the old car shed. Where the Kimball House† stands now was just a clump of trees. A creek went near by. There was swampy land, and the creek ran up to Pryor Street and turned across Alabama Street. Them wasn't no paved streets then, honey; I helped to fill in that creek. I remember on the spot where the Kimball House stands was a big spring with the best water, it was so cool. All along where the car shed was, women sold dinners and one could get all he could eat for 5¢. There was a marble yard near the Kimball House. People didn't have to buy much wood, for Atlanta was woods, woods. Where Peachtree, Whitehall, and Broad streets is today, there was nothing but woods and pig and cow paths, I used to go right out near the Kimball House and get wood to make fires for my family. So, honey, you can see how Atlanta has grow'd.

"Colored people had little shanties with stick and dirt chimneys. Where Morris Brown College‡ is now, no colored people lived there. A man had a little store in that vicinity where the West Mitchell Street C.M.E.§ Church is now standing. All white folks lived there and very few of them. I thank God I have been spared to see all those old landmarks changed from swamps, woods, and creeks to modern streets.

"I have seen the streetcars that were carried along by mules and had a bell on the car. The man who drove the mules would ring a bell, *ting-a-ling, ting-a-ling*, down the street he'd go. The mules went very slow. I remember once I was riding the car and I was in a

*Brother/Uncle Ben was a root doctor. For a perceptive analysis of root medicine, see Loudell F. Snow, "Folk Medical Beliefs and Their Implications for Care of Patients," *Annals of Internal Medicine* 81 (1974): 82–96.

†Atlanta hotel erected in 1870, now torn down.

‡Coeducational black college established in 1885 under the auspices of the African Methodist Episcopal Church.

§Colored Methodist Episcopal Church, renamed as Christian Methodist Episcopal Church in 1955.

hurry to get where I was going and it seemed the mules were going too slow. I just got out of the car and ran. I kept up with the car and passed it. The streetcar shop was on Butler Street, where they kept the mules and cars. Now to think I have lived to see electric-drawn cars. The Lord has blessed me.

"I worked for Mr. Forest Green, as yardman. I worked for him a long time. I then got a job driving for Dr. Stevens. No, chile, no car but a fine buggy and horse. I looked after the yard too. I worked for Mr. Rosenblack. Whew-ee! I've had some fine white folks, honey, and they were good white folks. I worked for another man, now what is his name? Babe, what was his name? You know, he would send me anything he thought I needed. What's his name, Babe? Oh, Babe, can't you remember it either? You know he would send me two tons of coal at the time. Oh, I hate to miss giving you his name, chile, because he was such a good white man. He is dead now.

"I married this wife, Emma, forty-six years ago. She was raised in Atlanta but was born in Marietta, Georgia seventy-four years ago, in January. She was a cook before she got too old to work and a good cook she was too.

"I sent my daughter, this was a child by my first marriage, to school. The first school she went to was Miss Packer's School which she held in Friendship Church. I paid 10¢ a week for her schooling. I never had any children by this wife. Honey, we have lived together all these years, trusting in God and that is why He keeps us. Young people is traveling too fast, they live too fast and they die fast too. Don't live to get old like me and Babe here. They just hurry themselves to their graves.

"Daughter, seems like I am telling you all the things that happened to me in slavery but I guess I have time to live and think in the past and that is the reason. I think of how slaves were auctioned off like cattle. The auctioneer would get up on a block, tell all of the things the slave could do, and he would tell it in the most glowing manner, so the bidder would offer a big price for him, or her. I can see the auctioneer now, standing here, 'Nell is a good nigger, a good cook, she is obedient, a good nurse and a good field hand. How much do you bid, $25, $50, $60, do I hear another . . . going, going, gone.' I've know'd them to take the slaves home after buying them and have them take off all their clothes to see if there was any defects.

"I've worked in the fields and when time come for dinner there was a horn blow'd or a bell rung for us to stop. Even the mules were so used to the bell and horn that when they heard it they would stop dead still in the middle of the row, or wherever they was and wouldn't go another step. We slaves had a hard time but we trusted in God. We stood together. If one stole a hog, chickens, or anything, the others wouldn't tell it for nothing. It would be a good thing if Negroes would stick together now. I don't believe in stealing and dishonest things, though. White people is good and they will help colored folks all they can if they is honest. God said, 'Together we stand and divided we fall.'

"White folks let us off on Friday and Saturday to get ready to go to church. Men put on their best shoes and red shirts and suits. The wimmin their best. We all tried to act like our masters and mistresses when we'd get out where they couldn't see us and oh, how we'd strut. Everyone went. We had baptism in the lakes and rivers. Them was happy times, for we felt big as the white folks. But, chile, we better not let the white folks know it though. The converts would come up out of the water shouting and clapping their hands, so full of the Holy Spirit.

"We had some good white people and my master was one of them. He was one of the best white men that ever lived and there is many a one.

"At times the slaves would run away. I saw a man who run away and went on another man's plantation by a creek and dug a hole, way back up in the bank, put planks in and he stayed there six years. His owner didn't know where he was. He and his wife stayed in that cave all those years. One of the children was born there. They would come out at night. They did all of their work at night, so they wouldn't be found. Some of the colored people know'd they was there and would carry food and other things to them at night. After six years a man's dog turned them up. A hound dog named Ruler. He went to the cave and scented and bayed, causing them to get suspicious. The dog dug and dug and finally the owner called in men and had them dig. Old Man Bill Grant, the meanest white man I ever saw, got picks and shovels and said, 'I bet I'll get him out.' He uncovered the cave and there was that family of four that had been in there six years. They didn't look like human beings when they were brought out.

"When I was young I went to see my girl. She was a fine, pretty girl and I loved her. Her owner came out and saw me there. 'Who is that nigger and what is he doing here?' He walked up and saw me, 'Why that's ole Luke Weston's nigger,' he said. He grabbed me by the collar and said he was going to whip me. Well, he didn't know I wasn't going to let him whip me before that girl. When he grabbed me by the collar, I caught him by the leg and raised it as high as I could. I wasn't going to let him whip me. He fell and when he hit the ground, I ran as fast as I could.

"After we was free I got dissatisfied and decided to come to Atlanta. I was always the leader in my family and all depended on me. I walked to Atlanta from LaGrange, Georgia with my mother, father, and two brothers. We walked it in a day and a half. We didn't have no money and just put our feet in the road and come on here. We toted our little possessions on our heads. My father and brothers would carry it some and then I would take it. When we got to Atlanta, we met a white man, Captain Fuller. I asked him where we could stay. He showed me an old house down the road in the woods a piece. It was near where the Kimball House is now. He said, 'The door is down but you can stay in it. Set the door up at night so no one can bother you.' I went in. He told me to go to his house, and showed me where it was, to get some food. I carried our things in that house. There was a piece of broom in it and I swept the dirt out. I went out and cut some firewood and made a fire. No one bothered us, for everyone was trying to get someplace to stay, after they had been freed. For them Yankees didn't have nothing to give us after they'd freed us and although some of the masters give their slaves a little something to start on, there was so many more that didn't do nothing but put them out and let us make it the best we could. I set up all night. Captain Fuller's wife, when I told her he had sent me there, gave me plenty of food and told me to come on up there, that there was a little house out in the back yard we could live in. It was better than the one we was in.

"Father was kinder scared of white folks. He hadn't been used to coming close in contact with them as I had and he was scared of them. He was scared to talk to them, but I wasn't and asked for what I wanted. Mrs. Fuller told me to bring Mother up there and when she saw her she said, 'Millie, you come and get anything you want.' My mother told her she would wash and cook, or do anything else she could do about the house. Mrs. Fuller showed her where the wash place was and the tubs. She gave us meats and all kinds of food. She asked me if I was a member of the church and said God would provide for me. She was a kind woman and a Christian too.

"When Captain Fuller came back we had cleaned up the whole place. Everything was as clean as could be. They wouldn't charge us anything for rent. We stayed there six months and then got a place to live in. Mr. and Mrs. Fuller gave us clothes and everything we needed. Yes, God told me to ask for what I wanted and I always did. They were some of the best white folks I've every know'd and I've know'd some mighty fine ones.

"I worked as a plasterer and made good too. I was paid $2 a day. I did this work for a long time and after I began to grow old I did yard work and house cleaning for different white folks. I'm too old to work now. I do piddle about in the back yard. I have a little garden there.

"When the government passed the old-age pension law I was the first one to get it, me and Babe here. Bless God, you don't know how much it helps. . . . I had always been able to pay my own bills and have a little money left for the little things we needed, and with the old-age pension coming in each month, I still have that. We are ole and unable to do much about the house and the government fixed it so we can have someone come in to clean and wash for us. She is sent from the housekeeping place. She is very nice. She ain't been here, though, in a week and when I saw you coming in I thought you was another one sent us.

"We get surplus food once a month, and, God Almighty, I am happy. Chile, this was the best President we ever had, he is a Christian man. He believes in helping poor people. God got into his heart and told him to help us poor people and he is doing the most blessed thing for us. Lawd, I wish he could stay up there in that White House forever.

"Honey chile, I am happy here, praising God for His blessings to me and Babe. I'se just living in His blessed glory and, bless God, I'se praising His name."

Geneva Tonsill

No Stick-Leg

SEABOARD, NORTH CAROLINA, 1939

I was here when Nat riz, when de stars fell,
when de war come, when de surrender was,
when it was de earthquake—and I's still here.

"Lettice Boyer is my name. I's a hund'ed and ten years old. My mind's clear, but my memb'ry's got short de last ten years.

"Lord, honey, I's been here from way back! I was here when Nat riz, when de stars fell, when de war come, when de surrender was, when it was de earthquake*—and I's still here.

"When my son lay dyin' a long time ago, he called me to him and says: 'Mammy, wake Delie'—I wouldn't let Delie sleep wid him whilst he was sick—'I got to ask her somethin'.' Den he turned to me and says: 'Mammy, does you see death in my eyes?'

" 'No, son. I don't see no death in your eyes.' But I did.

"When Delie come to his bed, he says: 'Delie, I wants you to tell me de truth. Does you see death in my eyes?'

" 'No, Henry, dat I don't.' Delie was fit to cry.

" 'Mammy, look good. Don't you see it now?'

" 'No, son, I don't see no death in your eyes.'

" 'Den you can't see good. It's dere. I's leavin' soon. But you gwine stay here. I can see you livin' to walk wid a stick, to look at folkses aworkin' in de field when you done past workin'.'

---

*She is referring to Nat Turner's Rebellion of 1831, which occurred near where she lived, possibly to Belia's Comet, which appeared in 1846 and 1852, to the Civil War, and to the Charleston, South Carolina, earthquake of 1886.

"Dat's come to pass. I can't git around nowhur widout my stick, and all I can do is look at folkses a-workin' in de field. I done past workin'. Last week my sheet and pillowcase, my apron and dress was so black dey was bound to be washed. But I hated to say anything to Hattie, much as she got to do. So I filled me up a tub o' water, found some mo' dirty clothes to put wid mine, and got out a tubful o' washin' on de line 'fore Hattie come from de field. Dat washin' 'bout done me up; my back ain't been right since. A little washin' and sweepin' o' de yards and patchin' clothes is all I's fittin' for now.

"De two months I's been here wid Hattie, I ain't been able to walk no furder dan to de bottom. De day I got dat fur, I jus' stood and looked and looked, but I couldn't see over dem trees in de bottom.

"One thing dat ail my back today is de witches. Dey ain't so bad now'days, but sometimes dey still rides a body o' nights. I knowed one man dat was a witch and rid folks. Long den de witches was ridin' me so hard I'd wake up plum wore out, and I suspicioned 'twas dis man. When I was down wid de fever, dey greased me in 'intment all over. Dis man come in and looked hard at me.

" 'Umph! Too greasy, too greasy!' he says.

" 'Too greasy for what? For de witches to ride me o' nights?' I put it plain to him. Den I told him if he ever rid me agin, I'd tell him to de world. De witches didn't bother me no mo' right away; dat made me know he was de one dat had been ridin' o' me. De only way I every knowed how to keep 'em off was to put a broom under de bed; de witches couldn't bother nobody till dey had counted all de straws in de broom. Cou'se dey's still witches! I don't has to reckon 'bout dat.

"Ha'nts?* Cou'se dey's ha'nts! I's seed plenty of 'em, but I ain't never been scared o' none. Dey ain't no harm in a ha'nt; dey's jus' dead folks come back to deir old range. I seed a woman jus' ahead o' me one day, but I couldn't catch her, how fast I walked; she kep de same distance from me, no nearer, no furder. 'Nother time I seed a woman settin' on a stump side de road. She was dere plain as my hand till I took my eyes off a second; when I looked agin, she was gone. A ha'nt won't never vanish long as you keep your eyes on it. My mammy always told me I'd see things 'cause I was bo'n wid a veil over my face. But de only thing I ever been scared of is de livin', not de dead, not ha'nts.

*Ghosts.

"Sometimes when I thinks 'bout dem days 'fore de war when we was all slaves and well tuk care of, I wonders if we wouldn't been better off widout freedom. Maybe not; some wanted deir freedom so bad. Dou'se a heap o' de slaves had a hard time back den. I was bo'n at de Brandon's plantation down on de Neck.* My mammy had twenty head o' chil'ren. My father was made ferryman crost de Roanoke River, and dis was his job till de surrender.

"I was 'bout two year old when Nat riz, but dat's too fur back for me to 'member. My mammy used to tell how dem slaves in Virginia killed up de white folks, but we never had nothin' like dat on de Neck. She say some o' de slaves on de river plantations got wind o' de risin' in Southampton, but dey never made no plans to jine.

"Long as my mistis lived, we slaves at Brandon's was treated good. No, madam, Mis' Louise Cline wouldn't 'low nobody to whup her slaves! It was her rule that no overseer shouldn't hit one of us widout fust bringin' de case 'fore her; dey was dasn't to touch one o' Miss Louise's niggers. One time when a overseer did whup a slave, soon as Miss Louise found it out she rushed out de great house like a streak o' lightnin', jumped on her ho'se, and rode tearin' down to de overseer's.

" 'What's dis I hear 'bout Eli?' she wants to know.

" 'He got unruly; so I had him to whup, Miss Louise.'

" 'Don't you know I forbid anybody to touch one of my servants till I's heard de case and settled it lawful? Yes, you knowed it. Now git out. Git out right now!'

"Miss Louise put him out in de road right den. I can see her now slingin' her leg cross de ho'se, ridin' a-sidesaddle down de road in a fog o' dust.

"We didn't have no marster, least he didn't stay home much. He was a missionary and rode from church to church to preach, whilst Miss Louise stayed home and run de plantation.

"I was raised in de great house to help nu'se de chil'ren and to wait on de table. When I started settin' de table I was so little dat I had to stand in a chair to reach high as de table. I stayed round my mistis in de great house till looked like I thought I belonged dere same as de white chil'ren. One of my brothers was de carriage driver, and some de rest had jobs at de great house too.

"Every winter we got two pair o' yarn stockin's and two pair o'

*Far eastern North Carolina, a peninsula bounded by Albemarle and Pamlico sounds.

winter shoes. Our mistis give us shoes for de summer too, summer dresses, and a shaker. Don't you know what a shaker is? It's a straw bonnet made out o' wheat straw dat kept our heads cool in de hot sun.

"Dere was plenty to eat at Brandon's—molasses, herrin's, butter, every kind o' milk, every kind o' meat. We used to kill a lotful o' hogs; dey'd be a string of 'em hanging' up fur as from here to de road, and it'd take three weeks to git done wid de hog-killin' and cleanin' up afterwards. We was fed so many herrin's dat to dis day I don't love herrin's for nothin'.

"De slaves had tole'ble good times. Dere was a dance every Satday night, sometimes oftener dan dat. We went to de white folks's church and learnt to sing deir songs and enjoy religion. I don't 'member de songs, none but de one 'bout 'Behold de Saviour on de cross.' Dat was Preacher Norton's favorite; he said he got a lot o' conversions on dat hymn. It was all changed atter Miss Louise died and de overseers took holt. I had a mistis! I love her in de ground!

"When dey sent me in de field, my hard times started. Lord, how dey did beat us! We was stripped and helt by our heads and feets while they lash was laid on our backs. De men slaves was staked out whilst dey was whupped. On de Pleasant Grove plantation dey used de bill-bo'; de slaves had to stick deir heads th'ugh a holed cut in a boa'd and lie dere whilst dey was beat. Deir ears was marked just like hogs.

"My father said, dough, we was treated better'n slaves was when he was a boy; he could 'member back to de fust war.* When de marsters wanted to punish de slaves, dey cotched 'em, put 'em in a hogshead driv full o' nails, and rolled de hogshead down de hill; blood run down de road like pourin' water.

"Every night when de nine o' clock horn blowed, all de slaves had to be in deir place or de paderoller cotched and beat 'em. If I was here in dis room and my bed was dere crost de hall, I'd get a whuppin' for bein' out o' place if I was cotched. My brother, my own dear brother, was beat to death by a paderoller. He was always weakly and couldn't work in de field like de rest; so Mistis had made him a shoe-mender. One day when he was out o' leather, he cut off a little strip from some old gin belts to patch his shoes wid. De overseer beat him so bad he had to be tuk to de sick house, and when dey brung him out it was feet fo'most. Eadie was whupped

*She is probably referring to the Turner Rebellion. See Stephen B. Oates, *The Fires of Jubilee: Nat Turner's Fierce Rebellion* (New York: Harper & Row, 1975), p. 145.

to death de same way, only she in de sick house a little longer dan my brother.

"We slaves knowed dere was a war comin', but we dasn't breathen it. My mammy's white folks at New Bern learnt her to read and write 'fore dey sold her to Brandon's plantation, and she read in de Bible 'bout dere was a war comin'. 'De sun shall be darkened and de moon give no light and de stars from heb'n shall fall, and brother shall fight agin brother, and every nation shall go to its own home and wash-up God under dier own fig tree.' Mammy read dat and said it meant war. She used to eel-drap and hear de white folks talkin' war too. De slaves knowed 'fore de marsters did, but we had to steal and talk it.

"Den when de stars commenced to fall from heb'n, everybody knowed de war was at hand. When night come dey'd be a big shower of 'em wid long streamers. De stars fell on de earth I reckon, but we never found none. All time de war went on, we could see de stars fallin' from de sky at night.

"When de war broke out, I was married and had two head o' chil'ren. We stayed home and raised de somethin' t'eat, whilst de white folks tended to de Yankees. De Yankees never stoled nothin', no madam! Dey come along and tuk what dey wanted right out from under you, but dey didn't call it stealin'. Dey never hurt nobody or burnt nothin' on de river plantations as I ever heard of. De Ransoms and de Barlows hid deir gold cups and saucers and plates and glass jars full o' money in de millpond, and atter de Yankees passed th'ugh folks went dere and stoled de gold dishes and money while de Ransoms and Barlows was off fightin'. When I seed de Yankees comin', I hid my chickens under de house and den run and hid myself and de chil'ren. Dem Yankees, wid deir buckles and swords flashin' in de sun, was a frightenin'-lookin' sight. Dey didn't ride like folks does now; deir ho'ses come 'long de road in a leap, jus' like dis: jumpty, jumpty, jumpty, jump!

"Our side met de Yankees at Bull Hill over yonder at Barrow's Hill and had a fight. De Yankees said dey was gwine kill Gen'l Ransom* dat day shore. Dey did shoot at him close to a tree de other side o' de millpond, but Gen'l Ransom runned away from 'em. Dat fight at Bull Hill ended de war. Gen'l Lee surrendered den.†

*General Robert Ransom, Jr., or his brother, General Matthew Whitaker Ransom. The latter was a United States senator after the Civil War.

†She is referring to some local skirmishes that probably occurred as the Civil War was ending.

"After de surrender, we stayed on at Brandon's plantation till my three chil'ren was grown—I lost one—workin' for what wages we could git. Atter while we bought a farm at Rehobirth and moved off de Neck dere. My sister paid for one half de farm of fifty acres and we paid for de other half; dere ain't a penny on it today. It was hard to make a livin', for de land was pore, but we scuffled along and got th'ugh somehow.

"Hard work? Lord, honey, I's done some hard work! Don't ask me what I *has* done, but what I *ain't*. I's plowed, dug stumps, chopped, broke steers, ginned cotton—I fed cotton to de hoppers when de gin wheel was high as dis house. De hardest work I ever done was keepin' de co'n back out o' de co'n-sheller. If it wa'n't ke' out, de sheller stopped up, and de bearin's was tore all to smash. Dat's de only time I ever flagged out at work, keepin' de co'n out o' de sheller. I fell down like I was dead.

"Jus' twice I cooked out for white folks, once over in Virginia and about two months at de Rapids.* My husband wouldn't allow me to stay no longer'n dat away from home. Dat's fur as I every traveled. My husband's been dead—Lord, I don't know how long. Atter he left me, I tended to de farm best I could, plowed my co'n and cotton, and lived by myself part o' de time. When I 'gin to git old, my sister's boy come holp me. Once I moved to Walkers' place and lived wid one o' my daughters. Sometimes I stayed round wid my other chil'ren.

"Church is de last place I give up gwine to. I belongs to Parker's Chapel Baptist Church. Dat's whur I was when de earthquake come, at de revival meetin'. De fust thing dat happened was de lamps all went out. Den de church shook. Somebody said: 'Who blowed out de lamps?' I says: 'De One who blowed dem out is gwine blow us all out.' We thought 'twas Judgment Day shore. De young converts dat was settin' on de mou'ners bench got 'ligion so fast dere in de dark dat de whole house was in a shout.

"I had done got 'ligion long time 'fore dat. Jesus 'peared fore me and says: 'I will redeem you and take away de cuss of Adam.'

" 'Redeem. I don't know no redeem,' I says.

" 'You is under de cuss of Adam in de Gyarden, but My Blood will redeem you and make you free.'

" 'Redeem. I don't know no—'

"But I never finished. I fell out dead. I woke up shoutin'. Dat's how I got 'ligion. I miss gwine to my church wus as anything.

---

*Roanoke Rapids, North Carolina.

Lord, dat I did shout! When de Spirit says shout, I shout; when He says sing, I sing. Shoutin's somethin' nobody can't help, whur dey in de washtub or sweepin' yards or nussin' little chil'ren or in de church.

"De las' time I heard de preacher he give it to de grown folks 'bout de way dey was raisin' deir chil'ren. 'I was 'bout to say,' he tells 'em, 'dat de young folks of today is gwine to hell for deir fast livin'. I'll change dat; it's de mothers and fathers dat's gwine to hell for raisin' 'em fast.' De young folks ain't raised now'days; dat's a fact; dey's too fast, too knowin'. You see how dem chil'ren is stickin' here under us 'stead o' gwine on out in de yard like dey ought to. When I was a gal, young folks wa'n't 'lowed to set under de old folks a-listenin' to deir talk. My mammy would've said, 'Lettice, git on out in de yard; what we's sayin' ain't none o' your business.'

"De gals now'days smokes cigarettes; dat's bad for deir health. I smokes a pipe, or did till I left it at home two months ago. A pipe's healthy. I dips, and when I can't git snuff I chews tobacco, but a pipe's de best way for a woman to use tobacco.

"All my chil'ren's dead now, nobody left but me, one grand-daughter, several great-grandchil'ren, and four great-great-grand-chil'ren. De closest kin I got in de world now is Hattie, my grand-daughter. Two months ago she sent Will over to bring me here to stay, 'cause she said I mustn't stay by myself at Rehobirth.

"I *has* stayed dere by myself. De last few years, my daughter lived dere at de home place wid me, but atter her death her husband kep' fallin' further behind till he got so he couldn't go. Last year he didn't make enough to pay de taxes on de place; so he quit and moved off. De land's lyin' out now, for nobody won't rent it; still de taxes has got to be paid and nothin' to pay wid. It can't be sold, 'cause it's heir-land; do, I'd shore git rid of it and pay Hattie and Will somethin' for takin' me in.

"It bothered me to have to come here and put up on Will, when I ha'n't never done nothin' in de world for him; he never eben eat a meal's vittles at my house. Dere's two chil'ren here, 'sides Hattie and Will, to eat off o' de one bale o' cotton he made last year, widout me crowdin' in. Sometimes when I gits to de table, I sets dere and cries 'cause I's so hongry and hates so bad to eat up Will's vittles.

" 'What you cryin' 'bout, Granny?' Hattie says.

" 'I hates to be on you, child,' I tells her. 'You needs your vittles.'

" 'Go on, eat,' Will says, 'for long as I got bread you has too.'

"I got a hearty appetite and can eat anything comes to de table, only I don't love herrin's for nothin', no madam! If you'll bring me some cheese and light bread next time you comes, I shore be proud of it. Meat tastes good to me; cou'se I can eat meat—I gums it, dat's how. Dere's two old tusk-es left dat ought to come out and when dey gits a little looser I's wring dem out like I done de other old tarrers. Ain't no tooth doctor never been in my mouth. Dere ain't been no doctor to me but twice—oncet when a moccasin bit me and my leg swolled all up over my ankles, and three years ago when I broke my leg.

"A automobile caused me to break my leg. I hooked up the cart and started to Jim's for some co'n. My daughter says, 'Mammy, I hears a automobile. You better drive off to one side till it passes. By dat time I heard de automobile close; so I drove my ho'se into a man's yard till de automobile passed. De ho'se got too near de palin's, upset de cart and throwed us out. My leg cotched under me and broke. When de doctor come, he told me he was gwine do de bes' he could for me, but my leg wouldn't never heal 'cause I was too old. Whilst dey was tryin' to set de bone, it hurted so bad I had to holler. Den dey got to pullin' my leg so hard I thought shore dey was tryin' to pull it off; so I hollered to 'em not to pull it off 'cause I didn't want no stick-leg. De leg healed up, and I can use it all right now. No stick-leg for me to drag round, no madam!

"I don't look a hund'ed and ten years old? Well, I's beginnin' to feel it anyhow. One eye is still good, but de other one's gone. My hearin' has failed some too, but I don't feel bad nowhur but my head and my back. I got no blood pressure as I knows of: it ain't never been tuk. De most doctorin' I's had is wid old folks's remedies—salt and kasine and vinegar. I reckon you smell kasine on me now. Knock dat fly away; dey so tame here dey's soon walk right in your mouth.

"I's seed a lot o' sickness, holp wid birthin' many a baby, and washed many a corpse. Diptree* used to be wus as de plague; when it struck a house, all de chil'ren died in a pile. Black tongue† tuk off a lot o' folks and cows too. I never had black tongue, but I's seed folks died wid it. Dere was small-pox and big-pox—I can't tell you 'bout it wid dem chil'ren settin' here under us.

"All de picture I ever had o' myself got burnt up in de bureau dat de rats set afire. We cotched de fire in time and saved de house. A man come from Rich Square one time dat said he was gwine to

---

*Diphtheria.
†Pellagra.

write 'bout me for de paper, but I don't know whur he did or not. I couldn't read it nohow. I never learnt to read or write my name; none o' my chil'ren could read or write.

"I don't git no help from nobody 'cept Hattie and Will, never got none. My son-in-law talked to 'em in Jackson* 'bout gittin' de old-age pension; some others has told 'em I ought to have it. 'Bout three weeks ago a man come here to talk to me, and when I told him 'bout de land dey ain't a penny on he said he 'fraid dat was gwine to keep me from gittin' help. De land ain't no 'count to me nor nobody like 'tis; it's heir-land and can't be sold: if it could, nobody buy it 'cause it's so unconvenient and hard to git to. Nobody won't rent it. Will wouldn't leave Mr. Carson to go way off down dere to live; he's sharecropped here for fourteen years, and he wouldn't start farmin' on land dat's got to be divided 'mongst de great-grandchil'ren soon's I's dead. He couldn't make de taxes nohow. So land ain't no 'count to me. I wish de gov'ment would take it. If dey's helpin' de old folks, I'd be proud of a little so's I wouldn't feel like I was a drag on Hattie and Will.

"De other day I was worried so bad over it I went out and set in de yard to myself. Will come to de do' and says: 'What you doin', Granny?'

" 'I's studyin'.'

" 'Bout what?'

" 'Trouble.'

" 'Don't set out dere in de cold. Come to de fire.'

" 'I's prayin'.'

"I didn't tell him how it hurted me to set at his fire and not eben be able to tote a stick o' wood in. I don't know how long I's gwine live. My mammy was 105 when she died. I wish I could stay here till I's 120. I knows I's gwine to heb'n and see Mistis and all my folks when I dies, but I'd like to live to be 125 fust. You reckon I can?

"Don't forgit my cheese and light bread."

Bernice Kelly Harris

*County seat, Northampton County.

Prices that had been sky-high in 1918
started tumblin'.
—Sharecropper

I reckon you can call me a successful farmer.
I come from a one-horse to a four-
horse farmer, with two sharecroppers
on my place now. From a steer cart to
a surrey we've climbed to an auto-
mobile. From a turnin' plow, I've
come to . . . disc harrows and plows,
though I don't own a tractor yet.
—Farmer

We are the least agricultural, least rural generation in American history. We wear blue jeans in profusion, but our domain is urban or suburban. Our fortunes do not ride on the next harvest (" 'Backer Barning"), the weather, or the price of cotton or tobacco. We define security in terms of pension funds, Social Security, savings, and maybe stocks and bonds, not as the farmer in "Just a Plain Two-Horse Farm" did: "When my wife died I was in good shape financially. I didn't owe a cent, and I had five bales o' cotton on hand. It took them five bales to pay the doctors' bills and her burial expenses, and I begin then to get behind." Our career paths do not ordinarily include trying to acquire land, improving it, and then using it to build a legacy for our families. Not only do we own little land, we are not very attached to land or locale. Nor do we know the joy of "smell[ing] plowed land" or in sensing that farming "is in [our] blood for keeps" ("Tobacco's in My Blood").

It takes a considerable leap of imagination to transport ourselves to the rural South of the 1930s, where two of every three Southerners lived, where almost one in two Southerners earned their too-often meager living from farming, where more than half of those farmers (1,831,475 in 1935) worked other people's land, where sharecroppers earned an average of $312 a year, and hired farm labor $180. And tenancy had increased steadily during the first three decades of the twentieth century: "I aimed when I started out to own me a farm, but it didn't turn out that way."*

Southern landowners never lacked sufficient hands (though they were not necessarily efficient); there was little alternative to working on farms because American cities and industries offered few unskilled jobs to the landless agrarians. Southerners, black and white, migrated in large numbers during World War I and the 1920s to factories, towns, and cities, but farm labor supply continued to exceed farm labor demand. So landless farmers endured being "cussed like a dog" ("Aaron and Mary Matthews"), occasionally getting some help from the government or from organizations like the Southern Tenant Farmers' Union, a short-lived radical farm labor organization ("Ain't Got No Screens"),† or trying to get

*From an unpublished life history, "The Lees," written by Bernice Kelly Harris, Seaboard, N.C., 1938, p. 8, FWP-Couch Papers, Southern Historical Collection, University of North Carolina Library, Chapel Hill, N.C.

†Encouraged by local socialists, a few black and white farm tenants organized the STFU in 1934. Its abortive cotton pickers' strike in 1935 and its brief general strike of

41

away from a bad landlord in order to work for a good landlord ("In Abraham's Bosom"). The realities of land tenure and tenantry—only 13.4 percent of black farmers owned farms of any size—meant that most blacks in Southern agriculture worked for whites. As a black man plowed a field near Columbia, South Carolina, he sang a song heard as far away as Missouri:

> See dat pecker-wood
> Settin' on de rail
> Learnin' how to figger
> All for de white man
> Nothin' for de nigger

But one-fourth of all Southern white farmers worked as tenants or wage laborers. Crippled by alcoholism and anxious that no one call him or even think him "poor white trash," Jim Jeffcoat drifted from Georgia to Virginia to the Carolinas:

Jim and me married twenty-three years ago and this is our seventh place. . . . We have never owned a horse or a mule or a cow or any tools or anything to ride in. Of course, we ain't never owned a house, and we never will. The houses we've lived in ain't worth owning. They ain't worth nothing to nobody except to furnish poor croppers like us who can't do any better.

Repeated disappointments soured relationships. In the interview "In Abraham's Bosom," Emaline, the daughter of ex-slaves, tells how blacks in Dillon, South Carolina, who believed they had been cheated by landlords settled scores. Like their slave ancestors, they stole, they destroyed crops and livestock, and they burned barns. Landlords claimed wanton destruction of their property ("The Landlord Has His Troubles"). Some landlords eased tensions between their tenants and themselves by being scrupulously honest ("Jackson Bullitt, a Small Landlord"); others exacerbated bad relations by seeking every advantage at the tenant's expense.

Regardless of individual relationships, nothing could alter the

---

cotton field workers in 1936 gained national attention for the STFU but few concessions from farm owners for members of the STFU. By 1937, the union claimed nearly 31,000 members in seven Southern states, though Arkansas remained the center of activity. The organization declined by the end of the 1930s; eventually the residue became part of the American Federation of Labor as the National Agricultural Workers Union. See George B. Tindall, *The Emergence of the New South*, vol. 10 of *A History of the South*, ed. Wendell Holmes Stephenson and E. Merton Coulter (Baton Rouge: Louisiana State University Press, 1967), pp. 416-21; Donald H. Grubbs, *Cry from the Cotton: The Southern Tenant Farmers' Union and the New Deal* (Chapel Hill: University of North Carolina Press, 1971). For the moving, brilliantly told story of a member of the farmers' union, see Theodore Rosengarten, *All God's Dangers: The Life of Nate Shaw* (New York: Alfred A. Knopf, 1974).

basic facts. Southerners who farmed in the 1930s struggled against farm prices that slumped after the boom days of World War I, then struck a plateau by 1925, then fell over the edge in 1929, and only recovered during World War II.

I made an unusually large crop of cotton the year I was married, and that fall the price was so good I got rich. And the next year, 1921, was favorable, and I got still richer. When 1922 came, I was sitting on top of the world. I rode around in a new automobile. I had bought new furniture for the house, and I had spent money freely for farm tools, and gotten to be a "constipated gentleman." If one had told me I'd be as poor as I am now, I wouldn't have believed it.

H. L. Mitchell, a founder of the Southern Tenant Farmers' Union, noted perceptively that when tenants dealt with landlords, they were "paupers trying to bargain with paupers."* But it was still a struggle of unequals. "De landlord is landlord, de politicians is landlord, de judge is landlord, de shurf is landlord, everybody is landlord, en we ain' got nothin'."

The New Deal tilted the struggle even more. Its basic farm policies, which were aimed at raising farm prices by crop reduction and government price supports, favored the landed, especially the owners of larger holdings. Farm owners received money from the federal government for taking land out of production and agreeing to plant fewer crops. This money allowed them to purchase new equipment and reduce their work forces. In "Horse Trader" a man confidently and erroneously awaited the comeback of the mule, formerly one of the pillars of the rural South.

Not only did Southern farm owners improve their equipment and retire their mules; they also developed better practices for livestock, they employed better techniques for conservation, and they diversified their crops ("A Day on the Farm"). Stimulated by government policies and prodded by the price declines of cotton, the Southern farm staple, from 34 cents a pound in 1920 to 14 in 1930 and 10 in 1940, Southern farmers turned to new cash crops—soybeans, hay, pulpwood, forage, and turpentine—crops whose production was easily mechanized and required less labor.

Another pillar of the Southern farm life toppled. Tenant farmers began to disappear in the 1930s. Improvements in Southern agriculture had been bought at a terrible price. The unneeded, unwanted hands became a human mass that scattered in search of jobs.

*Quoted in Tindall, *Emergence of the New South*, p. 421.

Horse Trader

Nearly every man in the South who did any kind of
business at all had to know something about mules and horses.

"If any man knows the mule business I ought to; been followin' it since I was a boy fourteen years old. That's a long time ago: I was born in 1867—Fernland County," he said.

He was sitting in the lobby of the Bond Hotel. There was nothing about his clothes to distinguish him from the average man; he affected no out-of-date modes to which his age might have entitled him. The suit was dark, white shirt with soft collar attached, and a slouch hat that he might have exchanged with any young man on the street.

He was five feet ten inches tall. He weighed 160 pounds and was of a wiry build.

"If I'd stuck right to that instead of shootin' off at this and that, I'd be a very rich man today. Nearly every man in the South who did any kind of business at all had to know something about mules and horses. Next to farmin' itself I reckon it was one of the most active lines of business. Fact is, mules and horses were the power of the farm. A good pair of mules is just about as good assets as a farmer can have when he wants to arrange a small loan. Never saw a real banker turn one down yet if everything else was in good shape.

"Lot of people think the livestock business is dead. Ain't nothin' in that. Mules will always be useful to the land and the farmer. There's just something about a mule that fits ploughin' a field with

45

a nigger behind him. They're both just built for heavy work—that is if you ain't in a hurry. A mule is a funny animal, been studyin' 'em all my life. George Washington was the first to raise mules in this country. The King of Spain sent him a jack and a jennet as a present. The jack got with one of the horse mares and as far as I know this was the first mule in America or anywhere else as we know the mule.*

"I was fourteen years old when I started out with the wagon train; it wasn't any train, just a two-horse wagon that we rode in and camped when night come. The mules would follow behind or we would halter them to the wagon if it was necessary. Then we would just follow every court week from county to county. When the court met, every farmer in the county would usually come to the courthouse sometime during the week.

"Made a pretty nice arrangement for us, and we did plenty of tradin'. Back in those times there wasn't any money in this country. That was about '81 or '82. Most of it was tradin' with us; old scrub cattle or timber or anything that we could turn into a profit.

"Those farmers needed mules in those days to start raisin' their cotton again. I'm tellin' you, all this part of the country was in a hell of a mess. Goddam if it didn't look like every son-of-a-gun and his brother would starve to death tryin' to get started again. I learned a whole lot startin' off in a two-horse wagon that way and tradin' for any damn thing a man had. I got to know the country pretty well. Knew who needed what and where to go get it for him. But the mules and the cows were the base of the business."

He stopped to light a cigarette. His hands were full and unwrinkled as he cupped them for the light. His face was ruddy and clean-shaven and the eyes were clear and alert. Alternately he looked through and over his horn-rimmed glasses.

"Yes sir, they were pretty tight times back in the middle eighties. A young fellow had to scuffle about to get any education or even something to eat. I got so I could write and figure; picked most of it up from hangin' around the courthouses. The lawyers and doctors were about the only folks with an education and that wasn't much good. My folks were all farmers and preachers. Outside of the Bible they didn't have any books. That was in the days though

*Actually, the mule existed in Asia Minor long before Europeans settled the Americas. Nor was the King of Spain's gift the first time mules were brought to North America, but the gift did publicize the usefulness of mules to American farmers. That use increased rapidly after 1800.

when a good trader was worth a lot more to himself than all the education he could get.

"The livestock business was a good business in those days for a young fellow. He had to be sharp, though. Travelin' around the country he could pick up a whole sight more information than just workin' on the farm; there was always a lot goin' on durin' court week aside from the actual lawin'. I followed this with farmin' part of the year until I'd got along to about twenty-one years old. During that time I decided to leave the farmin' off and start tradin' in what the farmer raised instead of makin' it myself.

"I set up a little store there in Lynberg with a small stable next to it. I kept tradin' mules and horses and runnin' my store for three or four years. I'd done got a good start then, but there still wasn't no money in the country. The farmers would bring in the scrub cattle from all around the adjoinin' counties. They didn't have money enough to buy the mules so I got on to the idea of takin' the scrub cattle in trade and whatever money I could get from them. Then I got me a great big pasture and fenced it all in. I'd take the bulls and all in trade; just scrub cattle anyway. Before we'd turn 'em loose we'd get 'em all together and saw horns and cut the bulls. I tell you that was a plenty bloody business. Didn't only cut the bulls but we clipped all the moles and stuff like that on their hides to clean 'em up. After we finished, they were a plenty sick-lookin' crowd for a week or so.

"Soon as they'd had a chance out in the pasture for several weeks I'd get ready to ship them on up into Virginia and Maryland and sell 'em for cash. They were pretty poor then, but those farmers would fatten them up for beef cattle. They had plenty of feed to do that on, and I didn't want to mess with it any more than I could help. All I wanted was the cash so I could go on out to the western markets and buy up more mules. The farmers needed them here in North Carolina for the cotton and tobacco crops. I did pretty well at that. Kept tradin' the mules for the scrub cattle and sellin' the cattle in turn. After some years the money got a little bit easier.

"I'd have a fine time on the trips out to St. Louis, Kansas, and even got as far as Omaha, Nebraska. After I got rid of the cattle, I'd go on into Baltimore, buy a new suit and get all cleaned up. Get me a bottle of liquor and maybe a woman.

"I rode and slept on the caboose. Anywhere along the way that the railroad had named for a feedin' and waterin' place, I could go ahead and trade right there in the pens. We let the stock out for a day or so's rest; the railroad had the pens kept up for that purpose.

Of course if a caretaker went with the load, and sometimes I'd send one, he couldn't do any tradin'. Only the owner could do the tradin' while they were on the road.

"I didn't do much tradin' of the cattle; fact hardly none, because they were just going to be fattened for the beef. It was better just to get to the eastern section up there beyond Norfolk and get shed of them as fast as I could.

"I stopped that kind of business as soon as they began to get some more money in this section. The farmers could then pay for the mules with money; if they didn't have it all, they could get fairly reasonable credit on a team of mules. Using money was a whole lot less trouble and cleaner than all that barterin' with the cattle. We had to do all that horn sawin' and cuttin' right there in the pasture to get 'em fit for shippin'. The stockyards use everything now when they butcher. We'd just throw the horns in a ditch or gully, and when we'd cut the bulls, the niggers would eat them things. I've known 'em to carry away two barrelsful in one day.

"My mule business had grown to be pretty well known all around this section. I had by far the biggest stables in the whole of the section. Wasn't any trouble for me to make money then. I used to go to St. Louis, pick up a carload and come on home. Sometimes I'd get no farther than Radville before I'd sold out. I'd pay around $50 apiece for the mules; cost about $50 freight to get back here, and they'd bring anywhere from $175 to $225 apiece.

"A carload would be between twenty-five and thirty head. Most of the time I'd try to put thirty in a car. Come on back by Atlanta, Greenwood, and any of them places the railroad used as rest stations. Sometimes I'd stay in Atlanta three or four days. Once or twice I sold out and had to go on back to get another load.

"It wasn't very hard for me to make money on them because I'd studied 'em for so long. I knew just what kind of stock our folks wanted and I knew how to buy it on the markets for them. That was the main thing with me, and I had a lot of good luck along with it. North Carolina was just beginnin' to open up then. It turned out to be pretty sure money with me.

"Judgin' a mule nowadays is fairly simple. So many books written on it and the agricultural schools turn out a lot of students that know about the science end of it. There wasn't nothin' like that in my day, so it was fairly easy for me to get the lead on most of 'em in my section.

"I got to know that a big-boned mule would more than apt to be lazy. Then a mule with stiff hair stickin' up on his head was nearly always bound not to have any sense. I've seen a lot of nigger gals with that mop of black hair on top of their heads and ninety-nine out of a hundred times they ain't got no sense; just something about it. Some mules are what we call rabbit-chested, little narrow chests, that mule will be short-winded and not very strong for the heavy work. Best mules were those out of Nebraska where they bred the jacks to them great big old Perchion* mares—draft horses we call them. That made a trim mule plenty big enough to do all the work that one of them draft horses could do. He'd usually be a big broad-chested fellow just about the size of his mammy. That was a little too much mule for our folks down here. They would rather have a smaller mule out of a standard mare. That was a little cheaper and plenty of mule for the plow and the general work around the farm. I stuck mostly to that type unless somebody wanted one of them great big teams.

"I'd got my stables well established; had a bookkeeper and plenty of help around to look after the stuff while I had it on hand. 'Course I'd try to turn over a carload as soon as possible on account of the feed. That could turn out to eat up a lot of profit.

"I did manage to keep a half dozen or more on hand the year 'round. You couldn't always tell when something was going to turn up. I remember one day a little Jew come ridin' up to the stable, had a little old horse poor as a snake and about done for; wasn't worth a dollar. He and his little boy was settin' up there on the little one-horse wagon, been goin' through the county buyin' up junk. He wanted a mule but he hadn't made enough money to really get started. I knew his horse wasn't worth anything. I had a mule in the stable that wasn't doin' anything so I decided to try that little Jew. I let him have the mule and told the bookkeeper to let him have as much as $200 to go out and buy up all the old iron and brass he could get his hands on. I had to go away somewhere on business. When I got back to the stables that little Jew had bought up two carloads of old iron and brass; had one of my lots near 'bout full of the stuff.

"We shipped the first carload to Norfolk; that was along about 1910. I let him operate along for about a year. At the end of that time we'd made $5,000. I told him to take $2,500 of it and the mule and work out another section. I didn't have time to fool with it

*Percheron.

anyway. But you talkin' about a happy Jew. He was one happy little fellow.

"Three or four years ago I had to go up to a place in the northern part of the state. I heard he was up in that section. I found his place: a ten-acre tract all fenced in with all the iron bought up in that section of the state. Looked like piles of buildings stacked around the place. I found out he was dead. Been dead four or five years, but the little old scared boy who sat on that pitiful one-horse wagon that day had done grown up and taken over his father's business. He remembered me and all about the beginnin' of the business. Now he's up there rated at over a million dollars.

"I didn't know that was goin' to turn out to be such a good business. Along about then I'd learned a lot about cotton futures— at least I thought I had. Anyway it was a money-makin' business when you hit it right. I was foolin' with that and buying farms and timberland, too. I was makin' money right and left, faster than I could in the mule business but I kept on with my stables in a small way.

"I got mixed up with a fellow in Lynberg that wanted to go into the liquor business. I had some extra money that I wasn't workin' at that time, so I went in with him. We didn't have any barrooms; it was a sort of a wholesale mail-order arrangement. Fernland County was wet, and those counties that were dry would let people order a quart or so a month or come get it. We did very well on that for a while: looked like I was goin' to make some money. I didn't pay very much attention to the business; looked like it was goin' all right, but I finally got word that the distilleries where we had bought the liquor, at first for cash, of course, had given my partner credit on my name.

"After the auditors got through checkin' the books, I found out that I didn't have enough money left hardly to get to St. Louis for a carload of mules. That fellow had damn nearly ruined me.

"By that time I had become a director of the bank in Lynberg. I got enough money to start up the mule business again seriously. I always bought timber and farms for about half down cash, so when this liquor business broke me up I couldn't turn a bit of those farms and timber lands into quick money. I always liked to buy that way though because when you did get a hit it wasn't any trouble to make $10,000 or $15,000. So the bank saved me that time. I would have had one hell of a time tryin' to come back.

"Cotton and tobacco was goin' very well at the time, and I did right much business sellin' mules and horses. I had a great big stable right there in the heart of the town, and I was supposed to know about as much about livestock as any man in the whole section. Didn't take me long to get on back to makin' money again.

"I kept on foolin' with the cotton future market. I was in pretty heavy in 1914 when the World War knocked the bottom out of all the markets. It caught me; not so heavy, but I just couldn't get a profit on a single contract I'd buy. The market just kept goin' down and down, but I managed to stay, along with the stable and the store which I still ran.

"The children were growin' up pretty fast then, and Whit and Folger wanted to go on over to Chapel Hill* when they could get in. I saw that boys were goin' to need an education more and more. I got married in 1891. Had three children, the two boys and Marlene, my daughter. I saw that they got an education: that is what they'd take.

"Whit got married along about 1928, and he's got three children. He started workin' with the Wachovia Bank and Trust Company; got up as high as a teller and it looked like he couldn't get any farther. He finally went into the State Banking Department where he's an examiner. I reckon that suits him pretty well; anyway he seems to be about as happy as most of them I see. But I don't think he'll ever make any money—not in him.

"Folger followed the life insurance game after he got out of the army. He was a lieutenant. He ran around Radville about ten years with that. He's managed to build up a fairly good little living—but he won't make any money. It's not in him; he's too lazy. You know he married Jenks Halborn's widow. Halborn's estate amounted to about $70,000. They say she's got sense enough to hold on to it; I hope she has. Folger's a funny fellow: if he had $10 tonight and didn't know where the next dollar was comin' from tomorrow, he'd spend every cent of it. I hope his wife will swing on to it.

"Marlene, my daughter, was the oldest. Let's see, she's about forty-five now. Her husband's with a power company. She's got three children.

"Yes sir, I tell you it's a good thing to get 'em all up. My wife and I got a home where they can come and stay if they want to. I paid $8,000 for the place but the mortgage is $4,000. I wanted to pay for it all at one time but when I got it there was a farm out in the Barnwell Mill section that I wanted to buy and cut up into lots for an auction. So I didn't pay cash for the house. I needed the money

*University of North Carolina.

for this deal. I've bought up several since I came to Radville to live.

"I left Lynberg back in 1930. Closed the stable and everything I had. I was flat broke. You couldn't sell a mule or anything else then. The farmers were starvin' to death.

"I thought we were goin' to starve until Roosevelt came in. Things begin to pick up a little bit then, and I was able to get hooked up on two auctioneering jobs. That was in 1935 and the first money I'd made since 1929. Got hold of about $10,000 in that deal. I bought up some more farms; paid about half down on them with the idea of cuttin' them up into residential tracts. Then I took some of the money and went out in Missouri for some more mules. I can always get goin' again if I've got enough money to get a load of mules. It always did put me on my feet except back in 1930. That was one time, and I've been through the Reconstruction of the Slave War, that a man simply couldn't make a nickel. It was the worst time I've ever seen or anybody else has that I know of for tryin' to make a dollar. It was all here, but no matter what you say nobody's goin' to be able to make money when there ain't none rollin'. You just let the banks and the rest of 'em tie it all up, and you'll see this country in worse shape than it ever was. I don't know a whole lot about the study of business that they teach in schools now, but I do know one thing: if Henry Smith's mule dies and he's made his tobacco or cotton crop and he can't get no money for it, then Henry Smith ain't got no money to buy another mule with—and there he is and there I am with mules to sell. If we have too many Henry Smiths and nobody's got sense enough to help 'em, then somebody like Hitler gonna get 'em all together and the first thing you know we'll have another type of government.

"I been a Democrat all my life; never voted any other way. But there's one thing certain in my mind, and that is we've got to make this kind of government modern enough to keep up with that crowd over yonder.

"Hitler can say something and fourteen regiments will be on the march and ready for business. Over here we've got to stand up and argue for two or three days to find out whether it's going to hurt somebody's feelings. It's the same way about anything else we want to do. No use to complain about it though.

"I've thought about it a lot. 'Course my education is just practical. I picked it up as I went along. Not much of it out of books either. I have read the Bible some, but I never had much time for religion. I was busy as hell tryin' to make money. Religion is a fine thing for women and children. But as I was sayin' I noticed in the

Bible where a man has had a hell of a time ever since he's been on this earth. Just like a lot of hogs in a lot; some of them will get all the food, and the runts will keep on gettin' weaker and finally get squeezed out altogether. The best farmer won't let that happen though. The little runt is a pig too, and when he grows up, he's worth more than he was to let starve to death. Any farmer knows that.

"I reckon I've had about as many ups and downs as any man who ever tried to raise a family. I've made as much as $25,000 in one year, and on the other hand during the last ten years I've gone for as many as two years without makin' a single dime. I should have kept right at my stable; but tradin' in real estate and cotton futures is pretty money when you hit it right.

"I've got that place out yonder that I've cut up into lots. I'm going to auction that off tomorrow. If I have the luck I expect to have, I'm goin' out west and buy two or three carloads of mules. I've got a half-interest in those old tobacco barns down on Blandon Street, and I'm going to turn those into a first-class sales stable and start my mule business all over. Think I'll stick to it this time."

Harry H. Fain

Ain't Got No Screens

HOLLY GROVE, ARKANSAS, 1939

Sho' ain' goin' to stay hyar no longer, ain't got no screens.

They were seated on the front porch of a three-room, unpainted shack. She, a portly Negress, was comfortably anchored in a swing behind a veil of honeysuckle vines. He was draped languidly about a tilted, cane-bottom chair, one leg of which was perilously near a gaping hole in the floor.

"Come in, suh," he unwrapped himself from his chair, and hastily brought another, which he placed safely away from the hole. "Dat noon breeze comes thoo hyar. Hit's fine, too, dese hot days.

"No, suh, I ain' been to de fiel' dis mornin', jus' puckerin' aroun' de house a bit; hit's mos' too wet to work in de fiel'—little mo' rain and dey won't be no cotton, though they ain' been near de rain we had de year of de Big Flood*—

"What year was de Big Flood, honey? It was de yeah after we come up fum Mississippi—must've been twenty-seb'm. And rain! Dey wuz fifteen families on ouah place; de landlord got his stuff out to high land, and he never left nothin' to hep us git out cepn' two ole pieces of waggins and a no 'count team of mules dat wouldn' pull more'n fo' men.

"Time hit come my turn, water wuz up to de wagin bed, and I couldn' see de road, though I knowed whar it was; but you know, long's I been on de farm I cain't drive a team 'til yet, and I got 'em

---

*The 1927 flood of the Mississippi River covered 20,000 square miles, drove 300,000 people from their homes, and left 246 dead.

too fur to one side 'tween two dreens, en de wagin tumpled over in de deep water, en we lost practick'ly all we 'cumulated, furniture en all.

"I give up de bottoms den; hit's better land, but I got be where I kin git out when I wants to git out.

"You say dis land look like bottomland to you? Co'se hit's black and strong and level, but hit's a heap higher dan de bottoms, I tell you!

"How do we farm? Well, dey's sev'ul diff'unt ways. Dare is de cash rentuh, but we has always sharecropped, on a third and a four—he furnish de house en de land en credicks you enough to live on, en den you settles at de end of de year. In de cotton we gives him a fourth, in de cawn he gits a third—ain' dat right, honey?" he asked his wife. "Anyhow, when you raise four bales of cotton de landlord gits one en you git three, and if you raise three wagonloads of cawn he gits de first one en you git the other two.

"Landlord's got a store on de place, en he 'low you so much a week on de books—dey wuz four in my family and he didn' 'low us but a twenty-four-poun' sack of flouah, en a twenty-four-poun' sack of meal, en eight poun's of lard, en maybe a bar of soap. Ef you got molasses you didn' git no sugah, en ef you got bakin' powdah you didn' git no sody—Meat? Whooo! We didn' git no meat, but we'd ketch a mess of fish now en den, en de nex' year we had ouah own meat.

"De landlord wouldn' give us no land foh a garden, er no wire to fence it, ef we could of got some land. He ain' like Mistuh Brewer down de road. Mistuh Brewer give his 'croppers land foh a garden, en if dey use it he doan' charge 'em no rent, but ef dey doan' use it he makes 'em pay rent on it, eight dollars an acre—but we had to plant cotton right up to de do'.

"Tolbert—dat's my oldes'—hired out sometimes drivin' tractor —he got six bits a day foh workin' fum kin to cain't, fum sunup to sundown. He got a dollah a day foh a while, but den dey put him back on six bits. No, suh, when it rain en he cain' work he doan' git no six bits for *dat* day. Tolbert he kin do anything to a tractor, he kin take one down and put it back up, en he kin tell jus' by listenin' what's wrong with one; learned it all jus' by studyin' a 'struction book. No, suh, you see, dey doan' use no colored mechanics hyar in Holly Grove, en I guess he woan' never git nothin' but six bits a day. Yas, suh, I guess he *could* go off somewhare, but I doan' speck he will—

"We misses screens de mos' aroun' dis place, pesky flies and mosquitoes is so bad. I said sump'n about it to Mr. Sparrow early dis spring, but I guess he forgot—or mebbe he ain' forgot, he jus' doan' *want* us to have no screens. Jus' like I wanted a patch of sorghum, make me some 'lasses with, but he say hit sour the land. What he mean was, hit sour dat ninety cents a bucket he gits for Steamboat.

"Most of us is credick men—you gives a dime foh a nickel box of matches, and a dime foh a nickel bah of soap—mebbe two foh fifteen, en you kin git flouah en meal in town foh about half whut it cost you out'n the comm'sary. We-el, yas, suh, I meant de cash price in town, dey ain' no credick in town, less'n yo' landlord stand good, en den dey marks you up en he git a percent off'n you. Sometimes where dey ain' no sto' on the plantation all de landlords goes in and buys stock in de sto' in town, en hit's jus' de same.

"De landlord is landlord, de politicians is landlord, de judge is landlord, de shurf is landlord, ever'body is landlord, en we ain' got nothin'!

"You take de acre p'duction checks de gov'munt gives foh not plantin' cotton: fust dey wuz made out so's we couldn' git 'em thout de landlord—dey wuz even sent to him—en he mark 'em up en mark 'em down, en mark you up in de comm'sary en mark you down, en den we didn't git no checks, we jus' signed en git whut he *say* we had comin'. En de landlord think he ought to have *all* the acre p'duction checks, cause it his land, en we oughtn' to git nothin', but de Tenant Farmers' Union* put up a kick, en now dey send *us* de checks—ef we evah git anoth'un. *Who* gives de checks out? I doan' know *who*, jus' de gov'munt. But dey comes thoo de county board, en dey is all landlords—

"I thinks mebbe nex' year I'll git a place on Sebastian McElroy's farm—he's a colored man—en he's mo' apt to treat me right, en den I kin have a garden, en a patch o' peanuts, en some Arsh 'taters, en some sweet 'taters; en Sebastian got screens on all his houses. I'd lots ruther work for a colored landlord than a white man one.

"I had a old Hudson Super Six two years ago, but hit tuck so much gas, en I spent all mah cash money en they come and tuck hit back foh de payments. I mos' gin'ally clears about seventy-five dollahs. Sometimes I doan', though; sometimes I comes out in de

---

*The Southern Tenant Farmers' Union, a vigorous but short-lived tenant farmer organization that was strongest in Oklahoma and Arkansas. See also pp. 41–42n, p. 43, and pp. 76–77n.

hole. But I'm goin' to move nex' year again; ef I doan' git on Sebastian's place, I'm goin' to git on somebody else's. Sho' ain' goin' to stay hyar no longer, ain't got no screens."

Walter Rowland

Jim Jeffcoat

*If you're interested in poor folks you don't need to
go no furder. They say children is shore nuff riches.
We's got five of them. But if you mean money
and things, we ain't got 'em. Never have had 'em.*

Jim Jeffcoat's family lives near the McDuffie's Baptist Chapel, five
miles from Chapel Hill and eight miles from Durham. But they
haven't lived there long. They have not lived anywhere long.

"We've been here only since December. Jim and me married
twenty-three years ago and this is our seventh place. Susan Johnson, she's my nearest neighbor, says there ain't no use in moving
so often. She says, 'A rollin' stone gathers no moss.' I don't want to
gather no moss. But I guess we have made a mistake 'cause we
ain't gathered nothing, or next to nothing. We have never owned a
horse or a mule or a cow or any tools or anything to ride in. Of
course, we ain't never owned a house, and we never will. The
houses we've lived in ain't worth owning. They ain't worth nothing to nobody except to furnish pore croppers like us who can't do
any better.

"We are now about where we wuz twenty-three years ago when
we started keepin' house down in Oconee County, Georgia. Jim's
grandparents and mine, too, lived in Oconee before the War. None
of our eight grandparents could read or write. Neither could our
four parents. And Jim and I don't know any more than they did.
Book larnin' never come easy in our families. But all of our men
folks and some of our womenfolks has been good at machinery
and tools of every kind.

"Jim's father spent his whole life fussin' around machines of some kind. He once owned an old-timey gin and at another time a wreck of a sawmill. A few summers he owned what wuz left of an old threshing machine. They called him 'Old Bob.' They used to say, 'Give Old Bob a nail, a piece of wire and a pair of pliers and he'll fix anything.' He couldn't get much business 'cause the people were afraid his machinery would break down, and they would be tied up for days. And he barely made a livin' 'cause he had to pay his help while they sat around waitin' for him to repair his machinery. But he wouldn't do anything else. He used to say and many sided with him, 'If I could only read and figure and could buy some new machinery or purchase new parts for what I do own, I could make money hand over fiss.'

"Jim helped his dad until we got married. He was about as good as his dad, but he decided that he had better go on the farm where the owner would furnish him with tools. Jim's a good man in many ways. But he will drink. He works hard and does good work. I help him, and our children have always worked. But he drinks it as fast as we can make it. We seem to move around in circles like the mule that pulls the syrup mill. We are never still, but we never get anywhere. For twenty-three long years we have begun each year with nothing and when we settled here in November we had the same. I bet you if we had saved all the money Jim has paid to the bootleggers, we'd be well on the way towards ownin' a farm. If he didn't drink so much, he could go into town in the winter months and work in a garage or a shop of some kind. He tried it two winters, but they fired him every time he got on a drunk. Finally he said, 'I won't try it again unless I find I can git on the water-wagon and stay on it. You got to be a temperance man to work in them places.'

"Jim's also got a high temper. He's 'touchy' about everything. I never know when I'm goin' to offend him. I set him off plenty times when I don't know what I've done. And he can't get along with his landlords. Whenever they differ about anything, he loses his head and cusses like a blue streak. Three of his landlords told him to 'git' and he beat three of them to it by announcing that he would pull out.

"It may be this fall or it may be a year later, but won't be long until he will say to me, 'Let's move again. Maybe it will be better in the next place. The landlord gets more than's fair here.'

"And I'll probably say, 'All right, Jim. Let's move to Virginia. Maybe if you can lose your old cronies, you can hitch onto the water-wagon and make a go of it this time. I hate to leave my friends but if it will help you I'll pull up stakes and go. We'll make a fresh start. You can't write the letters but next year the Lord will give you a bran new, white sheet. It will be as clean as any man ever had. That's one sheet you got to write on, Jim. You can hire people or git your children to write letters. But this sheet I'm talking about is something you will have to write on. It's your record. What you goin' to write on it? God wants you to write one thing, Satan wants you to write another. But neither of them can make you write his way. When the year's up and you hold that sheet up it will have on it what you decided to write. It's your record, Jim. It's your mark.'

"But it won't do no good. In Virginia it will be like it's been in Georgia, South Carolina, and North Carolina. He'll ride the water-wagon for a month, and he'll be soused for a week."

"It has probably cost you a lot to move these six times," I suggested.

"Now you're talking," she said. "From where you sit in the doorway you can see our two bedrooms. You can see three old wooden double beds covered with ragged quilts. I've got a lot of quilts stored away for next winter. They are all like these you see. I used to have sheets and pillowcases for every bed, but I can't afford them any more. I keep sheets and a pillowcase for the bed in this room. But the only time I use them is when a visitor comes, and they will probably be here a long time cause we don't have much company. That dresser and that settee look like they might have come out of Noah's Ark. That lace you see on the table is the only piece in the house. Sister Jackson gave me that last week. She's our pastor's wife over at McDuffie's Chapel. They live in Durham, and her husband runs a store over there. She came to see me last month, and she said, 'I see by your flowerbeds that you love pretty things, and if you will take it, I'm goin' to send you a cover for your table.' Bless her heart.

"I wondered if I should let her do it. I told her I'd take it. The neighbors say she's all the time doing something like that and that I did right 'cause she'd of given it to somebody else if I had turned it down. The cane-bottom chairs have been reseated twice. Jim will keep them rebuilt as long as the rounds will hold up. This little rag rug I made myself, and it's the only one in the house. I made my quilts, too, but the neighbors helped me on them. Those large pictures are my parents and Jim's mother. They never could get Jim's father dressed up enough to have his picture took. These old ragged shades were here when we came. We can't get the owner to put in new shades or screens. He says the mosquitoes around here don't carry malaria and that we will be so busy that the only time we will need to fight the flies is on Sundays.

"That next room has only the two beds, a dresser and a table. We eat in our cookroom. No, we don't have any ice 'cept on Sundays in the summer when we get Susan Johnson's old man to bring us some for ice tea. We buy a little milk from Susan now and then and we keep that in the well."

"You may have a small house, but I can see some pretty oak trees in the yard," I said.

"You said it! Them trees is shore nice in the hot weather. Jim says they bursts his farmin', though. The shade feels so good he has to lie in it two hours after dinner. But one thing about him is he's not lazy. He's plowin' halfway between daylight and sunrise, and he keeps at it half an hour after sunset. That's all the mule can stand. Them's long hours, mister. During the busy season nobody in this family says anything about an eight-hour day.

"If you're interested in poor folks you don't need to go no furder. They say children is shore nuff riches. We's got five of them. But if you mean money and things, we ain't got 'em. Never have had 'em. Jim and I both are from pore stock. Our folks told us that before the War, there wuz the plantation family, the small farm owner, the pore whites, and the slaves. Grandpa Jeffcoat says he used to rent as a sharecropper, and when he couldn't find nothing to rent, he worked for wages for the small landowner. He didn't mind that until slaves were hired from the plantation to work beside him. This made him look down on work, and he wuz tempted to steal rather than git down on a level with the niggers. The thing that made him boil wuz the fact that the slaves instead of looking up to him called him 'pore white trash.'

"When the war broke out Grandpa Jeffcoat was one of the first in the county to volunteer. He said, 'I'd rather git killed than have all these niggers freed and claimin' they's as good as I is.'

"Jim says that when he wuz a little shaver a rich man's son got mad at him and said, 'You ain't nothing but pore whites.' He asked Grandma Jeffcoat what that meant. When she told him, he made up his mind right then and there to leave Oconee County the first chance he got and if they still called him that he would leave the state.

"Nobody ever called him 'pore white' any more. But Jim still believes that people are thinkin' it. When they cuss him or 'pore

Jim' him, he gits sore and keeps rememberin' and rememberin' that his folks were down near the bottom before the War.

"Mister, I believe that's one reason Jim drinks so much. The only time he forgets that he came from pore folks is when he gits drunk. Boy! He's rollin' in clover then. The first farm we worked wuz owned by Mr. Tom Johnson, the richest man in Oconee County. At that time all our riches was our clothes, a bed, three chairs, two tables, and a cookstove. But Jim got on a tear one day and called Mr. Johnson out of his house and told him, 'Tom, I'm sorry for you 'cause most of your tenants ain't no 'count; but I'm making money fast, and if you needs any, you just come to me. Jim'll take care of you.' I went with him and tried to keep him from saying or doin' anything foolish.

"When he sobered up I told him how he had talked. Jim looked like a fool. He said to me, 'Jessie, Mr. Johnson is probably saying that no one but 'pore whites' would try to talk to him like I did. I ain't never goin' to be able to look that man in the face again. Jessie, I reckon I'm through here. Let's move.' I wuz so 'shamed of him that I agreed.

"We moved to a Mr. Wilson's place in South Carolina across the Savannah from Augusta. For a spell, we wuz happy, to be shore. We talked about how no one there knew us and how we could make good in a new place. But Old Man Liquor followed us across the state line and soon Jim was at it again. The children's coming meant doctor's bills and someone to work in my place in the field for two months. And then after a year, Jim fell out with the landlord and said, 'Let's move again.' We moved to the northern part of the state, and it took the last penny we had to pay for the truck. And this is the third farm we've had in North Carolina. Susan took me into her attic the other day. I wuz surprised at the things she has there that my children could use. I reckon the seven houses we've lived in has attics. I never thought to look 'cause we never had anything to store in them. Every time we move, we break something and throw away something and leave some little improvement we made in the place. As we roll, the extra moss rolls off.

"The children can all read and write, but it looks like they will all drop out after about six years of schoolin'. It's the old curse of book learnin' bein' hard in our family. Tom, that's our oldest boy, he's jist started to learn the garage business. He never liked to read but he jist eats up every pamphlet on cars they loan him. The other boy would like to work with machinery too; but Jim will keep him on the farm to help him. If only some school wuz nearby where they would teach my boys wheels, screws, and valves! Then they would study and not be slaves to the soil."

William O. Foster

The Landlord
Has His Troubles

SEABOARD, NORTH CAROLINA, 1939

The sharecropper is the landlord's child, in effect.

"Millard couldn't work like I had to when I first started farming. He throws away more money on cigarettes and gas for his automobile than my whole family used to have to live on. I started out by working on my mother's farm by the day, getting $75 a year and my board. I mean I worked too, day and part of the night, at hard labor—ditching, cutting cordwood, mauling rails, plowing, anything there was to do. We got by in them days without spending, though sometimes it was a poor get-by. For one thing, there was little sickness back then, or little that required a doctor. My daddy raised ten children, and I never remember him having the doctor but twice, once when one of my sisters had appendicitis and the other time when we had a case of pneumonia. Another thing, taxes were low and land was cheap then; it could be bought for one dollar an acre. I was able to save most of my salary of $75 a year.

"When I married the first time, I bought the Taylor farm, later selling it and buying a farm near Simpson from my brother. After my second marriage, I bought two more farms and started farming on a big scale, with sharecroppers added gradually till now I have fifteen families on the different farms. We used to work day labor; that's the way it ought to be now, for sharecropping's a mess. But after I built and moved to town, I done like the rest—filled farmhouses with tenants. That's how come us to have sharecropping here now instead of day labor; one man started it, and the crowd followed, like they do around here about everything.

"We've got in the habit of living according to the income we got ten or fifteen years ago, and now looks like we can't get back to the level that used to satisfy us. One child spends more on clothes now than our whole family used to. If my daddy could know what it takes to run my family a month, he'd rise in his grave! And he accumulated more by pinching and saving than I'll ever have. Last year my son's gas bill was $400; he has to have a car of his own to drive here and yonder all over the country day and night, and every two or three years he must have a new car. It's spend, spend all the time! Today he's off on a 200-mile trip for nothing. It'd take a two-horse farm to pay his automobile expenses. We have to send $70 a month to our daughter who is away at business school, not to mention her clothes. Katy works hard and tries to run the house as cheap as she can, but there's the cook, washwoman, odd help around the house and yard, groceries, etc., that has to be taken care of every week. We raise our own meat, keep a cow, have a garden practically all the year, and a cellar full of canned vegetables and fruit. So Katy keeps groceries down to around $4.00 a week when just three of us is at home.

"Folks are more expensive other ways besides clothes and food and colored help around the house. Looks like somebody's always got something to be treated. You never used to hear about sinus trouble. Millard has been treated several times by Richmond specialists, but he has still got it so bad that if he'd have flu or pneumonia he wouldn't have a chance. I've had four heavy hospital bills to pay since I've moved to town, three of them for operations. Then there are the doctors' bills for the tenants. Some doctors won't go to a man unless his landlord stands for him. Where poor folks used to doctor with herbs and teas, now they want the doctor first thing and the hospital next. Burial expenses for sharecroppers have to come out of the landlord with no guarantee in the world he'll ever get a cent back. Of course lots of 'em belong to the burial league, which is a good thing, though the dues has to come out of us in the long run. I remember Dr. Carter used to contract to doctor a family for so much a year. A man and his wife he'd take for $15 and in some cases cleared every cent of it, since there was no sickness for him to doctor during the year. Other contracts went as high as $100 or more, depending on the size and health of the family or the number of tenants that a landlord wanted included. Sometimes I reckon he got stuck.

"If a nigger gets sick or in trouble he looks to the white man. Sometimes on Sunday he shoots craps and gets involved in a fight, cuts somebody open or gets his side cut open, and then hollers for his landlord to get him out of jail. We are bound to stand for him, if he is any 'count at all. The sharecropper is the landlord's child, in effect. We can cuss and abuse him, but we humor and indulge him in a lot of ways. Sometimes it's forced on us by other landlords. A feller comes and wants a crop with me, a good farmer maybe; he's got nothing but old broken-up furniture, no clothes, not enough bed cover to keep his folks warm. The first thing he wants is an automobile. I know it's ridiculous when he's hungry and naked and ought to have a cow instead of a car. But if I don't get the automobile, another landlord will, and he'll get the labor too. So the car is bought and has got to be run whether they eat or not. Why, back in 1900 the average white man didn't have a driving horse; he walked or hooked a mule or a steer to a cart. Nobody then thought a thing of walking two or three miles to church on Sunday morning. Now it's too much exertion for a lot of our young folks to get up and drive a half mile to Sunday School. It's got into our tenants too; they're bound to ride now where they used to walk altogether.

"We make it easy for the sharecropper to waste his living on gas. We furnish him cash money, so much a week, depending on the size of his family, to run himself during the crop year. Of course he's going to take that money and buy gas or whiskey. What we used to do and ought to do now is furnish the rations instead of the cash. One of my tenants come to me Saturday wanting three more dollars he said for rations, when I knowed he wanted whiskey. I let him have a dollar. When a nigger gets his hand on money he's going to spend it; if he can't throw it away fast enough he'll give it to some other nigger. One year old Benjamin made $2,200 on his crop. He had a Ford car, which he traded for a second-hand Hudson, so he could ride the roads in fine style. When the crop year started, he didn't have a cent to run himself with. He had around eighteen or twenty in the family, but there wasn't no sense in spending $2,200 in three months. The year that Amos Farthing made $1,200 on his crop he said to me: 'Mr. Greaves, you won't have me to take care of next year. I'll run myself.' Well, there was three more bales of scattering cotton to be picked out at the end of the season, and by george if I didn't have to furnish money to have it picked out!

"It's a rare thing to find a sharecropper that's thrifty and saving.

The white ones as a rule ain't no better than niggers. They're usually the slums of the world. I had one white family a few years ago that sickened me with white labor. They come to me from one of the southern counties, a big family of about twelve, as destitute as I ever saw anybody. They was literally naked. The whole town through different organizations begun to take them clothes, bed cover, furniture; of course I was helping all along too. The girls took the nice dresses the missionary society give them to wear in the cotton patch. It was told that soon as a garment got too dirty to wear any longer they had a barrel in the barn they throwed it in—junked good clothes to keep from washing them. They didn't take care of a thing. While the men worked smart, I didn't like their attitude; after the new wore off, they wanted to figure their way through; the old man was always writing me notes. Some of 'em was always sick; three of the children was down at one time with colitis, with the old lady in bed with a broken leg. The baby died, and I had to furnish the plot for its grave and its burial expenses. Follow that family after they left me: the old man and old lady died after a little, one girl married a sharecropper, one boy took up with the Holy Rollers, and one of the boys is in the county jail now for criminal assault; his brother come here one night recently to ask me to stand his bond. If you'd give 'em a home they wouldn't have it. Sometimes a tenant buys him a little piece of land, but he mortgages it by the time he finishes paying for it. If 'twasn't for we landlords, what in God's world would become of this shiftless crowd?

"Folks are always pitying the sharecropper; he is to be pitied. It ought to be fixed so he could make a living. A nigger today can't make enough to feed his family like they ought to be fed, and we are not able to furnish them enough cash money by the week to take care of their actual needs. Bad as sharecropping actually is in a lot of ways, aggravating as it is to us, what would become of the sharecropper if he went back to day labor like he used to work? On the basis of the present prices of cotton and peas, we couldn't pay him over forty or fifty cents a day; we actually couldn't afford more. No doubt the government would have to take the farms. That's what's going to happen eventually. In three years we'll all be sharecroppers, and the government will be the landlord. I see the handwriting on the wall. There's no way out for we farmers.

"I've got about five hundred acres of open land. During the past two or three years I've made nothing farming. Instead, I owe heavily. It takes about $4,000 to produce a cotton crop for which I can get only $3,500. I borrowed $2,000 from the bank to run my farm this year. Let me go in the hole two or three more years, and the farm can go for taxes. The value of land has been cut in half. I bought a farm some years ago for $81,000, but luckily for me I got it off my hands before these times struck us. There wasn't any money around here till 1917. We farmed and made a comfortable living, but farming wasn't thought of as an investment on which big money returns could be expected. All we saved back then was by penny pinching and hard work. Along this time of year we farmers would be cutting cordwood till time to start crops, and then in August after crops was ready to be harvested we'd haul load after load to be shipped to town. That's the way I first made any money, cutting and hauling cordwood. Now we depend entirely on farming, on raising cotton and peas, and don't try to add to our income in ways we used to. The good years from 1920 to 1929, with a poor one now and then in that period, spoiled us. Just before Christmas I found a book in the attic in which I kept a record of every penny I spent, even the postage stamps. I allowed myself five cents a week for tobacco then. Now we just sow it and keep no record. It would take a two-horse farm to run Millard's automobile.

"The landlord has his troubles as well as the sharecropper does. The destructive spirit that seems to prevail among them is expensive to us. After every tenure the landlord has to spend a lot on repairs and building back what the tenant tore down. Sometimes he knocks down outhouses to burn instead of going to the woods to cut his firewood. I had one man to tear down the kitchen, that was made out of heart timber, for lightwood kindling. In the house I lived in before I moved to town the plastering was better than in the house I live in now—till I put a nigger in there. In one year he smoked the walls black as soot and shot holes all through the plastering. They drunk whiskey and fired shotguns all day Sundays. They break out window lights and expect you to replace them, when sometimes it's pure meanness that prompts 'em. Tom Mullen stayed with me fifteen years, and after he knowed he wasn't going to be there another year, he begun digging up all the flower bushes in the yard that had been there no telling how long. His idea was to pick a fuss, but when I passed and realized what he was up to I merely said: 'You all are certainly improving the looks of the yard,' and drove on. They're aggravating about cutting down our timber too; we tell 'em where to get firewood, but they pass right by that and cut down our nice trees.

"If sharecroppers didn't have a boss, they couldn't get nowhere. I never saw one yet that could be turned loose. I go around on Sunday morning to remind them that I want a certain piece of work started on Monday, then Sunday night I check by to remind them, and Monday morning I hurry off before breakfast to see that they start. If they're left to themselves, pretty soon there'll be a ragged farm; they'll plow around a bush the whole year instead of cutting it down. They don't want to cut a ditch to drain the land, though it's to their advantage as well as the landlord's, nor even cut the briars off the ditch. The well on their place they look to us to clean out for them; in fact, all they expect . . . to do is just farm and let you pay for the upkeep of everything. One man used to work as long as I was there, but soon as I left he got his fishing pole and went to the creek. Sometimes they worry us with an old cow or hogs, letting them get into our corn or cotton and do a lot of damage. Even if they have a pasture, they'd rather stob the old cow out to graze close to a cotton or pea patch. Just let the share-cropper get us in grass, and he'll come demanding a suit of clothes or money for something and threatening to leave if we don't come across. It's a holdup. We fork over the money, and it's throwed away for gas or whiskey or something trifling. As soon as one has a little prosperity he's likely to want to leave, try somebody else; he sees bigger things ahead somewhere else. Lots of times when the tenant comes to the landlord he claims he's got his own team and equipment. That means the landlord pays for all the fertilizer. Half the time what the tenant brings to farm with ain't worth nothing, so we have to go buy plows and things for him to piece out what he has called equipment. Then when the tenant leaves he moves it all along as his own.

"In the course of twelve months, a lot of stealing goes on. Not only does the sharecropper get corn out of our barn, but cotton out of our fields. He picks sackful after sackful, throws them in a ditch or in the woods, and at night collects them to sell. A cousin of mine, after finding rows here and there in his cotton patch picked out, tracked the stolen cotton to one of his tenant's houses and found 1,400 pounds in the loft. I've had men to bootleg cotton, and I was pretty sure of the white neighbor who bought it, though I couldn't say anything. Anyhow, the man was just a small farmer, and he carried more cotton to the gin than he could possibly have raised.

"There's the trouble about settling too. The sharecropper thinks we charge too much against him, but as a matter of fact we don't. The law allows us a time price,* and to go the limit is not cheating. Just consider that all the land had to be paid for by the hard work of the landlord, that all the risks, responsibilities, and expenses are on him. Most times the sharecropper gets what he's due and more. The nearest to serious trouble I ever had with one was the time old Manly pulled me out of the car and throwed me in a mudhole because I would not let him have some money he claimed he had to have. Another time old Hank Davis questioned my account and even employed a lawyer to bring suit against me. I had carried over one year's debt to another, and that's where they had me. But Hank died, so the case never come to trial. If a nigger makes $600 one year and $300 the next he thinks right straight he's been robbed. He don't consider that one year I made as high as $20,000 money crop when we raised 3,000 or 4,000 bags of peas and 175 to 200 bales of cotton, and that now I'm cut to a fourth. He didn't complain when he was making $600 or $700 a year that I padded the accounts, but now when we all go in the hole farming he seems to think that I'm cheating him out of his share. They tell on me that I run down my good tenants, telling around everywhere that they're sorry as hell, to keep other landlords from getting 'em. That ain't so.

"It's a fact that the government program has done a lot for farmers. I don't know what in the world we'd have done without the government help. Some phases of the program don't work out right, it don't seem to me. It ain't right for the sharecropper to have half the spring check; the land that is sowed in beans or peas or left idle for improvement purposes and cotton acreage reduction ain't his, and he don't have none of the expenses to pay for. The landlord furnishes the soybeans or peas, uses his tractor, hires additional labor, pays all the taxes, yet the check comes directly to the sharecropper who refuses to pay his half of the beans and other expenses. If he gets his hand on the money he won't let it go. He farms the same as ever, not having his pro rata share of idle land; it's my land that lies idle, though he reaps half the benefit. Now the parity check that's paid in the fall is different; the sharecropper ought to have half of that, and no landlord kicks on it.†

"Another thing we landlords have to contend with is debts the sharecropper owes us. If this year's crop fails, if a hailstorm hits

---

*The interest rate on capital lent to tenants by landlords.
†See pp. 76–77n.

the crop, we've got no way in the world to collect the debt, for it's against the law to carry it over to another year. When one gets in debt to us, he'll pull up and leave, and that cancels the debt. Old Benjamin got behind this year, and after staying with me twenty years he left, thinking I had cheated him. The Freemans stayed with me fourteen years, but most of them don't last but one, two, or three years. Any man that has to work labor has a lot to contend with."

Bernice Kelly Harris

Jackson Bullitt,
a Small Landlord

SEABOARD, NORTH CAROLINA, 1939

The Golden Rule is the method I've tried to farm by with my sharecroppers. . . . I'm good to them, and they're good to me.

"I was born over near Juniper, Virginia, where I worked on my father's farm till I was free. Then I moved to Deer Run in North Carolina and rented a small farm for three years. From there I moved to the old Anson place four miles from Hilton, buyin' the house and little farm the next year. I soon met Miss Della Huges, who lived in the neighborhood, and after a year we were married. What success I've had I feel like I owe most of it to her; she was close and savin' and helped me accumulate enough to pay for our place and buy a little land every now and then. From ownin' nothin', from bein' just a renter, I now own two farms, a comfortable dwelling and three tenant houses, and some town property in Hilton.

"Since my wife died eleven years ago, though, I've not done much, not even hardly held my own. My five girls has done the best they could for me, but a man needs a companion to get along any sort o' how. I've been with two or three girls since Della left me, and I'd have married the widow woman if my daughters hadn't objected so strong. At one time she'd've had me too, but Mary was so rank against it I kept puttin' it off. Now I'm in no fittin' fix to get married—and Mary's married and gone, as well as Lela. I still love to talk to the widow, to be in her company. They say Mr. Forsythe is about to cut me out, but I don't think she'll have him; she would've had me, at one time. I met a girl I liked when I was visitin' Mary at Ocean View last summer, but of course it couldn't amount to nothin'. I don't know whether I'd've had this stroke or not if I had gone on and got married like I wanted to. Worry over losin' my wife and bein' alone, as well as other things, brought on the high blood pressure and the stroke that crippled me up like I am now. It's a helpless feelin' after you've been workin' and goin' hard all your life to be in this fix. Yesterday I drug this leg out to the wood pile and throwed some wood in the house out of the weather; today I ain't hardly able to move around.

"About thirteen years ago we moved from the old place up here closer to Hilton so the children would be more convenient to the school and church. I was makin' right good money farmin' along then; in just one year I built and paid for this house we live in. One time I could've bought the place for $600, but when I did buy it cost me $3,200. Mary, Lela, and Selma went to Chowan College,* and the two oldest ones taught a while before they got married. My youngest one, Lavinia, will soon get through her nurse's course in Norfolk. Lily does the best she can keepin' house for me, but she's afflicted and can't do like the others. If Selma's husband just hadn't got drowned last summer—but I'm thankful Selma and Lavinia were rescued, for they had a close call down there at the beach. Selma's husband aimed, after he finished his crop down at Buckner, to come here and take hold of the farm for me, which would've been a fine arrangement all around. If Selma didn't have that cafeteria job at Hilton school now, I reckon she'd go crazy, losin' her husband just six weeks after marryin' him.

"In spite of bein' paralyzed, I manage my farmin' pretty good, because I've got tenants I can trust. Sharecroppin' is the best system for this country I think; anyhow it's best for me. I don't know what I'd do if we had to go back to hirin' day labor altogether. Bob Miller, a white man, has been with me nineteen years. I've got confidence in him. He works a two-horse crop and always pays out and makes a little money besides. In fact, he has made enough clear some years to buy him a house and farm easy, but instead he lets his money get away from him somehow, with nothin' much to show for it. It used to worry me for Bob to throw away his money, but my wife would say: 'Why should you care? If he saved up his money, he wouldn't work for you, and you'd lose a good tenant.' That is one way to look at it.

"From March to December I furnish Bob $4.00 a week for him-

*Baptist women's school, Murfreesboro, North Carolina.

self, his wife, and the child they took to raise; they've got no children of their own. My time price is 10 percent, which is understood between me and Bob; that's fair, and all tenants are willin' to pay 10 percent for the use of the money. Bob furnishes his team, while I pay for the fertilizer. I let him run the farm to suit himself, goin' down there to see about him only once or twice a month. This year, which was the hardest we've had in some time, Bob paid out all right and cleared $200.

"My men always clear a little somethin', though I don't see how Miles Richards did this year. With nobody but him to plow and with him pushin' seventy and not well either, it's right hard on Miles. He's been with me two years and is stayin' on again. Looks like when I get a man I generally keep him, if he's any 'count at all. I rather have white sharecroppers every time. For one thing you can trust 'em with your team and with havin' more judgment about runnin' a farm than colored tenants do. It seems to come natural for the colored ones to be a little roguish, while you can put confidence in the white farmer that way. Most of the stealin' you hear landlords complain about, though, is the landlord's fault as much as the tenant's. When the landlord takes shortcuts and deals unfair, the tenant knows it, even if he can't put his finger on where the cheatin' is; that's where, as a general rule, he takes to stealin'. I never had no stealin', practically none, to contend with. Tenants I've had to get rid of after a year were usually impudent or triflin', wouldn't work the crop to no advantage. Colored tenants worry you too sometimes about their old superstitious notions; some wouldn't plant to bless you except on the moon. Some white ones are that way, of course, but I've not had them to contend with so far.

"Miles Richards made one bale of cotton on his farm this year, and just half of it goes to him. His wife helps him what she can, but she has been to the asylum and can't be counted on. One daughter is married, and the single one— she just as well to be. She's come back home on Miles now, with her baby, and that's another one for Miles to feed. She's a good-lookin' girl, too; it's a pity she throwed herself away. Miles told me the other day that it takes $2.00 a week to buy milk for the baby. There's the little girl, too, that Miles and his wife took to raise. That's one thing about sharecroppers; they never seem to have too many children to feed and clothe but what they can find a place for one more. They're goin' to have children —and yes, dogs too—around 'em. Miles furnishes himself; how he does it I don't know, but that was his request. He's bound to owe somebody more than he can pay, the way his expenses are. I think it's better for the landlord to furnish so much money a week or month to run the tenant than it is to furnish ration like use to be done. The tenant can trade to much better advantage that way and feel more free too, I think.

"My other man is John Winder, colored, who I hire by the day. He lives yonder across the field and works here around the house —cuttin' wood, feedin' the stock, tendin' to the outdoor jobs I use to enjoy doin', as well as workin' in the field on my own home farm. I give him sixty cents a day and a pea patch, a house to live in, and board from my table. I think that's fair.

"I reckon I run my business a little different from most landlords. For one thing, I require the tenants to keep a set of books too. Every time I enter an item in my book I make them set it down in theirs as well. So when settlement time comes, they know good as I do how the expenses are goin' to run out. I never had no trouble settlin' in my life; sometimes maybe there'll be a difference of a dollar or two the tenant failed to enter like I told him, but he'll remember soon as it's called to his attention. All the tenants ought to be required to keep books just like the landlord and know exactly what's charged against them and what for. Then, too, I always let my sharecroppers have half the peanut vines, as well as pay my half to hire the peas picked off. They say I'm the only landlord in this country that pays my half of the pea-picker expense, but it's the only fair way, looks like to me. When it comes to ditchin' or other labor for permanent improvement on the farms, I always pay for that; some of the landlords kick because the tenant won't ditch his own farm, but I reckon that's our business. For repair work around the house, I furnish the timber and the nails and let the tenant do the work; he's usually willin' if he's any 'count at all, to do that.

"If it hadn't been for peanuts this year, I'd have gone in the hole sure enough. On 75 acres of open land, not countin' the acres I rented to the government, I made 5 bales of cotton and 400 bags of peas. Before the boll weevil hit here so bad, I used to make 16, 17, and 18 bales of cotton and 600 bags of peas. So many things has knocked the farmer late years. Like the rest, I got excited and bought one of them dustin' machines the year the boll weevil first got rank here. That had to be junked, for we found the dustin' wa'n't worth a cent. Then the value of land has been cut to half, though the taxes ain't been lowered to take care of the decreased valuation. The same thing is true of my town property, the store buildin' I rent for $20 a month. I invested $6,000 in it and now couldn't sell it for half that. The rent don't near pay the interest, the taxes, and repairs on this investment. On the side I used to make a little money sellin' peanuts, but a fellow in Hilton undermined me when a new boss took the place of the one I had been dealin' with for years, promisin' more business to the peanut concern than I had been handlin'. I still sell peanut bags, though there's not much in it now since I'm handicapped about gettin' around. I have to depend on Selma to drive for me.

"The government farm program hasn't helped me much. Roosevelt's intentions are good; I've no doubt of that, and I'd vote for him again if *he* was all that was involved. But the way things are in this country, you've got to have a pull with the ring crowd to get anything out of the government rentals. Some big farmers has profited by it. One county commissioner, that kept the farm agent in when he was on his way out for too much political activity, has been able to buy a farm a year because of his pull with the farm agent's office since then. Others has made a big thing out of it too. They manage to get 500 pounds to the acre, while the little fellows has to take much less. I got only 300 pounds to the acre last year, and some that don't have a bit bigger yield than I do get 500 pounds without any trouble.

"Then there's the question of rentin' land to the government. Some say the farmers can't cheat because of the map they've got over in Leesburg. Well, they do just the same. Some cut down bushes in uncleared land, sowed it in velvet beans that run up rank and tall and covered up the stumps, and then rented this land to the government. That happened just down the road on a certain fellow's farm. One man that has just cut the pulpwood off a piece of land aims to sow it down in beans this year and draw government rent. All I drawed last year for co-opin' with the government was $25, and half of that went to the sharecroppers.

"It's right, I think, for the sharecroppers to get half the two government checks. Some don't think they ought to share in the spring check, though they wouldn't kick on the parity check.*

*To improve farm prices in the 1930s, the federal government paid farmers (with the "spring check") to reduce the amount of land they farmed and (with parity checks) the amount of crops they produced. Tenant farmers believed that they should receive both payments since, although they were not landowners, their acreage and their output had been reduced. Landowners usually favored sharing only the parity checks with their tenants, and this was the general practice. Some landowners defrauded their tenants by keeping both checks. Thus, even when

"I don't know; I don't get enough to lose no sleep over it either way. I believe in fair dealin's, and it's enough to make folks sore to see how some gobble it up, how farmers linked up with the political ring in Jackson* are gettin' rich on the government. I don't want a cent don't belong to me from the government or nobody else. I want the tenant to have his share fair and honest, and I don't think you'll find one that'll say I cheated him. The Golden Rule is the method I've tried to farm by with my sharecroppers. The only problem I see is for folks to do right. There'll be a few worries along, for tenants can be aggravatin', but a man's children even can aggravate him, so that's just a part of it. When it comes to gettin' 'em out of jail, standin' their bond, buyin' their coffins— well, I'm always thankful it ain't my children I'm havin' to do it for. By happen-chance, I've not had that kind of thing to do for my tenants much. I'm good to them, and they're good to me.

"Speakin' of the farm program, I'll have to say the government has helped the peanut farmers by takin' the peas off their hands, storin' them in bonded warehouses, and allowin' them three and a quarter cents for them. Otherwise, peas would have been dirt cheap and many a farmer would have lost his place for debt. Peanuts is all that has paid expenses the past two years. The farmers are wantin' now to plant more peas, which will run the price down like cotton, though they seem to think the government will protect them. If I had a barn I'd plant some tobacco too, but barns are too expensive to build under the present uncertainty. Lots of farmers around here aim to plant some tobacco this year, since there's no tobacco control now. The boll weevil has discouraged the cotton farmers so they're bound to shift to some other crops some. But it's hard for us around Hilton to get away from cotton; we say we are goin' to cut, but when the time comes to plant we turn back to cotton or would if 'twa'n't for government control. The high cost of fertilizin' the cotton crop has disgusted farmers, as well as has the boll weevil; with the heavy fertilizin' farmers have practiced they can't hope to make much more than expenses under boll-weevil conditions. There used to be a time when farmers lived more at home than they do today. Why, now they even burn coal instead of wood.

"The prospects for farmers look very gloomy to me at present.

---

fraud was not involved, a New Deal program favored the more prosperous and more powerful.

*The county seat, Northampton County.

But we've pulled out of a lot of bad situations in the past, and maybe it'll be better than we think for. Eighteen eighty-nine was a bad year when farmers thought they was ruined, but cotton has been as high as forty cents a pound since that year. By 1950—but a lot of us won't have to worry about cotton by that time."

Bernice Kelly Harris

In Abraham's Bosom

Somebody sot fire to dat barn, an' I knows
who done hit, but I ain't never gwine tell, caze
Mister Shores sho' treated dat man powerful mean, dat he did.

The one-room tenant shanty sagged dangerously in the middle, its pine-block foundation having rotted years before. A greenish scum covered the mildewed shingle roof, and the weatherboarding buckled from the uprights, leaving large cracks. Rough wooden shutters with quarter-inch seams served as windows. A few hardy flowers struggled for survival in the bare, hard-packed yard.

The interior presented an equally despairing picture with its rough, pineboard floor and its smoke-stained walls plastered with old newspapers to keep out the cold.

The furniture, in keeping with its surroundings, consisted of two rickety iron beds that sagged like the house itself, and on which were piled musty, ragged quilts and old clothes. A wobbly, grease-stained table stood in the middle of the room. An ancient victrola rested precariously on an uncertain three-legged stool. In one corner, an old New Home sewing machine with half its parts lying beside it spoke of more affluent times. In another corner, its rusty pipe sticking through a hole in the wall, stood an old-fashioned "nigger" stove that boasted a Pepsi-Cola sign for a top, the original having burned out long before. On the mantel above the rough fireplace stood a motley collection of hair-grease tins, bleaching-cream jars, and Black Draught* boxes.

*Patent medicine for constipation.

"*Yassuh*! We'se movin' dis Jan'u'wery *sho'*!" Emaline, black, emaciated, fifty, leaned forward on her soap-box chair and threw a fat
splinter in the fireplace from which most of the bricks had fallen.
"We'se been heah 'leben yeahs, an' hit sho' looks to me lak we gits
deeper in de bog ev'vy yeah, yassuh, dat we *sho'* does! Mister
Stores, dats de man we wucks fo', tole Tee, dats mah boy, dat he
mought as well give him de cotton crop caze he warn't gwine meck
nothin' no-how. Hit do beat de nation how we'se allus in the de
pinch caze we *sho'* wucks an' mecks hit! De plain Gawd's truth is
dat Mister Stores done stole mos' ev'vything he niggers meck caze
we is ignunt an' cain't figger wid him.

"I'se jes' 'bout nekkid myse'f, but I kin meck out summers.
Hit's dese heah grandchillen what frets me. I went down to de
relief place what gives clothes an' sich truck, an' de lady what run
de she-bang ax me effen Mister Stores doan' teck kere of he han's,
an' I tole her, '*No, mam, dat he sho' doan't*!' She knowed right well I
wuz tellin' de Gawd's truth, an' her eyes kinda flash lak, an' she
sez: 'Damn em, dey wucks de po' niggers an' white buckra* mos'
to death in de spring an' summer, and fall, an' den loads em on us
after stealin' dere share de crop! An' den dey got de nerve to cuss
de relief! Why! *dey's* de ones meckin' money offen de guvment!
Damn em!'

"I declar' mister, dat young lady sho' ain't no fool, an' she doan't
teck no draggin' *offen nobody, nawsuh*. I reckon she wouldn't tack no
sassin' offen Mister Rosy-velt effen he wuz to come in blowin' off.
She say she gwine see de right done effen hit cost her her job, but
shucks, dey couldn't run dat gal off. De po' niggers an' white
buckra would tear down de jint effen dey did try hit! She sho' is
one good 'oman, effen she do cusses a little. She gived me a little
piece er paper an' tole me to teck hit to another lady an' tell her she
say give me some clothes fer dese here chillen, an' me too. An' dat
lady done hit too, an' hit sho' is help out, yassuh.

"Mister Stores, he is sho' one hard man to wuck for, yassuh, dat
he sho' is. He got a commissary what is sho' a gold mine. An' what
mecks hit worse, he turn out de hawgs an' say, 'Let em forage
'roun',' an' dey forages right in mah gyarden an' et up all mah
collards. De stock jes' naturally eat up an' tromple ev'vy thing I
plants. Hit sho' do seem hard, dat hit do. We ain't even got no toilet
no mo. De ole un is fell down, an' Mister Stores he won't put up a
new 'un. De guvment man come out an' sez he kin put up one

---

*A term of African derivation used to describe white men.

what de relief mens is meckin' fo' ten dollars. But Mister Stores, he jes' laugh an' sez, 'Let em go to de bushes lak dey been er-doin'.'

"I sho' wishes I could git wid Mister Richards, but he is allus full-up caze he so good to he han's. I 'clar to Gawd he sho' is one grand man, yassuh, dat he sho' is. He jes' as diffunt from Mister Stores ez day is from night, yassuh. I 'member when mah ol'est boy, Ed, traded wid him. Ed, he been useta stealin' what wuz his'n from Mister Stores, an' he kinda got de habit. He hadn't been wid Mister Richards more'n a week fo' he stole a bushel er peas, an' sole 'em up to de fillin' station on de road. When de ole man fine hit out, he call Ed up to de big house one mawnin' early lak, an' says right slow an' low: 'Ed, my niggers doan't steal from me. I treats my niggers good, an' dey treats me de same. I'm gwine look over dis caze yo' is new heah, but doa'n never let hit happen agin, yo' understan'?'

"Ed, he felt so orney an' mean dat he borrowed some money on he mule an' bought dem peas back for twice what he got for em, an' teck em back to Mister Richards an' 'pologize.

"Ed, he jes' lak all de res' now. Jes' loves de groun' de ole man walks on, yassuh. All he niggers is 'voted to him. De ole man tuck sick las' yeah, an ev'vybody thought sho' he gwine die, an' I reckon de ole man thought so too. He calls he niggers in an' tuck each one by de han' and says: 'I wants you to teck kere of Miss Lucy effen I die. Teck yo' share de crop an' put hit in yo' barns an' teck my share an' put hit in my barns. Stay on here an' teck kere of Miss Lucy lak you is allus done.'

"Gre't Gawd, Mister, but dem niggers did kerry on sumpin terrible, yassuh, dat dey sho' did. I could hear 'em er-cryin' an prayin' clean over here. Dey sho' wuz sum rejoicin' when de ole man pull through. I reckon de Lawd kinda reconsidered, an' let de ole man stay on to hep po' folks an' niggers what needed him so bad. I specks hit wuz partly on account er Miss Anne, Mister Richards fust an' only wife what wuz sech a grand 'oman an' died when Miss Lucy wuz bawn. I never seed sech a good 'oman. She tole Mister Richards to be kind and lovin' to ev'vybody what needed hep, an' not crush de life outen po' folks caze dey didn't git no chance in de worl'. Mister Richards, he sho' loved dat 'oman. I 'members when dey wuz both young an' courtin'. Mister Richards, he teck an' drive by here in a springboard wid a high-steppin' hoss, an' dere beside 'im wuz Miss Anne, all dress fit to kill, an' lookin' pretty ez all git out, yassuh. Dat man sho worshipped dat gal, more'n even de Lawd, I specks, an' yo' couldn't blame him, nawsuh. Dey wuz a sight er young mens courtin' her same time, but she didn't have eyes fer nobody but Mister Richards, nawsuh. I 'members de day he foun' out she gwine take him in pref'rence to all de res'. He wuz jes' about de happiest man in dese parts.

"Dey sho' wuz happy effen dey did start off po'. Miss Anne she wuz so sweet an' 'siderate, an' hit warn't long fo' all de bes' han's wuz on he place. He done prospered ever since.

"'Cose Mister Stores doan' lak him much, 'caze I specks Mister Stores wuz kinda stuck on Miss Anne too. Dey all wuz raised in dis part er de country. Dey is allus at it too. Mister Stores tell Mister Richards he gwine go busted messin' up wid po' whites an' niggers, an not lookin' to he business, but Mister Richards jes' smile sad lak he allus done since Miss Anne died, an' say: 'I treats my niggers good, Stores, an' dey treats me de same.' An' dey sho' is done dat very thing too, 'caze Mr. Richards got de prettiest house, an' de bes' barns, an' de mos' stock, an' a lot er money in de bank.

"But Lawd Gawd, Mister Stores sho' is had he ups 'en downs, yassuh. Last yeah, he los' a barn wid 1,800 bushels er corn in hit—burnt clean to de groun'. Somebody sot fire to dat barn, an' I knows who done hit, but I ain' never gwine tell, caze Mister Stores sho' treated dat man powerful mean, dat he did. He lak to los' all he hawgs jes' a little while back. Somebody put sody in dey feed. Looks lak de mo' he try to grab, de mo' he lose.

"I sho' will be proud when I kin git moved outen dis here shed. I 'bout freezes to death in de winter, and de skeeters eats me up in de summer. Mister Richards he comed by one day an' look at dis shack an' sez right pert: 'Stores, I wouldn't put stock in a shed lak dat!' Mister Stores he mumble something bout he ain' got no money to set niggers up a fine hotel.

"Mister Richards he keeps up he houses; leastwise, de tenants mecks enough to keep 'em up deyself. Mr. Richards, he gived each one a cow las' yeah, an' bought fence wire so dey could have a gyarden. Cose, he tecks hit outen de crop, but he is sho' one fair an' hones' man. I don't specks he tuck out enuff to even pay de cos'.

"Jes' to show you how Mister Richards is, I 'members when Zekiel's wife tuck down wid de appendeceedus. She wuz tuck right sudden lak, an' de doctor what Mister Richards gits to look arter he han's sez effen she doan' git to de horse-spital quick, she gwine die, sho'. Mister Richards nearly bus' a blood vessel gittin' out he fine cyar an' dey puts Sarah in de back, an' Mister Richards driv' her to de horse-spital in Florence, an' paid de bill in 'vance. 'Cose Zekiel paid him back. But he never ax fer nothin'. Dat's one thing 'bout Mister Richards, he doan' never ax you fer what you owes him. He jes' act surprise lak when you goes to pay him—lak he warn't 'spectin' hit right then, but sho' is tickled to death to git hit! Gawd bless dat man!

"Po' ole Catty Lynn what beens cookin' fer de Richards fer de las' forty yeahs cain't hardly git roun' no mo' on account her roomytism, she's so drawed up. I spects I'll git de job. Mr. Richards wuz over heah de other day to see me 'bout hit. Sed he ain' got de heart to hurt Catty's feelin's, so I better jes' act lak I'se heppin' her, so she woan't think dey is shunted her back caze she is gittin' ole. Mighty 'siderate man, Mister Richards is, yassuh, dat he sho' is.

"Well, anyhow, effen I does ever git wid Mister Richards, I sho' gwine burrow in deep, yassuh! I done had mah share er hard times, an' I sho' ain' gwine let dis heah chance slip to git wid dat good man an' spen' de res' er my days in peace an' 'tentment.

"I wuz bawn right near here 'bout fifty yeahs ago, I specks. I married soon's I wuz ole nuff to Susan Cory's boy, Abel, by her fust husban'.

"My Abel jes' kill hese'f wuckin' fer Mr. Carrington what is daid now, may de good Lawd rest he sinful soul. I warn Abel bout killin' hese'f in de hot broilin' sun. He tell me he got to keep goin' sun er no sun. He comed in fer dinner one day at lay-by time, jes' naturally burning up, an' mos' pantin' to death. He stretch out cross de bed, and teck de baby wid 'im whilst I gits he dinner fix'. When I went to git him up, he never answer when I calls, so I calls 'im again, and sez: 'What ail you, honey, come on, yo' dinner gwine git col'. Abel he say nothin'. Den I starts beratin' him from de kitchen, an' tell him he is a fool to kill he'se'f fer po' buckra what think mo' er de mule dan him. Abel, he still doan' say nothin'. I walked oer an shuck him, an' den I seed he eyes wuz wide open, an' so big an' glassy dat hit nearly scairt me clean to death. I knowed Abel daid. I tuck de baby way from him an' started to de house to tell Mister Carrington. De teahs wuz er-streamin so I could hardly see. I wuz about sixteen I reckon, an' wid mah fust baby, an' I loved my man. Hit mos' broke mah heart, yassuh, dat hit sho' did. I doan' specks a gal ever gits over her fust man. I sho' didn't.

"When Mister Carrington come out an' seed me standin' dere crying wid de baby under mah arm, he look kinda funny an sez: 'What ail you, Emmy?'

"'You done kill my Abel,' I sez.

"'Mister Carrington jes' laff, an' sez: 'Onliest way to kill a nigger is to hit him on de heel, he haid too hard to hurt him!'

"'Effen you doan believe hit, go see,' I sez.

"He did, an' comed back an' sez: 'Hafta git somebody to finish Abel's crop. Dat darkey done up an' daid sho' nuff!'

"Dat's all he sez! He ain' kere nothin' bout po' Abel, jes' de crop!

"I got Brother Wilson what wuz a good carpenter to meck Abel a coffin outen white pine. He done hit, an' never charge me a cent. Moughty good darky, Brother Wilson. He got somebody to dig a grave, an' somebody to hitch up de two-hoss wagin, an' carry Abel to he last res'. He died on a Wednesday, but hit wuz Sunday fo' we could bury him, caze de team wuz busy in de fiel'.

"I married agin 'bout fo' yeahs arter Abel died. My secon' husban' wuz a good man; leastwise, he wuz good to me wid what he had. 'Cose he had to wuck hese'f nearly to death, too. Some said he runned arter women, but effen he did I didn't know nothin' 'bout hit. Yassuh, he wuz a right smart man, but he died las' year. 'Cose, I never did git over Abel, 'caze I loved dat boy. A young gal loves her fust man. Yo' see dese heah widows er-marryin' agin, but mos' of 'em marry to git somebody to teck kere of 'em! Yo' cain' tell me nothin'; a gal jes' naturally doan' git over dat fust blush er youth wid her man!

"I jes' hopes now I kin git on wid Mister Richards. I'se too old fer a young man, an' I sho' ain' gwine have no ole man er-slobberin' roun' me! Nawsuh! I jes' looks forward to a peaceful rest fer de few yeahs I got lef' on dis heah vale er tears.

"Six feet er earth is sho' gwine meck us de same, Mister. An' I'se sho' er one thing. When yo' meets yo' Gawd face to face, he ain' gwine ax is yo' white or collud. Nawsuh! He jes' gwine turn in an' sep'rate de sheeps from de goats. Dat's all!

"When we gits up before dat golden throne de Lawd gwine say to Mister Stores: 'Stores, yo' ain' treated people right, nawsuh, dat yo' sho' ain't!' An' de Lawd gwine call St. Peter an' tell him to throw Mister Stores in de bottomless pit! Yassuh! An' when Mister Richards step up fer he turn, de Lawd gwine laugh an' say: 'Welcome, Brother Richards! I sho' is glad to see you! Jes' meck yo'sef right at home. Miss Anne is waitin' fer yo'.'

"Yassuh! Mister, dey's gwine be a scatterin' er black an' whites up dere near de throne. Heaben gwine be full er dem dat's kept de law of de Lawd, an' hell gwine be packed to overflowin' wid dem what *ain't*, yassuh, dat hit sho' is!

"I jes' hopes you'n me will be among dat glorious company. Ah'll git wid my Abel agin, an' ah'll love him more'n more till eternity en's! He wuz de onliest man I ever loved, Gawd bless him!

"Ho, hit'll be a glorious day, dat hit will! Po' Abel won't hafta plough in de hot sun up dere. Thank Gawd, dere won't be no landlawds up dere before Jesus's seat, and dat's what will meck hit heaben! Yassuh! Dat hit sho' will!"

F. Donald Atwell

Aaron and Mary Matthews

PLEASANT HILL, NORTH CAROLINA, 1939

He said nobody should keep no dam' books
on his place, and if we didn't like it, Goddam' it, git out!

It is the New Year. The Matthews have moved into their new "home," an unpainted cabin on the Gumberry–Pleasant Hill road. Aaron sits on the porch in the warm January sunshine, smoking a corncob pipe. Mary makes her way out the door and places chairs in the sunshine, avoiding the broken places in the porch floor. From the three doors that open into the porch negro children, ranging from toddlers to teen-agers, peer curiously.

"Watch, Aaron! You'll fall th'ugh the floor," Mary warns her husband as he moves from his chair across the porch. "He tries to walk widout his stick, but you see how he drags dat foot. He's had two strokes and ain't able to work none now. He's over seventy; he don't know how much more. I's fifty-eight, but I can tell you I feels older.

"Dey's eighteen of us stays here now, eight or nine of 'em gran-chil'en we took when dey mother and father died and dey had nowheres to go. We's had fifteen chil'en of our own; all but seven of 'em's married and away from home doin' public work—saw-millin', workin' in de mill at Roanoke Rapids, or livin' up No'th. James is de oldes' boy dat stays wid us; he works at de sawmill at Gumberry. Floyd was killed in a automobile wreck last fall; his wife and chil'en lives here wid us. Dora married up No'th in Baltimore. I went up to see her 'bout fifteen years ago, but I was glad to git back to de country. Dey's too much fuss in de city for me. I rather

86

do wid less and stay in de country. I don't know where I got enough names to go round 'mongst de chil'en. Some I got from de Bible—Vashti, James, and Mark—and de others I picked up; I didn't git none from de almanac. . . .

"I never had a child or a grandchild I felt like I could do widout. Course sometimes 'fore dey got here I felt like I didn't want to own no more, but when dey come dey was welcome. I ain't never had nary one I was willin' to spare.

"We ain't been moved here but two weeks. Dey's more room here—four bedrooms, de dinin' and cook room—where dey wa'n't but four at de place we come from. Three has to lie in a bed to git 'em all slept. Dis house is in tole'ble good shape. We pasted dis wallpaper in dis room since we come here and newspapers in de other rooms. All de furniture I got is jus' junk like you see. We hain't been able to buy nothin' much but jus' add a bed or two now and den as de chil'en come along. Don't break dat tea set!" Mary admonished a toddler who picks up a tiny green cup from the table in the best room and simulates tea-drinking. . . .

"We 'bout got straight now, and I reckon we'll like it here. We gits lonesome for our old neighbors; de Hardins crost de orchard yonder ain't been to see us yet. De neighbors from round Roanoke-Salem was good to us. If it hadn't been for dem, de chil'en wouldn't had a bit o' Santy Claus dis year. Dey all put together and give us some fruit and candy for Christmas and some o' dey somethin' t'eat. De neighbors saw how we had been treated and was bound we shouldn't go hongry Christmas. We miss de neighbors. But I reckon we'll git use to here. Dem two dogs ain't left us, but de cat's gone. She got homesick, I reckon, and went back home.

"Dey all tells us Mr. Williams is a right good man to work for. I don't know. We ain't seen him yet, but he sent word he was comin' tomorrow. Dey ain't been no bargain made wid him; he jus' told us we could move in his house, and we had to git somewhere. Mr. Lem Jones told us if we wa'n't out by New Year he'd put us out. Maybe he didn't mean it; he had told us dat a lot o' times befo', 'specially round Christmas when he thought we'd want some money. But I told Aaron we'd tried Mr. Jones long enough; looked like dey wa'n't goin' to be no 'mendments, and we jus' well's to make a break and see if we couldn't better ourselves. We had been wid Mr. Lem Jones nineteen long years, and it got wus all de time.

"Me and Aaron both was raised on de farm. Our folks was sharecroppers and renters, never owned no land, but dey wa'n't never ones for movin' round much. We was bo'n and bred up here at Vaughan. His folks went to Suffolk, and Aaron worked in a sawmill down dere. My folks left Vaughan and moved to Suffolk to farm. Me and Aaron got married and went to farmin' for Mr. Tom Wright Dunbar. We stayed wid him eighteen years, and I tell you I's cried a many a time 'cause we ever left him. Long as we stayed wid Mr. Dunbar at Suffolk we had money all de time; we never knowed what it was to be widout some change in our pockets. We got every cent from de crop dat was due us when we lived wid Mr. Dunbar.

"Den Mr. Lem Jones come up to Suffolk in 1919 and persuaded us to move to his farm. He sounded like sech a good man and made sech fair promises we thought he must be de best man in de world. So he fooled us away from Suffolk, and we moved wid him in 1919. Dey's been nothin' much but hard times since we come round here. I've wished a many a time we could move back to . . . where we come from or to Virginia and leave round here. But wid our big family it looked like it was de best to jus' stay on and keep a-hopin' times would git better.

"We never had a fair deal while we was wid Mr. Jones. Every time he settled wid us he took de inside track and 'lowed us what he pleased. We knowed it, but twa'n't no use to complain. Hattie Duncan use to have a row wid Mr. Jones all de time, but we never said nothin'. We knowed we wouldn't git nothin' dat way but cussin'. Dey tell me Mr. Jones is after de Duncans to go back wid him, but I bound dey ain't a-goin'. I don't mind workin' hard; I 'spects dat. But it is hard, after you done de best you can, to be cussed at and talked to like a dog. Aaron killed hisself a-workin' for Mr. Jones; he kept a-pluggin' away even after his blood got too high till dem strokes caught up wid him. I spent de best years o' my life on de Jones farm, and what has we got to show for it? Nothin'—nothin' but younguns!

"De most we cleared wid Mr. Jones was $600. Cotton was sellin' for 30 cents a pound, dey wa'n't no boll weevil much, and we made big crops 'long den. De average we cleared wid Mr. Jones was from $150 to $200 a year. De year we made 70 bales o' cotton and 971 bags o' peas we cleared round $500 or $600."

"What good did it do? . . ." [Aaron asks]. "Long den I put by $600 in de bank and bought me five mules dat cost $250 apiece. I was aimin' to buy me a piece o' land soon as I could 'cumulate enough. When Mr. Jones found out I had banked some money, he shut right down on us and refused to furnish us a dust o' flour or a strip o' meat till we had spent every cent I had put by. What can you do wid sech as dat? Mr. Jones's brother was in de bank, and dey wa'n't no way o' keepin' de money I banked a secret from Mr. Lem. Den next he got busy and worked us out'n de mules, one at a time. At de end o' de year he'd take 'em for debt, claimed we didn't pay out or owed him stuff we didn't know what for.

"Soon as he got de mules in his hand, he furnished de team and made us pay half de fertilize. We never could git him to tell us what de fertilize 'mounted to. 'What in de hell is dat to you?' he'd holler at me when I'd ask him."

"It was de same way wid de books," Mary [adds] as Aaron pauses, . . . "I bought me a five-cent book and ask him to set down what he was chargin' us wid. He cussed at me, said I didn't have no sense, I was a fool, and to move out."

"He said nobody should keep no dam' books on his place, and if we didn't like it, Goddam' it, git out!" Aarons corrects. "He charged us wid stuff we didn't know what 'twas for and wouldn't explain nothin'. We had to pay for pickin' off all de peanuts, ours and his'n too, as well as de pea bags. He claimed to pay half de fertilize, but it was worked out in sech a way we ended up payin' it all, I reckon. He furnished us wid $6.00 a week de year round; dat had to take care o' rations and every string o' clothes. I don't know how much dat come to, but I know we'd ought to cleared more dan we did much as we made some years. Mr. Lem told me several times I had made enough on de farm to buy de Vasser place if I had took care o' my money. Took care o' my money! When he wouldn't let me have nothin' in de bank, wouldn't let me have no peace till I had drawed out every cent! If I had had justice, we'd be livin' on a farm o' our own right now. I tell you one thing: hell's gettin' het up right now for some folks. De devil's waitin' for 'em; dey're goin' jus' as straight—"

"Hush talkin' so bad 'bout de man, Aaron. Everybody's got some good in 'em if you can find it. Dis past gone year we made jus' 15 bales o' cotton and 223 bags o' peas and 75 or 80 barrels o' corn on a four-horse crop. I can't tell you how much it ought to come to—more 'n we got, I know. Mr. Jones furnished us de $6.00 a week like Aaron said and paid half de fertilize, while we paid all de labor for pickin' peas and de pea bags and one half de fertilize. We never got no rental checks. Some has got gov-ment money on dey crops, but ain't none come to us. I don't know how it works. We never had no help from de gov-ment; Aaron's old enough to draw de old pension, but he ain't ask for none yet. When we settled dis year, Mr. Jones took de whole crop and claimed we was in debt $218."

"If you want to know what de settlement is like I can tell you:

"'Aaron, come 'ere! You're behind dis year. De crop's all in, and you ain't paid out.'

"'How much did my part come to?'

"'Not 'nough to cover your account.'

"'What did you say de account is?'

"'For fertilize, de 'lowance by de week, de money I let you have—'

"'Which money you talkin' 'bout?'

"'You're a dam' fool. It's all booked here. You think you can keep it all in your dam' head?'

"'How much did de fertilize come to?'

"'What in de hell is dat to you? I ain't robbin' you o' nothin'. I carried you de whole dam' year, and now you owe me two hund'ed and eighteen dam' dollars. Looks like dey's no end to carryin' your dam' crowd o' dam' niggers.'

"'I know de crop ain't much, but—'

"'Goddam' you! Git out o' my dam' house, you and your dam' niggers, don't I'll put you in de dam' road—'"

"Hush, Aaron! Don't talk so bad! . . . It's bad as he says and has been for most o' nineteen years. Soon as settlement was over dis year, Mr. Jones locked up de co'n, nailed boa'ds across de door of de crib, and left us blank, not even no co'n for bread. Den he said git out. I wisht we could o' gone back to . . . Virginia and left from round here. Dey ain't never been nothin' but trouble in dis country.

"Mr. Jones wouldn't even let me keep no cow. I tried when I come here from Virginia, but it didn't suit him. Everywhere I'd put my cow out to graze he'd come right along and have it plowed up. He ding-donged after me 'bout de cow till I got rid of her, for peace. De same way wid de chickens. I tried to raise some, but he claimed dey bothered de cotton. So I had to quit. I kept tryin' to raise me some pigs, and he objected to dat; he didn't want to spare 'em de co'n. Dis year I raised me one hog when I saw de crop was goin' to be a failure, so as to have some meat on hand for de chil'en. Mr. Lem sent his boy here to buy de hog. I told him I didn't want to sell. I knowed dey didn't want no hogs on de place, but I was bound dey shouldn't have my one hog dis year. Soon after dat, my hog was shot; de shots hit him in de leg and crippled him so bad we had to kill him. When we butchered de hog, we found de shots in de morrow of his bone.

"So dat little handful o' meat is all we got to live on from de smokehouse—no collards, no turnips, no 'taters, no co'n for meal, nothin'. 'Bout all I could raise widout creatin' a fuss was my flowers. I had de front yard packed full o' cosmos and zinnias. Dey ain't no flowers here. I don't know where I'll start any or no. Every cent we got to live on is what my son makes over yonder at de sawmill in Gumberry, 'bout three dollars a week. On dat we's had to live since crops was housed. All we buys is a sack of flour, coffee, sugar, and stuff we're bound to. If we had had any fruit I ain't had time to can none. De cookin', washin', ironin', and patchin' kept me straight. Dey was plenty in de field to keep de work goin'; de house took me. For breakfast we eats bread and meat and coffee; for dinner it's de same, unless we can git holt o' some dried peas and beans to help out; at supper it's bread and meat again. It don't bother me to cook for eighteen. I'm use to it; when you once git your hand in, it's as easy as to fix for three or four."

"Reckon what Mr. Lem told me 'fore we moved?" [Aaron asks]. "He said if I'd run all dese younguns away, he'd let me and Mary have a house to live in for de good we had done. My chil'en's as near to me as his'n is to him! He wouldn't done it nohow."

"We miss de neighbors" [Mary continues]. "We got no team or wagon to go to see 'em, and it's too far to walk. Durin' de nineteen years we was wid Mr. Jones we owned three cars. I believe if Miss Bettie had had de farm in charge times would o' been better for us. She always seemed like a good woman to me. Ramsey was bad as his daddy, 'cept he didn't cuss at us.

"We been lucky 'bout sickness and death, don't it would o' been still wus wid us. When Floyd was killed last November, de insurance buried him. I pays three dollars burial insurance for de family; right now I'm behind on it, but I'm hopin' dey won't drop me 'fore I can catch it up. Death would shore catch us at a bad time right now. Aaron has got high blood, and I suffer wid rheumatism crost my shoulders and arms right bad, but we stays pretty well, to be as many of us as is. Thirteen years ago I had a operation at Roanoke Rapids for appendicitis, but we got dat bill paid up. The doctor ain't been but three times since, once to Aaron and when two of de chil'en had pneumonia. I raised all fifteen o' my own to be grown; Floyd's de only one dead, and he was killed.

"De chil'en's never had much schoolin'. De highest any of 'em ever went was to de fou'th grade. None dat's here now has been past de third. Soon as one gits old enough he's put in de field. Dey ain't no time to go to school. I don't reckon nary one will ever git th'ough de grades. My schoolin' was so pieced up I don't know how far I got. Like dese chil'en now, I had to go when de crop was housed and quit when work started. I ain't never learnt to figger none, but I can write a little and read. 'Stead o' de chil'en a-readin' de Bible to me, I has to read to dem.''

"I never went a day," Aaron says. "My daddy was a slave, and times was so hard when he was tryin' to raise me dey wa'n't no chance for schoolin'. My daddy always told us his marster was mean to him; he'd be plowin' 'long in de field good as he knowed how, but his marster would stand at de end of de row and thrash him crost de back wid a lash, jus' for good measure, he'd say. He whupped one of his slaves so bad he had to throw him in de chicken coop to keep de dogs and things off'n him. Dat slave died. I've heard my daddy set and tell many a time 'bout how cruel dey was treated back den.''

"We goes to church at Roanoke-Salem, and all dat's old enough belongs to de church dere. I never moved my membership from . . . where I was bo'n and bred. Aaron don't belong nowheres. I've worked on him all I knows how, but seems like he won't give up. He thinks dey's too many bad uns inside and too many good uns out, but I tells him he's gittin' too ageable now to keep holdin' off. I wish I could git him to join de church.''

"I believes in de Lord" [Aaron replies]. "I believes in livin' fair and honest and treatin' folks right. I sees too many follerin' de devil and tryin' to hide dey meanness behind de church to talk much 'bout joinin'. When a man cusses you and talks to you like you ain't nothin' but a beast, like you got no feelin's, dat's de Devil's dealin's. De Lord's dealin's is nice and pleasant. Torment can't git too hot for some dat deals wid de Devil. If some dat's done gone dere could speak dey's tell you 'bout it.''

"De dead don't come back to tell nothin'. Ha'nts?* Dey ain't no sech a thing. You hear tell o' ha'nted houses, but 'tain't nothin' but 'magination. I never seed nothin' I couldn't make out.''

"Me neither," Aaron agrees. "Some folks claims dey can see things, but I never did. Dey's plenty right today dat believes in conjure and mess like dat, but 'tain't no sech thing. You know dey ain't no sech thing!''

*Ghosts.

"White folks comes round sometimes, not much now as dey use to, tryin' to sell stones and roots and one thing after another, to keep off bad luck, dey claims. I always told 'em I didn't mind buyin' nothin' dat would bring me good luck, but 'twa'n't [worth]while to talk to me; dey wa'n't no money for good luck at our place. I don't worry much about de bad lucks. Dey says it's bad luck for a woman to come to your house on New Year's, but if a man's along he'll make it good. If a woman comes de six' day o' Feb'uary, you won't have no poultry dat year.

"I ain't had much luck since I landed in dis country. I had nice times when I was single. . . . We never believed in dancin' and cuttin' up rowdy. Since we been married I went to de picture show a few times, and I's tried to let all de chil'en see at least one; but we ain't got around yet, dey's such a shower of 'em. I likes de pictures fine."

Aaron drags his foot along the broken floor and looks at the sun. "It's twelve o' clock. . . . Um-hum! Dere's de sawmill whistle at Gumberry blowin'."

Bernice Kelly Harris

'Backer Barning

SMITHFIELD, NORTH CAROLINA, 1939

I hadn't ought to be so tired. I've worked like this all my life.

Ransome Carson, tall, emaciated, and quivering with nervous energy, was busy stripping the green leaves from waist-high tobacco stalks. He had no time to talk but he straightened for a moment and stared at his visitor.

"Go on up to the barn where the women are," he spoke shortly. "We'll be in after we get this slide* full." As soon as he had spoken these few words he returned to his task.

All of the men were barefoot, paying no attention to the hot sand. They wore straw hats with frayed brims and most of them were as dark as Indians.

The women at the barn were laughing and joking. They had strung the last slide of tobacco and were resting, some sitting in the barn door, some on the empty slide, and some on nail kegs. Most of them were barefoot and the loopers† wore aprons made from worn oilcloth. Many of them wore blue overalls and blue homespun shirts open at the throat. Some of them wore perky little bonnets; some, straw hats, and the old ladies wore big dark bonnets that covered their necks. Ransome's wife wore blue overalls and a blue homespun shirt. She also wore a ragged straw hat and was barefoot.

---

*A sled used to haul tobacco from the field to the barn.
†Loopers tie "hands" (three or four leaves) of green tobacco to sticks. The sticks then are hung in curing barns to cure.

"I'd ought to go up to the house and see about Jean," she said. But the tobacco slide appeared. "Oh, I can't go now because there's the slide and I'll have to go on stringing."

"I'd never think of leaving a nine-months-old baby in a house alone for half a day," Granny scorned. "Poor little thing'll never learn to talk or act sensible in its life. It stays by itself all the time. Suppose the house catches on fire or suppose the child swallows something and gets choked to death. Why, suppose it crawls up on a chair and falls and breaks its little neck. There's a hundred things could happen to her. I wouldn't leave none of mine that way."

Frances laughed. "I don't think anything will happen to her. Everybody else leaves their younguns at the houses. Mrs. Creech ties her baby to the table leg with a hemp rope because she's scared it'll get in mischief or swallow something that'll choke it. I left mine in the yard once but it eat sand, chicken manure, and strings, so I decided to leave her in the house and take a chance on her eating buttons. If I left the 'backer every hour or two and went to the house to see about her, Ransome would raise the devil."

The women and children worked rapidly and the green leaves disappeared from the slide quickly. A visitor arrived and started to hand tobacco, but Frances called her over to one side and whispered, "Ruby's crawling with lice; you'd better stay away from her."

The girl gave a shriek and went and sat in the barn door. Frances returned to her hoss* and continued stringing tobacco. Now and then the twine broke and the looper gave vent to his feelings in impatient little exclamations, such as "Oh, there," or "Oh, damn." When the sticks were full there were calls of "Stick off," "Get this stick," or just "Stick."† One little towheaded boy removed sticks from all four hosses, and he was the busiest person present. A three-year-old clung to her mother's apron, bawling lustily. Small boys wrestled under the barnshed or amused themselves by running straws through the bodies of long green tobacco worms. One boy had perhaps a dozen of them on one staw. Frances joined in the laughter and the jokes, but her brown eyes often looked wistfully toward the weather-beaten, four-room house where her baby stayed alone.

Before the slide was empty another had arrived and then the

*A hoss is a rack on which sticks are placed while a looper ties tobacco to the sticks.
†Once a stick is full of hands of tobacco, the sticks are lifted up and hung in the curing barns.

work went on. The laughing ceased and only occasional exclamations broke the stillness.

Ransome came with the next slide. When he was near enough to be heard he stormed, "Damn it, what have you been doing that you can't keep trucks* in the field? I told Johnny that if it was his fault I'd skin his god damned hide. If you damned women wouldn't jabber so much you'd git done sometime." He walked up to Frances and, white-faced, she shrunk back.

"If you don't git a move on I'll git a 'backer stick," he muttered, holding her tightly by the collar. Her eyes dilated and her lips quivered. Then he let go of her and walked hurriedly back towards the field. Frances said nothing but rushed more and more, and she almost entreated the others to hurry. Nobody talked and nobody stopped for anything, and the slide was empty before the next one arrived. They did not get behind again, and at eleven o'clock Ransome returned and ordered Frances to the house to prepare dinner for all the help.

The girl didn't open her mouth but handed her apron to another girl and hurried to the house. She ran in, lifted the baby, and hugged it. It was dirty, but a glance at the floor and at the child's wet clothes explained it. The beds were unmade; clothing lay in heaps on the bed, the table, the chairs, and the bureau. There was no rug on the floor, and the dingy white curtains at the window were ragged and tied in big knots. There were no shades at the windows.

When Frances had suckled the child she built a fire in the stove and set her pots of beans, potatoes, and tomatoes, that she had cooked before dawn, on to warm. She ran into another room and changed to a clean but faded print dress before she made biscuits. She boiled a dozen eggs for salad and made a huge pot full of coffee and sliced a six-layer chocolate cake before twelve o'clock.

The help came up to the well and drew water to wash up. Frances carried soap and towels to them and then hurried back to the kitchen to slice tomatoes and cucumbers. The men, women, and children rubbed their hands with sand first and then scrubbed them with washing powder and washed them in the washtub. Most of the gum was off by this time, but they washed again with toilet soap and then rinsed with clean cold water.

Ransome didn't wait for the others. He washed ahead of the

*Trucks: probably another term for slide.

women and hurried to the table. Frances looked embarrassed and tried to reprove him gently.

"Ain't a man got a right to set down at his own table when he pleases?" he bellowed at her.

She said no more and the men filed in and seated themselves on kegs, rickety chairs, and almost bottomless chairs. They ate their food and scarcely spoke until they were in the yard again. The women went tiredly to the table as soon as Frances had washed the dishes and set them on the table again. They ate slower and talked a little, and when they were through eating, Jane Creech helped Frances wash the dishes and Granny put them in the old-fashioned safe.

"I'm tired enough to die," Frances remarked. "I hate 'backer barning, but I know we have to do it. We're off now till two o'clock, though, to let the mules rest. Thank God we've got mules to work or Ransome would work me to death. He's right good to the mules, but he does cuss them and if they make him mad he beats them, too. Think I'll stretch out here on the bed and rest a little.

"I hadn't ought to be so tired. I've worked like this all my life. Papa was a farmer and he made us work so hard that we didn't go to school half of the time. We had to stay at home in the fall and grade 'backer and pick cotton, and in the spring we had to stay out to plant it. That's why I never got out of the fifth grade. I went a little higher than the other six, too." Tears were rolling down her cheeks.

"I'll tell you what's so: tenant farming ain't no pleasure at all. My papa done it and Ransome ain't never done nothing else. We make mighty little after working ourselves near 'bout to death and we move just about every year. I've heard folks say that there was good landlords and bad ones. I ain't never seen neither one. They're all alike, looking for every cent they can, and landlords was born without hearts. I always thought so while I lived at home, and since I married Ransome, I know it.

"I married when I was sixteen and didn't care a snap that he drunk and fought and had been in jail a time or two. I thought he'd stop it when I married him, but he got worse. He drunk and stayed away two or three days and nights at the time. He still does, even in barning season, and I have to set up with the barn* all night by myself and then work in the 'backer the next day. When he comes

---

*Tending the curing fire.

home from being gone so long and I ask him where he's been, he tells me it's none of my damned business, and that's all I ever know about it. He keeps his jug of liquor in the kitchen and drinks when he pleases. If he wants to beat me or the children, he does, and that's all there is to it. He ain't got no mercy on nothing but mules and dogs. He don't think that I need clothes and, do you know, I love him better than most women love their husbands. I reckon women do love bad husbands better than they do good ones. I ain't got nothing, but I'm happy when Ransome's nice to me and the children.

"The little boy's five years old and the baby's nine months old. I ain't never been sick much, not even when they was born. I was up cooking and washing dishes the third day and when the last one was born I milked the cow on the third day. I felt pretty fainty, but there won't nobody else to do it. We had the doctor both times and that's the only times we've had a doctor in eight years.

"I don't hardly ever get out and go nowheres. I don't go to church, and I don't go to town once every six months. I ain't got no near neighbors and I don't care a straw about visiting nohow. I don't take no interest in reading and voting. I don't want to do nothing when I ain't working except rest. I'm tired all the time lately and I reckon I've got a right to be. We're trying to tend seven acres of 'backer, four of cotton, and twenty of corn, besides the garden and peas and 'tater patch. We're not going to make nothing like we done last year.

"Last year we farmed on another place and after we bought a second-hand Model-A Ford we didn't have enough left to buy any winter clothes. We've still got the old car, but we ain't had no money to buy numbers this year. When Ransome goes to town he catches a ride. Sometimes he goes on Saturday and comes back on Tuesday or Wednesday. I never know what to expect and that keeps life interesting. I manage all the year pretty well except during 'backer barning season and then I stay dead tired. Just look at the mess this house is in and you can see that I don't have time to keep it right. Well, anyway, after the barning is over I'll git a little rest, but grading ain't much rest. When you raise the stuff it's really 'backer all the time, pretty near all the year around."

Mary A. Hicks
Edwin Massingill

Tobacco's in My Blood

EASTERN NORTH CAROLINA, 1939

*I love tobacco, I love to fool with it and get the gum on my
hands and clothes. I love to sell it and I love to chew it and smoke it.*

Lee Hughes sat on his doorstep looking over his field of tobacco.
"Guess the worms'll eat it in spite of all we can do. We've been
worming and suckering since early May and we can't seem to
make much headway over the worms. We don't make nothing—
but still we stick to tobacco and cotton. We raise most of what we
eat during the summer and I try to work out enough to buy our
winter groceries, but sometimes I can't find a job. I'm a first-class
carpenter as well as a farmer. I've tried to get on WPA or PWA* but
they won't hire me because we own this land.

"Annie's mother gave her this land, a hundred acres. The old
lady bought it when it was an old field grown up ten feet high in
second-growth woods. She was a widow with twelve little children
and she cleared most of it herself. She plowed it, too, with a steer,
and in ten years she had a good farm. She bought the land across
the road, a couple of lots in town, and another little farm down the
road. She divided the land up several years ago, although she just
died a year ago. She was eighty-eight years old, and she could still
plow when she was eighty-five. My folks was all strong, too, but
me and Annie are both kinda weak. I don't believe our folks worried over crops like we do.

*The Works Progress Administration and Public Works Administration were New
Deal agencies.

99

"We got up before daylight, winter and summer, and by the time it's light enough to see we're out at work. We fix our plant beds for tobacco in January, and in February we plant the seed and cover it with canvas to keep out the cold. We have to pull out the weeds about twice or three times before the plants are big enough to set out. While the plants are coming up we break the land, put in a ton of fertilizer to the acre and run rows. We set out the plants as soon as it gets warm enough so they won't freeze, usually the first of May. Then the war starts. If it's too dry we have to water the plants after we set them out, and then it's sucker, worm, plow, and chop until the latter part of June when the lugs get yellow. We barn them first, and by the time they're cured the body-leaves are ripe and we barn and cure again. When they're packed down ready to grade, the tips are to barn.

"We're mighty glad when the last barn is killed out, but the work ain't over yet. The tobacco's still to grade, tie, and carry to market. That means work in the packhouse ten hours a day and sometimes by lantern light. It means worrying about getting the tobacco in order to move it and then setting up all night or getting up in the middle of the night to take it to town. . . .

"I love tobacco. I love to fool with it and get the gum on my hands and clothes. I love to sell it and I love to chew it and smoke it. Annie dips. She tried to get modern and smoke, but she got sick on it and went back to her snuffbox. I don't like to see women smoke, but when I see one with a cigarette stuck in her mouth I think to myself that means more sale for tobacco. I don't want to be harsh on them.

"We plant about four acres of cotton a year, and it's really more trouble than eight of tobacco. We have twenty acres of corn and two or three of hay, but nothing gives me pleasure like tobacco. I never have raised anything that I like to raise half so well.

"My father was raising the weed before I was born and my grandfather made it when it had to be sent to Virginia in hogs-heads. He made as high as thirty acres some years, but he had plenty of slaves to work it. His job was to oversee the overseer, and that's all he had to do. Now if that was all I had to do, I don't think I'd mind raising a hundred acres.

"When me and Annie got married we rented a farm and started raising tobacco. It was a wet year and our tobacco moulded, and we had dysentery. The next year we made four acres of tobacco, but the bottom dropped out of the price and our crop didn't bring enough to pay for fertilizer. Cotton was low, too, that was 1916,

and I never saw so many hoboes as was traveling that year. Eldridge, our oldest son, was born that year. Another bad year was
1917. We didn't make a good crop and prices was still low. It was
better in 1918, but the price of food and clothes had gone up, and
we had another son, Clifford, that year. The years that followed
were better, but after the old lady gave Annie this place the house
had to be fixed up and wired, taxes had to be paid, barns had to be
built, fertilizer had to be bought, and we had five kids to support
and send to school. It took some hustling, and Annie worked so
hard she ruined her health and had to have two operations, which
cost us over $1,000. That was more than the profit on our crop for a
couple of years.

"Ever since her sickness I've tried to make her be more careful,
but she won't listen to a word I say. She's a smart woman but she
carried it too far, firing the tobacco-barn furnace, drawing water,
cutting wood, and doing a heap of things she ain't got no business
doing. Our three oldest sons are gone now and the youngest one is
sickly, has epileptic fits. Eldridge is a mechanic and lives in Rocky
Mount.

"Clifford's a tobacco farmer and lives down on Neuse River, and
Charlie joined the Navy some three years ago. He's in Shanghai,
China, now. Our daughter, Mary Jim, who's fifteen, is still in school
and she's smart as a briar. She'll make some farmer a good wife
one of these days 'cause she loves tobacco just as good as me and
her nanny and her grandfolks. Some of the girls wants to wear
gloves when they hand tobacco, but not Mary Jim. She loves to get
the gum on her hands and she don't mind going barefooted around
the tobacco barn, neither. To show you how smart she is, she got a
dollar a day for handing tobacco when she was eight years old.

"I sorta wish that my oldest boy was interested in tobacco, but
he ain't. When I told him some time ago that I wished so, he said
that working in tobacco was filthy work and that he'd almost starve
before he'd do it. He said that one reason for his hate for tobacco
was the number of times we'd whipped him with tobacco sticks. It
wan't no use to tell him that mighty near every farmer in North
Carolina had been whipped with tobacco sticks and had whipped
their younguns with tobacco sticks too, but he says that knowing
that don't help a bit. Charlie's pretty much the same way, and
Clifford's so slow he'll never get nowhere. He's always trusting to
luck, and thinks he'll get rich sometime when he strikes a good
year. Tobacco farmers are like gold miners, always hoping to strike
it rich.

"And tobacco sure is fascinating. I reckon it gives more pleasure to more people than any other single thing. It is used by more different types of people than any other article in the world. Kings use it, millionaires, chorus girls, clerks, businessmen, gangsters, convicts, merchants, farmers, and every country in the world. It began in America with Sir Walter Raleigh. Yes sir, its history, travels, and uses are fascinating. I read all I can on the subject, and I have given it pretty close study, especially the advertisements. I never saw an old lady happier than when she is dipping snuff, or an old gentleman so contented as when he is taking a chew. Young people puff on cigarettes as though they furnish the breath of life, and businessmen suck on long black cigars which emphasize the executive's importance. I tell you, I've got a kind of passion for tobacco. I've worked the stuff all my life and I've barely made a living on it. I've blessed it and cursed it and loved it and hated it; still, I've never given it up.

"I don't think we'd ought to have crop control;* I think the government ought to leave us farmers alone. We don't mind our crops selling for nothing if we can get our food, clothes, and fertilizer for nothing, too. We want an even break, and it seems to me like the government could force down other prices easier than it can raise the prices of farm products. All we expect is a living and a little over.

"Now this year I expect to make around $2,000 on my tobacco, but half of it will go for expenses, and then there's the truck I bought to haul it in still to account for. There's a barn that'll have to have a new roof, some new harness has got to be bought, and fertilizer for another year, in addition to living expenses, and then I might not be able to get $2,000 for my crop. We always have to figure on starting a new year with nothing. There's one thing you can count on though; Lee Hughes'll have plenty of peas, corn, and potatoes, and he'll be raising tobacco as long as he's able to stir. Yes ma'am, tobacco's in my blood for keeps, and I've got a real honest-to-goodness passion for it."

Mary A. Hicks

*A government program to raise farm prices by subsidizing the reduction of farm output.

A Day on the Farm

CATALAN COUNTY, ALABAMA, 1939

It use to be nothing but cotton; now we raise our own food.

Mrs. Dora Healy and Miss Annie Franklin are two lone old ladies that have made a success of their farm without the help of a man. Miss Annie is about seventy and Miss Dora about sixty-eight years old. Miss Annie said: "It don't get you nowhere to tell your age, but I'll say this; we been right here on the farm since 1881. Our father had two other farms, but he was a slack businessman and sold them both; but he kept these 400 acres."

Miss Dora was married one year, and has been a widow thirty-five years. She is very deaf and uses an ear trumpet. Miss Annie has never been married. She is getting very feeble, but is the business head of the family.

Miss Dora said: "Now, honey, you got to eat dinner with us first and then we will tell you all you want to know about the farm. Our dinner is all cooked, yesterday being Sunday and all we got to do is to make up some biscuit and make coffee. We got a little nigger girl that helps us. She lives on our farm. Her mother washes our clothes. We have two Negro families that live on the place. We give them so much land; they give us a bale of cotton and help on the farm.

"Right now there is nothing much to do. We kill a beef most every Friday and sell it at any of the county towns. We kill on an average of fifty a year. There are not more than thirty-five head right now, but we have about eleven that will drop their calves before long.

"Our nephew from Chicago, that married Karen (she's the baby that we raised from two weeks old) wants to stock our farm this summer with 200 head of Hereford cattle, but we don't think we are going to let him. It will be too much work on us, and we are getting old. It wouldn't have meant nothing to us ten years ago, but not now. We might if we had a man, but we ain't.

"The weather has been so warm we haven't killed hogs but once this winter, but soon as we have a cold spell we'll kill again. We don't sell much pork; we cure it for ourselves and put it in the smokehouse. If I do say it myself, we make the best sausage of anybody in Catalan County."

Just then Miss Annie came to the door and invited us in to dinner. If ever a table "groaned," this one did. It was set with a snowy white cloth and napkins and with old-fashioned china that Miss Annie said belonged to their mother. Unusually large coffee cups completed the setting. On the table were platters of sliced turkey, country ham, fried chicken, and sausage. Other foods were turnip greens, peas, stewed tomatoes, pickle, brandy peaches, jelly, cornbread and hot biscuit, coffee, buttermilk, fruit cake, and coconut cake.

I said, "Great goodness, I have never seen so much to eat! It would be enough to last me a month." "Go on, honey," said Miss Annie, "if we had known you was coming we *would* have had something. We don't have to buy a thing except a little flour, coffee, sugar, and kerosene now and then. Everything is raised right here on the farm. We used to get up before day when we were young, and ride on mules all over the farm, but not now; we got too much sense. We sleep till eight and nine o'clock.

"We make a right smart selling cedar posts. We got so much cedar down on the creek. Then we make money on our timber; but we don't make nothing on cotton. We raise all of our feed for our cattle, hogs, and chickens and turkeys. Turkeys are hard to raise. They stray off so bad. We got about a hundred head of hens; sell our eggs for thirty-five cents a dozen now. Of course at Christmas time we get more."

"Our timber," remarked Miss Dora at this point, "is bought for a ten-year contract, but the man went broke and moved away. Now another man, Mr. Davis, wants it. We want to sell it to him as soon as we get everything straightened out."

Miss Annie then took up the thread of conversation with, "We get plenty lonesome here at night all alone. Karen's been away fourteen years; four years at school, then she's been married ten years. Her mother was a western woman, and she died when

Karen was born. We took her when she was two weeks old and raised her as our own. Her father died two years later. She called us Mama Dora and Mama Annie.

"She was a blessed child and beautiful. Law, but we had a time at first. Two old maids that didn't know nothing about no babies. We raised her on cow's milk, and everything was sterilized. Then when she was six months old we gave her pot-licker from collard and turnip greens, too. That's got iron in it. Then we gave her cow's milk with cream. Her cheeks were like roses, and she was fat as a little butterball. We would take her to town in our flivver, and everybody would stop and look at her. She is a beautiful woman now and has two lovely children, a boy and a girl. She married a man of means who is a fine fellow. She was going to school and living with her mother's sister when she met him. He sent us a check for $300 Christmas and Karen sent us a big Christmas box. Law, honey, I could talk forever about that child. We sent her four patchwork quilts and crocheted her a beautiful bedspread for Christmas. They are coming back for a visit in June, and we are going to bring them to see you. Her children call Dora and me Granny Annie and Granny Dora."

Miss Annie, speaking of the farm, said: "Well, honey, since we have diversified crops—cotton, corn, peanuts, velvet beans, sugar-cane, potatoes—and our vegetable garden, we have done much better. It use to be nothing but cotton; now we raise our own food. As I told you, we don't spend but mighty little on flour and sugar. We don't sell our vegetables. We can them to use in the winter. We still have about 300 quarts to last us 'til our spring garden comes in. We have a lot of jelly and preserves and marmalade. Our peach and pear trees and crab-apple trees are doing well, and we have the blackberry and huckleberry bushes, more than we can use. We make blackberry and elderberry wine too, but make more scup-pernong wine than any other kind. We don't waste nothing; save all of our leaves even. Leaf mould is one of the best fertilizers.

"Our stock don't take near as much feed in the winter. We just turn them a-loose, and they just graze from early morning 'til late in the afternoon. Now, from March on we have to put them up and feed them on corn and cottonseed meal. Of course we have some pasture. Our cotton seed we exchange for cottonseed meal. It don't cost us nothing. And we raise a lot of corn. Another thing we have is our pecan trees. We make some money off of them, but the price hasn't been good the last few years, and the crop has been poor, not enough rain. We ain't had near enough rain. But here we go, liable as not it will rain. Ain't farmers terrible? I am one and I know. Can't please them; even God Almighty can't; they're always grumbling."

Miss Dora reentered the conversation with comments about some of their other troubles. "We have had a time with niggers stealing," she said. "They just can't help it; it's born in them. But we can't stay here and watch things all the time. If you turn your back, the'll grab up a chicken, steal your eggs, and sell them to the rolling store.

"We were robbed Saturday night. Somebody stole twenty-six dollars out of my trunk. We were here all alone and heard the dog barking. I mean Annie did. I am so deaf I can't hear nothing, just like I am dead when I take my ear trumpet off. The dog kept on barking. After a while Annie got up and opened the door. There was a door, leading to the porch, wide open; the trunk was open and the purse gone. It sho' is worrying us. We have a gun and the dog, but that must have been a nigger that knew the dog or he sho' would have bit him. If we just had a man to stay out here with us. But we don't know who to get. We are getting old, and if Annie were to die and leave me, what would I do?" Big tears rolled down Miss Dora's old wrinkled cheeks. "We were smart girls in our day. Annie can shoot just like a man, but she don't do it now 'cause her eyes are bad.

"We got a lot of game on our place: quail, dove, and rabbits. In the season Annie would get up before day. I'd hear her gun *pop*, *pop*, at first light—that's when the birds start coming in—and in no time she would come in with enough to last several days.

"That's one kind of meat you get tired of mighty quick. There's a saying you can't eat birds twelve days straight running.

"The birds are beautiful out here. I tell Annie we ought to call our place 'Bird Heaven' because of the redbirds, thrush, and mockingbirds. Now, I don't like the blue jays; they are mean to the other birds. Peckerwoods are good to keep insects away, but they are aggravating sometimes. Sometimes they tap-tap-tap so loud, we say 'come in' and it ain't nobody but the old peckerwoods. It's spooky too with nobody there. They say old folks love birds best. I 'speck it's true. I didn't used to love them like I do now.

"Now, Annie is the hunter, but I can beat her fishing. I'm the fisherman. I could set all day and never get tired. It's convenient to have your creek in walking distance. I fish a lots on Sunday; I'm so busy in the week. Ain't no sin to fish on Sunday. That's when I see God most. Setting on the bank, it's so beautiful down there. In the springtime—that's my favorite time of the year—the wood violets, the lilies, the honeysuckle, yellow jasmine, and dogwood are all blooming at the same time. It smells like heaven. It's funny, but Annie's favorite time is autumn. That's because she likes to hunt. And mine's spring, because I like to fish. I ain't never fished at night, 'cause I'm scared of snakes. I always take our dog because he ain't scared of snakes. He kills every one that he sees."

Just then Miss Annie came in out of breath. She said, "Excuse me, honey, but I been out there talking to that nigger. I believe that son-of-a-bitch got our money. I caught him stealing eggs and chickens before. Now you are laughing at me 'cause I am cussing. But you got to cuss if you run a farm."

She said, "We pay the preacher regular, give him hams, sausage, chickens, butter and eggs and things. He knows I cuss—'speck he does, too—but nobody knows it. Now, Dora don't swear as much as I do, but she likes a drink better."

Then Miss Dora said, "There you go, don't you like a little toddy too?"

" 'Course I do," Miss Annie retorted; "it hopes me up; but I don't take but one and you take two. Now, honey," she explained to me, "we takes a little toddy in the winter and a little mint julep in the summer. As Pa used to say, 'a little for the stomach's sake.' "

Attributed to Gertha Couric

Just a Plain
Two-Horse Farm

PLEASANT HILL, NORTH CAROLINA, 1939

That's the way it is: I'm just a plain average
two-horse farmer with land o' my own, no money and
no prospects to make none. I don't look forward to havin' nothin'
in this life nohow; beyond makin' a livin', I don't crave nothin'.

"That's all right about leavin' my plowin'. I reckon the ground's a little wet anyhow; but it was such a pretty sunshiny day, after all this rain, looked like I just had to get out and break up some land."

Thin to gauntness, James Hale sits and wipes the sweat from his flushed face with a red bandanna handkerchief. For an instant he lets the balmy March breeze blow through the window on him, hot from plowing. The odor of sweat that is blown from the thin graying hair under the old felt hat and from the gray work clothes that cover his gauntness is fresh and of the fields.

"The mule won't mind restin' neither. Look at her a-makin' straight for that patch of oats! That green stuff looks good to her after all the dry feed she's had to live on all the winter. She won't eat enough to make her sick, I don't reckon. Do, it'll be the first time; I've raised twenty-six crops with her, and she ha'n't never been sick yet. If she was to play out on me now, it'd leave me flat in the world. My horse died in January, and so that throws all the work on my mule till I can make 'rangements to get her some help. That's how come me out here this soon after the wet weather; with just one mule to plow, I got to put in extra time to cover the ground. I told the nigger that works for me to go get him some work by the day anywhere he could find it, since I got only one plow to run at present. I never had no sharecroppers, but I let the nigger live in my house yonder and pay him by the day to help me farm.

"Farmin's pretty work. I love it. This time o' year when everybody starts breakin' up land, looks like to me I can smell plowed ground in the air, nights when I unhook my mule. Well, I ought to like it, for I've been a-farmin' the biggest part of sixty-two year, right in one spot you might say. 'Bout all the movin' I ever done was from one side o' the road to the other. We've been at this little cottage twenty year, and I 'spect to die here—I hope to.

"My father, George Hale, sharecropped all his life till we children growed up and help him save enough to buy some land. There was five girls and two boys, and we all worked hard; that's what I've known all my life, hard work. My brother died young, a year after he was married. We farmed, cut cordwood and pulpwood, and got together enough money to buy that place yonder on the hill. Every year we tried to add a little strip o' land, till Pa fin'lly had around 200 acres in his possession, slam to the road here. The land on this side the road belonged to a widow woman who mortgaged it up and let it get out from under her. Pa bought all this too.

"So far as schoolin', I never got much. Bein' the oldest boy, I had to take holt o' the plow handles soon as spring come. That give me 'bout two months a year to go to school. There was a one-teacher school up yonder in the woods where we went a little, and one year I walked to Wentworth School two months. Mr. Williams learnt me more them two months than all the rest o' the time put together. I give Tom what schoolin' he could take.

"Soon as I was free, I went to New River Mills and worked in the cotton mill about six months. It didn't suit me. I decided I was cut out to farm. I come on back home and got Pa to sell me a little piece o' land so I could start farmin' for myself, for I had fell in love with a girl at the mills and wanted to get married. The next year we was married, and we lived together in the house yonder for five year. We had four children, but all of 'em died except one little baby boy we named Tom. Then I lost my wife.

"Ma took care o' my baby till I got married again. My second wife was the daughter of the widow woman that had lost the land Pa had bought. When we was on our way home from the magistrate's, Janie said to me, 'I know I'm the happiest woman in the world today.' I asked her how come. ' 'Cause I'm goin' back to my old home,' she said. We went by Ma's to get little Tom to take him home with us. I noticed when I picked him up to tote him to the buggy, he begin cryin'.

" 'Me hurts,' he said.

" 'Where hurts, honey?'

" 'Me back hurts,' he said.

"That night he had a fit. I sent for Dr. Cain who come and said he reckoned the child had worms and to give him caloma.* It didn't seem to do him no good, though.

"When Janie was bathin' him one night, she called me to come look at his back. There was a knot big as my thumb at the end of his backbone. Later on I found out that one of my sisters in handlin' him had dropped him on the hea'th at Ma's and had been scared to say anything about it.

"The knot got bigger. Tom's leg drawed so he couldn't use it, and as he growed up he become a hunchback and couldn't get about except on crutches. He's never been able to do no work at all on the farm, though I run a little store at my house several years so he'd have somethin' to do. We busted on that. Tom got to trustin' out too much stuff to folks, and 'fore I realized it the books was filled with debts that couldn't be collected. So now there ain't nothin' for Tom to do but drive the car for us when we have to go to town and church. A few years ago when Preacher Hopkins was on the circuit, he took Tom to Dukes† in Durham to see if somethin' couldn't be done for him. They said at Dukes he had had spinalgitis or a bad fall when he was little how come he's hunchbacked and drawed so bad. He stayed there several weeks, and they did straighten his leg so as he can drive a car. Dukes is a wonderful place.

"My second wife was a smart woman. She pitched in and helped me pay off some money I owed and add this strip o' land to my little farm I bought from Pa. She was hard-workin', willin' to do anything that come to hand, in the house or in the field. Her health begin to fail several years ago; she took to havin' epileptic fits and fallin' out at her work. I had to quit the field awhile and watch her, for she wouldn't give up her work. One night I found her lyin' under the cow; she had been tryin' to milk when she had a fit, and if the cow had moved Janie might've been trampled to death. I had to keep a tighter eye on her after that. Five years ago she died.

"I reckon I shan't never get married no more. I ain't capable of a wife now. I'm sixty-two, and my health is failin'. A few years ago I

*Probably calomel, a purgative.
†Duke University.

had a stroke of the mouth and one arm. While I was lyin' on the counter of the store at twelve o'clock, restin' after a mornin's work in the field, I dropped off to sleep. When I woke up, I was in the curiousest fix I'd ever been in, couldn't speak and couldn't move. Fin'lly I got off the counter and found I could walk, but all I could say was, 'M-m-m-m-m-m.' My mouth was drawed way to one side, though you see it's back about straight now, and this arm was dead. I still can't grip nothin' hard with my hands, though I can hold to the plow handles pretty good. You see how my hands is; I can't even double up my fists. Since my stroke I ain't been able to cut a fire of wood; Tom's wife cuts all we use in the cook-room and in the fireplace too.

"Another thing that's kept me from marryin' a third time is finances. If I brought a wife here she'd look for more'n I'm able to give her. I couldn't take care of a woman now the way she'd expect. While I was thinkin' 'bout gettin' married two or three years ago, I heard in the neighborhood that Tom was 'bout to bring a wife here.

"'Look here, Tom,' I says to him, 'they tell me you're fixin' to get married.'

"'I am,' he admitted.

"'I was thinkin' 'bout the same thing, but two new wives here—'

"'You been married enough, Pa,' Tom told me.

"I concluded he was right. Just so we had a woman in the house, if didn't make so much difference whose wife she was. Down in my heart I knowed nary one of us wa'n't fit to get married. Anyway, Tom married my niece, a strong healthy girl that's been the greatest help to us to be sure. It didn't look right for first cousins to marry, and I wondered if I ought to tell her about Tom bein' so helpless and all. But since she had been knowin' him all her life I thought she ought to realize what it'd mean to tie up with him. She said, though, she loved Tom and wanted to wait on him. I can sure say she's done it; she even dresses him.

"When my wife died I was in good shape financially. I didn't owe a cent, and I had five bales o' cotton on hand. It took them five bales to pay the doctors' bills and her burial expenses, and I begin then to get behind. The next year I borrowed money to farm with, though I paid off my debt and had enough left to run us till March. Then I had to make another borrow to farm on, givin' a mortgage on my crop and team. That's been the ticket for the past four years, and I ain't been able to catch up. This year it'll be worse, 'cause I got to buy a plug of a horse to tend my farm, or else let a half it lie out.

"To tell you the truth I don't know what I'm goin' to do this year. They tell me the gov-mint is goin' to pay the farmers not to plant cotton; that looks like a good idea to me, much as is already on hand. The farm program mixes me up; I ain't never understood how it works. I got a check from the gov-mint last spring, but it was so little I done forgot what 'twas. If they'll pay me not to plant cotton, I'll just tend some peanuts, corn, soya beans, and food crops. I aim to plant 'bout half a acre of tobacco just for my own use, not for the market. So far as politics is concerned, I'm a Democrat, though it don't make so much difference 'bout who's in. There's good years and bad years, and you sure can't vote the boll weevil out. I've voted for Roosevelt twice, but I don't think I will no more; twice is enough. We need the right men at Jackson* worse'n at Washington.

"I still owe twenty-five dollars to Dukes for Tom's operation. Doctors' bills and operations and burial expenses hit a pore man hard, though I wouldn't begrudge nothin' if my folks could get well. Sometimes I hear folks say times now is a lot worse'n they use to be fifty year ago. Well, I ain't able to judge about that, for when I was a boy all I studied was eatin' and sleepin', and I got plenty o' both. But I reckon Pa lay awake nights studyin' plenty 'bout where the meat and bread was comin' from, the doctors' bills, even a roof over our nine heads. I reckon if he could come back he'd say we don't know nothin' 'bout hard times and doin' without.

"I'll tell you exactly my situation. I've got forty acres here, twenty-five of it open land, besides my pasture. There ain't no claim on it so far, and I'm tryin' to hold to it. This year I made 960 pounds o' seed cotton and 72 bags o' peanuts. My corn got drowned by all them heavy rains last summer, and what I use from now on I got to buy. Off'n six acres I got just one stack o' fodder. When I sold my cotton and peas and paid off my crop lien, I had seven dollars left. Since then I've been sellin' what chickens and eggs I could spare to live on.

"We have got a smokehouse o' meat to help out. One hog we killed before Christmas weighed 300 pounds. We had penned him close to the house and fed him scraps and slops till he was mud-

*The county seat.

fat. Besides this one, we killed two other pigs. We may have to buy some lard along in the summer, but we ought to have enough fry to last till the next hog-killin'—that is, if we have one. I ha'n't got but one hog this time, but I'm hopin' she'll find pigs by'n'by. We'll have a good garden if nothin' happens; last summer we raised more beans than anybody in the neighborhood. For a feller with high blood pressure, they say meat and bread's bad, but it does hold you together. After my wife fell under the cow that day, I sold the cow to keep Annie from doin' the milkin'; she would keep slippin' out and tryin' to do her work around the house. Since then there ain't been no money to buy another cow, though when I can get holt of a little change I buy Tom some milk and butter, he loves it so good.

"That's the way it is: I'm just a plain average two-horse farmer, with land o' my own, no money and no prospects to make none. I don't look forward to havin' nothin' in this life nohow; beyond makin' a livin', I don't crave nothin'. I rather not live from hand to mouth like I'm havin' to do, but I can say I ha'n't suffered for nothin' t'eat yet. If 'twa'n't for my high blood, I could go get a job at ninety cent a hour layin' brick for the new part of the court-house. I'm a first-class brickmason; my father before me was, and I picked up from him what I learnt about layin' brick. But whenever I've climb any lately, my head swims so bad I can't stand; even ridin' in a wagon bothers me, makes me dizzy. I have to stay close to the ground; so plowin' suits me the best, though I could make some money easier at Leesburg than tryin' to dig it out o' the ground. All the chimneys you see around in this neighborhood I run.

"My taxes this year is nine dollars, two more'n I made on my crop. I ain't paid 'em yet, but that's what they say is against me. Till this year I never asked for no help, but like things is I went over to Leesburg to talk with Miss Robinson at the welfare 'bout gettin' some help for Tom. I don't want nothin' for myself, for I can make my board somehow or other, and clothes last me right good; I been wearin' the same suit for two year, winter and summer. Miss Robinson wanted Tom's wife to try for a job in the sewin' room at Wentworth, but she ha'n't had no experience sewin'. Besides, it's five mile to Wentworth, by a rough dirt road part the way, and the sewin' room opens at eight. That'd mean risin' and cookin' breakfast and dinner before daylight and eatin' two cold meals a day—even if the girl could sew. If they'd let us have a little money by the month like they do some—but every time anything is said about direct help like that, they say: 'No, you own your own land.' Well, we can't eat the land, and we can't wear it.

"After I went a second time about some help for Tom, Miss Robinson told me T. G. Carroll would handle all such requests in this neighborhood. So I come back home and saw T. G. He said he couldn't pass on it, except in the case of minor children, and that Tom is too old. I told him, knowin' Tom's condition like he does, to fix some way to get a little help till another crop anyhow. He said I'd have to see Miss Robinson. That's the way they do, shift me from one to the other.

"Larry Martin, on T. G. Carroll's place, gets thirty dollars a month; he's got a boy at home big enough to work and one at the CCC* camp drawin' some money. Before the boy went to the CC's in January, he had a job in New River Mills. Now, I ain't kickin' on Martin havin' the thirty dollars; he's in the hospital and ought to have help—though it's his meanness that put him the hospital, Dr. Crocker says. After servin' a road sentence, Martin come home, but didn't quit his meanness; fin'lly it throwed him. That's the class gets help, looks like. The Martin family rents a house from T. G.; how come 'em to get that thirty-dollars. He meant to get his rent out of the gov-mint or somebody. They tell me he has patched up a lot o' old houses around to rent out to the gov-mint like that or to folks he helps get gov-mint money for. T. G.'s a good man, but he'll do them things. I see th'ough it all. They're settin' for my land; if I don't get no help they know I can't farm, not without givin' a holt on this place. They think they'll get my land, add it to theirs, and prosper on it. I aim to hold on long as I can.

"There's one thing I got to look forward to; when I leave this troublesome world, I'm goin' to a better place. All my life I've tried to live right, and I've got no fear of the next world. I'm goin' to a better place, though I ain't in no hurry about it. Pa raised us all to go to Sunday school and church, and I've kept it up. We used to belong to Peace Chapel, but we moved to Hickory Grove Methodist Church, me and Tom. His wife belongs to the Baptists at Bethel, and we go there mighty nigh as much as to our own church. This is a good neighborhood except for about two families; they drink and spree and beat folks out o' what they can. I got no patience in the world with drinkin'. Pa used to have prayer meetin's round at different houses in the neighborhood durin' the week, bein' as we was several miles from church. I was super'ntender at Peace Chapel

---

*The Civilian Conservation Corps, a New Deal program.

a long time, and I'm assistant at Hickory Grove now. After the revival at Bethel last summer, I told 'em all to le's start prayer meetin' every Sunday night. We been holdin' prayer service since then, though if 'twa'n't for me they'd drap it. I hang on.

"We all read the Bible at my house; we got us one apiece and a big fam'ly Bible with pictures in it. Not a day passes I don't read and pray; we don't have fam'ly prayer, but I kneel at my bed every night to pray in secret, and Tom and his wife does the same.

"I don't reckon there's a happier home in the country than we've got. It's a little house and it needs paintin' bad and we ha'n't got nothin' fine, but we ain't miser'ble 'bout it. There ain't never been a cross word spoke or a oath cussed in my house. Long as I had my health I never thought about askin' nobody for nothin', but now—if you got any pull with the gov-mint, see if James can't get a little help. Tell 'em I got no income in the world but what's in these two hands."

Bernice Kelly Harris

"I'm a landless man. . . . What chance have I got ever to own any land of my own? . . . I could make money at the mill, . . . I ought to be able to save enough in no time to buy a few acres. . . . How do I know how long the mill job will last? . . . I don't know the folks who own the mill. They don't know me. I don't like to work for folks I don't know. I don't like to live in a house either that belongs to a stranger. . . . What would you do, Phil?. . ." "What do you want to do, Tom?" asked my uncle Philip. "I want to improve my condition. . . . I want to educate my children. I want them to have things better than I have had them. . . . I'm ambitious and I'm strong. I'm going to do it. . . ." Finally one Sunday at Praters Baptist Church the preacher announced that Brother Tom Rampey and family desired to remove their letters of membership from Praters to Cateechee Mill Baptist Church.
—Ben Robertson,
Red Hills and Cotton, 1942

More than seven of every ten Southerners tried to earn their living from agriculture in 1870. Six of ten tried in 1910. And, by 1930, slightly more than four of ten tried. Economic desperation forced a great migration. In only one man's lifetime, masses of Southerners shook the dust from their shoes or bare feet and went to towns, mills, and scattered places. Towns offered better job opportunities and excitement. We might scoff at finding excitement in Petersburg, Greensboro, Durham, Spartanburg, Augusta, or Birmingham. We would also reveal our ignorance about the alternatives.

Jobs were the nub of the matter: jobs as laborers, clerks, domestics, jobs with little pay and even less security, but jobs. Calvin ("From the Mountains Faring") pieced together a living from odd jobs; his wife had worked in a laundry. Joe Johnson ("Green Fields Far Away") prospered as a contract miner in the Alabama coal fields in the 1920s. Then the Great Depression struck and the human flood slowed; the rate of urbanization declined in the 1930s for the first time in American history. Like many others, Joe tried farming. He failed, and he returned to the mines where his needs forced him to accept a low-paying, low-status position. His wife went to work for the government.

In the 1920s, the rig-builder moved from job to job, place to place, and injury to injury in the rowdy world of the oil boom in Texas and Oklahoma. Then, in the 1930s, hard times and technological change took their toll. The rig-builder joined the union which gained a strong beachhead in the labor wars of the oil industry during the depression ("The Rig-Builder").

A generation earlier, defeated farmers in the Southeast flocked to the booming textile industry of the region. They gave up their relative independence on the farm and acquiesced to the routine of "A Day on Factory Hill." In 1880, 16,741 people worked in mills; in 1900, 97,559 did; in 1930, 262,383 did. Dubbed "mill people" or "lintheads," they lived and worked in a segregated world. The few black workers were restricted by custom and law (in South Carolina) to the most menial tasks. Mills and mill villages were located in rural areas or on the edges of towns and cities. Mill workers worked as families ("Retired Mill Worker"). If their children didn't work, they usually attended mill schools rather than the regular public schools.

Declining fortunes crippled the Southern (and Northern) textile industry after World War I. Management attempted to cut costs by increasing labor productivity, primarily by speeding up the work (the stretch-out). Labor trouble followed ("When a Man Believes"). Unionization efforts began in earnest in 1929 and continued into the 1930s. A determined, overwhelmingly powerful management prevailed ("There's Always a Judas"), and Southern textile workers remained unorganized. Paternalistic mill owners may have softened the hardships brought on by the textile slump of the 1920s and the Great Depression, but the owners maintained the stretch-out and brooked no challenge to their personal authority.

Virtually eliminated from textiles, a major employer in the South, and generally forced to accept lesser positions, Southern blacks who left farms hovered on the margins of the economy, North and South. Some found a niche in the segregated economy by serving as preachers, physicians, dentists, undertakers, and small businessmen in the black community. A few found jobs reserved for blacks ("Chimney Sweeper's Holiday"), or, before the federal government adopted a rigid segregationist policy after 1900, as lower-level government employees ("I'se Still Traveling 'Cause I Got Faith in God"). Of course, even after the federal government policy change, black janitors continued in government service. More, especially black women, entered domestic service ("My WPA Man"). Throughout, blacks knew their place—they had to ("Tech 'Er Off, Charlie").

There just were not enough jobs for the surplus labor—unneeded and often unwanted human beings—from Southern agriculture. In 1940, Southerners were still more rural than most Americans and twice as likely to work on farms as were non-Southerners.

Thus, whatever their work, Southerners earned less than other Americans, and this had been so for many years. In 1880, they earned $151 per capita, one-half of what other Americans earned. Southern per-capita income rose to $198 in 1900, to $326 in 1920; at the same time, the national average increased to $414, then to $578. In the 1920s Southern incomes declined to $321, while the nation's rose to $640. For most Southerners, the Great Depression began in 1921.

From the Mountains Faring

Calvin and me come from the mountains . . .
[to] make a living in some way or another.

"Calvin and me come from the mountains, for Calvin knowed he could make a living in some way or another about town doing odd jobs. So we left the farm. We fared on down to Knoxville. Our times has not been easy here. But then times has always been hard with us. We was both born poor. Lived poor all our lives. All in all, though, it's a lots easier making out here than it was back there on the farm. We ain't never had to ask a penny off of no one. Never asked the government to put us on relief, neither."

Lola Simmons rocked slowly as she talked. Large bony hands rested on the arms of her chair. Her drab gray calico dress was tucked close under her to clear the floor.

"Calvin's handy with tools," she said, "and always has been. He can fix a chair or whatever kind of furniture you've got that looks past doing, and it will be stout as new. He can build things, just anything, from the ground up. He's good on porches and stairs steps. Most anything about a house that needs righting, Calvin can git it in shape. He does a heap of patching screens and painting roofs. He's not a regular plumber and electrician but he does some of that work, too."

She pushed a dangling hairpin back to place. Her straight black hair, streaked with gray, was tightly braided in one plait and balled on the back of her head. Her thin face was lined and worn but there was no hardness in her expression.

"This place here we live in, it's not any great shakes of a place. But we're going to stay on as long as we can. Every time we've moved from here to somewheres on the edge of town, Calvin's lost work. Here he's in close-catch of town folks that wants a job done right off. The biggest trouble about living in a basement like this is they's not any room for spreading. Well, three rooms is enough for me and Calvin and Cap, even if they're not big rooms. This here sitting room is space enough to hold the parlor furniture and Cap's bed. Cap's just only fifteen but he's near outgrowed that bed back yonder. He has to lay catercorners of it now. Ought to be some way Calvin could stretch it out, seems to me. I don't see no way we could put a double bed in that space even if we had cash to buy it—which we ain't.

"Me and Calvin takes the back room. They's no grate in it, but some heat comes from the kitchen. That kitchen has a sink with running water, and that's the closest we ever come to having a bathroom. Well-a-day, not having such means less to us than most. Coming from the mountains, we is use to a wash pan and a tub for cleaning up. We has a halfway sort of a little water privy in the kitchen closet, but it don't flush right. I can tell you, though, it beats trotting out in the back yard in the weather.

"The last of the three rooms we has is damp and cold without you keep a fire going all the time. And we can't do that. The basement's about all that's brick about the whole house. That's the reason our rooms stays that way. The house up above us is in awful shape. The roof leaks. It lets the water come right down the side of the walls. When a hard rain comes they's water all over the kitchen floor. I just reach the broom out. I keep sweeping it to the back door. The walls stay so wet half the time that wallpaper just pops off everywhere."

Lola shifted her position. She pointed toward the ragged corner of the ceiling. "And look at that plastering back there in the corner. Dropped smack off last week. Ah, Lord.

"I guess we can't expect just a whole lot for the rent we pay. The landlord never misses coming a Monday for our two-fifty. But fixing things up is another tale and it's never told. He won't do a blessed thing about this wetness and it matters not how much we howl. Tells us now that the government is planning to tear down every house in the block and put up some sort that ain't tenements. Well, 'twon't be no trouble to tear down. Just give a push, and not such a hard one neither, and the last one of these houses will come down and never a wrecking tool needed to help out. And the neighborhood is worse and far worse than the houses. Oh, I know it's no place to bring a youngin up at all. I thank the Lord that me and Calvin has got but only the one, and that's Cap. We can manage him all right with both of us studying on it. Most of the families in this block has from six all the way to ten youngins, and all sizes. Seems like about half of the mothers is sick. They just let the youngins run around as filthy as cow-dab. I tell you, most of these youngins learn to cuss and swear and take the Lord's name in vain when they's buggers of five years old and less. They start fighting amongst one another. Before long the mas and pas take sides. It ends in a cutting scrape or one or the other taking their leave of the street. Me and Calvin stays clear of it all.

"We don't want no more trouble with neighbors. That's the main reason we moved from the mountains. Trouble with neighbors. Trouble betwixt Calvin and the Osmans over what they'd done to Calvin's coon dog. Drum was a night-running dog and I will freely admit it, but he wasn't a chicken-killer. Calvin had trained him about chickens to where he'd leave them alone. Why, I've seen that Drum flatten out on his belly and whine like he was scared to death if a chicken so much as passed him near. Calvin had trained him so he was really feared of a chicken. But it was something using* around the Osman's place of nights and taking their hens. So they says 'twas Calvin's Drum. They'd shot him but they dassn't, for they just knowed what a hasty-passioned man my Calvin can be when it comes to his coon dog. So they tried one of their sneaky tricks. They caught Drum off in the woods and they docked his tail right slam up against his rump and they cropped his ears down to his head.

"Calvin flat-out accused them Osmans of doing the job. They swore they didn't, but you could see the daylight through what they said. So it was a hardness sprung up and before long Calvin hopped all over an Osman and beat the corn out of him. Then the whole tribe ganged on him and came close to beating him to death. Looked like it was going to have to be a killing on one side or other. We didn't have enough kin to fight that Osman bunch. Calvin and me both knowed wasn't room for him and the Osmans on the same mountain. So me and him pulled out and come faring down from the mountains to Knoxville, and ain't never going back again."

Lola's light eyes were far-shot and she nodded her head slightly.

*Frequenting.

"I miss them mountains sometimes. Yes, I miss that steep old land.

"Me and Calvin growed up in the same neighborhood. The schools wasn't much we went to. Still they learned us to read and they learned us to write and how to say words as we should in talking. Calvin and me took a heartburning for each other when we was in that school. Then Mammy died and I come down to Knoxville and I got me a job in a steam laundry here. No place there or home for me, for Pappy brought in a new wife and started in on a new bunch of youngins. I made four dollars a week. Worked ten hours a day in the damp wash end. It wouldn't be a dry rag on me at the end of them ten hours. Most of us that worked there was girls come in from the country and down from the mountains. We managed by rooming together and doing all our own cooking and washing. Now, you hear folks talk a heap about the way country girls goes on with men when they come to the city. Ah, Lord! We was so wore out by time work hours was over that we was good and glad to fall into bed and sleep. At the laundry I worked up to the finishing room and I made five dollars and fifty cents. But the hours was longer and I was so tired all the time I'd just as soon been dead and done with it.

"Well and all, it was right after the war that Calvin come down from the mountains. He talked me into going back and keeping house for him. It didn't take a powerful lot of talk. I was sick and tired of working like a slave. But I guess I'd sort of lost track of things I'd once knowed about living on a farm. That's a hard life. Anyhow, I went. I never had it in my mind that it was a thing wrong about me going. But the neighbors talked about us living together. Five years after I went to keeping house for Calvin, Cap come. I don't see no difference in the way me and Calvin feels about Cap because we never did have the time nor money to git a preacher or justice of peace to say a few words over us. It costs a lot of money to git married. More than five dollars some places. We never seen five dollars ahead till we come down here to Knoxville. Then it seemed like a plumb fool waste of money. They tell me that some good lawyer says a common-law marriage is just as good as a church or court one any day. So I ain't noways ashamed that me and Calvin has never got around to the regular kind. He's past fifty and I'm near to it and ain't neither of us ever trotted around loose like half the ones that blows about wedlock and such. We is poor but we's decent.

"Being poor ain't easy nowheres, but it's a sight better in the city than on a farm. City folks just don't know nothing at all about what country folks puts up with. Me and Calvin rented the farm we had in the mountains. It looked like it took the biggest part of what come from it to just meet the rent. Every cent from the tobacco crop went for rent.

"We never did git ahead to the point of having stock of our own. Had to borrow from the neighbors. That meant they'd git theirs plowed when the weather was right. Even if the ground was as hard as a brick, Calvin had to do plowing when he could borrow some mules or some horses. I didn't git nowhere trying to make extry with a garden. Pigs and chickens seemed like two things it just wasn't no way for us to keep from dying. The sort of cows we could pay for wasn't worth the feeding. We's had more butter and milk and meat and eggs here in town than we ever see on that farm. Farm living is plain slaving from one month to the next, from morning to night. And they's nothing left to show for all the hard work you do. Winter comes and you got to start toting wood for the fires. Have to tote it yourself when they's no sign of horse or mule to help you. Then every bit of the water you've a use for must be drawed from a well or fotch to the house from a spring. Here all you have to do is twist at the hydrant and out pours the water. Neither one of us ever wants to go back to farming.

"Calvin gits plenty of work here in Knoxville. He works cheap and that's the reason, I guess. He's not what you'd call a skilled worker. But he can do as good work as the best of them, I don't care what name you call them by.

"They's more folks here in Knoxville that wants cheap repairing than any other kind. The rich folks is the same way. Calvin knows where he can git supplies cheap. He can take a contract lower than most and still come out on top. If he could just go straight from one job to the next, why, I bet he'd make close to twenty dollars a week. Like things is now, he makes about ten. He loses money looking for jobs and figgering on gitting things in shape to git the contract. Old customers has always stuck with him. But things ain't going to keep dropping to pieces about the same folks' house if they's fixed right. And Calvin always fixes them right. Sort of cuts his own throat, but he does it.

"I do all the washing and ironing and cleaning and cooking. And I can stretch that ten dollars out for the three of us. Rent and coal and kindling and food eats up about seven of it. That leaves three for other things and the clothes we wear. It don't take no more than fifty cents a day to feed the three of us. We's country folks. Glad to git cornbread and beans and potatoes and greens. I've heard some doctors say you could live on cornbread and vegetables without meat. I doubt it. Not and be hardy. I try to git meat for us at least twice a week. Fix an egg apiece for us at breakfast. I pay a nickel a day for a pint of milk for Cap. I know he ought to have it, a growing boy like he is. We never have had to spend a red cent on doctors' bills for no one of us. Not even when Cap come. It didn't cost me nothing because the midwife was a friend of mine. She wouldn't hear of me paying her for helping me through."

Lola got up from her chair to straighten the worn strip of carpet her rocker had wrinkled. She shoved back the old parlor furniture, upholstered in red plush and placed at regular intervals in front of the fireplace, smoothed the rug, and sank back in the rocker.

"Me and Calvin wasn't only thinking about easy going for our own selves when we come to Knoxville. We knowed Cap would have a better chance at schooling here. And do you know what? That boy ain't turned sixteen yet and here he wants to quit school and go to work. Some ways I don't blame him. As hard as we work it looks like it just never is anything left over for us to throw to him to spend for fun. And they ain't a soul lives around here I care for him to run with. Well, both me and Calvin carries burial insurance. It'll git us out of his way without cost if anything happens to us. I don't see no sense in paying out for that on Cap yet. He's not going to die no time soon. If he's going to start out for hisself, I want him to have some sort of a good job. He can have every penny he makes for hisself, too. I don't believe in milking your children.

"I told him it's got to be some good straight job. Some boys git it in their heads that they can make a sight of money selling liquor. The law cracks down on them almost as soon as they git a start. We see it happen every day around here. You've got to keep the law paid off a good and plenty or else the penitentiary is where they's going to land. Now if they does pay off, where is the profit left from selling? Ain't none. So there they is. I told Cap if he had it in his head to do that, he better be clearing his head of it right now.

"I don't blame him one bit for having his mind set on making a little money to have fun on. Seems like me and Calvin ain't never done a thing ever but work hard all our lives. Some folks find pleasure in going to meeting on Sunday. But it's no church I've had sight of here in Knoxville where the ones coming in and out ain't dressed up fit to kill. Some says it's all the same in the eyes of the Lord about how you dress. But I knows if He's got sense at all, He knows our clothes is too wore out for Sunday strutting. I know they's shabby in my own sight.

"Calvin and me both can read right well. In times back we use to read the Bible pretty much. But seems like you always come across something you can't make out straight. So we just stopped reading it. Looked a pure shame, as wore out as we was, to read things that upset your head.

"I guess I got on to the main of it, though. I know that Jesus Christ died to save sinners. And all that me and Calvin have to do is trust in Him. And we do. And we believe in Him. I don't see where they's any way to keep me and Calvin out of Heaven. Calvin moved away from the mountains to keep a killing from happening. That clears what's said about not killing. We ain't never stole and have always told the truth. We never brought false witness against nobody. They's more to it, but I counted them off one day and we is all right. Calvin and me ain't never harmed a living soul in our lives. So I ain't bothering about Hell if I never gits inside the door of a Knoxville church. When me and Calvin gits there I'd be more than glad to do what I could to help others git in.

"They's some folks, not a thousand miles away from here, that are going to need a heap of helping. Ah, Lordy, yes!"

Dean Newman
Jennette Edwards
James Aswell

Green Fields Far Away

BIRMINGHAM, ALABAMA, 1939

*We're gettin' along all right now. . . . Those
"green fields far away" was green all right, but
the green happened to be the grass that had to be hoed out.*

" 'I forbid you ever to see him again, and if he keeps on seeing you after what I've just said—well, I guess there's nothing left but to shoot him, and damned if I won't do it.'

"And I was afraid he meant to do just what he had threatened," said Dera Davis.

"My father didn't know Johnson very well, or he would never have said those things about him. You see, he was judging all coal miners by the ones that came up for trial in his court at North Birmingham. He had been justice of the peace there for twenty years, was a member of the Chamber of Commerce in Birmingham, and was influential in politics. He had given all his children a college education and had instilled in us all the highest ideals, yet he looked down on the laboring class.

"In our home, his word was law, but he didn't have the understanding my mother had. Somehow she always seemed to know just how I felt about everything almost soon as I did. It hurt me to disobey my father and keep on seeing Johnson, but what else could I do? I was in love with him.

"I loved Joe Johnson the very first time I saw him . It was funny how we met. I was teaching school in the country and had come home for the weekend. We had the only phone in that part of town and all the neighbors used it. While I was at home, a young man came to use it. All the family had seen him in the neighborhood, but nobody seemed to know his name. I watched him the whole time he was phoning, and he wasn't backward about using it, like so many were.

"He picked up that phone and talked with such assurance! 'My,' I thought, 'this man is worth knowing.' He was a big, strong-looking man with broad shoulders, and his face was kind. I guess his friendliness is what really struck me first. He had on a good-looking blue serge suit, with blue tie and blue socks to match, and neat black shoes. You see, I didn't miss a thing. I noticed that he looked at me, too, every time he caught me looking away.

"I didn't meet him that day, but I soon did. I knew then and there that I'd met the man I would marry if I could get him. He must have felt the same way about me, for in less than three months he had told me all about his wife dying and leaving him with three children, one three, one eleven, and one fourteen—and about his trouble in trying to keep a housekeeper that would be good to them. Soon he started talking about how lonesome he was, and everybody knows that when a widower starts talking about that, a woman's battle is half won.

"Sure enough, after we had been going together for eight months, we slipped away and were married. My mother and sisters knew all our plans, and strangely enough when my father found out that we were actually married, he changed completely and invited us to come to see them whenever we could. Later, he learned to admire Johnson, too.

"I took a great deal for granted when I thought that I could go into that home and easily make well-mannered, right-thinking, useful American citizens right away out of those children that I had only seen a few times. I guess that's a good illustration of the old saying, 'Ignorance is bliss.' But I really did it and without much trouble. They'd had a good start. They certainly had a fine father anyway.

"A few days after we were married, Johnson said, 'Dera, Rachel needs a new pair of shoes. She's fourteen now, so supposin' you tell her to go down and get a pair and charge them to me. She'll like 'em better if you do the tellin'.'

"Well, I did that very thing and Rachel couldn't get to the store fast enough. That night, as soon as her daddy came home, she showed them to him and he asked her where she got them. Grinning from ear to ear, she pointed to me and said, 'She told me to.'

"I knew I had won my first victory. My husband had helped me, of course.

"The very next morning while I was cooking breakfast, the baby came to the kitchen and stood, half-ashamed for a minute, then he said, 'If you let me be your grocery boy, I'll let you be my mama.' From then on, he was my grocery boy, and we were devoted.

"I had lots of ups and downs with those children, but they're all grown and married now. Two of them are doing well in Georgia, and Buck, the youngest one, is working in Sayreton mines and lives just five blocks from us. Any trouble the children ever gave me faded away a few years ago when Rachel put her arms around me and said she wanted to die before I did. 'What in the world are you thinking about, Rachel?' I asked. 'Oh,' she said, 'I want to get to Heaven first so I can be there to get my mother's hand and put it in yours and tell her how good you always were to her children.'

"By that time we were both crying. That will always be one of my mountaintop experiences.

"After I had been married three years, my first baby was born. In the three years that followed, I had three more babies, but they were all premature and lived only a few months. Then for two years I didn't have a baby. A little later, I discovered that another one was on the way. When I told Johnson about it, he was disappointed. He's sixteen years older than I am, and he was afraid he wouldn't live to see it raised. The whole time, he made me very unhappy about it. I didn't show him any of the little clothes as I had always done with the others, because it seemed to worry and fret him just to mention it.

"Finally, when my little girl came, I let them put her over by herself and I didn't pay any attention to her. After a while, Johnson came to me and said, 'Dera, do you know you haven't even asked to see the baby?'

" 'I haven't felt like it,' I said, still not looking toward the baby. All the time, my arms were fairly aching to hold her.

"Johnson went over to her crib and picked her up gently and placed her close to me. 'Just to think,' he said, 'this little baby gal didn't have a thing to say about being born, and she's not wanted by her daddy or her mammy, either.' He put his arms around us both then and nearly smothered us with kisses.

" 'Well,' he said, 'from this minute on, she's wanted by her old daddy. Dera, I've got a lot to make up for.' Johnson never knew why I cried then.

"We named that little girl Rebecca, and called her Becky. She's always been happy and carefree, and she grew up fast. She's sixteen now, and she's been married a year. I hated to see her marry so young, but she married a fine young man, a graduate of Auburn Polytechnic Institute. He's twenty-five and is an engineer working for a good company. Their success almost convinces me that early marriages aren't so bad after all.

"Buddy, that's my boy, is twenty-one now. Five years ago he stopped high school and went to work in a machine shop. He simply refused to go to school another day. Well, I kept right on hoping that some day he'd realize his responsibilities and go back to high school. He was a good worker and everybody at the shop liked him.

"Suddenly he began talking about saving his money to go back to school. I didn't discuss it because I wanted him to make his own decision. Then he made his own arrangements about books, clothes, and spending money and went back to high school, where he graduated with good grades. He got a scholarship to a two-year course in a Georgia college by playing football, and last March he graduated with honors.

"He thinks now that he can't afford to work in the shop that hired him before he went back to school. He can't get the jobs he wants; and he won't take the job he can get; so I'm not so sure that extra schooling helped him as much as it hurt him.

"I was giving Buddy money for haircuts, picture shows and clothes when Johnson began to warn me that I was going to ruin a perfectly good boy. One day he said, 'Dera, you'll have to break that boy's "plate" before he'll be worth a damn.'

"Well I stopped giving him money and in less than two weeks he had a temporary job and was about to get a permanent one.

"Johnson has no patience on earth with people who won't work. It is probably because he started to work so young. His father had eight sons, and he was a Methodist preacher on Sunday and a blacksmith on weekdays. They lived in Tennessee where seven of those boys went to work in the mines and the other worked as a blacksmith. Not long ago, there was a picture of Johnson's blacksmith brother in a Tennessee newspaper saying that he was the oldest blacksmith in Tennessee. Johnson, the youngest one of the brothers, started at the mine picking slate when he was only twelve years old, and he's been coal mining ever since.

"He went to school only nine months before he started to work. Twenty years later at Brookwood, Alabama, several of the miners went in together and hired a teacher to come to teach them and get them ready to stand mine foreman's examination. Johnson passed that examination, and his grades were second to the best.

"Since we've been married, I've helped him a great deal, because he is so anxious to learn. Of course, his English is still bad, but I have drilled him so often with sentences leaving blanks to be filled with 'see' or 'saw,' 'took' or 'taken' that he never makes those mistakes any more. He still says 'foire board' for 'mantel' and 'chist' for 'chest,' but I love him so that I don't want him to change altogether, or he wouldn't be the same man I fell in love with.

"I can't for the life of me see where people get the idea that coal miners are rough and brutal. Why, Johnson is the most tender-hearted man in the world, and that's one characteristic of coal miners in general, especially where widows and orphans are concerned. Johnson has been a steward in the church here in North Birmingham for years and years, and I've been a teacher of the matrons' class for about as long. Johnson is a good man, but he never believes in letting his right hand know what his left hand does.

"I remember one time, there was a widow with three little children at Sayreton mines, and they didn't have a bite to eat and nowhere to get it. Well, Johnson heard about it, and he went to the commissary and bought two big baskets full of staple groceries. He took them to her back door, and slipped them in without a soul seeing him. He always was in his glory when doing just such things.

"It made no difference who had a streak of bad luck in his family or mine. He would always send for them and say, 'Come on and stay with us until you can get straightened out, and think nothin' of it.'

"I remember one time we kept my cousin and her three children for a whole year. Now lots of people have the heart to do for others, but not the money, and then lots of people have the money but not the heart. Occasionally, you'll find the man with the heart to do and the money to do it with, and Johnson was one of those few.

"You'll hardly believe it when I tell you how much money he has made. The first month after we were married, he brought his envelope to me, and all deductions had been made—such as groceries from the commissary, doctor's fee, and cuts of other kinds. He still had $204 left. Johnson brought me the envelope and threw it in my lap. 'There it is, gal,' he said. 'Take it and do what you can with it. If it takes it all, that's O. K. by me. That's all I'm working for, a living for you and the kids.'

"He made as much as $900 a month, and he averaged $600 a month for many years.

"I used to take Johnson to work and go after him every day. On paydays, I'd park the car where I could see everything and wait for him. All around, collectors would be scanning each group to see if they could find their man and collect some of those easy payments. Three or four big slick Negro women would be busy selling barbecue. I can shut my eyes right now and almost smell that barbecue and have always wondered if it could possibly taste as good as it smelled. Then there was the company deputy with a big gun on each hip, and eyes that could spot trouble a block away.

"On one end of the commissary porch was a preacher and singer, for they could always be sure of a crowd on payday. Some of the miners would be grouped here and there telling jokes and eating and drinking. There were always two lines of miners going up to [the] pay window, one for the whites and one for the colored—no pushing, everybody waiting his turn. Somehow or other, they have always reminded me of faithful mules going home after a hard day's work. They have earned their pay, and they've come to get it.

"Negro girls wearing their Sunday best, would be switching this way and that way, trying to attract the Negro boys. Well, on the payday just before the last Easter, one of the Negro girls attracted just one too many boys. It was the Saturday before Easter and spring was in the air. A boy took his girl into the commissary and bought her a pair of Easter slippers. Later on, that same afternoon, another boy did the same thing. To each one, she gave her word that she would wear his slippers to preaching on Easter Sunday morning.

"She had a terrible time deciding which pair to wear first, but finally she decided to wear one pair to preaching in the morning and the other pair to preaching in the afternoon. You see, in mining camps on special days, the Negroes have preaching just about all day. One preaches till he gives out, and then another takes his place.

"Well, the girl had just come home from preaching and was eating dinner, when one of her beaux came to the door and asked her if she wore his slippers to church that morning. She confessed to the awful fact that she had worn the other boy's in the morning, but added that she was just fixing to put on his slippers to wear that afternoon. All the time they talked, he had a gun in his hand.

"'Well, gal,' he said, 'put yo' foot out dere and let me be shore. I heard all about whut you went and done, but I wanted to see with my own eyes. You see you tol' me you wuz gwineter wear mine, but you lied to me. Well, you won't never lie ag'in, 'cause I's gwineter kill you right now,' and with that, he shot her straight through the heart. The sheriff's still looking for him.

"Each payday, we always set aside a certain amount for saving. Seven years after we were married, we had bought and paid for a nice home, paid for a good car and had lots of insurance, didn't owe a cent and had $3,000 in the bank. Then we built more houses. I remember one year when Johnson figured his income tax, he reported that he had collected $2,300 in rents.

"The last house we built for ourselves cost $6,500 as the Negroes would say, 'scusin' de lot.' It had a hot-air furnace that dried out my throat so bad that Johnson had it replaced with gas heat. In winter, our gas bills ran from $18 to $20 a month.

"At the time Johnson built the home, we had five houses in the clear. Then Johnson mortgaged them all and built four more. That was in 1930, and just about the time the company did away with the contract system and threw Johnson out of a job. The company offered him a job as shift leader at $6 a day, three days a week. We only had $1,500 in cash, and we had set such a high standard of living that we knew we couldn't possibly live on the job they offered, and we knew that our savings would be gone in no time. Johnson refused the job, and because some of them were leaving their jobs our renters started slowing up with their rent. We had payments we couldn't possibly meet. We finally sold our own lovely home for $2,500 and tried to save the others; but we couldn't. We ended with one house clear and a debt on another one.

"Worried and wondering what in the world to do, we finally decided to buy a farm while we still had enough money for the first payment. None of us knew a thing about farming, and we set out to learn.

"We went all the way from the Georgia line to the Mississippi line, trying to find exactly the right place. Finally, one day we went to a forty-acre farm at Corner, thirty miles from Birmingham. I didn't pay much attention to this one, for by this time I thought I knew what kind of a farm Johnson was looking for, but I was shocked when Johnson said, 'Well, Dera, I think we'll take this one. I can fix up the house and I'll wire it.' I thought at first I was imagining things. The place was no man's land. The nearest neighbor was a mile off, the water in the well was muddy, and the front porch was as unsteady as a chair. I could see Johnson was worn out looking, and that his mind was made up, so I swallowed twice, and told him that I had always looked to him for a living, and that he had never failed me, so I would keep on.

"Well, we moved in. Johnson screened the house, wired it, fixed the roof, built a new front porch and painted it. We had a nice house when he finished it. We had pretty good furniture for the country. All of us had plenty of good clothes, raincoats, galoshes, shoes, and we had an ample supply of linens and bedclothes.

"We all worked morning, noon, and night, simply for something to eat; after two years of this farm drudgery our clothes had become worn and shabby, and we had no money to buy more, because we had paid $1,000 down on the farm and much more for the improvements. Johnson seemed to think that if we worked hard enough and long enough after a while we would get straight, so he not only cleared land, but he dug up the stumps. None of us ever worked as hard before or since as we did then.

"When feeding time came, we almost needed a traffic cop. One was going this way to feed the cows, another going that way to feed the mule, another to feed the chickens, pigs and rabbits.

"There wasn't a single minute to sit and rest, from early till late, except after supper, and then my conscience hurt because it didn't seem quite right to sit. When I think about that place I know why people like the little rhyme:

> I wish I was a little rock
> A-settin' on a hill
> Without a single thing to do,
> But just a-settin' still.

"My, those were heavenly times when I could finally relax at night, sitting in front of the fire and listening to Johnson play the guitar and sing. Johnson had been playing that same guitar and singing the very same songs for years and years, but I never paid any particular attention to them. Those old songs, 'Spanish Fandango' and 'Love, Oh, Careless Love,' somehow seemed beautiful while I was rocking and eating roasted peanuts. I was tired and the warm fire made me feel at peace with the world. I'm sure when the angels sing the Hallelujah Chorus, I won't enjoy it any more than I did Johnson's singing on those long winter nights on the farm.

"Early one morning, I was standing on the front porch, when I looked up the road and saw our nearest neighbor, old Josiah, coming. He was riding a big gray mule. Josiah had one foot tied around and around with yards and yards of string. His head was tied up and around with an old flannel scarf, and his lip was full of snuff. He had an old dominecker* rooster under one arm. I asked him what he meant to do with the rooster.

" 'Wal,' he said, drawing the mule to full stop and leaning way over to spit between two fingers, 'I'm takin' hit to the store to swap hit fur some o' that store-bought snuff. I'm plumb wore out a-dippin' this here homemade stuff. Yes, I knowed I wouldn't get much fur it, but I shore want one more good dip afore I die.' And with that, he went on up the road, his long legs dangling, and part of the string hanging down.

"Swapping gets in a person's blood after staying in the country awhile. One day I told Buddy to take some eggs to the store and swap them for some salt, coffee, and sugar. That nearly killed him; he was ashamed to let the storekeeper know we didn't have the money to buy what we needed. I explained how thankful he ought to be that we had something to swap. Even after all I said, he went away resentful, talking to the mule and hoping he'd fall and make him break every one of the eggs. Just to show how he changed— six months later, he'd swap eggs for anything, even a ticket to a picture show.

"There are things about those three years on the farm that I'll never forget, one in particular. Late one afternoon, old Mr. Reeves, our nearest neighbor, came to tell me that his wife had died that day. When I got over to his house, the neighbors had already laid her out. The coffin was a plain pine box, covered with black cloth and lined with white sheeting. It was trimmed all around with paper lace—the kind that's used for kitchen shelves. Six brass dresser handles, three on each side, completed the job.

"There old Mrs. Reeves was, all dressed in black, with her hands folded across her bosom. She had nickels on her eyes to keep them shut, and a rag tied under her chin to keep her mouth closed. A camphor cloth was across her nose and mouth so she wouldn't turn black. It was a very cold night, but the windows had to be kept open, and every once in a while, a neighbor would get up and saturate the camphor rag again. Toward midnight, I went to the kitchen with one of the neighbors to cook a midnight meal. Everybody except the cooks enjoyed it thoroughly.

"The next afternoon at two o'clock, the funeral started. It was a cold, drizzly afternoon in late October. All the cars, buggies and wagons stopped as close to the church as possible, but even then

*Dominique or Dominick, an American breed of domestic chicken.

nobody missed the red mud that was all around. As we went into the church, the men went to the left and the women to the right. The fire had just been started, so the room was still chilly. The dust from the last sweeping was on the rough, splintery pine benches.

"There was no use on earth for that family to try to be brave and not break down, for the preacher took his text and proceeded to preach a sermon about getting ready to go to meet their loved one. Things were entirely too peaceable to suit him, so he started reciting story after story from Mrs. Reeves's life, until he had every man, woman, and child in that church crying, some wailing at the top of their voices. Success at last had crowned his efforts! Then he moved a little toward the front and with a benign smile said, 'Everybody can pass around and view the remains of all that's left of the earthly body of dear old Sister Reeves!' Between wails and sobs, they managed to get around while they sang, 'Oh, Bear Me Away on Your Snowy Wings, to My Eternal Home.'

"It was almost dark when I finally got home from that funeral, and I noticed that there was only one dim little light in my house. When I got inside, I found that the electricity had been cut off because the bill hadn't been paid. I'll never forget that night. I played the victrola while Johnson held the kerosene lamp for me to change the records.

"Things had gone from bad to worse. That same fall, after we had been on the farm three years, we couldn't afford schoolbooks for the children. That year, we made 80 bales of hay, 150 bushels of corn, 100 gallons of syrup, 60 bushels of sweet potatoes, besides peanuts and popcorn. Oh, yes, we did make two bales of cotton, but the government paid us to turn under one of them.

"Well, the end of our farming came when Johnson at last realized where we were headed. It was Sunday morning in October, and I was out in the garden cutting tender collard sprouts for dinner and Johnson came out to help me. There was no preaching that day, as we only had preaching once a month. When he stood in the garden without saying a word for a few seconds, I could tell Johnson had something on his mind. 'Well, Dera,' he began, 'what kinda shape's our clothes in? If they're not ready, press 'em up and get ready, for you and me's goin' to town by sunup in the mornin' to look for a job. When it came to the pass that every one of us works as hard as we can from sunup to sundown, and sometimes later, and then we can't buy schoolbooks for the kids, I think it's time to call a halt. I haven't got a thing ag'in' my kids, but you'd think I did by keepin' 'em out here workin' 'em to death. I've always been used to puttin' my hand in my pocket and findin' a dollar. We will just let this place go. We owe more on it right now than we could get for it, even if we could find somebody that wanted it, and I doubt if such a person could be found. We've sold everything but the hay, and we'll save that and give it to somebody to move us back to town.'

"Now, all that was music to my ears, for I had been wanting him to say it for months, although I was determined to let Johnson call 'enough' first. I never enjoyed anything more than the job of pressing our clothes. At least we could both say that farming was out of our system once and for all.

"Well, the next morning we got out our old Ford and started bright and early to the place that had grown dearer to all of us every day. Johnson drove straight to Sayreton Mine and they seemed as glad to see us as we were to see them.

"Johnson went to work the very next morning and I went back to the farm to move. They gave Johnson the rock foreman's job at $3.80 a day. We moved into the house that wasn't quite paid for. We had to use kerosene lamps until Johnson could get a payday, and the children wanted me to leave the house dark so their friends wouldn't know. I didn't do it though, because I wasn't ashamed of something that couldn't be helped.

"Without telling me a thing about it, Johnson changed his work from a foreman's job at $3.80 a day, to a coal loader's job at $6 a day. He was a martyr for the food that went on our table and every time [I] started to eat I'd nearly choke. By this time, his health was failing fast. The company had passed him for company work, not loading coal, and as soon as the doctor found out what work he was doing, he stopped him from all work. He had high blood pressure and arthritis and was forced to rest and diet.

"I slipped off to Birmingham and applied for a place teaching in an F.E.R.A.* adult education class. They put me right to work and I organized my class at the Sayreton mine school. I had only men in the class, for it was a kind of specialty work. They wanted to get ready to stand the mine foreman's examination, and they all worked hard, for they had a reason. I taught English, spelling, and mathematics, and there was an average attendance of twenty.

"At first I had to handle them carefully, for miners are very sensitive, but in no time at all, they'd speak up in class and answer

*Federal Emergency Relief Administration.

questions. They even got to the point where they would speak up before the visiting teacher. On Friday nights we always had a short spelling match.

"That class was a lifesaver to my family. I taught it for a year, and his rest had improved Johnson so much that he went back to work, and they let him work every day at $6 a day as rock foreman. That's the job he has now.

"I'm so glad to be back at Sayreton, but there's one thing that I really enjoyed on the farm, and that was the thought that Johnson was safe—that he wouldn't be brought home burned or crushed or crippled for life. Saturdays and Sundays now are really the only days I can enjoy to the fullest. While he has only had one injury in all his experience, and that was a minor rockfall injury, every woman worries about her menfolks in the mine.

"Buck, that's my stepson, got his arm caught behind a rock the other day, but he didn't report it because an accident goes against a miner's record. The company takes the attitude that if a man is careful and obeys the safety instructions, he won't have an accident. All mines have classes in safety, and the men are required to attend them.

"Not long ago, I had a terrible fright. I heard an awful noise, just like an explosion, and the mine whistle blew loud and long. I got in my car and went to the mine as fast as I could, and found that the big engine in the boiler room where the electricity is generated had blown up. It threw the engineer out of the window and only scratched him up a little. The ventilation stopped in the mine as soon as the electricity was off, so all the men had to come out as soon as they could get out. I waited right there until I saw Johnson come out safe and sound.

"I guess I wouldn't have been so scared if an explosion hadn't occurred at Dogwood mine a few months ago. We could hear the whistle blow from here, and the sound of terrible shrieks was awful. Only those who have somebody they love in the mine know the fear those whistles cause. The whistles blow in the morning at five o'clock, then at twelve, and again at quitting time. Somehow we get used to those; but let another blow, and you hear it the first time. You know at once that those shrieks spell disaster of—maybe an explosion, the most feared of all.

"As soon as Johnson heard there had been an explosion at Dogwood, he went over to help if he could. I'll never forget the expression on his face when he told us about it. He said if our house was paid for, he wouldn't go on the inside of a mine again for all the coal there was. Here comes Johnson now, and I'll get him to tell you about it himself."

Mr. Johnson is still a big man, but I would hardly have recognized him from his wife's description. He is a tall man, stooped and with one shoulder higher than the other, and he walks stiffly. His hair is thin and gray, and his eyes blue and soft. He looks squarely in the eye of the person with whom he talks.

"Sure," he said, "I'll try to give you a description of what I saw, but I'm afraid I can't find words enough to tell it as it really was. When I got there, the hillside above the mine was filled with women, wild-eyed and dazed. Some of them had their cook aprons on, for it was about time to start supper. Little children with red eyes was holdin' onto their mammies for dear life, and the littlest ones cryin' and didn't know why. There they was, their eyes fastened on the mouth of the mine—not speakin' a word, just waitin'.

"The track leadin' out of the mine and up to the tipple was cleared. Volunteers to go inside was called for. Gas masks and safety lamps and first-aid material was all ready. Once a man volunteered, he didn't know what he'd find when he got inside. In fact, he didn't even know whether he'd come out alive, for sometimes other explosions follow.

"Well, at last the rope that pulled the cars started to move, slow at first—then a little faster. That meant that a body was on the way out—whose, nobody knew. They were put on stretchers and covered with blankets. Well the fact is, those bodies was burnt so that you couldn't tell whether they was black or white, and one of the bosses straightened that out right quick for he said there wasn't a single Negro in that part of the mine where the explosion occurred. I heard one Negro woman say, 'You know, I feels just as sorry for these folks as if they was my own color.'

"The only way you could identify those men was by the check number on them. They all have a brass number they get if they go inside every day. As each body was identified, it was turned over to relatives. In all my life, I'll never forget the look on those faces—they just couldn't be convinced that the charred bodies were actually their sons, sweethearts, or husbands; but when they were finally convinced that they had the right body and all hope was gone, they just looked sort of numb.

"Altogether, thirty-two men was killed and eighteen burned so bad they died a few hours later in the doctor's office. It was no use to take them to the hospital. The sufferin' and groanin' was awful.

I don't know which was the worse, those dyin' or those who were losin' their loved ones.

"Rescue business is mighty slow. Every minute seems like an hour. Some of those men had to be taken out from under rocks, and some of them was trapped in that mine for two days. Now that's the thing I hate worst of all about the whole thing.

"If I can be killed in a mine outright, then that's all right—but don't let me be trapped for days and days—slowly starvin', and knowin' that death is almost certain unless help comes in time. It just naturally gives me the creeps to think about it. I always tell Dera to put plenty in my dinner bucket—enough to last two or three days. It's much better to have too much than not to have enough.

"We work in a stooped position so much of the time that indigestion is common among miners, and they always take soda into the mines with them. I carry mine in a little tin can. We don't take anything heavy like peanut butter and we can't take crackers either. They get soggy in just a little while. We have water, coffee, or tea in the bottom of the bucket, and the food in the top. Workin' in a stooped position so much has caused my right shoulder to be higher than my left.

"There's not much in or around the mine that I haven't done at one time or another. I started pickin' slate when I was just a kid, then I started spraggin' at seventy-five cents a day. Then I was a mule driver, a track man, and later a coal loader, and then a digger. About thirty years ago, I got my first contract here at Sayreton. At first, I made from $200 to $300 a month, then I began to make from $600 to $900 a month. From 1914 to 1931, I made my highest money.

"The mine superintendent gives out the contracts. I usually got good contracts, because I was always considered a good pillar puller. The pillars in the mine are the big props of coal to hold up the roof. Later when the mine is worked out in a fashion, you go back in the mine and pull the pillars. The whole trick in that job is to pull them in such a way that the roof won't fall. Of course some other props have to be put in, to take care of the protection that is taken out. You would hardly believe how much coal is in one pillar.

"The size of the pillars is dependent on the coverage. The distance from the roof of the mine to the ground above is what we mean by coverage. You can see that if the weight overhead is heavy, you need to leave bigger pillars to protect the roof. Here at Sayreton, the coverage is usually about 500 feet. The pillars for that are 50 feet wide and 300 feet long. If there are 5 feet of clean coal

—leaving out the rock and slate—there will be 3,500 tons in that one pillar. In getting this coal out, you shoot as little as possible, because that cracks the coal too much. We pick it and work with it, so as to get it down as easy as possible. The workers always keep in the clear, that is, with backs toward the mouth of the mine.

"I hired from eight to fifteen men, depending on the size of my contract. I always like Negro labor best. At first the superintendent would let the contractor hire and fire all his men, but later on the superintendent began to have more and more to do with the hiring, but we still did the firing. They would do better work for a man that they knew could fire them.

"During the World War, the price of coal went way up. Steam coal that wasn't worth anything much, sold for ten and twelve dollars a ton. I had a shift leader for the day and one for the night. I paid for everything that had to be bought, such as tools, picks, shovels, dynamite; in fact I stood every expense and the miners' money was clear. Each man's task was five cars a day—three cars for the worker and two of the contractor. The price the company paid us varied slightly but was usually two dollars a ton.

"Long about '28, the miners at Sayreton came out on a strike, and since I am more or less a company man, I didn't have to come out. But I am and have always been a union man, so I came out with them. Well, the upshot of that strike was that the national wouldn't recognize the strike, and we lost. That wouldn't happen now, because they're better organized.

"Anyway, I felt so bad about the way the strike turned out that I wouldn't go back and ask for my job. In a few days, they sent for me to come to work, but I didn't go. Then they sent again, still I wouldn't go; but the third time I went. A few days after I went back to work, the superintendent met me and said, 'Joe, I was mighty disappointed in you during the last strike. I know you belong to the union, but you are kind of a company man, and you didn't have to come out. I've got a fine place that I was thinkin' of givin' to you when you worked out your present contract, but it looks like I can't exactly depend on what you would do in case of a fight. I don't exactly know what to do.'

"I didn't like the way that sounded one bit. What he wanted me to say was that I was sorry for comin' out and that I wouldn't do it again, but I don't run my business that way. I just turned around and looked him straight in the eyes and told him that he knew how I ran my contract, and if he wanted to give me the good place, I would do my best and I'd be mighty glad to get it, but I wasn't makin' no apologies for the past and no promises for the future. Well, when the time came, he gave me the place.

"I always tried to help the company in every way I could. For example, the inside track was always laid right up to the pillars. I moved that rail every night to take care of it in case we had a rock fall that would cover it up and cost the company money to place more.

"In 1931, all the companies did away with the contract system. It was done because of the new rule about collective bargaining. It was decided that no miner should make money off of another miner. The contractor didn't hit a lick of work and he drew from $300 to $900, and sometimes lots higher than that a month, while the ones who did the actual work earned only a meager living of $6 or $7 a day. I guess it was right to stop it, even if it did cost me lots of money to give it up.

"Well, I'm not making much money now, but then I haven't got the responsibility that I did have. Anyway, it's not how much you make, but what you do with what you do make. I can't see where we have any less than we used to have when I was making so much. Dera always has some left over anyway.

"We have a comfortable house—living room, two bedrooms, dining room, kitchen, and bath. We don't have a furnace, but you'd be surprised how the coal stove in the kitchen and the heater in the living room keep the whole house nice and warm. Dera has an oil stove to use in the summer, but I think food cooked on a coal stove, especially boiled victuals, just naturally tastes better if it's cooked a good long time on a coal stove.

"We're gettin' along all right now, and all right's hard to beat. All of us are well and we enjoy what we've got. Those 'green fields far away' was green all right, but the green happened to be the grass that had to be hoed out of the same mighty poor corn and same cotton that had to be plowed up, out on the farm."

N. S. McDonald

A Day on Factory Hill

LANDGROVE, NORTH CAROLINA, 1938

Next day starts like the one before and ends about the same.

"You'd like to know what a day in my life is like? Well, taint no trouble at all fer me to tell you because every one is so much like the other I've learned the pattern by heart long ago.

"Pink goes to work at seven. I get up at half past five to get his breakfast so's not to be rushed and so's we can have a few minutes for talkin' before he leaves.

"Every mornin' I cook oats for the younguns. They like it and it's cheap. Me and him eats it too, but now and agin we get a little bacon meat. A body just seems to want a little bacon meat once or twice a week. The children ain't learned to crave it yet. They get up when they hear the dishes rattlin', and we're done with breakfast a little after six. Sometimes they ain't much to talk about and we just set.

"After he's gone I help the younguns dress and then start cleanin'. 'Gin I get the dishes done, the beds made, and the floors swept, it's nine o'clock and almost time to start cleanin' agin. You see, them all bein' girls except the baby, I have to keep 'em in the house most of the time because the boys around here play so rough I'm afraid my girls 'll get hurt if they play with them. Then, too, they's no place for children to play but the road out there and it's full of black cinders put there to keep the road from washin' worse than it is.

"Most days around half past nine I start fixin' Pink's dinner. I leave here at half past eleven to take it to him. He works in the dye room, and the kettles has to be kept boilin' all the time. He can't take no time off, and he eats scatterin'-like when they's a slack in his work.

"When I get back from the mill me and the younguns eat. Most days it's biscuit-bread, potatoes, and beans of one kind or another. After I'm done with the dishes, I wash or iron, or maybe sew when they's anything to sew on. The other day I bought a quarter's worth of cloth, and I've just finished makin' a dress apiece out of it for them two least ones. I usually look at a picture in a catalogue and cut me a paper pattern from it. Most times they fit right well.

"Two evenings a week I wash, and even then I ain't able to keep my children noways like clean. I don't reckin they's a dirtier place in the world to live than here. It takes two evenings, too, for ironin'.

"At four o'clock Pink comes home from the mill. In a little while I start gettin' supper. We gen'ly eat before half past five. When I'm done with the dishes, me and him sets in the swing and watches the younguns play. A body don't even visit their neighbors because they'd feel foolish doin' it. We are that jammed up together we see one another too much anyway. Hardly a day passes that every one of us don't see the other run out and grab her younguns out of a fight. Like as not we'll meet one another emptyin' trash in them big garbage cans put out there by the mill. No, they's no reason much for visitin' in the evenin'.

"Around half past seven or eight I put the children to bed and me and him sets on till about half past eight or nine.

"He's sleepin' this summer on the single bed in the front room. Usually he sleeps with them two biggest ones, and I sleep with the two least ones, but they're so frenzy-like durin' hot weather, it keeps him from sleepin' as much as he oughter and him workin'.

"Next day starts like the one before and ends about the same. Of course, on Fridays and Saturdays it's a little different. Both of us enjoys Westerns, and we gen'ly go once a week to the picture show. I go on Friday night while he stays with the children, and then he goes on Saturday. They's always a bunch of women goin' on Friday, and I go along with them. It'd be nice if me and him could go together sometimes but they's nobody to leave the children with. If it wasn't for that movie I don't know what I'd do. Course, we ain't really able to spend the fifteen cents apiece for foolishness when he's just makin' nine dollars and sixty cent a week, but a body cain't stand it if he don't have a little pleasure sometimes.

"Pink just gets three days a week in the mill now, but we get up at the same time on the days he don't work. He's so tired since they put on the stretch-out* that he lays around the house and rests a good bit when he's off. Sometimes he goes down to the store and sets and talks with other men from the Hill. The past spring he made them two swinging boxes out of old car tanks and got him some red paint from the ten-cent store to paint 'em with. They make good boxes for petunias. He hauled me dirt from West Asheville to make them two flower beds by the doorsteps. That's his truck settin' out there but we don't use it much since they's no money for gas. It used to be a car but he fixed a body on to it. I put out a sight of diggin' makin' beds for them petunias and phlox but no place seems like home without a few flowers.

"The year goes round bringin' very little change but the weather. Poor folks don't have no vacation, you know, when they's time off from cookin', and washin', and worryin' about the grocery bill. The only money I've spent for pleasure this year went for the picture show and for them flowers. I'm glad my flowers done so well. It's nicer settin' on the porch when they's somethin' to look at besides a red, ugly hill."

Ida L. Moore

*See pp. 119–20.

A Retired Mill Worker

ATHENS, GEORGIA, 1939

*To make a good textile worker you had to
start young, say around the age of eight.*

"Well now, I don't know where to begin. . . . If I'd known you
were coming I could have thought it over and had some interesting
things ready to tell you. The modern cotton mills of today and
those that were operated in the days of my youth are quite different.

"You take this place, for instance. I came over here when this
mill was first started. Now it's most rotted down. In my time they
worked 750 hands. Now I expect 150 names would cover the entire
payroll. The old mill hands have been replaced by modern machinery. Now, for instance, let me give you an illustration. At the
time when they were working so many hands, there were 4½
looms to each weaver.

"My grandfather—I was named for him—spent his life in the
Athens Manufacturing Company's plant. That was way back before
the Civil War. He made seventy-five cents a day working in the
finishing room, where it was his job to get the cloth ready to be put
in bales for shipping. Tell you why I remember that so well. It's
because that was the standard wage for that particular kind of
work. Some made fifty cents, others made one dollar a day, according to the type of work they did. That was in my schoolboy
days.

"My grandmother kept house while my grandfather, my mother,
two uncles, and three aunts worked in the mill, and at that time

they did real well. Our family lived in a two-room house of an old style that was customary in Southern mill villages at that time. While it had only two main rooms, they were both large. They had a real large kitchen that was built off separate from the house, and it served as a dining room too. There was no roof over the plank walkway that went from the house to the kitchen and if it was raining you had to come and go just the same, if you didn't want to miss a meal.

"To make a good textile worker you had to start young, say around the age of eight. In those days you didn't see so many idle people walking around as now.

"Mr. Bloomfield was president of the Athens Manufacturing Company. In fact, he was the whole cheese when I was growing up. He was a devoutly religious man, and was good to the people that worked for him, but at the same time he was a strict and careful man; there was no foolishness about him.

"This is facts. Well now, we all went to school. Mr. Bloomfield provided a school for us three months in the year, but if he caught a child under twelve years old idle, he picked it up and put it to work. It was go to school or go to work when you lived in his mill village. That was all right with his mill families. Every man, woman, and child among them simply worshipped him.

"We were paid off once every four weeks, and once a week the heavy groceries were sent to our doors. They were meat, meal, and flour. Mr. Bloomfield had these groceries sent around in a two-horse wagon, but to tell the truth those wagons were pulled by mules. Anyway, the wagons were sent to your door for you to select what you needed, and the amount was deducted from your pay envelope. There was everything in that company store but matches and kerosene.

"Some few bought small lots and built homes on them. To those that did, Mr. Bloomfield paid seventy-five cents a head for everybody living in that house to work in his mill; otherwise some of them might not have made more than fifty cents a day, but he wanted to help those that tried to own homes of their own. He visited every house and knew every man, woman, and child that lived in his village by their first names.

"Now, it is customary around a mill village that if a family wants to change houses, they make arrangements with the manager. If it suits him you can move, but if it doesn't you stay where you are. That was not the way with Mr. Bloomfield; he decided for you. If he found that some member of a family had been sickly for awhile, he would have men, wagons, and teams go there while the family was away at work and move their things to some house that he considered was in a healthier spot. When that family would come back from work they'd find a note from him on the door telling them where to go, and when they reached there they found everything in its place; even the wood was in the wood box.

"My father bought himself a little lot that was a low and sort of swampy place, and he built a neat little house on it. Some time after we had moved into our new house Mr. Bloomfield stopped by one Sunday afternoon when he was making his round of calls on the mill families. He found my father sick with chills and fever. He didn't mention anything about our moving or ask my father anything about it, but the next morning, bright and early, he sent his team around to our house and moved us out on Bloomfield Street, where it was higher.

"Watermelon season meant a holiday to us. The mill closed down, and the hands went to the country or did anything else they chose, but the object of the vacation was to give us the opportunity to enjoy eating watermelons. During the rest spell, hands were allowed to get food from the company store and pay for it when they returned to work. To tell the truth, 90 percent of the hands owed the mill, and 10 percent was taken out of every dollar of pay earned until it was all paid back. I've known several families that owed the mill as much as $100 at one time. Their households were large, and the debt was held up off of their payroll accounts whenever their families would have suffered for lack of necessities if the regular deductions had been made.

"In my days at the mill, there was no hiring and firing like there is now. There were so many little children growing up to take their parents' places that they often worked in this manner. When a father or a mother, or an older sister or brother were sick, a younger one was sent to work in that person's place and the youngster continued to hold the place until the absent one returned. I'm telling you the truth, lady; many a child has started to work when they weren't no larger than this dog. . . . Lots of those kids didn't have the sense this little dog has. Once I went off and stayed several months and when I came back he was the first to greet me. Knew me just as well as when I left. Do you know what breed of dog he is? He is a mixture of fox terrier and Boston bull.

"I never heard of a strike, or of anything that came near amounting to one, but once. At the time, there two rough sort of fellows working in the mill, and they decided to get up a strike. The mill was run by water power, and one day they went out and stopped the mill wheels; that stopped the machinery. Those fellows tried to get the rest of the hands to take part in their strike, but they wouldn't follow. The manager rushed to the scene, gave 'em all a good talking-to, and fired the men that had stopped the wheels. The mill was started again at once, and the others went back to work. What brought about all this trouble was this: we had been working six months without pay because Mr. Bloomfield hadn't been able to sell his cloth to get the money to pay his hands with. That was the nearest thing to a strike I ever heard of in that mill.

"Want to hear about the first money I ever made? School was over, and I was playing around in the ruins of Mr. Bloomfield's boiler room that had burned down and was enjoying my vacation. Mr. Bloomfield came and said to me, 'Hal'—they called me that for Henry—'there's an iron arch in those ashes. If you'll go in there and scratch it out of those ashes, I'll give you a quarter.' You should have seen me digging for that piece of iron. Anyway, I found it, and he kept his promise and gave me the money. Do you want to know what I did with it? Well, in those days, they sold sugarcane in the stores and I spent every cent of that quarter for it. To me that was the best sugarcane I ever tasted. I'm fond of the stuff yet.

"My grandfather and grandmother Fant came here with their children from South Georgy, and they had passed on before I was old enough to remember much about them. I've even forgotten the name of the place where grandfather worked as overseer for a wealthy plantation owner during the war. From what they said, there's just no telling how many slaves were on that plantation. An overseer's place was the only job a decent man could get in those days if he didn't farm himself. After the war, he brought his family to Athens to work in the mill.

"My mother, Edna Fant, married Henry Hunt, and I'm their only child. Mother was a spinner and father was a beamer. He made seventy-five cents a day for a while, and was then raised to one dollar a day, and later on he made even more than that. The modern term now is a slasher. A slasher takes the place of six beamers.*

"One thing that seems funny to me now is, why don't they let the hands work all day? I used to go to work long before sunup

---

*Slashers size yarn to make yarn easier to weave. Spinning is the final drawing out or drafting and twisting of the yarn.

and it was dark when I got home, and we didn't have 'lectric lights then like we do now. . . .

"You know, since I've gotten too old to work I have an awful time. When I was working way back yonder it didn't take so much to live on. Our lives were simple, and our wants were few. We worked from sun to sun, ignorant but contented. Now a ten-year-old boy knows more than a grown man did when I was growing up. I mean he knows about more different things, and can do more things.

"I'll be sixty-eight the 17th day of February." He chuckled as he added, "And I just missed being a Valentine by a few days. When I was fifteen I was working steady in the mill, and while I can't remember just exactly how long I worked there altogether, I'm sure it was as much as thirty-five years. I'd be working there now, but I'm too old and am not suited to the modern way they operate the mills now.

"My first regular work was slashing, that is, starching and processing cloth for the bolt. After I had worked at that for a long while I stopped and went to the Athens Foundry and Machine Works to learn that trade. Mr. Thomas Beal was my boss at that place. Lord, I reckon I do remember old man Tom Beal. He paid me eight dollars a month the first year, twelve dollars a month the second year, and fifteen dollars a month the third year. I learned to be a moulder. We had to make the cast by hand and then the melted iron, or sometimes it was melted brass, was poured by hand. All of that's done by machinery now.

"Mr. Beal was a mighty fine man to work for. He was so good to his hands. In summertime he took us boys out on fishing trips at his own expense. That reminds me, just as soon as the weather opens I'm going to try to catch me a mess of fresh fish. I don't know anything I'd rather have. But, I was telling you about Mr. Beal, wasn't I? Well, when he started to work in that same foundry under Mr. Reuben Williams, to learn the trade, he didn't have a penny. He worked hard and saved his money and was worth quite a bit at one time. However, at the time of his death he didn't have scarcely anything left and was almost totally blind. My reason for leaving the foundry was that he didn't have orders enough to keep the men busy. By that time there were several other foundries in town. Concerning Mr. Beal's foundry, the only regret I have is that right there in that foundry is where I started drinking. I fell in line with the other boys and the older men that worked there. Of course, Mr. Beal didn't drink and wouldn't tolerate drinking in his men, if he knew it was going on, but you know there was always a way to whip around the ball. My father always kept whiskey in the house, but it was never served, only on Sunday mornings.

"After the foundry failed, I went back to the old check mill. It was known as the check mill because they made cloth woven in check designs in that mill. They made those checks on old-fashioned box looms, in this manner: say you wanted to make a bolt of brown checks, you put four strands of brown thread in the warp and four in the filling, and when the loom shuttled back and forth it wove the material into checks. All the common people, both white and black, wore those checks. We made a variety of jeans cloth out of wool and cotton, and it was used for winter garments for men and women.

"Long before Mr. Bloomfield had to shut down his mill, my father got well of his chills and fever, and we moved back to a little two-room house right near the mill. This little house had about a quarter of an acre around it that we used for a garden. Everybody had a garden in those days. Father had sold the little place he had bought and built on.

"When Mr. Bloomfield was no longer able to get enough orders to keep his mill going, he had to close it, and then we moved over here to the Southern Mill. The old part of it had just been finished and was known as the batting mill. There was where they made batting for quilts, and all the work was done on one floor. Soon after we moved here, they begun weaving in what was then known as the waste mill. The reason for that name was that they took waste from other mills, mixed it with some good cotton, and made the mixture into cloth. They first put in 64 looms, and at the time I left there they had a little better than 700. Before I left that mill they had added three new buildings that were known as No. 2, No. 3, and No. 4. That plant was built up to a million-dollar mill at one time.

"Do you see that oil tank and compress down the street there? Well, when I moved to this village they were grading it for a race-track. It ran all the way to Barber Street. Where Chase Street School is now was famous as a circus ground. Oh, the changes that have taken place in my time! There used to be a heap of houses over there across the railroad track, but they are mostly rotted down now. This was a pretty rough place to live in when I first came over here. They used to have dances right over there, and every night they would get drunk and cut up. I have stayed out the most part of many a night going to those frolics. That hill you see over there was known as Happy Top, and they've called it by that name 'til this good day.

"When I first started to work in the Southern Mill, the standard wage was $5.10 a week. When Mr. Taylor took up the piecework plan, all the workers in one department quit but two, and those two averaged twenty dollars a week. The others just wouldn't try the piecework. Said they would starve first. The smallest salary paid there now is twenty-nine cents per hour. The weavers make thirty-five cents per hour. I worked until they changed managers. The manager that came after Mr. Taylor left was a hard man to work for, so I decided to quit before I got fired.

"My father and I had saved up a little money, not so much, but we decided to quit work, and we rented a house at Linton Springs. Mother was dead and father was old, so I had to stay there and look after him. That was the beginning of my downfall. We kept house for more than a year and then boarded a year before my father died. We were both sick in bed at the same time, and neither one was able to wait on the other. Oh, we had hard luck, and such a tough time! The doctor coming every day and bills piling up. The folks around us said the reason I was sick was because I was such a hard drinker; that wasn't true. At that time I hadn't touched a drop in four months.

"When father died I tried to die too, for it seemed to me I had nothing left to live for. I had $6,000 in cold cash at the time of father's death. I got to drinking harder than ever. I couldn't have blamed the family I was boarding with if they had driven me off, for all I done was drink and lay around. My mind was so crazed with whiskey I didn't have sense enough to take care of my money. I never let anybody down that came along asking for money, and everybody came. Why, on Sunday mornings they would come to my room even before day, for liquor and money.

"My landlady used to say, 'Hal Hunt, you're crazy. Why do you let 'em ride you?' I'd tell her, they're not getting much out of me. I didn't realize how much I was spending. I let one man have $200. I thought he was honest and didn't make him give me a note of any kind. When all I had was gone I begged him to pay me back a little at a time, and he wouldn't do it. He always argued that he was hard up and couldn't pay me. I went away for a while and since I came back he won't hardly speak to me, and won't even give me a mouthful of victuals. If I had money today I'd remember that it's safer to lend money to a stranger than to your best friend.

Yes, dear lady, when you have money you have friends, and when your money is gone you can't find em.

"Back in the early times that I can remember there was no public relief in regard to sickness, death or want. There was no such thing as public relief. When someone died in a mill family and that family was not able to bury their dead, a collection was taken up in the mill among the hands. This is the way they handled it. A responsible person was appointed as chairman, and he passed the paper around to everybody. Each one wrote down by his or her name the amount they felt like giving. Then the paper was taken to the office and the money was turned over to the chairman in charge, and was spent for the purpose it had been raised for. When we were paid off, the amount we had subscribed was deducted from our pay envelopes. In sickness we helped out from the things we had at home.

"One boy that had a wife and child contracted TB, and we begged him to give up his work, for we knew he couldn't live long. He felt like he just couldn't afford to quit work, but finally we overpersuaded him and he did quit. We boys took enough out of our own wages to make up the wages he had been getting, and gave it to him on each payday as long as he lived, which won't long. After his death we gave the same amount to his wife and child 'til she was able to go to work.

"I don't never expect to see times like that again, and I wouldn't have them if I could. In them days, folks didn't crave the dollar like they do now, but I must say that this old world is a better place to live in now, in many ways. If anybody had told us all these modern conveniences would be invented and come into use, we wouldn't have believed 'em. Yes, it's much better now, if only the people would be more contented with what they have."

The 4:50 train was passing. . . . "We call that little train the hooker, because it's so small. My mother was seventy-one when she died, and do you know she never rode a train in her life? She never had but one automobile ride, and that was when she had to go see about one of our relatives that was sick. Father was eighty-three when he passed on. If he ever was in an automobile or a train it must have been when he went to the Civil War or when he was coming back from there.

"I told you the old check mill was first run with water power. Well, I fired the first steam engine that was installed in that factory. That engine was named 'Lizzie' for Mr. Bloomfield's daughter. Mr. Broom was the engineer, and his health was real bad. I was hanging around the mill in vacation time and often he would let me help him. Pretty soon I'd learned to operate it, and then I often had to look after it for him. He made $1.75 a day, and paid me 40¢ a day out of his own wages. When school opened up that fall my father told me if I didn't want to go back to school I could continue helping run the engine at the mill and he would give me all the money I made to buy myself a suit of clothes and a watch. I never will forget that gray suit I bought that year, and I still have that old watch. I thought I was the best-dressed dude on the hill, and acted it.

"There is no comparison in the conditions under which mill hands worked in my young days and the present-day conditions. In my young days the life of a mill worker wasn't very long. The close confinement, long hours, lint and dust that they had to breathe, all worked together to shorten their lives. 'Most everybody had a cough. I've had this cough ever since I can remember. Men and women all had sallow complexions, and the younger folks didn't have any color in their cheeks either. The mills of those days didn't have any way of controlling the dust and lint, and the air we breathed was dry and stale. Now they have humidifiers that keep the air moist. And another thing, in those days sanitary conditions were mighty bad sometimes. That was because so many lived crowded together in the same house, breathing the same air that came from the lungs of the sick ones. Now they have sanitary inspectors to go around ever' so often and inspect the premises as well as the houses.

"Oh, no! It wasn't all work in those days. We boys used to go to ball games and we played football and baseball too. I used to follow the Georgy boys and their big games, but now I can't go and so I have to sit at home and listen to their games over the radio. My first trip to Floridy was to see Georgy play Floridy at Gainesville. That was the best trip I ever had in my life, and it was the first time I ever saw the Atlantic Ocean. I'm just as big a fool over a football game now as I was at twenty. My father liked 'em too.

"No, ma'am, I've never been very religious. However, I did join the Methodist church with my mother. Father didn't belong to no church. When he was sick the preacher come and sat with him a long time, and once he said to father, 'Henry, do you realize you will never be well again? Don't you think it is time you were serving the Lord?'

"'I've been serving the Lord all my life,' answered Father. 'I went to Sunday School at old St. Mary's Church 'til I was a grown man.

And as children, how we did look forward to that Christmas tree at St. Mary's! Good old Mr. Bloomfield built and owned that church that he provided for the hands working in his mill, and he furnished all the entertainments held there. We could always count on him to do the nice thing by us.' . . .

"I'll never forget our Sunday School room. It was built right by the church, and we knew very well that children were to go to that Sunday School room first, and not enter the church proper until time for church services, when Mr. Bloomfield would come and invite us to take our seats with the congregation. When we got in our Sunday School room Mr. Sayers, the sexton, would lock us in. When Miss Mattie Carver finished teaching us our Sunday School lesson, Mr. Sayers would come back and unlock the door. Some of those little boys would run over him in their eagerness to scamper out where they could play and frolic. Children ain't made to go to Sunday School and church and behave like they were then. These days, Sunday is just another day to be spent playing ball, skating, and doing anything they want to do. . . .

"Now, miss, I believe I've told you all I know that could be of any interest. . . . Good luck to you. If you had come along a few years ago, when I had a drink or two in me, maybe I could have told you a livelier story. I was noted for talking then."

Sadie B. Hornsby

There's Always a Judas

*I don't reckin . . . they calculate
a sermon like that'll do 'em much harm.*

"He preaches because he's got the gift of preachin'; it's not from education, for he never got none."

Molly Sharp picked up a little blue-flowered scrap and a little pink-flowered scrap, and with minute attention fitted their edges together. She squinted her eyes, selected the exact spot for a beginning point, and plied her needle along the cloth edge. "He's out avisitin' the sick but I 'low he'll be in before long if you care to wait. This is what you call a double weddin' ring quilt. You can't get no idea of it from these little scraps, but here's how it looks when it's pieced up." She unfolded the half-finished quilt which lay on the nearby chair. "See, the curve on this square joins with the curve in this here square to make a ring. Flowered ring and solid center. Then these bigger squares makes a ring around the first. A ring inside a ring. That's how come they named it the double weddin' ring. Used to, I never had no time for fancy quilt piecin'. I just made cover. But this year, stayin' with Annie and the preacher, they ain't so much work for me to do like it was on the farm. Nothin' but housework, and Annie does the biggest part of it. Course, it's a big house but ain't so hard to keep because it's full of conveniences.

"The company furnishes a house for all its preachers rent-free. Good ones too, good as bossmen's houses. We've got a furnace; we've not had cause to use it much this winter. The grate'll warm

157

up this room where we set most of the time when the weather ain't rough and it's a sight cheaper'n usin' the furnace. . . .

"Annie was the first of my children to come to the cotton mill," Molly was saying as she searched among her scraps for the color she desired. "I had a sister that had done give up the farm for the mill and when she come avisitin' us one summer she said to Annie, 'Since you've had that paralysis and can't stand no hot sun, why don't you just come on down to the mill with me?' Doctors have said since, Annie never had no real paralysis; her trouble was caused from a nerve gettin' killed in her jaw when she had a abscessed tooth taken out. It left her mouth twisted and one of her eyes so it don't focus with t'other one. She was eighteen year old then and that summer she wan't a bit account for field work. Seemed like the hot sun would throw her into a spell if she went out in it for any time at all. We never had what you'd call a big farm up there in the mountains of Burke County . . . [but] it took all hands aworkin' to make a livin'. I studied about what my sister'd said to Annie and I told her I 'lowed it wouldn't hurt her none to go and try the mill. So when Sister Ola went back to Hickory, Annie went with her.

"Annie done right well in the mill from the first. She'd worked there five year before her and the preacher was married. He wan't a preacher then, just a eighteen-year-old boy workin' in the mill beside her and attendin' her Sunday School class of a Sunday. Annie said she'd noticed he could answer might nigh every question in the lesson, and it surprised her some to find out after they was married that he could bare read and write.

"It was his good recollection that helped him out with his Sunday School lesson. A body could read it to him and he could tell it off of a Sunday like he was the best reader in the neighborhood. I noticed what a good recollection he had the first time I ever met him. I'd come down to Hickory to be with Annie when her first baby come and I said to her one day, 'It wouldn't surprise me none to see you make a preacher out of him if you was to try. When I go back I'll send you the Bible storybook we've got at home, and you can read him them stories till you learn him to read 'em hisself.' I done what I told her I would and the next time I seen him—that was when the second baby come—he was right well learnt up on the Bible.

"Annie says David was around twenty-three when he first commenced to talk about feelin' the call to preach. It disturbed her mightily because no matter how much she prayed she couldn't see no way openin' up for startin' him in the ministry. But she give him what encouragement she could and times come now and agin when he was called on to do lay preachin'. Deacons* begin to take notice of him and some said he had the power.

"David was might nigh thirty when a accident happened to him that made up his mind. The mill had been closed for ten days, short orders I reckin—and David had held a meetin' of a nighttime. The tenth night brought more conversions than air other and the folks wan't willin' for the meetin' to close. But David worked on the night shift and he never knowed how to go about askin' his boss for time off, considerin' the mill had been astandin' for ten days. All day long he tried to get his own consent to lay out that night but he couldn't. He went to work. His job was up on the second floor of the mill and he'd started down the stairs to see a fellow on the first floor. He hadn't more'n put his foot on the top step when he got tripped up some way and fell down them steps, the basement steps, and right on to the cement floor. It broke his hip bone and when they carried him home the first thing he said to Annie was, 'I ought to been at church.' He'll tell you hisself that while he lay up in bed with a broke hip he wrestled with the proposition, fightin' agin it, and finally one day when he was might nigh dead with pain he says, 'Lord, I surrender, I'll fight the call no longer.'

"As I said before, he never had no education much but he'd done a sight of studyin' since he took up preachin'. Then, ever' year since he's been ordained, he's got his congregation to send him off on a trip, and travelin' helps him a whole lot. He'll go to the Association† and hear big preachers talk and recollect might nigh everything they say.

"The first trip he took was to Washington, D. C. It was the year Annie's last baby, her fourth, was born, and she was in bad shape. I'd been there with her for two weeks already and I knowed I was needed back home. But the preacher, he had his mind so set on his trip, it didn't seem like I could knock him out of it by leavin' Annie. I figgered the schoolin' he'd get from a trip like that would do him so much good, I was bound to help out all I could. So I stayed with Annie and he went to Washington. He ain't failed a trip air year since.

"Travelin's more common than it used to be anyhow. I was a middle-aged woman with a house full of children before I ever left

*Elected lay leaders of a local Baptist church.
†Voluntary association of local Baptist churches.

Burke County. My man had done a right smart knockin' around before we was married. He was pretty Irishy. Now, Pa, he was a right smart Dutchy. There's the preacher now, I think. Sounds like his step."

The doors slid open and I looked up to see the preacher standing in the room. Molly introduced him and he came forward with outstretched hand, "Sister, I'm glad to meet you. . . ."

"Yessum, I'm pastor of the Baptist church right across the street, a church with a membership of 518. After I baptize what was converted at a meetin' a few weeks ago it'll run us up to 525. That is the biggest flock I've ever been pastor for, though in my years of preachin' I've seen hundreds of souls brought to Christ. We got our start in meetin's and for many a year we fought against full-time service to the Lord. But we surrendered after a accident that happened to us when we ought to been at church. We said, 'Lord, we are yours. We depend on thy promise, Follow me and I will supply thy need.' We've been given the necessities though we haven't made the money we might've made if we'd stayed in the mills.

"I'der probly been a super somewhere by now if I had stuck to the mill. I'll be forty if I live to see June and at thirty-two when I quit to give my life to fulltime preachin' I'd worked up to overseer of the weave-room.

"I entered the mill at fifteen and learnt fast. I'd seen hard times on the pore little farm where my father was strugglin' along with us six children and him ownin' nothin' but one little plug of a mule and a homemade carryall. I worked hard in the mill and they soon took me off sweepin' and put me to weavin'. From weavin' I went to fixin' looms. Durin' war times I worked in the company store of the Brookford Mill at Hickory. When I went back in the mill it wasn't long till they put me on as second hand and in a few more years I was overseer. Yessir, I sacrificed to preach the gospel, but the reward has been great. I was savin' many souls even before I was ordained.

"The first meetin' we held after bein' licensed was in a county schoolhouse between Mooresville and Statesville. The county commissioners had the partition between the two rooms removed, throwin' the little schoolhouse into one big room. They built me a Bible stand out of a hickory log. 'We turn it over to you, Brother Brown,' they said, and sister, I'm tellin' you, that was a soul-stirring meetin'. The opening night we had four preachers settin' in the congregation listenin' to us and at first we was a little scared. We stayed pretty close around the hickory log till we begin to feel the power and then we gained confidence. We preached a sermon that brought 'em to the mourner's bench. The whole entire meetin' netted some thirty-five souls for the Kingdom.

"Three years later we was ordained. Since then we've had a regular church, five years at Pamona and three right here. Of course we don't know how much longer the people will want us but they seem to like us mighty well. The new brick church across the street has been built since we've been on this charge.

"This company is the most liberal in its gifts to the churches of any I know of. For buildin' a new church they put up $4 to ever' one a congregation can raise provided the church is put on the company's premises. And then ever' year they give $500 on the pastor's salary, treatin' one and all alike—Baptist, Presbyterian, and Church of God. Then there's special times they give, too. If I was to go to Mr. Herman Cones and say, 'Mr. Herman Cones,* the people of my church has sent me to ask you for $50. We need so-and-so and we don't feel like the church can get along without it, but the congregation can't raise the money.' If I was to do that I'd go away with $50. They don't let the churches suffer. And our church, sister, does what it can to keep the people from sufferin'.

"There's hardly a week passes we don't pound somebody in need. The deacons stand at the church door some Sundays and either take a special money collection or a collection of groceries. Sometimes the brothers and sisters meet here at the parsonage durin' the week, bringin' groceries to pound someone that's been out of the mill sick for two or three weeks.

"This company is awful opposed to any of its people gettin' help from the county or city welfare, and that makes a big responsibility for the churches. Of course I guess you know the company has its own welfare department, a nurse that goes around and tells you when you need a doctor, and a social worker that reports any real bad needy cases she finds. If there's cases the church and the community club just absolutely can't take care of, the company sometimes lends a little assistance. We've found it right strainin' in our church to look after all the calls we've had for help. Our church pays us a salary of $2,060 a year. Maybe you're familiar enough with the gospel work to know that pastor's salary is only a part of church expense. But, sister, this congregation has never sent me to an association with a backward record. And not once have they

*Herman Cone, one of the second generation of owner-managers of Cone Mills.

waited till Monday morning to pay this pastor. Forty dollars [is put in] my hands every Sunday night as regular as the weeks come and go.

"Not long ago we felt the need of new song books. We wanted two hundred. They cost ninety dollars. We said to our congregation when the service was over: 'Now all that will give fifty cents rise to your feet. Next, all will give forty cents stand up and let's see whose heart is right.' We got the ninety dollars.

"Now, we preach tithing to our people. We preach it because it's New Testament gospel and we believe in it. We think that a Christian should try to give a tenth of his wage to promote the Kingdom of Christ. But when we go to many of our people, they say, 'Preacher, we don't have nothin' to give. We had to pay the furniture man, the grocery man, the insurance man, and there's not a brownie left.' We know it's true and we don't bawl nobody out for it, but we do keep after them to give. 'It is more blessed to give than to receive.' It's a idea we think should be kept before church people."

The Reverend David Brown arose from the couch, strode across the room, picked up the coal scuttle, and stood before the grate, scuttle tilted, gazing for a moment into the fire. With measured deliberation he poured coal into the grate, returned the scuttle to its corner, and brushed his hands one against the other. There was about the whole performance an air which made of it a ceremony enjoyed rather than a task performed. The Reverend David Brown resumed his seat just as his wife came into the room.

The introductions over, Annie sat down in the chair close to her mother. "The Estes are in need," she said to David. "It means another poundin', I'm afraid, and the people have just about pounded out."

Molly, who had been quiet for so long a time, peered up over the rim of her glasses to speak. "In lots of ways these times is better to live in than the days when I growed up, but in a few ways the old times was best. Then, folks—pore folks—could manage to get along without askin' for help. We never knowed anything about unemployment, and now livin's hard on them without jobs in a time when they've got no manner of means of makin' a livin'. If I've got to be pore I'd rather been pore then way back on a little farm where I done nothin' but work to store back bread and meat and beans for the winter, than to be pore at a mill or any kind of industrial where my livin' ended when the wheels stopped turnin'."

The preacher cleared his throat. "I don't know whether you know it or not, young woman, but cotton mill people live a week at a time and always a week behind. From Thursday to Thursday is the way it runs here. This Thursday when they draw their pay they pay for what they bought last Thursday. That's why they get so scared when for one cause or another the mill closes for a week or more. They don't have nothin' to carry them over." . . .

"That's why the people lost in the strike last summer" [put in Molly]. "That's why after bein' scared for a whole week they said, 'We'll go back to work. A half loaf is better than no bread at all.'"

"Mother is right," the preacher said. "Of course we tried not to take sides in the strike, our work not bein' mill work but the salvation of souls. It was natural, though, us bein' their pastor, that many of the brethren would come to us and talk their troubles over with us. We give them what comfort we could. . . .

"We stayed in our house and said nothin' that could be called takin' sides. We told the children not to talk and, Mother, she said nothin'. But while that strike was goin' on we done a lot of thinkin'. We decided the South ought to be organized, but how? There's always a Judas to sell his people out. He'll get into the union and find out its secrets. Then he'll go to the company man and whisper in his ear, 'They're organizin'. They're plannin' to strike when you cut again.' Why does he do it? I don't know and you don't know, but gifts can be give at other times than Christmas. The people are cut, they walk out, sayin' among themselves, 'We can't live on no less. We won't let nobody go in that mill to work until we get our old wage back.' What happens? The mill owner with his foot on the head of the law asks for help to open up his mill to let his people work, or he asks for help to keep his mill closed if that be his will at that time. Whichever way his fancy goes, he gets the help. The law comes out and fortifies him against the people. Ah, sister, it's a hard thing to do to get ahead of a power like that.

"What happened here last summer? When the cardroom struck, the bossmen said, 'All of you might just as well go home, the mill can't run without the cards.' Many folks that hadn't aimed to strike at all went home. The company could've found plenty willin' to work to run one shift but they didn't do that. They closed down all of the mill. The people begin to think, 'We'll just stay out till they promise not to cut, we'll join the union, we'll be took care of.' They was out a week and much talkin' went on. Groups met here and there and a speaker would get up and make a speech, 'Do you want Lewis* or do you want Cones?' they'd say. 'The mill will open when the people answer.' At first the people didn't care to make an answer because they thought they had a chance of winnin'. Provisions would be given them by the union or the unemployment compensation, they didn't know which.

"The week went by and all the stores except the company stores cut off their credit. 'We can't give you credit except when you're workin',' they said. There was much excitement in the land and fear begin to creep in.

"Then while folks was still tryin' to get a little hope to hold on to a delegation went to Raleigh. They went down there and said, 'Mr. Hoey,† the people of the Cones mills has sent us to ask you for aid and assistance in openin' the mills. The people want to go back to work but we don't want to have no trouble with the roughnecks that may try to stop us.'

"Now Mr. Hoey bein' a big industrial himself up there at Shelby —just like Max Gardner‡ before him—said to the delegation, 'The government of North Carolina will give what assistance is needed.'

"The same day the delegation come home a piece come out in the paper here saying the people had stated their desire to go back to work and the mill would open up Monday. Scores of people had signed the paper they took to Raleigh without knowin' what was in it. Some of 'em even signed a blank piece of paper and was told by the fellow signin' 'em up it was just a way of seein' how many folks wanted their jobs back. They didn't actually know what was goin' on till they read the piece in the paper. But they knew then they was defeated. They tore up their cards, their union cards, and they cried, 'Give us Cones.' And among themselves they muttered, 'A half a loaf is better than no bread at all.' So the company started their wheels again with the promise of a bean, a bean today, a bean tomorrow, but never two beans on the same day. Aye, sister, it's a proposition. Bondage, slavery, a bean. The multi-million-airy is hard to beat. . . . §

*John L. Lewis, leader of the United Mine Workers and a leader of the 1930s movement to organize the unorganized by industry rather than by craft. In 1936 Lewis was expelled from the American Federation of Labor. He and his associates founded the Congress of Industrial Organizations.
†Clyde R. Hoey, lawyer and politician, Democratic governor of North Carolina, 1937–41, later United States senator.
‡O. Max Gardner, lawyer, textile manufacturer, and Democratic governor of North Carolina, 1928–33.
§Caesar and Moses Cone established the first of their textile mills in North Carolina in 1895 at Greensboro. In 1899 they defeated the first attempt to unionize their

"Old Caesar Cones, when he lived, cried, 'These are my people, my very own.' It is easy to cry, 'These are my people,' when you take the butter from the biscuits and give the people dry crumbs, crumbs, crumbs from Dives' table.

"As the people went back to work that Monday mornin' I thought of a joke I heard at the association a few years back. This was durin' slavery time, a old colored man named Daniel belonged to his Marster John. Marster John beat pore old Daniel might nigh every day and the old nigger not able to help hisself no way took to prayin'. Late of a evenin' he'd go down to a big oak tree in the pasture and he'd talk with the Lord. 'Dear Lord,' he'd say, 'pore old Daniel is treated mean and beat like a hound dog. Won't you come, high Marster, and take old Daniel home?' Well, one day Marster John overheard Daniel at his prayers. The next day while the old man was still at work he clumb up in the tree and hid hisself amongst the leaves. Daniel come and prayed his same old prayer. And when he'd finished, a voice spoke softlike from the tree, 'All right, Daniel, I'll come for you and take you home if that's what you want.' And soon as the old nigger could make his voice speak he said, 'Lord, high Marster, can't you take a joke?' "

With a gesture of resignation the preacher declared, "That's the people, that's the people."

"Old Daniel's prayer, and specially the end of it, was pitiful," Annie declared, "but while we was at Pamona I heard the most pitiful and the most beautiful prayer I ever heard in my life."

"When was that, Mother?" [asked the preacher].

"Durin' the end of Hoover's time and on into Roosevelt's time, we fed from two to three people a day that was passin' through Pamona, people that had been throwed out of their jobs and sometimes their homes. One day there come a crowd of six men, six jobless men. That was the day that the whole family cried. We took them in and fed them, they could hardly talk, only one man kept saying, 'I've got a Christian wife at home and three babies. I've got nothin' to give them. They seems to be no sort of job in the land for me.' He had old pieces of shoes tied on with a string. He was the

---

mills. They had, Caesar Cone repeatedly said, come to the South to avoid unions, and they would destroy their mills before they would submit to unions.

When a series of strikes occurred at Southern mills in the late 1920s, Benjamin Cone, one of the second generation of Cones to manage the mills, said "the laborer does not need the union; the union can do nothing for him."

In June 1938, almost all the workers at the Cones's White Oak Mills struck. The strike ended as suddenly as it began, lasting only two weeks. See the *Greensboro Daily News*, 12–16 July 1938.

one that stumbled in the door when he turned around to thank me. He stepped on the end of the string and it broke. I never have forgot how he looked when he asked me for a string.''

Annie's voice was unsteady now and she paused for a long minute. . . . "But what I started out to tell was about the old man come by one day when David wasn't at home. I didn't make no practice of askin' 'em in the house when David wasn't there, but this time I said to the children, 'He's old and I'm goin' to fetch him in to the table.' He set there in the kitchen lookin' while I fixed his plate, never sayin' a word, but when he set down to the table and looked at his food he begin to pray. Every word of his prayer has stayed with me like no other prayer I ever heard. I stopped right still in the doorway when he commenced and listened, feelin' like I never could move again. This is what he said, 'God in Heaven, it's good to be settin' at a table and eatin' victuals agin. I've got no work and I'm agettin' old. The mill's done with me. I'm weary and footsore, Lord, and I'm not knowin' where on the face of the earth I ought to go. I'd like yore guidance, God, and I'll try to listen. I'll ask you now to bless this kind woman that fixed these victuals.' He eat his meal while the tears streamed down in his plate. He never spoke no more till he got ready to leave. All he said then was, 'Thank you, kind woman, and God bless you.' " . . .

"The people have suffered, lady. Many of the people are sufferin' still. Somethin' is going to happen and I don't think it's far off. You can keep pushin' people to the wall but when they get close against the wall they'll turn and fight. The pore man is beginnin' to think as I never knew him to think before that the law is against him and there's no reason for him to respect it. A man we knew in Pamona had to move away from the mill and finally he found a little shack out in the country but the country itself had nothing for him. He'd been a good man at the mill, a respected citizen. I was at his home a year later when his daughter lay dead. He said to me when the two of us was in the room talkin', 'I've done time on the road since you last seen me. My wife was sick and she was sick'—pointin' at his dead daughter—'and I sold liquor to buy them bread. There's a hundred men in Greensboro that's done worse, but they're men of money, men that pushes me and the other little men to break the law, but the law'll never touch 'em. As long as I live I'll never have no respect for the law agin.' I was able to understand that man as I set there listenin' to him and I had only pity in my heart for him. . . .

"I am reminded now [the preacher continued] . . . of what I

told my congregation after I come home from Washington, D.C. They had sent me up there to the presidential inaugural of Mr. Roosevelt and I was relatin' to them what I'd seen and heard. I begin with tellin' em this joke on Hoover. Hoover was out fishin' and his boat turned over. A old fisherman was out there close by in a little bitty boat. He run his boat over to where Hoover was and tugged him in. When Hoover found out he was safe and sound he said to the man, 'You've been a hero and I'll give you a medal for this, a fine gold medal. I'll have it engraved, To So-and-So from Herbert Hoover.' The fisherman looked at the president and he said, 'Near mind about the medal. All the reward I ask of you is don't squeal on me and let the country know I saved you.'

"Of course they got to laughin' at that and then I went on to say, 'We went on the rocks with Hoover, folks, and lots of us might've felt just like the fisherman. But as I stood up there in that vast throng watchin' Hoover go out and Mr. and Mrs. Roosevelt come in, I felt like weepin'. I thought, one man of big promises goes out and another comes in, and like always the people go on in need. When the people is helped, it'll be when they've waked up to their rights.'

"Not long after that I preached my sermon from the fifth chapter of James. And I'll tell you, sister, when you get to foolin' around James you're tramplin' on ever'body. It sets down hard on the rich—ah, what it says about the million-airy is enough to set the woods on fire—I'll say this much for the Cones: there's never been one word of complaint from the company about that sermon and it's got many a sting in it too. Let me get my Bible; I'll read that text to you. . . .

"'Go now, ye rich man, weep and howl for your miseries that shall come upon you. Your riches are corrupted, and your garments are moth-eaten.'" He read on for six or seven verses and then with great solemnity closed the Bible. "After finishin' with that scripture . . . I begin to preach. I say, 'Do the multi-million-aries of our country have a hard time now? No,' I answer, 'they have their palaces, they have their servants, they can write a check for a million dollars. But the day will come, brothers and sisters, the day will come. You run their looms, you run their cards, you keep their yards, and you live on a little weekly wage.' And this is where I start to warmin' up, sister. Then I say, 'But what does the Holy Bible teach? Hellfire is waitin' to receive the rich man who gives no thought to his soul but spends his time fillin' his store-houses with earthly goods, and you, you, the faithful, are storin' up treasures in heaven where neither moth nor rust doth corrupt and thieves do not break through to steal.' Yes, ma'm, I preach hell, and I don't mean maybe, because it's there, it's all the way through that Book. That's straight talkin', sister, but I've never been called down for it yet."

"I don't reckin," Annie said slowly, "they calculate a sermon like that'll do 'em much harm. It's time I was startin' supper. You just set on in here with the preacher. It won't take me long to fix what I'm going to have."

"I'll be in to help you t'rectly," Molly said, gathering up her workbox. "Think I'll go upstairs and see if I can't find some yellow scraps. I've not got enough yellow in it yet."

Molly and Annie had both gone about their duties and the preacher sat gazing into the fire. "Sister," he said presently, "a pastor sees and hears many sad things as he goes about the Kingdom's work. Not long before Christmas a man and his wife come to me, both of 'em cryin' soon as they commenced talkin', and they said, 'Brother Brown, we want you to come and reason with our two daughters. They're not livin' right and the company has said unless they change their ways we'll have to move out of the village. It don't seem like we can pay big house rent out of what we make. It's just lately they've took to runnin' around and if you'll talk to 'em and reason with 'em maybe you can get 'em to give up their life of sin.'

"I went and talked with them girls, both of 'em nice-lookin' girls—and they promised to come to church. They haven't been there yet. About two weeks later the old man and woman come back and asked me if I'd try to persuade the super to let 'em stay in their house. So I went to him and stated my business and his answer was, 'What can you do with the girls?' I told him I could go once more and read the Bible to 'em and pray with 'em but he said he thought it was too late. They moved out of the village a week after Christmas.

"Now, I'm not one to be hard on folks that goes astray because I know the flesh is weak. I'd do all I could to help a fallen brother. back on the straight and narrow path, but so many folks, sister, is just too willin' to give 'em a kick to send 'em deeper into sin. You take me, I'm a strong healthy man, full of blood, just full of blood, never been sick a day in my life, feel good all the time. Well, Mother, she's a weakly woman, and a pastor meets all kinds of folks, them up in society and them out of society. Sister, I resists temptation every day of my life, but I don't believe in bein' too hard on them that hasn't had enough grace to stand firm. A pastor's life ain't an easy one, but we've been rewarded for all the sacrifices we've ever made for the Kingdom.

"Forty dollars a week may sound like a right smart money but it ain't so much for a pastor. He's got more expense than a laborin' man. He's got to be dressed up. Who wants his pastor goin' around lookin' like a hobo? I've said lots of times I'd like to sit around home in my overalls but it wouldn't do. I've got to have three suits cleaned a week and then these shirts costs me sixteen cents apiece to have 'em done up. Mother, she's not able to wash and iron."

The loud buzzing sound of the doorbell broke the silence and David Brown got up to answer the door. . . . "Come in, Sister Michael, come in, Brother Michael. Right on in here by the fire."

After introductions Mr. and Mrs. Michael seated themselves on the couch. "He come down to build a fire in the church," the woman explained, "and we thought we'd just stop by till time for choir practice."

"Glad you come, Sister Michael, glad you come," the preacher assured her. "I reckin you'll use the new songbooks tonight, Brother Michael?"

"Yes, I guess we will."

"Fine, fine. You'll see that they're gathered up afterwards and put in my study, won't you, Brother Michael?"

"I'll 'tend to that."

"Brother Michael is sure a big help to a pastor. We've got as fine a congregation as you'll find anywhere here at White Oak. Generous-hearted people. How is the collection for pastor's expense to the Association comin' along, Brother Michael?"

"A little slower'n it was this time last year, preacher. Course, the cut last summer has put most members behind. Then, we've had a lot of poundin's lately, besides the money we had to raise for the songbooks."

The preacher smiled and looked at Brother Michael. "The White Oak Baptists will come across, though. They've never failed us yet, not a single time. We reap so much from the Association and we try to bring the benefits home to our people. The White Oak Baptists likes to keep up with the times."

Ida L. Moore

When a Man Believes

RUDD, NORTH CAROLINA, 1939

I come to the crossroads when I was eighteen
and I took the road that led me to the mill.
I came to the crossroads again when I was fifty-one and
I took the road that caused me to be kicked out of the mill.

"I come to the crossroads when I was eighteen and I took the road that led me to the mill. I came to the crossroads again when I was fifty-one and I took the road that caused me to be kicked out of the mill and onto the farm again. There's always been a question in my mind about the first choice. I've never had no doubt about the second one."

James Edmonds's, voice, gentle and dispassionate, was in keeping with the serene expression of his face. We sat before a big, blazing fire in the freshly papered room of the five-room tenant house in which he and his family live. The cheery, flowered wallpaper minimized to some extent the drabness of the furniture. There was a wardrobe, an old iron bed, a machine, and the two chairs which we occupied.

James and his family had moved, he'd told me soon after my arrival, only three weeks before, and they had been busy painting the interior . . . of the house and papering the remainder. It was, he'd said, the best-built house they'd lived in since his return to the farm, but the inside was in bad shape. He and his wife had been at work all morning painting the back room, but soon after dinner Lottie had gone to see their son Percy and his wife who lived about a mile down the road.

I sat there now waiting for James Edmonds to speak again. He reached for the poker and shifted one of the glowing poplar logs to the back of the fireplace and dragged two smaller oak ones to the front. He was tall and lean, with closely cropped grey hair, and as he bent over the fireplace he seemed to be both more than and less than his age. His body moved with the slowness of accumulated years while his face in the firelight looked for the moment younger than the actual number of years he'd lived. His mind, it seemed, had approached a thought which he intended to express, and when he straightened himself in his chair he began at once to speak.

"You said you'd like for me to tell you the story of my life," he remarked. "It's been, I'd say, the story of a pore man's life, any pore man who can't help believing in equal justice for all men, and in trying to live by that the best he knows how, begins to question the ways of the rich man toward him and others of his kind. . . .

"The branch of the Edmonds family that I belong to started in North Carolina with Dr. Fed Edmonds about thirty years before the Civil War. Dr. Fed, my grandfather, was educated in England for a doctor and, as the story has been told to me, was sent to Turkey by the government to oppose Mohammedanism. I'm not a educated man, and why the English government would've sent him to oppose the religion they had in Turkey is something I'm not informed enough to talk about. But it turned out that Dr. Fed hadn't been in Turkey long before he was converted to the religion he'd went to oppose. He left Turkey—I've heard it said he had to leave—got together his savings and with his brother come to the United States. Both brothers bought up big sections of land in Richmond County, North Carolina, and also slaves for working it. Later Dr. Fed sold out his part of the land and moved to Halifax County. He owned thirty-two slaves at the time he come under the influence of George Fox's Quaker teachings. He begun to feel that slavery was wrong, and as the years went by he started freeing his slaves. He had freed all except four by the time the war broke out. He let the ones that wanted to stay on in their quarters and done what he could to help them get started in any sort of work they could make a living at. One of his slaves had accumulated before he died what you might call a pore man's fortune. He learned to make mats and rugs out of cornshucks, weaving them into special designs and coloring them, too. About ten years after the war he bought him a house and fifty acres of land. In crop times Dr. Fed hired some of his freed slaves for day laborers, paying them what was considered a pretty fair wage.

"My grandfather and his two oldest sons enlisted on the Confederate side soon after the war started. One of the sons was a captain, and Dr. Fed served as a doctor. My father then was about sixteen years old, and he stayed at home to look after my grand-mother and the children. Dr. Fed took the yellow fever during the third year of the war and died. One of the boys was killed not so long after that. Captain Jack come home at the end of the war, but he was never a steady hand at managing. The burden still rested on Pa, and he put off marriage until he was thirty.

"Ma was the daughter of Dr. John Franklin of Nash County. I owe what little schooling I have to Ma. I never went to a day of public school in my life. But Pa was sick even before Ma died—she died when I was thirteen—and I had to spend most of my time in the field. Brother Elisha, two years older than me, was always delicate and couldn't do no work, so Ma spent lots of time teaching him.

"My grandmother give Pa seventy-five acres of land when he married, and he never was able to add any to it. Times had been so hard right after the war that Grandma had had to sell off about half of her land to take care of first one expense and then another. So that seventy-five acres was all Pa ever got out of the estate, and at that he got more than the others because he'd stayed at home and looked after the farm after they was married. There was eight children in all.

"When Ma died I was already just about managing our farm because Pa was in bed most of the time, sick with a head trouble he'd had all of his life. When I was eighteen Pa died and that left me with my first real big decision to make.

"While Pa hadn't been able to help none with the work, it'd been worth a lot to me to know he was there to give me advice. Brother Elisha had left home the year before to study for the ministry under Aunt Maude's husband, a Methodist preacher. Now my sister Marthy was twenty and as fine a girl as you'll ever find. She worked side by side with me in the field and turned off a day's work a man needn't to've been ashamed of. But it was hard on her, awfully hard. Virginia, she was the next after me and sixteen when Pa died. She worked in the field, but she hated it. There was three other girls, fourteen, eleven, and seven.

"Aunt Maude come from Rockingham to see us when Pa died and she said, 'James, you can't raise these girls on a farm. The best thing you can do is to take them to a cotton mill where they can find work light enough for a woman to do.' Aunt Maude didn't have any children then, and I sorta felt that she was trying to make plans for us before somebody asked her if she was going to keep one or two of the younger girls. Marthy and Virginia both said they thought Aunt Maude was right, the mill was the best place for all of us.

"But I did hate to leave the farm. I went in to Enfield and talked with Robert Thomas, the county superintendent of education, and one of the best friends Pa ever had. He said, 'Boy, don't you let your womenfolks persuade you to leave your place. If Marthy and Virginia are wanting to move to town so bad, let them try the mill to see how they like it. They'll likely be back before you get ready to plant corn in the spring. The mill's no place for you and your sisters.'

"I went home that night well determined to stay on the farm, but Aunt Maude and the girls hadn't changed their minds a bit. First thing I knew, Aunt Maude had me on my way to Burlington to get jobs for me and the two oldest girls. Her husband had preached at the mill church there, and she thought I'd have a pretty good chance to get on. Two weeks later I'd done rented the farm and moved the family to Burlington. About the time we got settled, Brother Elisha come to us on a visit, and while he was with us taken pneumonia and died. He would've made a good preacher, Elisha would. One of the best speakers I ever heard.

"We stayed at Burlington three years and moved from there to Proximity. We'd been at Proximity about a year when it come to me for the first time with full force that my lot for the rest of my life would probably be with cotton mill people. And I begun to wonder if there was any way I could work with the people about me and together improve ourselves and our lot in life. I was ignorant and I felt it, but there was so many worse off than I was. A large part of the cotton mill people of that day had come up through poverty and ignorance, and they took without much complaint whatever was handed out to them.

"I'd started keeping company with Lottie then, and she'd tell me how she used to go to the mill of a early morning when she was just nine years old. She'd gone through the second grade at school.

"We was married in 1904, and the two youngest sisters lived on in the house with us till they was married themselves. Elizabeth, the youngest one, married the same year our second boy was born.

"It seemed about this time that the company was beginning to take a special interest in how its people lived.* They put up a wel-

*Around 1910, many Southern mills started or expanded their employee welfare programs, which included schools, libraries, recreational facilities, and company-paid welfare workers. All of this was a form of benevolent paternalism. It was also a "business necessity to begin at the bottom with day nurseries, kindergartens, pri-

fare building and they started having welfare meetings. The owners and boss men was to meet with representatives of the people and discuss different ways of improvement. A member of the program committee come to me one day and said they wanted me to make a talk at one of the meetings. I told him I'd never done such a thing in my life and I knowed nothing to speak on. He said, 'We've got you down for gardening and I know you can talk on that. You have about the prettiest garden in the village.'

"That subject suited me all right enough, because I felt like I did know a little something about gardening. When my time come to speak, I got up and told the audience how I managed to have vegetables for a good many months of the year, giving them instructions on my way of raising certain vegetables. I finished up my garden talk by saying I didn't see how me and my family could live on the wages I made if we didn't raise part of what we ate. That brought on two or three little coughing spells out in the audience, and after stopping for just a moment I said I had a right sad story to tell and I hoped the chairman of the meeting wouldn't mind giving me just a few more minutes. 'It's my understanding,' I begun, 'that these meetings are going to be held for the welfare of the people as well as for the advancement of the company. It would seem to be right helpful if from time to time we'd bring up special cases we happen to know about where the people are having a hard time getting along. I've got in mind a family I'd like to tell you about. I don't see Mr. Cone* here tonight'—he was setting on the third row back—'but I'm sure if he knew the condition of this family he'd set to work tomorrow to relieve their plight. It's just such circumstances that our foreign missionaries comes home to tell us they've found in China and to ask us to give a little more of our wage to help the Chinese to a better way of living.

" 'In this family I'm speaking of there's ten children, the mother, and the father, all living on the man's wages which is ninety cents a day. If he was a Chinaman he could probably buy his crowd enough rice to keep them from being hungry. I believe it's such things as these that Mr. Cone would like to know about and it's our duty to tell him.'

---

mary departments, [a] . . . nursing and medical department if we were ever to develop a nucleus of capable and efficient workers" (H. R. Fitzgerald, president of Riverside and Dan River cotton mills, to W. D. Anderson, Bibb Manufacturing Co., 1928, quoted in Robert Sidney Smith, *Mill on the Dan: A History of Dan River Mills, 1882–1950* [Durham, N.C.: Duke University Press, 1960], p. 242).

*Caesar Cone. See also the life history, "There's Always a Judas," pp. 157–69.

"I set down and never did let my eyes turn to Mr. Cone. Two or three others made talks, and then the chairman got up to say that we'd all be glad to have a few words from Mr. Cone. Mr. Cone stood up in his place down there on the third row and after a few remarks on how much he'd enjoyed the meeting asked all the speakers to remain for a few minutes. We had friendly chats amongst ourselves, and Mr. Cone complimented all of us on our speeches. He turned to me after awhile and said, 'Mr. Edmonds, you're right, I didn't know there was a family in the village in the circumstances you described. If you'll bring the man to my office tomorrow we'll see what we can do about it. Tell your overseer I said not to knock off any of your pay for the time you lose.' I thanked him and told him I'd bring Mr. Taylor around ten o'clock if that suited him.

"Mr. Taylor was pretty nervous when I first told him Mr. Cone wanted to see him, but after awhile I convinced him it was for his own good. He was the kind of fellow that had a sort of whipped-dog look about him and was awful uncomfortable always when he was around anybody wearing good clothes. After awhile though he loosened up, and told Mr. Cone that his wife hadn't had a pair of shoes in two years, and lots of times his children went to sleep crying because they was hungry. When he'd finished, Mr. Cone said, 'That's too bad, Mr. Taylor, and I'm going to give you, just give you, because I'm already paying you as much as your work is worth, twenty-five cents a day more than you are making. It'll be added to your pay every week, and the one demand I make of you is that you don't let this get out. There'd be dozens of others not needing help who'd come and ask for it.' Of course Mr. Taylor made the promise not to tell and so far as I know he kept it. Gift or not, I was glad then to see them little children have a little more food.

"It was a good many years before the welfare committee asked me to speak again, but I was right active in church and prayer-meeting work. I've always believed in the good of prayer. It used to help me when I first started my labor-union work and was accused of knocking religion, to remember the family prayers Pa always held twice a day. No matter how fast the grass growed in the fields we took time to read the Bible and pray and sing. Pa was a fine singing master, and before he got sick he could sing the old hymns so that anybody would feel better after hearing them.

"It was about 1911, I believe, when I made a talk at prayer meeting that sorta threatened my job. I got up and said, 'Brothers and sisters, I've got a true story to tell that I hope will make all of us feel shame that it happened in our community. It's too late for us to help the old people I'm going to tell you about but I pray God we won't set by without saying a word if it happens amongst us again. There was a old man lived three houses down from me that went to sleep on his job the other night. It was careless . . . [of] him but he was getting old. The weather was awful raw so when he set down by a good warm fire he went to sleep. He's been called one of the faithful ones, and for three or four years he's been night watchman at our boss's home. He was found alseep on the job and fired right then. The deputy sheriff come out the next day and ordered him to move. He did, because he knowed what would happen if he didn't. But it was one of the most pitiful movings I've ever seen. His wife hadn't been able to walk for over six months, and her neighbors took her to the streetcar in a rocking chair. They took her off the streetcar and put her on the train. They'd bought their tickets to Altamahaw where the old man hoped to get some sort of job. Word come back the other day that the old woman was dead. Something's wrong with a community, brothers and sisters, when a thing like that can happen in it.'

"I saw heads bowed but nobody said a word.

"The next day the superintendent of the mill sent for me. He warned me that if I wasn't careful how I talked I was liable to lose my job. I said, 'Mr. Cromer, before you get ready to fire me, maybe you'd better try to recollect where you was and who you was with two weeks ago last Friday night. Maybe you know I've been holding cottage prayer meeting around in different homes in the village, and that particular night I mentioned I passed by a house where the man of the house is night watchman around the mill. Some husbands are awful jealous.'

"He was surely one confused man. He turned right red and sputtered awhile and then said, 'Keep your mouth shut about me. Nobody's thought of taking your job away.' He didn't tell me, though, to stop talking in prayer meeting. I hated to have to use that threat on him but it seemed like the only thing to do was to hand out threat for threat.

"I was busy in these days working as hard as I could in the mill and doing what odd jobs I could find. The farm had already been sold, and the little money divided amongst the children. I started me a bank account with my small sum and added to it whenever I could. Me and Lottie together raised all the vegetables we needed in the summertime and had some to sell to the store besides. The mill wasn't crowded with help and nearly every week I got to put in extra time. We was managing to get along right well in a plain simple sort of way, me and Lottie and the three children—we have nine now but then there was just Percy, Henry, and Ruth—but somehow I could never be unmindful of the folks around me that was having life a lot harder than us. Percy had started to school, and it done me good every time he brought in a report card. I hoped then all my children would get a pretty fair education, and I wanted all cotton mill children to have a chance to go to school.

"It was along then that talk started in our city about a compulsory school law. From the first minute I heard about it I was for it. I felt that if laboring people ever bettered their lot it would be when the most of them had got a little common schooling. Mr. Cone called a meeting to find out what the people thought about such a law and I was asked to come to the meeting. Most of the representatives that had been chosen was advised before time to vote against it. Nobody come to me.

"That night the run of the talk was against the law. One man would say mill folks wasn't able to buy clothes and books for their children. Pore folks couldn't keep their children in school until they was fourteen. Another would get up and say about the same thing. Mr. Cone talked, not ever coming out and knocking education but knocking any sort of compulsory school law. Along toward the last my turn come.

"As soon as I got on my feet I said I wanted everybody to know I was for a compulsory law and would support any candidate that came out on that platform. I turned to Mr. Cone and said, 'Our leader here, the president of the mill where we all work, can tell you that one of the greatest blessings on earth is a education. He knows that if his father hadn't made any effort to send him to school he might be where he couldn't buy shoes and books for his children. He's a just and a reasonable man, and if the question was asked him whether the people in his mills would have to work for what they do if they was educated I'm sure he'd answer, "Of course they wouldn't." Once the people are educated, they'll have a little something to say about their wages and they won't have to say, "We won't send our children to school because we've got no money to buy them books." Gentlemen, I'm going to be for the compulsory school law whenever it comes up.'

"After the meeting was over Mr. Cone come to me and chatted a while. He said, 'Mr. Edmonds, you expressed yourself right plain tonight and that's nothing against you. If that's your opinion, you have a right to it.' I answered 'Thank you, Mr. Cone, and in all due respects to you that's exactly how I feel about it.'"

James Edmonds turned to me. "Maybe you're getting tired of hearing about these different meetings?"

"Not at all." . . .

"Well, I've been telling them to you so you could see I didn't up and join the labor union in 1930 on the spur of the moment. I'd been thinking for a long time on the rights of the working man, trying in my ignorant way to point out whenever I could that his life was as sacred to him as a rich man's life is to him.

"My two oldest boys had went to work after they finished the ninth grade and that made it easier for me to save more money. There was weeks in the summertime when I put my whole pay in the bank. I was saving to build a home.

"In 1922 we built our house, a pretty six-room cottage costing $3,200. We moved in it and lived for two years. Then I decided to move back to the village—we was working at White Oak then—and take the rent money I could get out of my house to pay for some improvements on the place. I rented it to a young fellow that was just getting married. He wanted everything nice for his bride, and he said if I'd buy the varnish for the woodwork inside he'd put it on himself.

"He built a fire to keep the room warm while he worked, and it was still burning when he went home that evening. He left a can of varnish on the hearth and that night about eight o'clock my house went up in flames. All my life savings lost in a few minutes' time. It was awful hard to get over.

"One bad break seemed to follow another all through 1924. About two months after the house burned, I was in the hospital for seven weeks, making a bill of $350. In all I was out of the mill for three months. Late in the year my father-in-law was killed in a automobile wreck, and his burial cost me $150. I was glad to see 1925 come in.

"But 1925 didn't bring much promise. It was to be my lot in that year to raise my voice against what I think is one of the most inhuman things that ever hit any industry. Hundreds of folks go to jail every year and spend the best part of their lives there for doing things not half as harmful to their fellow man as the stretch-out*. The Cone Company was one of the first in the country to begin it.

*See pp. 119–20.

The handwriting was on the wall early in the year, but it didn't reach a showdown till June.

"They'd got hold of a idea somewhere that the looms run faster and made better cloth if the weave room was kept at a awful high temperature. So all the time that they kept making the work load heavier they kept running the thermometer higher. One snowy day in January the thermometer went to 104. I couldn't stand it myself so I raised two or three windows. About the time I got them raised and before the thermometer had had time to drop, the superintendent come through. He yelled out, 'Who raised them windows?' I told him I done it and why I'd done it. He said, 'You can work in here with the windows down or you can get out.' 'If I do get out,' I answered, 'I won't stop this side of Raleigh. We may be pore working folks without much way of helping ourselves but I believe there's enough people in North Carolina in high places to object to men and women working like we are working in a temperature of 104.' 'It's not that hot in here,' he said, mopping his forehead with his handkerchief. 'Look behind you at that thermometer,' I said. 'When you reduce the steam in here, I'll pull down the windows.'

"He took one look at the thermometer, muttered something, and went out. After a while I could tell the steam had been cut down and I pulled down the windows. You see, lady, I had seen women, one of them my own daughter, going all day long in that unbearable heat with their clothes stuck to their bodies like they had been dipped in a pool of water. Going up and down their alleys weeping, working, all day long, and though the company was gaining from the stretch-out by saving in wages it wasn't gaining a thing by using such awful heat. I've wove enough to know that cloth makes better with the temperature at 90 than it does when it's at 104.

"When all the reorganization had finally took place, every fourth weaver had lost his job.

"They did add battery fillers for the weavers, mostly young boys and girls, and that brought the number back up to where they was working just one third less people than before. But they had created more of what they called unskilled jobs with low pay. Battery filling is one of the easiest jobs in the mill to learn, I reckon, but one of the hardest on you physically. The continual bending of your body and the heavy load of filling you have to carry around in a apron makes it awful unpleasant work. A child can learn it, but it soon gets the best of a child.

"Now in June I was making a pretty fair wage. I had so far as I was concerned myself something to be thankful for. I had been kept, while the fellow next to me had been dropped. My work had been doubled up on me but I had the physical strength to stand it. But there was plenty about me that didn't. Day after day, weeping women had come to me and said, 'We've heard you in prayer meeting, we've believed in you. Surely there's something somebody can do for us. We cannot stand the load they've put on us. Won't you try to think of some way to save us?'

"My mind was already thinking. It wasn't a pleasant sight to see my own daughter coming home worn to a frazzle. It was enough to keep a man awake at night to remember the two men that had broke under the strain and had to be took away to Morganton.* And it seemed to me that I could look out there in the years and see the awful misery ahead for working people. Thousands throwed out of jobs and the rest drove like machines till they died before their life was half over. When they was gone there'd be plenty others to take their place, young folks with hopes for living to be ground out until they had no life left, just to feed the selfishness and greed of people in power. And to me then the saddest part of it all was that the people, because of their lot in life, was too ignorant to protect themselves from what was being forced on them. It was like taking advantage of a child. I knew what a man was up against if he tried to point out some sort of way. I felt awful ignorant and not big enough for the job. But I had seen all I could stand.

"I organized the weavers and set the day for a protest. Every man, woman, and child in the weave room promised to stick by me. On Tuesday morning we went to our jobs. The overseer come around at seven minutes to seven. I had give him a little hint the day before of what we was planning so he could warn the superintendent and the general manager and have them down early. He pulled out his watch, looked at it and said, 'All right, let's get things to going.' He was awful nervous. Somebody yelled out, 'We will when seven o'clock comes.' He rushed on out of the weave room and got back just as we started marching out two by two, women first and the men following. The crowd went out and took their place between the mill door and the gate. Pretty soon the overseer and Mr. Gordon, the general manager, and Mr. Hopkins, the superintendent, come out. Mr. Gordon said, just like I'd ex-

*Location of the state mental hospital.

pected him to, for us to go back to our jobs or to go home. He was right well excited.

"I said, 'Mr. Gordon, there's no cause to be excited, because we're not after violence unless it's forced on us. We stand before you unarmed except with a awful determination to have adjustments made in our work so's we'll again feel like free humans living in a free country. We mean to stand here, though, in this mill yard until a promise of adjustments is made. Every man, woman, and child is pledged to defend his job at the cost of his life. We hate violence but we hate slavery worse. To work under the stretch-out system is the same as committing suicide, and we've made up our minds not to do it. But our jobs is not to be taken away from us. We mean to defend them if necessary until our blood runs down the streets of White Oak. It's your time to speak.'

"The crowd set to clapping and yelling. Mr. Gordon was so mad that he wanted to curse us all, but he wasn't a fool. He tried to be reasonable. He said it had been necessary to cut wages or to use the system they had worked out. I had expected him to say that. I pulled out of my pocket a copy of the *Greensboro Daily News*. Then I turned to the crowd and spoke. 'Mr. Gordon tells us it was necessary for him to give us a job and a half to keep from cutting our wages. And he surely must think he has reason for saying what he did. There's lots of things I don't understand and, being a ignorant man, I have to learn the little I know from the newspapers. In our daily paper here I see that according to the quotations of the New York market cotton has went down \$5 a bale and the price of denim has increased 2 percent. Maybe Mr. Gordon is right when he says the stretch-out had to come.'

"Mr. Gordon looked at Frank Hopkins but didn't get any encouragement. Finally he said, 'Maybe cotton has gone down \$5 a bale, but we're not using cotton bought at that price. We already had enough for two or three months on hand.'

"'But, Mr. Hopkins,' I said, 'that don't change the point that denim's gone up 2 percent.'

"The crowd give out another loud yell at that, and somehow it come so unexpected, Mr. Gordon jumped. I really think he was afraid somebody was going to hit him in the head with a rock, but I knew the crowd wasn't going to use violence unless force was first used against them. When Mr. Gordon spoke it was to promise the people that if they'd go back to their jobs and finish out the week the proper adjustments would be made by Monday.

"The people said they would but there would be trouble if they was double-crossed. We went back to work Monday on the same schedule we'd had before the stretch-out."

James Edmonds reached for an oak log and threw it on the fire. He looked out of the window toward the road which ran by the house. "I see my youngest daughter and my little grandson, my oldest daughter's child, coming," he said. "They're a little later than usual getting home from school. Maybelle finishes high school this year. James is in the fifth grade. His father was one of the men that had to go to Morganton."

A dark-eyed, rosy-cheeked youngster ran into the room and emptied an armful of books, both his and Maybelle's, onto the bed. "Grandpa, me and Maybelle's going to Uncle Percy's," he said. "Grandma said we could come after school."

"All right, young fellow," James Edmonds replied. "Can't you speak to the lady?"

Young James gave a hurried nod in my direction and rushed out of the room.

"His father was a awful good man," James Edmonds said, "but he never did have overly much physical strength. He'd always held out mighty well, though, till the extra work was put on him.

"We had won a victory in our first protest against the stretch-out, but I wasn't so sure it was a victory that would last. It wasn't long until men started coming to the mill, mostly from the North, I think, and they'd try out a new piece of machinery they'd had sent, or they would work at speeding up a few of the old type machinery. The fastest weaver would be put on a machine and his work would be timed. That went on for about two years and by 1928 they'd gradually turned off about one-fourth of the weavers again. Another stretch-out had been put over on us but so gradual that folks didn't get aroused. Through 1929 they added a little more work to each man's daily task.

"As I think back over it now, it seems the craziest sort of thing that people in the South has raised such a fuss about labor organizers coming from the North. They've called it meddling from outsiders, but the very folks that's done the complaining has never once thought anything was wrong with getting experts from the North to figure out a system for Southern labor that's actually killed men and women by the hundreds and throwed others out of work that had families looking to them for bread—little children and women with no food, no clothes, and no shelter. There's always a crowd to holler foreign influence when labor makes a move. But wasn't the fellow that worked out the stretch-out some sort of foreigner? Him that was going to be a sort of campaign manager for the Duke of Windsor on his intended trip to America. It looks like such ideas as his wouldn't pass unnoticed if the leaders was really interested in keeping what they call the American way of living.

"A bunch of us, that realized the stretch-out hadn't been took half as far as the company meant to take it, got together to try to think of some way to help ourselves before it was too late. We decided to write to William Greene, president of the Federation of Labor,* and ask him if he'd send a representative to Greensboro to tell us about ways and means of organizing. They asked me to write the letter, and I did.

"Mr. Greene sent a representative and I signed my union card on March 1, 1930. Sometime in May I was elected president of the local, and my son Percy was elected secretary.

"Now and then talk reached my ears that I was being accused by company officials of being the cause of the union organizing in Greensboro. We was getting members pretty fast and I begin to have hopes that we'd soon be strong enough to check the stretch-out. On June 20 as I walked out of the mill at quitting time I was handed a little yellow slip. As each member of my family come out, they was give the same. The slips meant we'd all been fired.

"I waited a few days trying to think what was the best thing to do and then I went to Frank Hopkins. Frank was expecting me, I think, and he hated to see me coming. Me and Frank had run together a right smart when I first come to Proximity as a young man, done a lot of courting together, in fact. When I asked him why me and my family had been fired he stalled around for awhile, doing some talk about the company having to cut down on the number of employees.

"'Frank,' I said, 'we've knowed one another long enough to be honest. Why don't you come out and tell me why I was fired? You know that as far as work goes the Edmonds family has always been rated amongst the best workmen you've got. It ain't likely that when a company gets ready to cut down on its employees it starts with them whose work it's always liked.'

"Frank twisted his watch chain a minute while he looked down at the floor in a deep study. Finally he turned toward me. 'James,

*The American Federation of Labor (AFL), now the AFL-CIO. See F. Ray Marshall, *Labor in the South* (Cambridge, Mass.: Harvard University Press, 1967), chaps. 7, 11.

there's just one thing you have to do to get your job back,' he said. 'I can't tell you what it is but you ought to know.'

" 'I think I know what you mean,' I told Frank. 'If I'll write a little piece for the *Textorion*,* the voice of the people, saying that I don't believe what I do believe, that I'm sorry I ever joined the union, that I think it would be impossible for a company to be better to its help, that no person to my knowing is overloaded with work in the mill, if I'd write them things I could get my job back, couldn't I, Frank? I want to go back to work; I don't know what's to become of me if I don't, but if I go it'll be as a free man. It ain't pride or stubbornness that makes me hold out, it's a feeling that I'd rather starve to death than sell my soul for bread. I've had my moving orders, but I felt like maybe I could come to you and you'd try to do something about it.'

"I felt sorry for Frank. I knew he hated to be put in the place he was in. 'There's nothing I can do for you, James,' he said. 'I get my orders from higher up.'

"We found a house at Hamtown, about two miles out from White Oak. Henry and Percy and their families moved in with us because we all knew we had to be as saving as we could with the little bit of money we had. It might be a long time before any of us had a job again.

"It seemed to me I'd never have a better time for working to organize the people. I had no job to lose and I'd have time for a while to give to the union. We held open-air meetings, and they begun to draw large crowds. Gorman† came down and spoke, though his speech was too radical to do much good. What he said was true, but the people wasn't ready to accept it. A man can't change overnight a whole lifetime of thinking.

"The company started using the *Textorion* for all it was worth to poke fun at the union. One week they had a cartoon showing a man with a empty pitcher in his hand trying to pour something from it into a glass. The pitcher stood for the union. They talked it around that the man in the cartoon was me, and it did look a little bit like me. Right under the cartoon was a editorial saying that the devil tried at one time to organize a union in heaven and was kicked out.

"We had a meeting scheduled for Sunday evening. It turned out

*The company newsletter.
†Francis J. Gorman, vice-president of the United Textile Workers. The moribund union revived in the early 1930s, led the dramatic, but abortive general textile strike in the South in 1934, and then stagnated again.

to be one of the biggest we ever had. People from every walk of life in Greensboro was beginning to be curious about the union, and they had come out to listen. I built my little speech around that article in the *Textorion*. I said if the textile companies wanted to start the practice of settling their disputes with labor by the Bible I was with them 100 percent. But I wasn't for taking a part of it, such as, 'Servants, obey your masters,' a favorite text with preachers who stood in well with the company, to prove that a Christian oughtn't to protest when his bread was being taken out of his mouth. And as for the Devil and his union, I said, that 'according to Scripture the Devil had attempted to break the union and was kicked out and that he was at work in the world today trying to break the union of peace and brotherly love.'

"We had hundreds to come up after the meeting to sign their cards. In a few months we had signed up 94 percent of the people working for the Cone Mills. I was a happy man because I could see a little light ahead for the cotton mill people.

"The company, of course, hadn't been sleeping. It had done everything in its power to check us and finally used the one sure way of winning. Word was circulated around that every person who wouldn't disclaim the union would lose his job, and if the worst came to worst the Cones would close down their mills because they had enough money to live on anyway. So when they finally started questioning the people, they went to them one by one, and in their talking give them the impression that the most of the folks had already disclaimed the union. The people got confused and scared; they had no way of knowing how most of the rest was standing. They begin to reason, 'What good will it do me to stick by my word unless the rest stick by theirs? My job is threatened, the job that means bread for my family.' So, one by one, they give in, and all day long they come in groups of twenty, twenty-five, thirty led by a overseer, or sometimes by a preacher who'd stand witness they'd drawn out of the union.

"Now, I've never had any mean, bitter feeling for them people, because I could understand what they was up against. My own son Henry hadn't been able to stand by his convictions. He had a wife who was complaining of the trouble he'd got them into, he had two little children. One day he called up Mr. Cone and told him he wanted to come to see him, he was ready to retract everything he'd said about the company. Henry wrote a piece for the *Textorion* saying all the things he had to say to get back his job. It was a great victory for the Cones. He's left the mill now and has him a good job as policeman uptown.

"I never talked to Percy about sticking but I knew he would. Percy is that way. He just ain't the kind of man who can put any job above his self-respect. I think he'll get to be a fairly good farmer some day. He's managing to clothe and feed his family in a plain way.

"There was seventy families in all that wouldn't disclaim the union. They stayed in their houses until the law come and throwed their things out on the street.

"If I tried to tell you just a little part of what them people suffered, I'd be talking here until after midnight. It's as sad a story as you'll find in any book. You'll excuse me, I know, if I don't go into the particulars of what I saw the people endure.

"We still had a little money left, so I took that and bought what food I could to divide amongst them that was in the worst shape. It didn't go anywhere. I went to a wholesale place here in Greensboro and got $200 worth of beans and flour and meal and meat. I give the man a mortgage on my car as security. I would have sold the car and paid off the debt then, but I needed it to go looking for a job.

"I had a feeling that me and the seventy families had been blacklisted, but I was a good hand in any weave room, so I thought some mill might take me on because of the work I could do. I rode through South Carolina and a part of Georgia, stopping at most of the mills. Three or four times after I had talked with a superintendent and he saw I knew my work they'd be almost ready to hire me when they'd ask me my full name again. Then they'd say, 'Come back tomorrow, Mr. Edmonds, and we'll see what we can do for you.' Always when I'd go back in the morning they'd say they didn't need me. I felt like they had a list and put me off to have time to check up. So I decided to change my name. One of my ancestors had been a Thomas, so I called myself James Thomas. I stopped at a little mill in a town in South Carolina one morning, talked to the superintendent, and he told me to come back that evening before five o'clock and he'd let me know if he could use me. I did and got the job. He told me to report for work next morning. At nine o'clock the next morning I was halfway to Greensboro, satisfied in my own mind they had me blacklisted.

"I sold my car and Percy sold his. We bought us enough staple groceries to last us seven or eight months, bought a mule and a plough, paid off the $200 debt, and rented us a little farm.

"The winter was awful hard on us, but when spring come and we got some crops planted things looked brighter. The crops growed off well, and we was beginning to have a little hope, when the mule took sick and died. The neighboring farmers was awful good to us, though, and first one and then another let us have the use of a mule. We've had more tough times since then and it's still not easy. But last year we raised fair crops and this year we've got the best place we've had yet. I'd like awful well to buy this place but of course I never will. I hope, though, if the place is good as I think it is we can keep on renting it year after year.

"I like farming but I wish I could have come back to it in a different way. I'm still good at gardening and in the summertime I sell a lot of vegetables to the company store. They seem to like my vegetables. They won't let me work in the mill so I'll just tend my little farm and raise something to eat for them that do.

"Though I'm not taking any active part in [the] union now I still have a interest in what it's doing. And I've got hopes that in not so many years the laboring man will actually have justice, he'll no longer be a pore creature that will bow his head and not open his mouth when a manufacturer says, 'You'll do what we tell you, you'll shut your mind up and let us think for you, or we'll starve you to death.' Labor has been stirred and it's going to think through. There might be violence; that depends altogether on the capitalist. Labor don't want to own the property, as some seems to think. It just wants a fair return of what it produces in the form of wages. I hope the labor laws passed by the New Deal administration will work out like they was intended. It's foolish to set back and say that nothing could happen in our country to bring on a revolution.

"I had a belief that's the strongest kind of religion, and I was called on to pay the price for it. They almost starved me out, but they didn't change my way of thinking. I'm still certain I took the right road back there in 1930. Peace inside is worth a whole lot to a man."

Ida L. Moore

No Union for Me

. . . "That strike last summer when the mill shut down for a week was what got us behind.There's always a few to make trouble for the rest."

"Did many people join the labor union then?" I asked.

Clara laid down her scissors. The five feet two inches of her was instantly like a sentinel standing guard. "I don't know nothin' about labor unions except they cause a lot of trouble. I'm havin' nothin' to do with 'em and nothin' to say about 'em. . . .

"The first time I ever saw what labor unions done was in Danville.* . . . What was the strikers doin'? Settin' out in the bitter cold weather around fires built in the street. I didn't like the looks of it and I've had no use for the union since. And they didn't get a God's thing to eat but pinto beans, I know, because that's what the folks had where I was stayin'. No, sir, no union for me.

"The folks here at the Cone Mills ought to know to leave the unions alone. Didn't old man Caesar Cone leave it in his will— well, I reckon it was his diary—anyhow, he wrote it down—that before he'd recognize a union he'd shut down all his mills? And Julius Cone† has had it put down in black and white that he'll do

---

*She is referring to the Danville, Virginia, strike of 1930–31. The American Federation of Labor focused its efforts to organize Southern textiles on the Riverside and Dan River cotton mills, the latter then being the largest mill in the South. These efforts and the resistance of management precipitated a strike that lasted from September 1930 to January 1931. See Robert Sidney Smith, *Mill on the Dan: A History of Dan River Mills, 1882–1950* (Durham, N.C.: Duke University Press, 1960), pp. 294–324.

†One of the second generation of owner-managers of Cone Mills.

the same thing. Folks can talk all they want to about their right to join a union but right don't count much when money is against you. The governmint can say it'll make the Cones let everybody that wants to join the union but the Cones is still totin' the keys to the mill. They'd be as good as their word too; they'd shut down. It wouldn't hurt them, they would live without the mills runnin'— they got millions saved up—but we couldn't. We've got to have wages to live on. . . .

"And besides . . . them Cones is awful good where big things is concerned. It wasn't long, not more'n six months, anyhow, before the cut* that they give us $14,000 on our new church. Yessir, all we had to raise was $6,000. One of the Cones come down there and made a talk, sayin' that he knowed they was more able to give than us, and they was glad of the opportunity to help build our church. They understand it ain't easy for us to get along on what they can pay us. I've got nothin' to say against the Cones, and I'll have nothin' to do with no labor union."

From the life history, "Clara Williams"
Ida L. Moore

*Wage reduction.

The Rig-Builder

In work, outa work; outa work and in again—but mostly out.

"In work, outa work; outa work and in again—but mostly out. That's rig-building. Work a month and off six; or usually, work a day and off a month. And the wages we get, that sound so big when you talk about it, just aren't enough to keep a man's stomach hooked on the rest of him. And that goes double when he's got a family.

"When I first started in the oil business, the little towns out on the prairies were all on the boom, and if there wasn't a town, the companies made one. Oil was high, and it looked like it was going higher all the time, and we'd all be millionaires. I had a brother-in-law at Drop Right, the little boom camp on the Canadian River that they later named Markham. There isn't anything there now to mark the town but some greasy lumber that the natives haven't hauled off yet for firewood.

"I was fourteen when I went there; that was in 1915. I went there on a vacation, while school was out, but I got tired of lazing 'round my brother-in-law's house and went out in the field. I was big and husky, so I tried for a job on a casing crew and got it. Men were scarce then, and I got a job the first place I tried. It was on six-inch casing crew, wet casing. And that's hell. We had to pull the casing, or lower it, while the well was flowing, and oil soaked us from hair to toenails. We looked like we'd been painted kind of greenish-black, we always had so much oil on us. And if there was salt water flowing too, and we had cuts any place on our body, that salt water got in the cuts and made festers, big sores that stayed for weeks.

"I always managed to get in about four days a week, and could have got in more if I'd wanted 'em. They paid us $10 a string, damned good money then or now. I worked at that for six months or so and quit; I had too much money. Before I went to Drop Right, I'd worked in the cotton fields, chopping cotton, for fifty cents a day; and what I'd managed to save out of working on the casing crew was more'n I'd of made working in a year in the cotton fields. And I hadn't saved much either.

"I went on home and went to school a while longer. Then my brother-in-law got a job as a rig contractor at Drop Right, and wrote me I could have a job if I wanted it and could stand up to the work. That last part made me kind of hot, thinking I couldn't take it, so I lit out for there again. I was fifteen, but looked a lot older.

"I only made $5 a day running rigs, but that was still a lot of money to a kid. I worked on till that fall, and then both of us lost our jobs. My brother-in-law left for another boom, but I had to go on back home and school. The next fall I went down to Yale, another boom field, and got a job running rigs at $3.50 a day. I worked there almost a year, and then when I heard my brother-in-law was contracting rigs at Covington, I lit out for there and went to work for him.

"I got hurt for the first time up there at Covington. Working on those wooden rigs we had to lay them out—saw the wood right there on the lease ourselves—and then put them up. I was using an adze to carve out a walking-beam—the part of a rig that moved up and down; you've seen a thousand of 'em—and the adze hit a chip of wood and bounced off. The blade went clean through the leaders and tendons in my left leg, through the back part of it, right back of the ankle.

"I set down and grabbed it, holding my knee up as close to my chest as I could get it, and trying to stop the blood. Everybody quit work and run over there. The crew pusher told me not to straighten my leg out or the leaders would crawl clean up to my knee. We only had one car in the crew; they bundled me in it, and we lit out for Covington. On the way, the contractor—I wasn't working for my brother-in-law then, but for another fellow—told me that if the doctor wanted to give me ether for me not to take it, I'd be sick for a week.

"There wasn't but one doctor in the whole town, and they had to go out and round him up. I waited in his office, and finally they brought him in. The rest of the crew had come to town in buck-boards, and they crowded in the office to see it. The doctor got out his cans of ether, and started to give it to me. I told him I didn't want any. I could stand a little pain. He cussed me for being a damned fool, and I cussed him right back for being a quack. Finally he went out and got a quart of whisky and handed it to me and said to drink ever' damned drop.

"I downed all of the quart I could, and laid back on the table. The doctor put two men on each arm and each leg, and then he cut my calf open. He had a pair of ordinary pliers he'd dipped in alcohol, and he took them and started reaching up there to pull the leaders down. I give a big heave and knocked all eight of those fellows clean acrost the office. The old doctor got mad and held me down on the table and poured the whisky to me. I must 've drunk all of it; I was weak anyway, from losing so much blood and the shock of seeing my leg laid open and all, and I passed out.

"They made me puke after it was all over and got me up. The old doctor had a pair of crutches in his office, and I walked out—just about an hour after we'd started. But I was still weak as a cat. You know, that old fool tied those leaders in square knots, so they couldn't slip or break, and they pulled my heel clean back against my ankle.

"I couldn't walk a step. He told me to get a wood block to use for a high heel for that foot, and every little while to shave off a piece. I did, but it was over a year before I could work again. I had to pay my own doctor bill, but the contractor paid me back later; and I had to lay off on my own time all the time I couldn't work.

"Well, just about a year after I went back to work, I was running rig at Yale, Oklahoma, and a fellow come up on the job and asked me if my name was Charlie Stone. I said yes. He said he was from the insurance company, and if I would come to Tulsa, Oklahoma, on a certain day the company would settle with me. Well, I was a damn-fool kid, and didn't even know the companies and con-tractors had to carry insurance on the men; that insurance fellow could have kept quiet and I'd never knowed any different.

"But I went on up to Tulsa, paying my own way on the train, and went up to the insurance office. The fellows in there had me walk around, lift things, and hop and skip. They said I wasn't hurt so bad, but they'd pay me off anyway.

"And do you know, those sonsuvbitches give me a check for forty-five dollars! Yessir; forty-five dollars, and I had to pay my own way up there and back! Well, if something like that happened today, I'd certainly know what to do about it! And it wouldn't be for any measly forty-five dollars, either!

"Working then was pure hell, 'specially for a kid that didn't have any sense. We had to hit a hard lick every time we raised our hands, and keep it up all day long. I've seen rig-builders piss while they was working; they didn't have time to take out to the brush, and they was so damned tired they just couldn't control themselves anyway. I've worked till my shoes would squish every step I took, with the sweat that'd run down in them. And I couldn't get my hands closed at nights; holding a rig-hatchet or a cross cut saw all day long, working with it, the muscles in my hands would get so cramped I couldn't close my fingers. I'd have to take one hand and bend the fingers down to grab something small, like a match.

"I've been pretty lucky about my hands; I don't have a blemish on them any place on the backs. But you can see the palms of 'em are so corny nothing could hurt 'em. I never had a blister on the insides of my hands in my life. One time, right after I was married, I came home and laid down on the sofa while my wife fixed supper. She woke me up picking at my hands. I didn't feel any pain at all; she'd already pulled twenty-three splinters out of one hand, and her jerking at 'em woke me up.

"Handling rough wood all day put splinters in my hands, all right, and other places too. The way they'd build a rig in those days, the rig-builders had to do everything. We dug the cellars, made the footing, sawed out the lumber for the rig, and then built it.

"When we sawed the lumber, making the rig according to the plans the contractor or company had, we called it laying out the rig. The pusher would get his orders to build a rig 22 feet wide at the bottom, say, and maybe 5 feet, 2 inches at the top, which was, say, 72 feet from the ground. The contractor would point out where the hole was going to be, send out the lumber, and then leave it to us.

"Well, we had to figure that there was so much slope—drop-off—to every section in the rig. On a rig that size, 72 feet, we usually figured a 20-inch drop-off for every section, or 2½ inches to the foot. The first girt—the straight crosspiece in the rig—was always 10 feet from the ground; that made a 25-inch drop-off. So we'd take a 2 x 12 board, saw it to 19 feet, 7 inches, and nail a 2 x 4 board at the correct slope on one side.

"Then we'd put a brace against the sloping inside of the 2 x 4 and on the other end of the 2 x 4 and on the other end of the 2 x 12; that was the first girt. From there on up the girts were 8 feet apart; so for the second one, we'd measure 20 inches back on the 2 x 12—eight times 2½ inches, see; the third one, 20 inches more; and so on, till we'd laid out the eight girts and braces. All we had to do then was pile up the boards and saw 'em.

"Steel rigs like they use now come already cut to size, with bolts and nuts, and the bolt-holes already drilled. A man can't possibly make a mistake on one of them; there just isn't any way to stretch out a piece of steel or shorten it.

"The first steel rig I ever worked on was down in Texas in '26. It was a little 72-footer, but damned if it didn't take us three days to run it. The company was just starting to build steel rigs, and they had to send a factory man down there to help us. The manufacturers used to have their men out with us all the time at first; they wanted to find out what was wrong, what kinks had to come out, they asked the rig-builders. You wanta know how your stuff works, ask the man who has to use it, that's the best way.

"And carpenters weren't worth a damn in building those wooden rigs, either. Down in Fort Worth one time, a company called my brother-in-law, who was contracting at the time, to come out and try to repair a rig. They'd hired a carpenter to put it up in the first place, but he hadn't had any experience, and made one helluva mess of it. My brother-in-law took one look at it and called up the company headquarters and told 'em he was going to build a new rig—there wasn't a big timber in the whole damned thing he could use.

"A carpenter could be a rig-builder, but he had to start from the ground up, from the beginning, and learn everything. He had to forget all he ever knew about finish work and learn how to do rough stuff; and he had to learn how to cut lumber in a different way from any he ever knowed.

"[When] I left Yale, Oklahoma, I went to Eastland, Texas, in 1919. I run rigs there for a while, during most of the boom, and then I went to Breckenridge, Texas, right at the beginning of the boom there. I got in there late one evening, and tried to get a room but couldn't. Only buildings in town were a hay barn, couple of houses, and three old rickety buildings. There was a pool hall in one end of a building, and I went in there and got to talking with the guy that run it.

"I thought he stayed open all night—there was a helluva lot of drifters come in for the boom wages—but he wasn't. He didn't have any place to stay either, and he'd been sleeping on a pool table. He told me I could sleep on one if I wanted to, free. If he'd charged me anything, I'd been out of luck.

"The second night I was there I slept in the hay barn, along with about two dozen more fellows. I stayed in the barn about a month or maybe a little more, until they got some shack boarding-house put up and I could rent a room. Living down there, or in any boom town, was hell, but the wages was good. I made twenty-two dollars a day, average, all through '19 and '20, and sometimes getting as high as twenty-five dollars a day. I wasn't a crew-pusher either, just a hand. In the last part of '20 they cut the wages to twenty dollars a day, and then in the first part of '21, to eighteen dollars a day.

"I didn't like to get my wages cut so much and so often, but I stuck it out. They were paying even less than eighteen dollars a day up in Oklahoma, and I didn't want to come back.

"I got hurt again down in Breckenridge. We were skidding a rig down there just outside the town for Magnolia Petroleum Company. We skidded it with steam. The way we did it was to cable onto a tree or a dead-man—a long pipe buried in the ground, to use as an anchor—or anything else solid, and then put skids under the footing of the rig and throw the steam to it.

"We worked like hell till noon, and got it moved about halfway to where we wanted it. We went and ate, and then four of us went over and began letting the engine house down. We wanted to get the job done by night, because we had another one to start on the next day. Me and another fellow were standing by the exhaust pipe, knocking the sheeting off and fixing to put skids under the engine house.

"Steam's always kept up on a rig, and 'specially if there's a job like that going on. The driller, who'd been handling the boiler, didn't know this fellow and me was behind, and he walked over and fed it to her. That live steam blew outa there and scalded me from waist to my heels. I couldn't do a damned thing. It hurt so goddamned bad I couldn't even holler, just dropped on the ground and laid there, trying my best to holler or do something to relieve myself.

"The other fellow didn't get burned bad; he rushed around and begin hollering, and they shut down the boiler. We was just a little way from town, and they picked me up and run me in, carrying me in their arms. They took me up to my room, and then most of 'em run out to try and find a doctor. I hurt so goddamned bad I'd of done anything to ease the pain. I had one of the boys go get a fan, and I cut off all my clothes and cocked my legs up on a table, and let the fan blow right down my legs. It was the worst thing I could of done, but if it happened to me again, I'd do the same damned thing.

"By the time the doctor got there I had big blisters raised up under my thighs and the calves of my legs that looked like footballs, only bigger. He give me a big shot of dope, and then took out his doctor's knife and ripped the blisters open. A half-gallon of old blister water poured outa each one of them blisters. It would of hurt like hell, but I had so much dope in me I hardly felt it.

"Then the old doc smeared me with salve and give me some more dope and left; somebody else had got hurt, and he had to go tend to them. I stayed around fourteen days and got well; he must've known his stuff because there isn't a scar on me now. I thought I'd never get over it at first, and it surprised me more'n anybody when I found out I was healing up all right.

"I did a lot better on my compensation, too. I got twenty dollars a week while I was off, and I got all the doctor's bill paid by the contractor. I didn't get any lump compensation, but I was so damned glad to be alive and without being crippled up that I didn't even care.

"The doc griped at me all the time he was treating me. He was a crusty old fellow, but he knew his stuff. He told me, and I had a doctor a year ago tell me the same thing—that all rig-builders have some kind of a rupture. This one last year said that eighty-five percent of all rig-builders have a semi-rupture; they might not even know they're ruptured, but all of 'em's got piles, and some of them pretty bad.

"In 1922 I came to the Osage Nation,* where there was a big boom on in the Indian lands. Me and another fellow come together; we piled off a train and had to walk a couple or three miles to get to the fields. When we topped the hill at Kaw City, it looked like all the rigs in the world was down in the valley. We stood there and counted over a hundred rigs under construction, and we thought sure as hell we had work enough to last us the rest of our life.

"We got a job easy; all we had to do was walk up to a rigging

---

*Forced from Arkansas and Missouri, then from Kansas, the Osage Indians were given a "nation" in the northeastern part of the Indian Territory (later Oklahoma), "a rocky waste . . . which no white man would have" (John Joseph Matthews, *The Osages: Children of the Middle Waters* [Norman: University of Oklahoma Press, 1961], p. 776). Happily for the Osages, a large reservoir of oil was discovered beneath the "rocky waste."

contractor and ask him, and he told us to put on our overalls and come out in the morning. But damned if that field didn't shut down eight days after we went to work. I never did find out why, either. At ten o'clock one morning the contractor rode out and told us to climb down outa the rig; he was closing down. And every other contractor, except just a few that were doing the contracting on their own stuff, shut down too.

"That was in March 1922, and I didn't get another job till July 4 that year. I got in a few repair jobs once in a while, tightening up a rig or nailing wind-braces on, but nothing I could call steady till July 4. I stayed at a little town called Apperson, another boom town not far away. And that little old town's gone, too, just like Drop Right.

"In '23 I kicked off from the Osage Nation and went back to Texas, to Breckenridge and Albany. Both of them were on the boom; Albany was a new boom, and there seemed to be lots of work. I got in enough work that I thought I couldn't lose, and in '26 I bought a house there in Albany. Nineteen twenty-six was a good year, and seemed like everything meant money. I paid $3,100 for that place, and it was a nice one, too. I put all I had into it—more'n $700—and was supposed to pay it out at $20 a month.

"But in '27 I didn't get in a lick of work for months at a time running rigs. I did get in twenty days with a casing crew, but that was just enough to keep bread in the house, and no butter. And finally I lost the house. I had about $1,000 in it by that time, but I couldn't have got out with half that.

"I moved the family—wife and girl—to a shack in the town, and we tried to get along with whatever jobs I could get. In November of '27 a friend of mine that was working for Magnolia in Oklahoma wrote and said I could get a job with him; he was pushing a crew. I came on up and worked till early in the spring of '28, when the job played out.

"I sent the wife and kid to my daddy's, over near Muskogee, Oklahoma, and a friend of mine and me hit out for California. We heard there was quite a bit of work there, and we decided to see if there was any truth in it. But that state was lousy, no work at all, no rigs being run, no nothing. They'd quit building wooden rigs out there and were using steel. I didn't know from hell about a steel rig, those big rotaries, you know, except the one I'd helped run, but I hit 'em all up anyway. I didn't get as much as half a day's work for all the walking I did. This buddy of mine got a job roustabouting, but I wasn't as lucky, and finally I came on back.

"I met my brother-in-law out there in San Diego and came back as far as Wink, Texas, with him. When he turned off south, I turned north, and hit the highways to Wichita Falls. The boom was just about to play out there, too, but I managed to get in two days' work there. I hit up a contractor one noon there, and he said he'd put me to work the next morning, for me to be ready and meet the truck at a certain spot, at four o'clock. I wondered what the hell we'd be doing out that time of day, but I didn't say anything.

"I was there about three o'clock; the truck come by and away we went down to Graham, Texas. I found out why we left so early—this contractor wanted us to build a 112-foot rig; he wanted us to lay it out, dig the cellar, and run the rig all in one day. Well, mister, I needed a job, and I really balled the jack. All of us did. We worked like a bunch of demons, and by five o'clock that evening we was through.

"The guy was happy about it, and gave us another day's work—the same kind. We finished that one about ten o'clock that night, and, of course, only got paid for a day. And that was the end of the work for us, me especially.

"I went back to my daddy's farm and worked 'round there for him, and picking up what work I could till the Oklahoma City field opened up in the fall of '28. I busted down there and got in fifteen days, and then they shut down a while. There wasn't enough work around there for a rig-builder to keep a boy busy—leastways I didn't catch any of it.

"I walked over to the Fox Rig and Lumber Company office one morning, about a five-mile stroll from where I was staying, and asked 'em for a job. The pusher said sure, he'd give me one, twelve dollars a day. I was to git a lunch ready and come back and go out with the gang next morning. I hustled back to the room and spent the rest of the day trying to get some lunch ready for the next day.

"Bright and early the next morning I was over there: I squatted down out in front with about fifteen other rig-builders for a smoke, when the boss called me in. He took me back in his office and asked me if I was the new man, the one that was to be paid ten dollars a day. I said, no, I was to get twelve dollars a day. He said, no, ten dollars was the regular wages. I said all right, and walked on out.

"I stood up in front of those other rig-builders and said, 'Boys, I just got in town here a little while back, and I don't know what's customary. Your boss here just offered me ten dollars a day; is that the customary wage?' Every damned one of 'em bellered: 'Hell, no!

We get twelve dollars a day!' So I walked back in the office and told the fellow that he'd made a mistake; twelve dollars a day was the customary wage. He said: 'Ten dollars, take it or leave it.' I left it.

'I'd managed to bring my wife down with me when we left my daddy's, but we didn't have any money. I went on home and told her what I'd done, and she begun taking on. We only had a dollar and a half, and no damned chance of going to work. But I told her if I'd taken the job, I'd of made me about fifteen enemies; that in the end it would have cut the wages of every damned rig-builder in the city. She didn't like it, but she took it.

"That next Saturday I went over to where they were building a big garage and hit the foreman up for a job. I told him I wasn't no carpenter, but I could make him a damned good hand. He told me to get to work, to go across the street where they had the material piled and carry sheeting over to the carpenters. I begin giving that sheeting hell. I carried enough of it to last every damned carpenter there a month, and when I saw I had plenty, I picked up a hammer and started to help 'em. But they wouldn't let me; they said I wasn't a union man and for me to sit down. So I upended me a nail keg and sat down to wait 'em out.

"The foreman came by and saw me sitting there and told me to grab a hammer and go down and start on the other end of the building, nailing on sheeting. I didn't want to get fired off this job, too, so I grabbed up a hammer, filled my pockets with nails, and set out . And do you know, by God, I finished half that damned roof myself; I met four of those carpenters halfway on that building!

"Well, anyway, when it come time to pay me off the next Saturday, the foreman called me over to one side and told me he was ashamed to pay me just four dollars a day, like he'd said he was going to. He said if I wouldn't say anything about it he was going to pay me eight dollars a day, the regular carpenters' wage. I was as quiet as a dead dog; I couldn't said anything about that extra four dollars for a drink of whisky.

"I worked on that job about five weeks, and then it folded up when the building was finished. I hustled all over the whole field but couldn't get a thing. One night I was setting at home when somebody knocked on the door. A fellow asked me if I was the one who turned down the ten-dollar job at Fox Rig Company. I said, yes; why? He said he liked the idea of me doing that, and that he was a rig contractor, and if I needed a job to come out and go to work for him.

"Did I go? I worked for that fellow all through '29 and '30 and damned near cried with him when the Depression hit him.

"When it got really tough down here, in about '31, I had a helluva hard time. My daddy died, April 21, 1931. I only had about a hundred dollars left out of my savings, and it took damned near all that to put him away. I left my wife up there in Muskogee with my mother after the burial, and I came on back. But it was '34 before I could get my family back down here. I couldn't seem to make more'n twenty-five dollars on any job; they'd last about two-three days and then fold up, and there wouldn't be another one for a month.

"One Christmas I was working down at Anadarko for a rig contractor. He was a tight guy; he never paid me off till he'd got his pay, and sometimes he forgot I was even working for him. He owed me about sixty dollars that Christmas, and I got a ride up from Anadarko and came by his house to get my check. I wanted to go up to Muskogee and see the family. But his wife said he'd gone to Houston, and wouldn't be back till after the first of the year. She handed me a check he'd left for me—for twenty-five dollars. So I had to stay in Oklahoma City that Christmas.

"In '35 I was working for a contractor in the Oklahoma City field. I'd got in eight days, when one noon the contractor came out and told the pusher to tell the crew that he was cutting the wages from eight dollars to seven dollars, and that the cut started the first of the month, which was about two weeks before that day. When the pusher walked over and told us—we were sitting around on the rig floor eating our lunch—we waited till he got through with his little spiel, and then I told him he wasn't cutting my wages a nickel.

"The contractor heard us arguing and come over, and I told him the same thing. I said I'd gone to work at eight dollars a day, and that was what he was going to pay me, if he didn't want to go to court about it. He took me off to one side and tried to argue me out of it, but it didn't do him any good. I told him I had eight days coming to me at eight dollars a day, and by God, I was going to get it all. He said he'd pay me the sixty-four dollars, and did I want to work on the rest of the day at seven. I said, No; I'd work for four dollars for the half day, not for three and a half. He finally saw I meant it, and said all right.

"But that afternoon there were two men, rig-builders, standing around the rig waiting for me to quit, so they could try to get my job. Times was tough, but I was damned if I was going to be chiseled like that.

"I got a job with another company, and then I pushed crews for a contractor for four years, in Oklahoma City, St. Louis, Ray City, Seminole, and all around the state. I went to work for Fox Rig and Lumber Company for a while, and got along pretty good with them, too.

"They tried to organize a union in '35, but didn't have much luck. In '37 the boys tried again, with a CIO* organizer helping them, and they had a pretty tough time getting some of the boys to join. They went on strike once; I went out too, but lost it. There was a big meeting down at Seminole about that strike, whether we'd go out or not.

"They all thought I was a damned radical. The contractors were trying to get us cut from ten dollars to eight, and I told the whole damned bunch of 'em at that meeting that I wouldn't pull on a glove for any eight dollars a day. Well, they finally all walked out, but we lost the strike anyway. I managed to get in a little work after that with the Phillips Petroleum Company; they paid me ten dollars a day, too.

"They had a bunch of leases that they had to drill on or the leases would be voided, so they had to put up a rig on each of them—that's what the leases called for, a rig on each one. During the strike the boys wanted me to go out to a lease and call the men off, try to get them to throw in with us. I started out there and met the contractor on the way. He stopped me and said: 'Stone, I know you're going out there and call my crew out on strike. If you do, I'll see you never get in another day's work in Oklahoma City!'

"I told him I was sorry, but I was doing what I thought was right, and he shot his car in low gear and lit out for town. The boys seen me coming, and shut down the job till I got on the lease. I hollered up at 'em and told 'em to come on out, and ever' damned one of 'em throwed his gloves high as he could, and picked up the tools and come on back to town.

"After the strike the contractors was sore as hell, and lots of the rig-builders was, too. There was only two contractors in the whole state paying ten dollars a day, and both of them was mad at me. I thought I was going to have to live on dirt and dew from then on, but one night this Apple, the contractor who said he'd see I never got to work again, called me up and said he wanted me to go to Perry, Oklahoma for him and go to work.

*Congress of Industrial Organizations. For background about efforts to organize oil workers in the South, see F. Ray Marshall, *Labor in the South* (Cambridge, Mass.: Harvard University Press, 1967), pp. 194–201.

"I forgot about being mad at him—especially after he said he'd pay me ten dollars a day—and went up there, and worked eighteen months for him. We got along fine, too—never a cross word between us.

"Then the union started again, but I stayed clear of it till I saw the boys meant business. I wasn't going to be the one that got my neck out like a Christmas turkey so somebody could take a whack at it. The ones that'd been the hardest ones to get out on strike was the first ones to try to get the new union started, and before long, about three months after they begun, a pretty strong union was up and going.

"I signed up, and I've tried to make a good member. Right now I'm setting here on my Royal American because there aren't any union jobs any place. I could go out and scab on the boys, but that'd hurt me as much or more'n it would them. Women don't quite understand that idea; I know my wife don't, but I think most men do.

"We got some heels in the union, but hell, there's heels every place, and rig-building's no better'n other jobs. We just take the good with the bad and try to line them up straight.

"The union's done a helluva lot for the rig-builders, I know that. Back several years ago, when we didn't have one, the pusher got around three or four dollars a day for using his car. He had to haul the crews out to the job and back, and then he had to hook on a cat-head to his car wheel and use it to pull up the steel in the rig. A cat-head's a kind of pulley; you just bolt it on your car wheel, sling a rope around it, and start up your car. It'll pull the top out of a rig if the car's anchored solid.

"Now, under our union rules, the pusher gets seven dollars a day for the use of his car; and wages all around are better than ever before. That is, they're more regular, even if the work keeps getting slacker. A green man gets six dollars a day; an intermediate man, who doesn't have enough experience to be a full rig-builder, gets ten dollars, and a rig-builder gets twelve dollars. A pusher draws fourteen dollars a day. If a man can get in enough days a year, he can get by on those wages.

"Another good thing about the union is that they're getting rid of a lot of things that cause accidents, and making the men realize that accident prevention's a helluva lot better than gambling on pulling through. For one thing the union won't let anybody but the contractor—nobody else but the crew, the pusher, and the contractor—on the rig when they're running it or tearing down. Too much danger of somebody getting hit.

"And we won't let any Caterpillars or any other tractors or any bulldozers—tractors to push the dirt out—on the lease when we're working. With one of them working on the same lease, there's too much danger of somebody not hearing what somebody else is hollering at him, and he might get killed.

"I remember once, about as bad a job as I ever went on, an old wood rig had to be tore down, right smack over a wild well. The gas was blowing up outa the hole like a dozen cyclones, and the tools had been blown up in the top of the rig and hung there. The tools and the gas pressure together had damned near ruined the rig, and they sent us out to tear it down. We couldn't of heard the last trumpet, and the gas damned near blowed me out of the rig a couple of times.

"The only way we could make each other understand, or the pusher could tell us anything, was to write on a piece of board and send it up on the line. We finally seen we could take it down the regular way, especially without taking a chance on striking a spark and setting that well on fire and us too, so we unhooked the guy wires from the top and run-around platform, climbed down, and pulled the whole rig down.

"That was down in Seminole, and believe me, I'd think a while before doing a job like that again. About as dangerous a job as a man can get hold of is a rig that's been burned. They're treacherous as hell; the steel is all twisted and warped, and you can't tell when the piece you're standing on will give way and send you to hell. The only way to do one of them is reinforce it as you climb it, then when you get to the top, begin tearing down. You have to put extra guy wires on it, too.

"Lots of rig-builders have been killed because the pusher or contractor jumps on just one side of the board. You see, when we're building or tearing down, either one, we have to use a platform of 2 x 12s, four of them; the men on the ground have to test them for us; the green man, usually, who has to drag up the steel or carry it away, puts one end of the 2 x 12 on the floor of the rig and the other on his shoulder, and then somebody jumps on it to see that it won't crack or split.

"If the board isn't jumped on both sides, one of 'em might have a knot in it and when they sent the board up the rig-builders might get the wrong side up and walk on it with a load of steel. They do that, and their wives are as good as widows. But our union makes 'em jump on both sides of the boards.

"We've had a lot of changes like that, all of 'em for our good and the contractors', too, come in the fields, but everything isn't rosy—not by a helluva lot. The oil fields keep moving away, and all a man can do, rig-builder or whatever he is, is keep following 'em. A man rents a house here like I done, buys his furniture, and begins trying to live like most white folks do, and he'll have to pull up and follow the oil. Either that, or leave his family there and go by hisself, and maybe not see 'em for months at a time.

"We've got the wages and hours settled; now all we gotta do is get the whole damned oil industry lined up, and keep it there."

Attributed to Ned T. DeWitt

A Woman's
Like a Dumb Animal

TALLADEGA SPRINGS, ALABAMA, 1939

*A woman's like a dumb animal—like a cow
or a bitch dog. You got to frail 'em with
a stick now an' then to make 'em look up to you.*

For forty-two years, George Fallaw has been pulling and shoving at the handle of a crosscut saw. He is a big, slouch-shouldered man, 6 feet 3 inches tall, 220 pounds of bone and muscle. He is 62 years old, but he says proudly, "I don't never ask no rest time—I ain't never been white-eyed but once, an' I got to tell you 'bout that." His skin is dark and leathery, his eyes black and squinted, his coarse, black hair streaked with gray.

It was Sunday afternoon, and he sat there on the slanting porch of his shanty, with his willow-bottomed chair propped against the wall. His huge feet were covered by rough cotton socks, out at the heels and toes. He pulled hard at a cob pipe through a slender cane stem, and he said: "A old man gits purty lonesome-like out to hisself this-a-way; but I ain't got no cause to grumble. I been 'round lots in my day, an' I done buried two ol' women. You couldn't give me another'n. They's too many runnin' 'bout that you don't have to feed.

"Gittin' down to what you axed me, I been loggin' an' foolin' 'bout sawmills since I was a duck of a boy. Ol' Man Blanton, over at the valley, says he wouldn't give me fer four common men. He oughter know. He's seed a lot of loggers.

"Why, when th' ol' man was runnin' a mill over thar in th' holler, buyin' his lumber tree by tree, he says to me, 'George, I got to make a profit. I got to git trees that'll make fine, clear boards; an' it's go'nter be up to you to git 'em.' Well, sir, I got enough of 'em to make him rich. I jest go up to a tree an' look it over, an' I can tell you what kind of lumber it's go'nter make. I can spot th' knots 'way up 'mongst th' limbs. I can even tell 'bout how many feet of good boards of floorin' there is in a tree.

"He ain't never paid me right, but I don't need nothin' much now. When I was a young duck I worked fer fifty cents a day, sunup to sundown; but I weren't workin' fer him back then. Th' ol' man pays me two dollars now, an' me s'posed to be th' boss logger. I ain't s'posed to work but eight hour a day, but I could count on my ten fingers how many times I got out o' th' woods fore good dark.

"One time I went to him 'bout my pay, an' he put on a mouth that was as pore as a widder woman. He says, 'George, you know I'm yore friend; I'd pay you more if I could. But my sales is 'way down. If I'm go'nter keep eatin' myself, I can't pay my help no more. It'd bust me, an' then we'd all be out in th' cold.' Well, I ain't been to him since that day. He thinks I'm a damned fool, but I ain't blind. A man that's been lumberin' as long as me knows a few things. I can look at th' stock in his sheds an' know that he was lyin' with a face as bare as a baby's rump. I know what I cut in th' woods, and I know how much lumber it'll make.

"He's got plenty money to keep him th' rest of his life. He don't bank it over at Sylacauga. He banks some of it in Birmingham, an' some in Mobile. Tony told me 'bout that, an' he ought'er know; he mails most of th' ol' man's letters up at th' Springs. Tony's th' commissary man, an' he says ol' Blanton is so stingy he wears buttons on his pants made out of his own wood. He's that tight, all right."

George stretched his towering frame, lifting his huge, sun-baked arms above his head. He shuffled his chair nearer the edge of the porch, where he could prop his feet against the 2 x 4 railing. He knocked the ashes out of his pipe.

"I been 'round," he said at last, "an' I ain't proud of some of th' things I done. I never did know no mammy an' daddy. Some said I was a woods colt, but they never said it to my face. Anyway, I was gived away. I was gived to a ol' man named Mears over on th' river—me an' a girl they said was my sister.

"That ol' man nigh 'bout worked me to death. He had a big farm over thar an' it got to whar I was doin' jest 'bout everything. I stood it 'til I'se fifteen year old, an' then I runned away. He kotched me th' first time an' whooped me 'til my ol' jacket stuck to my back, it was so full of blood. But I made up my mind he wasn't go'nter keep me. Next time I runned away, it was in th' night, an' I crossed th' river an' set out down th' road. I kept on goin' an' 'fore I knowed it, I'se in Selma.

"I tell you, I was so hongry when I got thar, an' I'd drunk so much water, that my belly thought I'd took in washin'. I've heerd folks say they wouldn't beg fer nothin' if they was starvin' to death; but they jest ain't never been hongry enuff. I went up to a house an' I begged, an' I got some coffee an' some cornbread. I ain't never tasted nothin' so good as that, an' I seen good vittles in my time.

"They was a circus thar in Selma, an' I'd not seed one before in my life. I jest comed up on it while I'se walkin' an' I went up, boy-like, to listen to th' music. They was takin' down one of th' tents, an' when I'se standin' thar goggle-eyed, a man come up on me. He says, 'Boy, you look stout; you wanta work?' An' well, I was needin' a job 'bout as bad as a body could. I pitched in right thar, an' I done so good that they took me along in th' work gang.

"I done all right, too. I was 'bout six foot high then, an' weighed close ter two hundert pound. I was like a ox, an' couldn't none of them men outwork me. But my dander kept risin' up, an' if I'd had bug-sense I'd a knowed trouble was comin'. I'd keep gittin' my dander up when th' boss-man'd come 'round with his cussin' an' bullyin'. I'd b'il in my innards when he'd kick a nigger, an' I got to thinkin' what was go'nter happen if he ever kicked me.

"He weren't high as me, but he was broad an' built close to th' ground. He didn't have no good side to him—he was jest mean as hell—an' even when he was in good humor, you knowed he was jest a rattlesnake in th' sunshine. You knowed there weren't nothin' 'bout him that was any good a-tall.

"Well, sir, I let a rope slip one day, an' he comed 'round to whar I was. We was at a little town in North Car'lina, an' that's a good piece from hyar. He started cussin' me, callin' me things that showed me thar was go'nter be trouble. Then, 'fore I knowed what was happenin', he kicked me.

"I reached down on th' ground, an' I got my fingers on a sledge-hammer that was lyin' thar. I said, 'You son-of-a-bitch, you kick me jest one more time an' I'll kill you. So he'p me my good God, I'll knock yo'r brains down yo'r throat.'

"I'll say this fer him; he weren't no coward. He jest looked at me a second or two, an' then he comed t'ward me. I knowed he meant business; I had to perteck myself. I raised that hammer an' I knocked him in th' head so hard that he fell like a sick ox. I run like hell, then, but didn't nobody try to kotch me. I guess everybody was glad.

"To this day, I don't know what become of him. He might a-died, fer I hit him a solid lick. Since I got religion, I pray 'bout it sometimes, but I ain't never been able to feel sorry 'bout it. He axed fer it, an' if he got well, I bet he didn't kick nobody else fer a long time."

George stuffed his pipe with sack tobacco again, struck a match on the pineboard floor, and puffed silently for a few moments.

"It took me mor'n a month to git back hyar. I was ragged an' hongry, an' didn't have no friends to go to, but I made up my mind I weren't goin' back to ol' man Mears. I'se feelin' grown now, an' I knowed I weren't goin' to take no more beatin's from him. I knowed I'd kill him if he ever laid a hand on me, fer I couldn't even think 'bout him an' not burn in my head. Sometimes I thought 'bout that gal that was s'posed to be my sister, but I never knowed that she was. She was a little ol' skinny, light-haired gal, an' she never favored me. Some folks say I got Indian blood, I wouldn't know. But I guess I done things in my time bad as a Indian.

"I done things that th' good God won't ever forgive me fer. When I come back, I didn't have no friends 'cept Tom Cooley, a nigger that lived down in Coosa County 'bout th' bend. I went down thar with him, an' he was as bad a nigger as I was a white man. I took to card playin' an' whiskey drinkin' down thar, an' we raised so much hell that we driv' his ol' woman plumb out-a th' house. When we'd give out-a whiskey, we'd jest make us some more an' go right ahead raisin' hell.

"A bunch of niggers who worked at th' Jackson sawmill over at th' Springs useta come down to Tom's house on Sundays, an' Tom an' me'd play cards with 'em an' take what they had. That's one of th' things I won't ever be fergive fer. There was them po'r niggers who'd git paid maybe three dollars on Saturday, an' then Tom an' me'd git 'em drunk an' take everything they had. You see this scar on th' side of my head? Well, I got it right thar. A crazy nigger gived it to me with a butcher knife.

"I stayed down thar in them woods 'til I was goin' on twenty year old. Tom an' me was makin' whiskey an' gamblin' an' fishin' a little fer a livin' an' we was doin' good. But then one Saturday, Tom got full of likker an' went over th' mountain to a sawmill that had started runnin' over thar. They was a bunch of niggers workin' at the mill, an' one of 'em was a nigger named Doc, who had a tall, yaller gal fer a woman that made Tom's mouth water. Tom saw her once, an' then he comed to me an' said that he couldn't look at 'er an' stand still. Th' thoughts of her jest runned all over him; an' then, that Saturday he got likkered up.

"He headed straight fer that Doc's shack 'spite all th' way I begged him to stay away. He had a pistol in his overall pocket, an' I knowed that he was goin' after what he wanted. I begged him right to th' door leadin' up to th' shack, but they wasn't nothin' could be done. He went up thar and walked in th' door.

"He wasn't no sooner in than Doc's woman started hollerin'. I was standin' out in th' road watchin', fer I knowed Tom was drunk enough to shoot me if I tried to stop him. The door was open a little, an' I could see him wrastlin' with that yaller gal, an' her screamin' like she was in a bed of snakes. Niggers started runnin' out of all th' shacks, an' some of 'em headed straight fer th' sawmill boiler room.

"I knowed then that thar was hell to pay, fer that was whar Doc was workin'. In no time a-tall, he come runnin' t'ward his shack, an' he had a rifle in his hand. He stopped out in the front yard, an' he called out, 'Come outa my house, nigger, or I'm comin' after you.'

"He hadn't no more than said it when Tom come to th' door. Tom didn't say a thing, he jest leveled down with his pistol an' started shootin' at Doc—I don't know how many times. But Doc jest stepped back of a tree thar in th' yard an' waited 'til Tom had finished. Then he raised that rifle to his shoulder.

"I never seed a shot gauged better'n that one. Tom stepped back from th' door, kinder to one side, but Doc seemed to know whar he was standin'. He shot through th' wall, 'bout two feet from th' door, an' that bullet got Tom right through th' belly. We runned up to th' house an' he was dead. Th' gal was under th' bed.

"Now I'm th' sort that knows what side my bread's buttered on. I knowed them people might say I was Tom's friend an' have it in fer me. But when I seed he was dead, I knowed that a dead man can't do nothin' fer nobody. So I started cussin' him right and left, an' tol' Doc that I'd see th' law didn't do nothin' to him. I did that, too, fer I went over to th' county seat at Rockford an' helped see that they didn't bother him. They jest had a little hearin', an' then they turned him loose.

"I didn't lose nothin' by tellin' what I knowed. They was a young man named Godfrey who was runnin' th' sawmill, an' he told me that he was to thank me fer what I'd done fer his nigger. Well, sir, I seed that th' time was right, an' I axed him fer a job. He gived it to me, an' that's whar I started out sawmillin'.

"I was a grownup man, an' I was as tough an' as stout as a mule. At first, I helped fire th' b'iler, totin' slabs fer it, but then one day Mr. Godfrey come up to me. He says, 'I'm short in th' woods, George; I need loggers out thar. How'd you like to try yo'r hand at it?' I tol' him that I'd like it fine, an' th' next day, I was pullin' at th' end of a crosscut saw.

"Well, sir, I had som'pun happen out thar that gived me a lesson. I don't min' tellin' you 'bout it, fer it's got funny to me now. They was a little ol' man helpin' me named Davis, an' he weren't nothin' but a runt. Th' first time I seed him I wanted to laugh, fer it was funny to think he could keep up with me on a saw.

"Th' second day I worked out thar, he was goin' into th' commissary fer som'pun, an' I give him a dime an' axed him to git me some 'baccer. He was gone a couple of hours, an' when he come back he seemed mighty worried. He come right to me, an' he said, 'George, I done lost that dime of your'n; I'll pay it back come Saturday.' An' I was wantin' 'baccker, an' I got mad as hell. I said, 'You stole my money.'

"Well, sir, he straightened up his little old wizened self, an' he said, 'That's a lie.' He was white as a sheet, an' he was tremblin' like he was go'nter fall to pieces. I knowed he was scared as a rabbit, so I took a step t'ward him an' said, 'If you say that ag'in, I'll slap yo'r face.' He come right back at me. He said, 'It's a lie—a double-dogged lie!'"

"They was just us two away out thar in th' woods—miles away from th' closest soul. I riz up my arm, an' I slapped his face so hard that it cracked like th' stinger on a cowhide whip. I slapped it that hard, an' then I turned to walk off.

"I've stirred up a yallerjacket nest many a time, an' I've had 'em git over me faster'n a country boy pickin' a banjo, but I ain't never had nothin' git on me as fast as that dried-up little ol' man. We was standin' on th' side of a hill, an' he come at me head first. His shoulders hit me in the belly, an' I went down on my back, with my head p'inted down th' hill, an' my feet p'inted up. It was all sudden-like, an' I couldn't a got up if it'd bin th' end of th' world.

"I tried to hit at him from whar I was lyin', but he wasn't nowhar I hit. He was jest like a banty rooster, an' he hit me in th' face so fast that you couldn't a counted th' licks. He jest sit on my chest an' beat on my nose an' eyes an' mouth like he was beatin' a drum. I couldn't do nothin', so I said, 'You have whooped me.' He got up then, but my eyes was swelled 'til it was all I could do to see, an' my mouth felt like it was big as a ham.

"It's a funny thing, but I got to likin' that little ol' man. He tried to pay me back my dime, but I wouldn't take it. We went on cuttin' logs together, an' it weren't long 'fore we was mighty good friends. An' it was him that I was goin' to tell you 'bout—th' only time in my life I ever was white-eyed.

"It was all on account of a ol' cheap watch. Bein' out in th' woods as we was, we couldn't hear no whistles fer quittin' time, so th' man that owned a watch did all th' time-callin'. Well, this was my watch, an' it was up to me when we was to rest. It got to whar I allus called time for 'bout fifteen minutes every mornin' so we could go over to a spring close by an' git us some water. When we'd drunk, we'd lie down awhile an' talk.

"Things kep up like that a long time, and it come to th' point whar Davis weren't doin' much work. He wanted to rest all th' time, an' we couldn't keep up with the teamsters. Well, sir, th' notion struck me that if I'd let him call th' time he might do better work, so one day I took out my watch an' handed it to him. I said, 'You keep th' watch awhile, Mister Davis, an' you call th' time.'

"Now, I've made lots of mistakes in my life, but that'n was th' worst. That little ol' man went crazy as a bat. He was allus takin' out that watch an' lookin' at it like he was a boss, an' he couldn't git to workin' early enough. It got to whar he wouldn't even lie down when we'd go to th' spring, an' he was stingy 'bout goin' a-tall. We'd git down thar, but jest th' minute I laid down, he'd take out that watch an' say, 'Got to git back on th' job, Fallaw; got to keep th' trees fallin'.'

"It tickled me fer a while, but it got to whar it weren't funny. One hot day in August we was cuttin' logs, an' he was worse than ever. He worked like we was th' only loggers in th' woods, an' by dinnertime I was blowin' an' sweatin' like a mule. That evenin', he jest kept me on sawin' like he was fightin' a fire, an' I knowed I couldn't make it no further. I took my hands off my end of th' saw an' I says to him, 'You better let me have th' watch ag'in. We'll take turns keepin' time, week by week.' But I never did git 'round no more to lettin' him carry it.

"I was beginnin' to make fair money fer them times—dollar an' a half a day. I was growed up, so I got my mind on havin' a woman of my own. I got to castin' 'round fer one, an' I got my mind sot on a little ol' gal that lived over on th' Peters' place. Her ma was passed on, an' her pa wasn't doin no good at keepin' her up. She was ragged as a can of kraut. Her pa was too busy raisin' hell to mind atter her, an' I knowed he'd be glad to git rid of her.

"One day I axed him 'bout it, an' he said he didn't mind. I traipsed over thar a couple of times an' did a little purty talkin' to th' gal, an' one day I tol' her I wanted her to come an' live with me—that it was all fixed with her pa. She studied 'bout it fer a minute or two, but I guess she was glad to come. She'd had a hell of a life thar whar she was. I tuk her to my shack that night, an' she kotched on right off. Weren't no time 'fore she had th' place lookin' better—scrubbed clean as a whistle—an' she planted some flowers out in th' yard.

"She never was much purty, but she was a good woman. Her name was Texas sum'pn-er-other; I don't recollect her pa's name. She weren't half my size—didn't weigh a hundert pound—but that jest suited me. I allus have liked a little bitsy woman. They don't give no trouble, and they don't eat much.

"I guess I loved her some. That is, I loved her for awhile. But like I said, I'se useta raisin' hell, an' it weren't long 'fore I got my mind on that ag'in. I guess I'se purty bad, but shouldn't no woman ever think she can put bits in a man's mouth. I recollect that I come home one day at dinnertime, an' I was hongry an' t'ard. She allus had my dinner ready fer me, but this time th' hoecake weren't quite done, an' it 'peared to me that she weren't doin nothin' to help things. She was sittin' at a quilt she had hangin' from th' ceilin', an' it made me madder to see her sittin' thar workin' with a needle an' thread when I was starvin', an' she should a been in th' kitchen. Well, sir, I jest give a runnin' leap, an' landed square in th' middle of that damned quilt. Down it come, railin's an' all."

George laughed boisterously, stamping the floor with one of his huge, socked feet. He slouched forward in the chair, his elbows on his knees.

"I'm tellin' you this, fer I'm headin' up to a p'int. That little ol' woman was a-feared of me, an' she kept her mouth shet, no matter what I done. But all th' time, she weren't keepin' her mouth shet fer ever'body. She was goin' up to Mister Godfrey's house behin' my back, an' she was tellin' him how bad I was treatin' her. That shows no woman can't be trusted. If they are like a mouse 'round you, well, you can bet th' shirt off'n yo'r back that they're talkin' to somebody. An' her talkin' her head off to Mister Godfrey weren't doin' me no good, though I didn't know 'bout it till later. If I had knowed, I'd a busted her wide open.

"It all come to a head one mornin' when I weren't doin' nothin' that most any man wouldn't do. They was a gal lived up on th' hill 'bove my shack, an' she was a sight fer sore eyes—big-chested an' broad hipped. Well, I ain't denyin' that I'd been watchin' her fer a long time, an' I knowed that she had her eyes sot on me—any man can tell when a woman wants 'im. She come to my place every mornin' fer buttermilk that I'se lettin' her folks have; an' on this pertic'lar mornin', she jest happened to kotch me right. That miserable little ol' woman of mine was big with a baby, an' I didn't have no eyes fer her.

"This gawky ol' corn-fed gal come saunterin' into th' kitchen that mornin', when I was sittin' thar gettin' my grub. I looked up an' seed her, an she looked better'n I'd ever seed her look before—an' she was smilin' at me like she was thinkin' 'bout th' same thing. I guess that's why th' notion struck me all of a sudden. I knowed that my ol' woman was out at th' lot, an' things was sot jest right.

"Now, I'm tellin' you this, fer I'm leadin' up to a p'int. I got up from th' table an' walked over to whar that gal was standin'. She didn't move a leg. I says, 'Ye'r kinder frisky, ain't you?' an' she giggled woman-like. Well, sir, I jest eased my arm 'bout her then, an' she was soft as a featherbed. I was huggin' her like all hell—I had ev'rything jest like I wanted it—when my ol' woman come in at th' door.

"She didn't say nothin' at first, jest stood thar with her eyes buggin' out like a chipmunk's. I weren't goin' to let her faze me, so I jest kept on huggin', but th' gal was squirmin' an' pawin' so bad I couldn't hold 'er. Then my ol' woman said, 'George, what are you doin'?' An' I come right back at her. I says, 'I'm havin' a good time, Mama.'"

The giant figure straightened in the chair, and the huge hands came down upon the huge knees with a resounding smack. A burst of laughter rumbled from the leathery, bull-like throat.

"I guess ye'r wonderin' what th' p'int is," he said after awhile. "Well, this is it: thar ain't no sin 'bout nothin' like that 'less you git kotched; that's all th' sin they is—gittin' kotched.

"Well, sir, my ol' woman couldn't keep her mouth shet 'bout that neither. She went straight as a pigeon to Mr. Godfrey, an' she must-a tol' him a bellyful. Anyways, he comed up to me on th' job a few days later, an' I could see that he had his dander up. He called me to one side, an' he says, 'Damn yo'r hide, you ought'er be killed. Somebody ought'er take a shotgun an' blow th' skin off'n yo'r stinkin' bones.' I tol' him somebody had been totin' a passel of lies, but he says, 'Don't be layin' nothin' off on that little woman. I'd fire you if weren't fer her. As it is, I'm go'nter run you off this place if ever I hyar of you mistreatin' her ag'in.'

"That shows you can't put no trust in a damned woman, but I knowed Mister Godfrey meant what he said. It got to worryin' me some, fer them was hard times, an' I couldn't 'ford to lose no job. If it hadn't a-been fer that, I'd a busted that woman wide open, but I knowed if I tetched her she'd go runnin' to him. So I jest bided my time.

"They was a meetin' goin' on 'bout that time, an' I done a lot of studyin' 'bout it. I knowed Mister Godfrey was a churchly man, an' I got to thinkin' that I'd put myself in good with him by j'inin' up; he'd done a heap of talk to me—'bout how I'd ought'er git myself right with th' God A'mighty.

"Th' hardest thing I ever done was that. Ol' Reverent Shealy from over at th' valley was doin' th' bellerin', an' he was th' damndest hypocrite you ever seed. He run a little ol' store when he weren't preachin', an' when a gal'd come in th' store, he'd try to hug 'er. I 'member they tol' me that one gal comed in fer a sack of sugar, an' that when he tried to love 'er up a little she busted that sack of sugar over his damned head. They said that he could comb his hair fer a week an' git enough sugar to sweeten his coffee with.

"Well, I went up thar to that meetin', an' my ol' woman traipsed along with me as proud as a mother wren. She didn't know nothin' 'bout what I was doin' it fer, so when we went in an' sot down, she begin lookin' about happylike, with her little ol' eyes wet as a baby's behin'. I sot an' listened to th' sermon, thinkin' 'bout what a hypocrite ol' Shealy was up thar on th' platform, bellerin' like he'd bust his throat open. I never listened to 'im, but when they started th' signin', I went an' j'ined up.

"I wasn't never in a churchhouse before, an' I felt like a damned fool. Ol' Shealy shuk han's with me, then sot me down on a banch in front of ever'body. They was th' most takin' on thar I every heerd, with them fools all a-bellerin' an' a-jumpin'. Some of them was a-cryin', an' that was right down my way. I allus could cry easy, thinkin' 'bout what a hard row I'd had to hoe. So I beginned a-cryin' with th' others, an' they comed down to th' front, pawin' at me an' makin' me feel like I was in th' crazy house.

"Atter it was all over, Mister Godfrey come 'round an' tol' me how glad he was. He called me 'Brother' an' I knowed I'd got him whar I wanted him. I kept him thar, too, fer I went to that church-house regular. They weren't but one thing that was good 'bout it. Ol' Shealy couldn't 'ford to preach at th' mill but twice a month, fer he had another church some'ers. It was a hard job, but I stuck it out—I stuck it out fer six damned years—'til ol' Shealy was dead an' in hell, an' a new preacher comed—an' 'til Godfrey went busted an' had to quit sawmillin'.

"I had three young-uns now, so I had to git me up another job. But th' first thing I done was to git me a hick'ry stick an' beat th' lard out-a that damned tale-carryin' woman. I beat her 'til she was down on her knees hollerin' fer God's love, an' I teached her a lesson she didn't never fergit. She never did carry no more tales on me. She never did say nothin', neither, when I got me up a woman that I wanted to fun with, an' I got me up a-plenty.

"But don't you never do that, son. I'm a ol' man now, an' I know all thar is to know. When you fun with mor'n one woman, you never do seem to fun as much as you want to; you want-a foller ever' woman that comes along. You don't hav' to do that, but I do. I'm so weak.

"It didn't take me long to git another job atter I left th' Godfrey mill. I was th' best logger in that country, I knowed my trees like they was people, an' I was th' stoutest man anywhar to be found. I went over to Shelby County, clost to Four-Mile, an' I kotched on right off with Ol' Man Bradburn. He was th' kind that never give a damn what sort of man you was, jest so you was a good worker. Well, that suited me fine, fer I didn't have to go to church no more, an' I could git out in th' pasture an' paw up sand with th' cows.

"I guess I pawed up enough of it to fill th' Coosa River. That was one place whar they was enough women to suit me, an' I runned after 'em 'til my tongue was rollin' out like a damned dog's. My little ol' woman didn't open her mouth, neither, fer I had learned her how to keep it sewed up. Th' best times I ever loved her, I reckon, was right after we beginned livin' together, an' when I stood lookin' down at her dead face. She died a-havin' a kid. She shouldn't ought'er a had it, fer Doc Long had tol' her she'd die if she did.

"They was a woman name of Nora livin' thar that I liked a heap, but I had done made up my mind that I weren't never goin' to feed no other woman regular. They's a lot of things to be done 'bout a shack, though, an' a man can't do all of it—'specially if they's a passel of kids runnin' 'round. I tried batchin' it fer nearly a month after Tex died, an' I weren't doin' no good at it. One Sunday mornin' I got to thinkin' about it, so that evenin' I went over to Nora's place an' tol' her how I felt about it. We'd funned 'round a good while, anyways, so she got up her duds an' comed over to my shack.

"But right after we beginned livin' together regular, I tol' her how things was go'nter be run. I knowed she hadn't hardly lived whar she had been, fer her ma was a widder woman, and thar was a gang of other brats thar. I knowed that meat an' bread et regular would be enough to keep 'er with me, an' I was right. She was a good worker, but she never did take a likin' to my other woman's kids. I had to git her up some of 'er own, an' that was all right with me. I allus did try to keep my women totin' a little bitsy baby. That keeps 'em from studyin' devilment."

Again, the roar of laughter burst from the big throat, and again the huge hands were clapped hard against the huge knees.

"I don't guess I'se as rough on Nora as I was my fust woman, but that was on account of her workin' to keep me in good humor. Sometimes I'd git drunk an' whale th' hell out-a her a time or two, but mostly I treated her as good as any woman ought'er be treated. Don't never be too good to one of 'em. A woman's like a dumb animal—like a cow or a bitch dog. You got to frail 'em with a stick now an' then to make 'em look up to you.

"Why, I tell you sump'un; they's been men workin' at loggin' camps whar I been that handled their ol' women like they was gold dollars. They'd pet 'em up, buy purties fer 'em, an' keep their backsides kivered with glad rags; an' then Ol' George hyar'd come along an' take 'em fer hisself. I've seed men that didn't have no sense 'bout handlin' women. You never ought'er tell one of 'em that she looks good, er that anybody'd have 'em 'cept you. She'll git to believin' it if you tell 'er that, an' she'll start struttin' 'round like a rooster that's whooped ever'thing in th' countryside.

"I tol' Nora how things was go'nter be run, an' they was runned that way fer mor'n 'leven years. She gived me six young-uns while we was livin' together, but she got to whar she weren't wuth keepin'. She got to creepin' 'bout th' house like a wood-legged woman, an' her hide got as yaller as a persimmon. I got thinkin' once that I'd run 'er off—she weren't doin' me no good—but it was fer th' best that I didn't. She was tuk with a chill one night, an' she went out a awful way.

"It's go'nter come my time some day, but I pray to God I don't go out like that woman. It was awful. She'd got to whar she talked a lot 'bout sinnin', an' how me an' her was doin' wrong by havin' kids an' not even bein' married. 'Bout a month 'fore she died, she says to me one day, 'George, le's go over to Sylacaugy or some'rs an' git a preacher to talk over us.' That was funny as hell to me, an' I thought she'd went bug-crazy. But you know, I'se thinkin' of what she said jest th' other day. Do you s'pose that's why she died that-a-way?

"When she was lyin' thar tremblin' with th' chill, she kep raisin' up her hands an' yellin', 'He's in th' kitchen now! Th' devil's in th' kitchen, an' he's comin' after me!' She went away yellin' things like that, with 'er eyes wide open. I wonder if th' damned devil was in thar after her?

"Well, if he was, he's go'nter to be thar with feathers on his head when it comes my time. He's go'nter do a frolic, fer he's got a heap a meat to fry when he gits to me. Reverent Taylor, that young feller over at Harpersville, tol' me th' Lord could save anybody. He tol' me, 'Though yo'r sins air of scarlet, I will wash 'em white as snow.' That's what I'm countin' on. That's what I went to Judge Tillman fer an' got him to give me one of his old Bibles. I ain't never read a lick in my life, but I got to thinkin' I didn't want to go out without a Bible in my damned shack.

"It's go'nter take a heap of washin' fer me, fer if it's a sin to have young-uns an' not be married, I done a lot of it. It's got to whar anybody could come up an' say, 'How're ye, Pa?' an' I wouldn't know if I ought'er knock hell out-a him or kiss 'im. But I got religion, even if I don't go to no church. Reverent Taylor said he was go'nter pray fer me, an' I guess that'll wash me off a little.

"I done los' track of most of the kids I had by my two women. I kept 'em with me 'til they jest drifted off an' didn't come back. One of th' little ol' gals—she never was bright—went to Sylacaugy to work in th' mill, an' somebody tol' me she was runnin' after ev'ry pair of britches in sight. If I ever kotch up with 'er, I'll bust some of 'er ribs loose. My oldes' boy was makin' likker down on Cohagie Creek last I heard—I don't know whar he is now. I don' know whar none of 'em is, so don' ax me 'bout 'em.

"I been workin' fer Ol' Blanton a good spell now, an' I reckon th' place is as good as ary'n I'd find. But he don' pay me like he ought'er. They ain't nobody knows a tree better'n me, an' they ain't nobody can do harder work. Ol' Blanton thinks I'm a damned fool, but I been 'round.''

As he talked, the black, squinted eyes kept turning with increasing intentness upon a narrow, weed-flanked trail that ribboned toward his shanty over a stretch of bottomland. Now, he roused his big frame from the chair and glanced inside the bare, two-room structure. His eyes paused upon the face of a cheap alarm clock that ticked above the fireplace.

"I ain't rushin' you off," he said after awhile. "This place is yo'rn to stay at long as you want to. But I thought I better tell you they's some fo'ks comin' over hyar atter awhile—they's Bud Adams an' some of them Eustis boys. They go'nter have some likker an' some gals along, an' we mought try raisin' a little hell. I thought I better tell you 'bout it, but that yo're welcome to stay."

. . . The sun was disappearing behind the fringe of pine trees over on Sulphur Mountain. Already, there was hoarse laughter down the path, punctuated with an occasional shrill outburst. Somebody in the approaching crowd was plunking "Red River Valley" on a banjo.

Jack Kytle

My WPA Man

You know, son, white folks think niggers is crazy anyhow.
So you got to be crazy sometimes to get what you want from 'um.

Marguerite Jonas says she is a good woman. She attends Zion
Travelers Baptist Church regularly, and prays on her knees. You
won't find Marguerite's name on any of the church's executive
boards, nor will you find it listed in the church clubs, but Marguerite is an influential member and is a "hoping soul." She is
hoping that Zion Travelers' members are praying with her, and she
is hoping that her galloping, slue-foot, light-brown, lazy husband,
Buster Jonas, will soon find a job.

"Marguerite better hope that Buster quit looking at that brownskin gal who lives around the corner," said a neighbor. "That gal
ain't giving Marguerite any trouble with Buster yet, but she has her
mind on it."

"You could describe me as a chocolate black," said Marguerite.
"I'm forty-seven and weigh two-ten. Any man ought to be able to
keep his mind on me and on nobody else. I know how to treat a
man, everybody says that. What makes me so mad is that even the
church says it. And the church says that Buster ain't treatin' me
right. That's why he don't go to church no mo', and that's why the
church is prayin' fo' me, I hope!"

Marguerite says she isn't superstitious, but you can't pay her to
mention the name of the girl who is offering her competition. "I
reasons that it ain't good to be callin' women's names 'cause that
helps mo' than anything else to make 'em take your man," Mar-

guerite said. "I hates to think of her with her arms around Buster's neck. And she must be doin' just that, 'cause there ain't nothin' better that Buster likes than havin' some woman runnin' her hands around his neck. He's sho weak fo' that. Old fool!"

Buster had just left the house when we called. "If he was here, he wouldn't talk. He ain't sociable," Marguerite said. "All he wants to do is bum in the streets. He won't look fo' work fo' nothin'. He must think that work is goin' to come to him."

Marguerite is a cook by heart and by profession; she works on Saint Charles Avenue for Mrs. Cline. Marguerite likes to be seen walking in her madame's palatial door in the early morning and out of it in late evening. "My madame lets me walk right through her front door in the mornin' and in the evenin'," she says, "and I'm a proud sumpin'. She likes to see me walk, but she don't like to hear me talk. She says I talk too much about my troubles."

Marguerite has been working for Mrs. Cline about ten years; she lives in one of her houses. Her room is very shabby and crowded with furniture. Clothes hang on the wall, and there are several pairs of shoes under the bed. Marguerite has many excuses for her untidy room.

"It's a hard thing to keep this room clean. Excuse it. There's so much dust in this neighborhood. And there ain't enough room to take care of things. I'm goin' to fix it up as soon as I get a little time. Buster should be cleanin' up, but he's in the street somewhere. I'm ashame' of him and I'm ashame' of myself fo' lovin' him. Son, I got troubles with that man. You don't know what it means to have a man on yo' hands who won't work. Do you know that Buster ain't had nobody's job in three years? I calls him my WPA man 'cause the last job he had was on the WPA. He come sayin', 'Baby, don't call me no WPA man, call me yo' stomp digger.' I can't call him that. He ain't diggin' no stomps. Old fool. He's waitin' fo' his WPA card ag'in. And if you ask me, it ain't comin'. I keep tellin' that fool that, but he won't listen. Old fool! When they laid him off, the man particular told him to find a job 'cause they had to cut the rolls. Instead of him lookin' fo' a job he went to all them offices and fussed with the people. Everywhere he went they told him to find another job. He makes me mad, 'cause he ain't got nothin' on his mind. He done even wrote to the President. I was just wishin' the President would of told him to find another job, he ain't had no time foolin' wid' him. But the President wrote him. Was he happy. That fool got that letter in his wallet, and his wallet is empty. I don't talk to him no mo' about work, 'cause when you wants to make Buster real mad just talk to him about work. Never seen a man gets so mad.

"I'm tellin' you, I don't know how we make it. After I takes my insurance money out my salary and pay a few bills, I ain't got nothin'. Do you think he'll ask questions? Huh! All he wants to do is sit around till I bring them white folks' pots home. Mrs. Cline done asked me how many mouths I'm feedin'. That Buster is got three, I feel like tellin' her sometimes. But I'm scared she'll get mad and run him plum out of this room. This is her house, you know. And you know how white folks is. They'll run you clean away from 'em when you ain't doin' what's right.

"And people wonder why I pray. Shucks, I got troubles. Just like I say. After a few things come out of my salary, it looks like a silver dime. Worse than that even.

"I'm local. I was born right here. Born on Sixth Street. I ain't had no pa. Don't guess my ma had time to keep up wid that. She told me I ain't had no pa. I didn't argue; she ought to know. Not me. I'm here by the hardest. I don't know why but I'm sho' glad of it! I betcha that! And I ain't askin' too many questions about it; 'cause somebody might find out that I ain't got no business here and send me on back where I come from. I hear 'um talkin' about Senator Bilbo* wants all the cullud people to go back to Africa. Africa ain't did me nothin'. I don't see why I got to go back to Africa. I'm doin' all right here. I don't need nothin' in Africa. Who started that, anyhow? Them people can think of some of the worse stuff. I thought Buster was bad enough, but I reckon some white folks is just as bad.

"My ma raised me all the way. She was cook and wanted me to be one. My ma could make any dish put on the table. They used to call her 'Toot-it Tot' 'cause when she turned loose a pot it was Toot-it Tot. That means it was ready. My ma had me workin' wid her. No, I ain't had much schoolin', but I got good mother-wit. I can read and write. Ain't nobody can beat me out a dollar. I betcha that. I been around the white folks. When I was little I used to run on errands fo' white folks. Used to eat in their kitchen, mind their children and things. Facts was, that was the first job I ever done got. School? I went to the third, did all right too. I didn't like school much. If it wasn't fo' 'rithmetic, I would of done all right, I reckon. That's what used to whup me. Just couldn't make it go, that's all. I was a bright child fo' everything else. Got my readin', spellin' and

*Senator Theodore G. Bilbo of Mississippi, notorious for his racist diatribes.

stuff. I went to McDonogh Number 24. Mr. Priestley was the principal. He sho' could use a strap. That man ain't had no pity on you. He use to fold that strap and slam you across the 'hine wid it and almost knock you crazy. I 'members one day he caught me in the hall fo' bein' late, and he came down on me wid dat strap. Did that hurt!

"I can 'member that my ma went to work early every mornin'. Her name was Marguerite Sloan. She was a short brownskin lady. She says my pa was brownskin, too. I used to ask her why I'm so chocolate, and she used to laugh and say, 'We plucked you out of a dark cloud that was hangin' low one day.' Fo' the longest I believed that. Me and my ma used to live in a room just like this, only hers had a fire grate in it. We used to sit down in front of that grate and make popcorn and eat 'um. Mamma used to tell me about her old days on the farm. She was from Harahan, used to work for some rich white folks when she was younger. Yes indeed, me and my mamma was good friends.

"Yes, Mamma went to church. That's where I got the habit from. She took me to church every Sunday, didn't miss a Sunday. Mamma thought all the world in goin' to church. Used to say, 'Divinity is the word. Pray fo' what you want and want what you pray fo'.' Them was her true words.

"There was nothin' stylish about my ma. She was just a plain woman. She didn't do no runnin' around, neither. I ain't never seen my ma wid no man. I tried to grow up and be just like her. She was a hard workin' woman, and she brought the pans right home. Then we'd sit down and eat out of the pans, and she'd tell me all about how them white folks like her cookin' and what they said. That's sumpin' me and Mamma sho' like to do, make them white folks talk about our cookin'. You is cookin' when you can make them white folks come pat you on the shoulders and say, 'Marguerite, that dinner was sho' nice, child.' That's the way they say it, you know. Sometimes they give you tips and things. My people does that all the time. They is always sayin' sumpin' nice about my cookin'. It makes you feel so good.

"Well, things went well. Then Mamma commenced gettin' old. I was hittin' around sixteen years old and gettin' kind of lively. There was a heap of fellows comin' around tryin' to get me, but I kept my head up and my mind on Mamma. 'Cose, you know I was scrapin' around. Gettin' some washin' here and there, makin' a li'l sumpin' and puttin' it right in the house. Well, Mamma got sick and she put me in her place. I was workin' fo' Miss Graves. It sho' was funny.

Miss Graves says to me, 'Honey child, does you think you can do my cookin'?' I says, 'Yes'm.' Shucks, in two days I had Miss Graves sayin', 'Honey child, I want you to be my regular cook.' She give me five dollars a week fo' cookin' and cleanin' up the house. It was some house, a two-story house. The only thing I didn't like about Miss Graves was that she always messed around the kitchen. She was always sayin', 'Honey child, is you got enough seasonin' in the food?' I wasn't no sassy thing, you know. I always says, 'Yes'm.' But I ain't paid her no mind. Just says 'Yes'm.' You got to say sumpin', ain't you?

"I worked fo' Miss Graves two years all by myself. Mamma was home sick. We had some scuffle. I took care of my mamma off of five dollars a week. Talkin' about makin' a dollar stretch. Cose, I nearly go blind lookin' at my li'l money, but I been makin' them dollars go fo' a mighty long time, son. I don't know how it would feel to have some big money. Don't guess I could arrange it much. Cose, me and my ma didn't wear no stylish clothes, but our clothes was sho' good enough to go to church in. I wasn't no high steppin' gal, 'cause I loved my ma too well and I wasn't rightly fixed. But if I'd known then what I know now, I'd been a solid mess. Don't you know that our preacher had his stuff, and he used to keep his eyes on me. Used to tell me all the time, 'Sister, I got my eyes on you.' I didn't say nothin' much, but I did a heap of thinkin'. You see, in them times I didn't know them preachers was runnin' around.

"Things went on mighty bad wid me pushin' here and pullin' there fo' a long time. Mamma was gettin no better. I was gettin' up in years, and the boys commenced comin' around. All of 'um wanted me to pull up my dress. That's all I could 'ear. 'Pull up yo' dress. Pull up yo' dress.' I commenced wonderin' what would happen if I'd pull up my dress. That's what you get. Some nice boys used to ask me that. And does you know one thing, like a fool, I waited till old Buster came along and then I pulled up my dress. That was the finals. What Buster didn't put on me, Lawd! I told that nigger he'd hafta marry me 'cause I liked it. He did. Both of us loved each other. But a heap of womens loved Buster. My ma used to tell me all the time that Buster wasn't the kind of man fo' me. I know, I used to hear people talkin' all the time, sayin', 'Don't let Mamma find nothin' out fo' you, find it out fo' yo' self.' So, boy, you got to 'scuse my talk, but I got me two or three mens, but they ain't satisfied me none. I was right. Old Buster is the man fo' me. That's the only thing my ma was ever wrong about!

"Yeah, Buster did all right then. He used to work down at the cotton warehouse. But I didn't get too much of his money, 'cause he had to take care of his mamma and papa. Then, old Buster spend plenty money on his back. He like to look fine, you know. That's what's hurtin' him now.

"We was livin' in a three-room house. The rent was ten dollars a month. I was still workin'. Did Buster eat them pans, like a goat eats paper. That man used to fall in them pans sumpin' awful. Man, pans is good eatin'. Ain't you never ate none? You get all that comes off the table.

"But let me tell you how I got Mrs. Cline to give me her pans. When I went there I says I slung pans. She says, 'What's that, Marguerite?' I says I slung pans, Mrs. Cline, that's all I knows. She commenced laughin'. Oh, she got a big kick out of that. Finally she says, 'I don't know what you is talkin' about, slung pans, but I give my cook all she can eat here, and I don't allow her to take anything home because I use the food the next day.' I ain't said no mo'. I just stood there. She says, 'What's the matter?' I says nothin'. She ups and asks me if I wanted to work under them conditions and I says, 'Yes'm, I'll work fo' you under any conditions, Missus Cline.'

"Well, I went to work. Buster and my ma started worryin' me about the pans. We was in a bad fix then. Li'l money comin' in, Mamma sick, and li'l food. Went on three months like that. I don't care if Mrs. Cline asked me to climb the house, I did it. Just do what them white folks want you to do—no matter what it is, do it. Man, I was doin' everything round that house. I was only suppose' to cook but I went to washin' and ironin', took the maid's job. Made my dinner. Set down and asked Mrs. Cline to read to me the new recipes in the book.

"I was nice with Mrs. Cline, but Buster and my ma was givin' me hell. Buster told me that [if] I didn't quit that job he was goin' to quit me. My ma told me I was an old fool to be workin' fo' people who didn't give her cook the pans and pots. I ain't said nothin'. You know, son, white folks think niggers is crazy anyhow. So you got to be crazy sometimes to get what you want from 'um. Well, I did all this work and mo' besides. So I gets myself together one day when Mrs. Cline was givin' a big party. The house was goin' to be flooded with people. She was fixin' things here and I was fixin' things there. I folds my hands and I walks up to Mrs. Cline. I says, 'Missus Cline, I got you a fine dinner today, and I done all my work.' She says, 'Yes, Marguerite, everything is finished.' Then I walks away from her and I says, 'Missus Cline, I'm quittin' less you let me slung some pans to my house.' She says, 'When is you

quittin', Marguerite? Would you be dirty enough to leave me now?'
I says, 'No, ma'm. If I was goin' to be dirty, I'd left you b'fo' all this
was done. But is you goin' to make me lose my husband by not
givin' me some fo' us[?] The only thing we cullud people can do is
get home and eat a little sumpin' you white folks can't eat. Has that
ever crossed yo' mind, Missus Cline? Is you humanity?' I could see
the change on her face. She says, 'You know damn well I'm humanity!' I says, 'Then give me them pans and pots.' She says,
'Why, you Marguerite. I got a mind to fire you.' But she only had a
mind. She wasn't goin' to fire me now. She looked at her watch
and then she told me, 'Get back to that kitchen, Marguerite, and
never talk to me like that again.' I says, 'No, mam, Missus Cline,
I'm sorry.' And I cried, 'cause I was sorry. She says, 'I'm goin' let
you take home my pots and pans, but I want you to come and go
out my front door, 'cause I don't mean fo' you to take home my
whole kitchen.'

"The party was fine. I heard all them people talkin' about my
cookin'. They wanted to see me. Missus Cline, she likes that, you
know. I met them white folks. Was I happy! Well, let me tell you.
Boy, it's no word of lie. Buster was packin' his clothes to leave me.
Come tellin' me, 'I ain't seen a woman yet who couldn't get the
pans from her white folks. The trouble is you ain't askin' fo' no
pans.' Don't you know I asked fo' them pans just in time. If Buster
would-a left me, what was I goin' to do[?] He did run around, but
he was some consolation at night. No, Buster ain't had much education, but he's got a heap of sense.

"Then around 1925 my ma died. I bury her. That was the first
time I ever missed work. Man, I been workin' fo' Missus Cline so
long I'm on her dead list. I hope she dies befo' me so I can get some
of that heiress money. I ain't the only one waitin' fo' that money,
neither. She's got a nephew there who is layin' in the hold fo' that
money. She'll leave a heap of thousands. But, that old woman is
goin' to outlive all of us and leave that money to Hotel Dieu* or
some place. That's where them white folks leave that money. They
never gives it to po' folks. Lawd, what is Buster goin' to do then!
Come askin' me was I sho' that Missus Cline got me in the will. I
says yes. What you reckon he says, 'I just want to know, that's all.'
She tells me she's goin' to give me some money some day and look
at me circulate it. Lawd, she won't see me circulate it, but she'll see
Buster circulate it. There's only one thing worryin' me. It's that
cool-lookin' brownskin gal. Oh, you got to give it to her now—

*Catholic hospital in New Orleans.

she's cool. I think she's got Buster. But let the fool go. She's a young gal, she'll wear him down one day. If she don't, the Lawd will.

"Buster's people all dead, and mine too. No, we ain't got no chillun. Don't guess we had the right system. Can't have none now 'cause our joints done got too old. Sho', I likes chillun. Wouldn't want but two—boys. Maybe they could help me out of this storm. Be my social security. I thinks people ought to have chillun. But they ought not to have mo' than they can take care of. Now, what would I do wid three or fo' kids? We'd starve fo' true then. I got a WPA man, I tell you. That's the only work he wants to do. He gets in with the foreman and gets one of them easy jobs. But I guess Buster needs an easy job to have an old and young womens. Poor Buster! I don't know where his mind is, but it sho' ain't on no work. And Buster sho' can't be thinkin' he's no pimp or nothin' like that. Talk to him? Man, Buster gets blood mad when I talks to him. I just let him be. He's raggety, ain't got nothin'. I got to mend his pants and sew mo' buttons on his shirts than anything in the world.

"About this education. It's all right, but where is the cullud goin' to use it? There ain't no good-payin' jobs in this part of the country fo' us. I say learn a trade or get good porter jobs. Work fo' good white people. They is wantin' intelligent cullud people now. I heard a lady say the other day she wish she knew where she could get a good college cullud girl to nurse her baby, 'cause them other gals is too dumb. Missus Cline says them college gals is too damn smart. There was one ag'inst the other.

"People should marry young and belong to the church, 'cause when you got a Christian heart you can do no wrong. Missus Cline says I'm right on that. She always tellin' me, 'Marguerite, you is glad you is black, and you is so happy.' I says, 'Yes'm, Missus Cline, I'm what I am. And I is proud of it.' I got what I wants. A li'l home, a good job. And to tell the truth, I done got used to a triflin' man. If he'd change now, I'd be sorry.

"Me and Buster ain't never been sick in our life. A little cold, yes, but nothin' else. We go to church sometimes. But, son, I spent most of my time foolin' wid Buster. He gets half-drunk, drunk, and re-drunk, and I got to make him sober. Got to feed him and fix him up. You know, I'm goin' get tired of that man and kill him. Might not do it, 'cause I love him. Ain't that a shame? What can I do?"

Robert McKinney

Chimney Sweeper's Holiday

NEW ORLEANS, LOUISIANA, 1938 OR 1939

That's the trouble with niggers now. They pray
too damn much. Every time you look around you see some
nigger on his knees and the white man figurin' at his desk.

The chimney sweep was taking a day off from work, and he sat on the porch of a dilapidated tenement house in a street of similar houses all occupied by Negroes.

He was a little drunk and was having an argument with an old woman, a neighbor.

His wife, sad-eyed and skinny, stood watching as a male crony at the gate urged the chimney sweep to join him at the corner saloon.

There was a little whiskey left in the sweep's flask and as he drank it the old woman began to talk.

"I remembers the day that boy was born," she said. "It was on a Tuesday night in 1894 in Westwego. And there was a big to-do at John Montgomery's house 'cause his wife Stella had just birthed her first and only child. Them niggers was raising it up. Yells was hittin' the ceilin' and whiskey was all over the place. Stella had shown she could bring a child to the world even if she had done run around with so many different mens.

"The crowd waited all day to see the thing happen, settin' on the front steps and in the side yard while the midwife looked on Stella, hoping she would prove her point. They was sayin', 'Come on, Stella.' And Stella was lyin' there gruntin'; her eyes was movin' around in her head like a top spinnin' on the ground. But Stella came on all right. A little black boy popped out and he commenced hollerin'. I was one of the first ones to smack him on his behine,

227

bam! He jumped! I remember it so well, like it happened yesterday.

"I don't know, but I'm willin' to bet that John Montgomery, Junior, opened his eyes to a pint of whiskey and some woman doin' a shake-down dance. 'Cause ever since that day he's been drinkin' whiskey and makin' women do shake-down dances. Them is dances where you slide back and pull up your dress; show your linen, you know.

"I drank with John Montgomery, Junior, befo' he was born, when he was born, and I been drinkin' with John Montgomery, Junior, ever since. I can't do no shake-down dance but I can have my fun."

It was Susie Coulter talking, a rheumatic brown woman, little taller than a midget. She is on the Department of Public Welfare. When she is drunk, she is friendly; when she is sober, she is hard to locate. It is necessary to have Susie around when you're talking to John Montgomery, Junior, because she is the only one who can handle him. She says boastfully, "Didn't I pick that black bastard up and put him on my knee when he was a baby? If I handled him then, can't I handle him now?"

John Montgomery, Junior, dressed in shabby blue overalls, drunk and forlorn, was standing next to Susie, and heard her introduction to his life without saying anything. He approved with a shaking head. John is a tall, slender black man with big eyes and white teeth. He walks proudly and talks at random. Susie says, "He is the best chimney sweeper in the world."

He is also a problem and a menace to his light-hearted common-law wife, Emma Daniels, who is never allowed to say what she thinks for fear of his fists.

Emma whispered, "You talk to him; I can't. He might sweep me away like he sweeps them chimneys."

John Junior began to talk. "Me, I'm a chimney sweep from way back—a chimney sweeper havin' a holiday. My pa was a chimney sweeper. . . . my ma was a chimney sweeper. Ask Susie." He wanted to say more about his mother and father but Emma interrupted him to remind him that his mother wasn't a chimney sweeper, but was a washwoman. "Lissen, bitch, keep your mouth closed," John said.

"I was born in Westwego. Took after my pa and ma. She born me in whiskey. My pa drank whiskey like the tank that bottles it. He was a laborer in the roundhouse of the T. P.* My ma didn't work at all. She was a good-time woman. But when she married my pa she

*Texas and Pacific Railroad.

settled down. She got into an argument with some people and bore me to prove she could have a baby. I'm sho' glad of it. No, my ma didn't have to work. She had enough to do takin' care of my pa when he got drunk. I ain't got nobody to take care of me."

This time Susie interrupted him, saying, "You is a damn lie, John Junior. Emma takes care of you when you is drunk and when you is sober." John Junior argued this point, telling her to go home before "I knock your damn head off."

He moved away from the post and eased himself down on the step. "I ain't got no education. Went to the third grade. That was enough fo' me. My pa stopped me, made me get a job on a milk truck. I was makin' two dollars a week. What I did with my money? I had a good time, that's what. Sho', school is all right fo' them who wants it, but I figures all you got to know is how to read and write, then nobody can cheat you out of nothin'! Ain't figures enough?

"I believe my pa and ma liked large families, but they tell me—now I don't know—but they tell me my ma had such a time bringing me she swore she wasn't goin' bring no more no difference what happens. She and pa drank so much they don't even remember how it all started, to tell the truth. Sho', I drank, too. Pa used to make me drunk, half the time. I've always liked whiskey and who don't like the way I do, they know what they can do.

"I quit the milk truck, couldn't have my fun like I wanted to. Had to get up too early. I was only ten years old then. What I didn't like about the milk truck was I couldn't be wid that sweet little gal next door to me long enough. Mister, I don't know if we was doin' nothin' or not, but it sho' was good. She at ten! What you think? Then, I got me a job ridin' a bike. Three fifty a week. I went to work so I could buy the clothes I wanted. My pa and ma wouldn't give me nothin'. I always did like to be dressed up. I like it now but my money ain't right. That's all a po' man can do—dress up, and have a good time."

Susie reminded John Junior that he spent $300 of his bonus on clothes for himself and his women.

But John had a defense: "Ain't we got to look fine when we walk down the street?" Susie reminded him that he pawned most of his clothes for whiskey, which encouraged John Junior to shout back: "A good bottle of whiskey is worth a suit in pawn any day. Then again, a man as ugly as me is got to spend money on women. Ain't that right? It ain't no need fo' me to fool myself. I always did spend money on women and I'm goin' to keep on doin' it.

"Sho', I done other jobs besides workin' on a milk truck and ridin' a bike. I worked at the roundhouse when I was a man. Made twenty-one fifty. Used every bit of it up, that's right. Man, I used to buy mo' fun than a chicken had feathers. They used to call me 'lil John Junior, a chip off his daddy's block.' I was a mess. Had women shakin' down and doin' the Eagle Rock* wid dollar bills in their hands. Have fun, live. You don't live but once. When you die square up the Devil. No, indeed! There never was a Christian in my family, we don't believe in that stuff. My pa used to say, 'Get me a bucket full of wine, I'll join the church.' Spare time? Man, I ain't had no spare time. Don't have none now. In my spare time I have my fun!

"I came to this part of town when I was about twenty. Bought so much stuff I had to go back on the other side. The policeman says, 'Boy, go back where you b'long. You is got these womens jumpin' naked.'

"Well, I tell you. There ain't nothin' wrong with being a chimney sweeper. The work might be dirty but the money is sho' clean and long. Yes suh! You get bucks when you clean chimneys! SWEEPER! ROOAP, ROOAP, SWEEPER! CHIMNEY SWEEPER! GET 'UM CLEAN 'FORE YOU SCREAM . . . FIRE! ROOAP! ROOAP! SWEEPER! I charge some people two dollars, and some two dollars and a half, mostly two and a half. I charge by the day and by the chimney. Jews make their own prices. You can't jew them up. The only thing I don't like about cleanin' chimneys is when them womens hangs around me. They sho' can give orders. What they know about cleanin' chimneys won't fill a book, but they hang around you. Sometimes I feel like tellin' 'um, 'Don't cry around me, lady, I'm not the fireman.'

"How I started cleanin' chimneys? Let me see. Say, you wants to know everything. Well, I was friendly with a fellow named Jeff Holt. He's dead. Jeff was makin' plenty money and needed help. So, me and him made up as partners. We used to make as high as twenty dollars a day fo' both of us. Wasn't bad, eh? Them was the days. That was before all this streamline stuff. Even the chimneys is streamlined now. Ain't no money in it now. Everybody is using gas and electric lights. And then again, nobody wants to pay. Can't make but about four or five dollars a day in the season . . . that in the wintertime. Some say let's get a union, but not me. I don't want no union. Fo' what? Fo' a bunch of black bastards to land in jail.

*Probably refers to the song, "The Eagle Rock Rag."

"How we get our jobs? Well, most of 'um is from our customers. They send us to people. And the fire stations send us lots of business, too. But, we just go along the street hollerin'. The reason why the fire stations wants to give us work because it saves them from a lot of work. See?

"It feels alright to clean chimneys. It's a job. And a good job. Sho', I'm proud of it. All them people who laughs at us is crazy. I used to make mo' money in a day cleanin' chimneys than some people who laugh at us make in a week. Money was just that good. Then again, there is a lot of places that feed you. Everybody likes a chimney sweeper. People think we is Mardi Gras. We don't care. We pick up a lot of tips like that.

"This is how we clean a chimney: we take them long corn vines and tie 'um together and sweep the soot down from top. It takes two men to do it. We draw down a small fire in the chimney by throwin' salt up the chimney. Salt is a strong acting agent fo' fire. It can't stand salt.

"I don't know why we wears beaver hats and them kind of clothes. I believes them is the uniforms because they don't look dirty. Nobody minds dirty clothes gettin' dirty. Does they? A white man gave me my beaver. The coat and pants is mine. We tie rope around our waist because we have to use it sometimes, to pull ourselves up and down the roof. We use that rope like a ladder. Man, sometimes we almost go down in one of them chimneys. I seen the time when I was in one of 'um like Santa Claus, reaching down in there like a baby reaching for candy. We take our pads, rags, salt, and stuff and wrap them up in a bundle.

"The trouble with this business is that them bastards cuts the prices all the time. Some of them womens tell you, 'The other man said he'd clean my chimney fo' fifty cents.' All that dust and stuff gets in your eyes. Man, that's dangerous. Suppose you get consumption? Cleanin' chimneys is bad on your lungs. I drink milk and liquor to keep from losin' my lungs. No, I ain't never been sick in my life.

"Man, I been tryin' to get on the WPA but I can't do it. There ain't no mo' money in cleanin' chimneys, ain't nothin' to it. Everything is modern and streamline. I'm tryin' to be streamline myself." He laughed and the women laughed with him. "I was so streamline I fell off a woman's roof one mornin'. The woman had done said, 'What you goin' do way up there?' I said, 'I'm goin' to examine things.' She had to examine my head. Say, man, them chimneys make you so dirty that when you get home you got to take a bath in kerosene. Everything on you gets black. That work makes you nervous. A white man sho' could never be no chimney sweeper. He would look like he was carryin' his shadow aroun'.

"Some white folks like to talk with you, especially them from the North. They say they ain't never seen nothin' like us. They wants to know where we live and how we live. One white lady ain't had nothin' fo' us to do, she just called us in and gave us wine and two dollars to talk with us. Man, we ain't told that woman nothin'. I ain't goin' to never let nobody know all my business, 'specially no white folks. We get cigarettes, clothes and things from people. All in all we do all right. But we don't take things instead of money. Some of them white folks try to get you to do that, but not me. I tells them to pay me money, sumpin' I can use. I can get bread, clothes, and what I wants with my money. It ain't coneyfit.

"I strictly have my fun. No, I ain't 'tendin' bein' no Christian. That's the trouble with niggers now. They pray too damn much. Every time you look around you see some nigger on his knees and the white man figurin' at his desk. What in the world is they prayin' fo'? Tryin' to get to heaven? They is goin' to get there anyhow. There ain't no other hell but this one down here. Look at me. I'm catchin' hell right now. I'm drunk and I ain't got no money.

"If I had some? Man, don't ask me no question like that. What else is I'm goin' to do but have my fun[?] I pay rent, give my old lady what she takes to pay the insurance, buy food, and get her sumpin' and that's all. What I'm goin' to do? Ain't no need fo' me to save nothin'. I ain't never been able to save nothin' in my life. I don't want to save nothin'. You want me to have troubles?

"I went to war—didn't get killed. Come on back—got my bonus. And then got me a load of womens and threw it away. Ain't that being a sucker? When you spend your money you ain't got nothin' to show for it. When you spend your money on whiskey you got whiskey to show fo' it.

"My wife is a good woman. She ain't had to work in two years. I took her out the white folks' kitchen. She wasn't makin' but three dollars a week, anyhow. That ain't no money. Sho', she brought the pots and pans home. But what was in 'um? A lot of leftovers. Man, as long as I can make a dollar sweepin' chimneys I ain't goin' to eat nobody's leftovers. I can buy what I want and I'm my own boss. Do you know that I been sweepin' chimneys off and on fo' eighteen years? Before I did that I used to be a common laborer. If I can help it I'll never be a common laborer agin. I likes to be my own boss. Don't want no white folks hollerin' at me.

"I fo'got to tell you that sweepin' chimneys is a hard thing in the wintertime; it's mighty cold five o'clock in the mornin'. I'll never fo'get. Man, I went hollerin' under a politician's window one mornin'. ROOAP . . . ROO . . . AP . . . ROOO . . . OAP! CHIMNEY SWEEPER . . . RO . . . ROOAP . . . REEE . . . REE . . . EEE . . . ROOAP . . . CHIMNEY! Man, the politician poked his head out of his window and told me, 'Say, you black bastard. If you don't get the hell away from here I'm comin' out there and rope your damn neck to one of them trees!' His wife stuck her head out the window and just laughed. It was early in the mornin' too. She just laughed, and said, 'Darlin', leave him alone. I think he's cute.' The man looked at her and looked at me; I was ready to make haste. He started cussin' agin, 'You black bastard, if you don't get goin' you'll be cute. You won't have no damn head.' Then, he looked at his wife. 'Cute, hell. You run your damn trap all night and here comes that chimney man runnin' his mouth early in the mornin' and you say he's cute. I'll kill that nigger.' Man, did I leave from away from there! That's why we don't go out early in the mornin' no mo'."

The man with the bottle said, "Come on, John, quit talkin' and let's go to that saloon on Washington Avenue."

Emma said, "John."

He looked at her and said, "Baby, get my dinner ready. I'll be back."

But the woman knew that he was off with his friends. Old Susie was angry; she shrugged her shoulders and said, "Damn fool, there he goes bummin' with rats when he has a nice gent'man to talk with."

A black man called to John Junior from a passing automobile, "Where you goin'?"

He flipped his fingers and shouted back, "I'm goin' make some women shake down and show their linen. Everybody is worrin' about John. Can't a man have a holiday?"

Emma was "plum disgusted" with John. "All he knows is work, more work, fun and more fun. That fool has more holidays than the President. He ain't never had nothin . . . ain't got nothin' and ain't goin' to never have nothin'. He's the best money circulator in the whole round world."

Robert McKinney

WHITE OVER BLACK:
ANXIOUS TIMES . . .
AN UNCERTAIN FUTURE

I think of the tale of the rattlesnake and the bear. The rattlesnake was in the fire and a bear came along. The snake asked the bear to take him out and the bear promised, if he would say he wouldn't bite after getting out. The bear took the snake out after his promise, and they walked on down the road. The bear noticed the snake continuously licking out his tongue. He'd think of his promise and then draw in his tongue. On down the road they went, and again Mr. Bear noticed Mr. Snake licking out his tongue. Mr. Bear said, "Mr. Snake, I'm afraid you aren't going to live up to your promise." Mr. Snake said, "Well, Mr. Bear, it is my nature to bite. I can't help it."

—Black minister,
Atlanta, 1939

Senator "Cotton Ed" Smith of South Carolina stormed out of the national Democratic convention in 1936 when a black minister rose to invoke the divine blessing upon the political donkey. Amid the tidal wave of support for Franklin Roosevelt that year, the senator's one-man march went virtually unnoticed.

The senator's angry walk was a timely political gesture for a man seeking reelection in the South in the 1930s. He graphically under-scored the Southern limits of the Democratic coalition. The South —most of it—embraced Franklin Roosevelt and his New Deal, but the embrace slackened whenever the Democracy drifted from its lily-white ways and gave even the slightest sign of welcome to blacks. In the 1930s, as before, *the* Southern white question was how to keep blacks in their place.

Slavery had provided a starkly simple answer to the question. Then, the Civil War came, and new answers had to be found, especially after blacks asserted themselves during Reconstruction. They voted. They sought and won public office. They tried to become land-owning farmers. They even formed separate churches when they discovered that after the abolition of slavery they were still expected to remain in the back pews.

Southern whites developed new answers: violence, fraud, in-timidation, discrimination, disfranchisement, Jim Crow. Initially, the first four were the primary tools of white supremacy; and these tools were never entirely discarded. Disfranchisement and the in-tricate web of Jim Crow legislation came in the 1890s. But even after Southern whites regained political control when Reconstruc-tion collapsed, blacks continued to vote in considerable numbers from the 1870s into the 1890s. Some held elective offices in the South until about 1900; Southern blacks served in Congress until 1901, while others held local elective positions. But then, black voters and black elected officials became virtually extinct species. Even the opportunities for blacks to get appointments to lesser federal offices declined sharply after 1900 ("Yes, Lord, I'se Tried to Serve You Faithful").

Economic advantage, however, remained the most effective means of maintaining white supremacy. Southern whites had had and continued to have most of the capital and virtually all the land. Thus, blacks lacked money, land, and access to credit in a predomi-nantly agrarian region where all three were integral to success, even to modest self-improvement. Consequently, blacks in the rural South sharecropped, farmed as tenants, and worked as farm laborers, almost invariably for whites.

Kindness and genuine warm relations between blacks and whites sometimes softened the harsh realities. Moreover, there were some common bonds: poverty, a localism that made migration a wrenching ordeal, and a common past though viewed from contrasting perspectives. But subordination remained and defined the limits of black-white relationships. According to whites, subordination did not require coercion because blacks were content. Some blacks may have been. Others were not but knew they had better appear to be. People played roles, developed tortured rationalizations, and became confused about their own identities. There was no confusion, however, about what could happen to blacks who got out of their place. Despite the claims of whites, acts of violence and the pervasive threat of violence were necessary to maintain white supremacy ("Tech 'Er Off, Charlie").

In the 1930s, blacks challenged the caste system. "Cotton Ed" Smith was aware of that. His march from Convention Hall in Philadelphia in 1936 was hardly the spontaneous gesture of an unreconstructed Rebel. When he ran for reelection in 1938, he refined his theatrics into a campaign piece, "the Philadelphia Story." "[When a] slew-footed, blue-gummed, kinky-headed Senegambian . . . started praying . . . I started walking, and as I . . . walked . . . it seemed to me that old John Calhoun leaned down from his mansion in the sky and whispered . . . you did right, Ed." Whatever Calhoun thought, voters in South Carolina were pleased. They reelected Smith.* They and he correctly sensed that their answers to the question were becoming inadequate, that the real cause of concern was not events in Philadelphia but the sort of things that were happening in places like Northampton County, North Carolina.

Superficially a sleepy, small rural county in northeast North Carolina, Northampton had and has a black majority. In 1930, most of its 17,000 blacks and its 10,000 whites farmed. Others worked in farm-related businesses—feed stores, cotton gins, and the like. Sawmills and nearby textile mills provided virtually the only alternatives to agriculture. However people in Northampton tried to make a living, most got meager returns.

Beneath its calm surface, trouble brewed in Northampton in the 1930s. A substantial collection of oral histories from the Federal

*Daniel W. Hollis, " 'Cotton Ed' Smith—Showman or Statesman?" *South Carolina Historical Quarterly* 71 (Oct. 1970): 249, 251–56.

Writers' Project recorded the trouble. Blacks and whites struggled over the severely limited economic opportunities.

And when we old heads is gone, they won't be no more farmin' except what niggers does. This young crowd a-growin' up ain't a-goin' to slave their lives away on farms. They're goin' to git jobs and make money a easier way. The county'll be turned over to niggers then. It's somethin' to think about I tell you, with ten niggers to one white man here now! In a few years a white man can't live on a farm, not safe, as many mean niggers as they is a-growin' up.—*White sharecropper*

Racial trouble had occurred before in Northampton. In 1832, Nat Turner led his famous slave rebellion in Southampton County, Virginia, which bordered on Northampton. Memories of the Turner rebellion lingered and festered in Northampton in the 1930s.

Just a few years 'fore I was born, the nigger risin' over at Cross Keys took place. I use to hear 'em tell about how Nat picked up babies out o' their cradles and busted their heads open on the hea'th, sayin': 'Nits make lice.' One woman that was hid from the slaves got so mad when she saw 'em tryin' on her dresses that she busted out o' her hidin' place and was killed. There's been scares since then, once not many years ago when the report got out around here that another nigger risin' was about to take place. They said the niggers was goin' to cut the telegram wires so nobody could send for help from other counties. I lost a many a hour's sleep 'long then.—*Widow of a farmer*

White folks 'll all move to town when we old heads is gone; they won't be no more white churches and schools. The country will be turned over to the niggers. I don't know what'll happen then—another Nat Turner risin', I reckon. I've been all through the neighborhood where Nat and his followers slayed the white folks. At Cross Keys the old Francis house is still standin', though nobody lives in it. I've been all over that house, seen the blood where Nat splattered on the floor when he killed his marster and mistress and the little baby he had helped nu'se.*—*White sharecropper*

I won't never forget some years back, since we been married, when the report got started that the niggers in Northampton and Southampton was goin' to rise. Most of our neighbors took quilts and blankets and spent several nights in thickets, 'fraid to stay at home. We didn't leave the house, but I never slept none for a night or two. I remember plannin' if we

---

*In this instance, historical fact has been altered by oral tradition. Though undoubtedly the leader of the rebellion, Turner killed only one person, Margaret Whitehead. At the Nathaniel Francis house, Turner's followers killed the overseer, Henry Doyle, and Nathaniel Francis's two young nephews. Mrs. Francis survived with the aid of some of her slaves who hid her in the attic. See Stephen B. Oates, *The Fires of Jubilee: Nat Turner's Fierce Rebellion* (New York: Harper & Row, 1975); Henry I. Tragle, *Nat Turner's Slave Revolt—1831* (New York: Grossman Publishers, 1972); and Henry I. Tragle, *The Southampton Slave Revolt of 1831: A Compilation of Source Material* (Amherst: University of Massachusetts Press, 1971).

heard the niggers comin' we'd run hide in my butter-bean vines; they was real thick that year. It wa'n't just a idle report neither. Some white folks e'dropped on the niggers and heard 'em plannin' a risin'. So the head ones was arrested and put in jail. Some folks is so scared o' ha'nts and ghosts, but it's the livin' I fear, mean niggers and such.—*His wife*

After the Civil War did what Turner could not do—end slavery —blacks figured prominently in the politics of Northampton. As late as 1901, a black congressman represented the district which included Northampton. In the 1890s, the whites rebelled. Determined to end black dominance at the ballot box and to prevent blacks from holding public office, the whites used violence, fraud, intimidation, and discrimination to restore white government locally, and they continued to do so in the 1930s ("Roger T. Stevenson: Justice of the Peace"). By then, however, whites in Northampton felt their grasp slipping. Blacks were demanding schoolbuses for black children, equal pay for black schoolteachers, and the vote ("Sam Sets It Down"). Some whites foresaw a day when there would again be a black majority and blacks once again in public office.*

So far as the racial question is concerned locally I see no immediate problem. There's no doubt it will have to be faced by the next generation. —*Farmer*

Too many of the present generation remember former Negro postmasters, county commissioners, and registers of deeds to feel exactly easy about the Negro vote.—*Local judge*

There's no doubt that the Negro is going to be our greatest problem in Northampton, where nearly three-fourths of the population is black.[†] More are registering every year, and when they fulfill the requirements you've got to let them vote. I'm told that the schoolchildren are being taught to that end. The next generation is going to have the problem of Negro candidates and officeholders, without doubt.—*Merchant*

Those whites were right. Today, blacks are a voting majority in Northampton, and blacks hold some local public offices. In 1972,

*Blacks, especially those in eastern counties like Northampton, had an integral part in the election of Governor Daniel L. Russell, a Republican, in 1896. North Carolina Democrats counterattacked massively in 1898—the "White Supremacy Campaign." Terror and fraud triumphed. Then, once in control of the legislature, the Democrats solidified their position by disfranchising blacks. See Hugh Talmadge Lefler and Albert Ray Newsome, *North Carolina: The History of a Southern State*, 3d ed. (Chapel Hill: University of North Carolina Press, 1973), chap. 39.

[†]The merchant miscounted. The actual figure is closer to 60 percent.

Northampton was one of only two North Carolina counties that gave a majority of its votes to George McGovern.*

The modern civil-rights movement began long before the more dramatic events of *Brown* v. *Board of Education* (1954) or the Montgomery, Alabama, bus boycott (1955). That movement was deeply rooted in the soil of places like Northampton.

*The other was Orange County, site of the main campus of The University of North Carolina.

Yes, Lord, I'se Done Tried to Serve You Faithful

ATHENS, GEORGIA, 1939

He thought a white man should have the job.

"Well," he began, "Doc was right about you."

"I don't understand what you mean," I replied.

John laughed and said, "Well, the minute I come out on this porch I knowed you, for Mr. Mercer had done told me you was comin' to see me, and he said you was the livin' image of your father. I knowed your father from his boyhood up. He was a mighty good man. If he told you he was takin' you to jail, you'd might as well go 'long, for you had to anyway. But, if he said he was going to grant you a favor you knowed he meant that, too. Negroes all trusted what he said, for he never went back on his word."

I thanked him for his kind recollections and then I sought more of the facts of the old preacher's life story. "Dr. Mercer tells me that you're the first carrier to deliver mail in the rural area in this county." . . .

"That's right," John said, "and I'd like to start back further 'n that and say I was born and reared in Clarke County. My mother was a slave owned by Judge White, and I was born January 4, 1868, at the White home-place at White Hall, Georgia. When the war ended Mother was a widow with four children to rear. While I growed up in this country I have since then rolled around from place to place, and it seems like I can make more anywhere else than I can here. I've earned me a good name here in Clarke County, and mark my word, it follows me wherever I go.

"When I was still quite small my mother moved to Athens and she sent me to old Knox Institute for three months. That's all the schoolin' I ever got 'cept now and then I got three months a year at little country schools. I didn't like life in town, so Mother said I could go back to the country. She hired me out to work on the farm for twelve dollars a year, and my clothes, eats, and three months of school. Mother hired us all out like that, and she collected the cash for us at the end of the year, but she'd always give us a little of what our work brought her. My father died before I was born—so they told me—and so, of course, I never seen him.

"Whilst Mother only got twelve dollars for my first year's farm work, she was paid eighteen dollars for my second year, and for the third year they paid her twenty-five dollars. That was good money for a little boy to earn them days. After that third year I left the farm and come back to town to live. I worked in a place where they made wagons and farm tools. They called it an implement company. Making six dollars a month made me feel rich, it was so much more'n I'd ever had paid to me in cash before, but I didn't get no clothes, or board, or schoolin' throwed in free with that job, so it didn't mean so much more pay after all.

"I quit the implement place and went to work for a contractor at seventy-five cents a day. That was almost as much in a week as I'd got in a whole month before. I was workin' there when the steeple was put up on the white folks' First Methodist Church. Ever' time I passes there and looks at that fine, grand steeple, I'se glad I helped to put it up there. There was many workmen hired to carry on that work of buildin' the First Methodist Church, but I believes I'se right in sayin' now that of all that crowd of white and colored men there's only two left livin' today. One of 'em's a mighty prominent white man now, but at that time he was just the little water boy that trotted all over the place totin' water for the workmen. The other one is myself.

"Mother left here and went to Richmond, Virginia, with some white folks, and so I had to look out for myself. I worked on several years for the contractor and then I got to wantin' to git back to the farm, where it wouldn't take all the cash a pore boy made to pay for his eats, a place to sleep, and a few clothes. So I quit and went to the country where I done farm work for wages and worked a patch of my own. Bein's as I was engaged then and gittin' ready to git married, I planted my patch in wheat and raised me a hog.

"On December 25, 1886, we got married. . . . Well, miss, we started off with plenty of bread and meat. I worked on the farm three years then, but money was so slow comin' that I had to quit farmin' again. I went to work in a machine shop in Rome, Georgia, and I was the only colored man in a shop that hired seventy-five hands. I made pretty good wages there for two years, and then I got homesick for the farm I just couldn't stand it no more.

"I went right back to that same old place on the farm, but this time I tried it out different. I rented me a farm, bought some good stock, and went to farmin' for my ownself. It was a pretty hard pull, but I was stickin' it out, and was makin' a pretty good livin' after I'd stuck to farmin' steady for several years, when all of a sudden, I was 'p'inted mail weigher. This was during President Harrison's administration.* On February 12, 1892, I went to work under Superintendent Ferrell. I kept my farm goin' while I worked as mail weigher on the trains of the Fourth Division of Railway Mail Service. After I quit weighin' the mail, I kept on farmin' and studyin'. I realized after I married that if I was to git ahead in this world, I had to study. Whilst we lived in Rome, I went to night school, and after we come back here to live I kept on studyin' at home. I'd buy me a good book and study it through till I knowed what was in it, and then I'd buy another'n and start learnin' it. I kept that up a good many years.

"I disremembers the 'zact date I started carryin' the rural mail, but it was some time around 1897—during the time Matt Davis was postmaster here. I was the first man to carry rural mail in the state of Georgia. They'd been running what they called star routes a long time, but there hadn't been no mail being delivered to homes out in the country in what was called the rural areas. We had mail delivered to homes in cities for years. I went in my buggy and drove my own horses. In fact, I had to furnish all my own means of transportation to git around with the mail. It was just a 'speriment to see if it could be worked out to pervide regular delivery of mail to farm homes. They tried to survey a route of twenty-five miles for me, but that wouldn't end right at the post office, no way they could 'range it, so I had to make twenty-eight miles a day. The mail was heavy and the goin' over them rough, muddy roads was bad.

---

*Benjamin Harrison, Republican president, 1888–92. Even after the end of Reconstruction, Republicans did not abandon the idea of building a Republican party in the South. For a description of Republican Southern strategies in the Gilded Age, see: Stanley P. Hirshson, *Farewell to the Bloody Shirt: Northern Republicans and the Southern Negro, 1877–1893* (Bloomington: Indiana University Press, 1962), and Vincent P. DeSantis, *Republicans Face the Southern Question: The New Departure Years, 1877–1897* (Baltimore: Johns Hopkins University Press, 1959).

"I had good horses and I was young and strong, so I made it, but it was the roughest ridin' and the coldest weather I'd ever witnessed. It's sho the truth that I've come in lots of times with icicles in my whiskers. That was one awful winter. There just wasn't no roads, and where I had to go was all cut up knee-deep in mud. There wasn't no automobiles then, but if there had been plenty of 'em they wouldn't have done no good on them trails, for it was nigh to impossible for a horse to git over 'em some days. Several miles to my old route is paved, and they call it a highway now. Well, it sho won't no highway then. It was just mud wallows knee-deep and stiff as everything. For all that work and risk they paid me just thirty dollars a month, and I didn't git nothin' for pervidin' my own horses and buggy. I had to feed them horses plenty, too. It took a heap of repairs to keep my buggy goin', but I never got a cent on that. It was lucky that I held on to my little farmin' business, for even if I couldn't do all the work myself I could put a renter on it, and I got enough off the farm to feed my stock. That was a heap of help, for that thirty dollars a month wouldn't have fed them horses and my family too and covered our other necessities.

"People along my route was mighty nice to me. During that bad winter weather they knowed when to 'spect me, and they would have hot coffee for me and hot things for me to eat. I can tell you that sho did help. Many's the time my feet have been frostbit by the time I got back to the post office after strugglin' through ice and snow for twenty-eight miles over them rough roads.

"I was a reg'lar post office on wheels, for I carried everything with me you could buy in a post office, 'cept money orders, and I took applications for them. I sold all sorts of postage stamps, stamped envelopes, and postal cards. There's more brain work in carryin' the mail than most folks thinks.

"Nothin' ever kept me from gittin' the mail through on time. It meant goin' in all sorts of weather. I thought the cold, the sleet, and snow was awful, but the hot summer weather and sudden hard rainstorms was bad, too. I'll never forgit one of them bad storms. The wind was terrible. It turned me completely around in the road. Horse and buggy was goin' 'round like a piece of paper; big trees was tore up by the roots. I couldn't stop, for the wind just carried me along. Sometimes it would seem like my horse and buggy was being blowed sideways off the road, and next minute we would be goin' backwards. I thought sho I'd die in that there storm.

"It's sho a wonder I don't have to go on crutches from them awful exposures and the many times I've come back with frozen feet and hands. Finally I had one of the wagon shops here in town build me a reg'lar mail wagon that had a nice little heater in it. I planned it so that I could drive right up to the boxes and put the mail in without gittin' out myself. It was a dandy, and while I had to pay for havin' it made myself, it was worth it for the sake of my health.

"The first hard years of gittin' the route started off at that small pay; nobody wanted the job. But when everything got straightened out and the salary had been raised to around seventy-five dollars a month, then folks started tryin' to git my job away from me. Pretty soon there was a hot race for the place as congressman and one of them candidates made speeches all over this district promisin' the people that if he was 'lected he'd sho see that my job was give to a white man. He was 'lected, and sho 'nough I was put off my job on August 1, 1913, after I'd served as rural carrier for fifteen years, six months, and two days. Them two days was the time spent breaking in the new white mail carrier.

"That congressman wouldn't give me no reason for firin' me, 'cept that I was a Negro. He testified to that in all the newspapers. I've got the clippings now in my trunk. There wasn't nothin' ever charged against my service record or my character. Even the congressman that got me fired testified to that and said I'd served faithful and well, but he thought a white man should have the job. That same route is now payin' over $100 a month.

"From the time I started in weighin' mail till I was put off my job as rural mail carrier, I served under six presidents. They was Harrison, Cleveland, McKinley, Roosevelt, Taft, and Wilson.

"Some of the older people along my mail route tried to help, but they couldn't do nothin'. Them good old men of them days was the salt of the earth. Long as I was carryin' their mail they never forgot me at Christmas time, and I didn't just git little old shoe-boxes full of stuff neither. They filled big boxes for me. One of my patrons always had me a ham baked when his ham was baked for Christmas dinner. Them old hams was some fine eatin'.

"I went right on back to farmin' when they took my job away, and I 'complished a right smart little bit of property. Later, in a bad deal I lost over $10,000. In fact, everything I had went except this house, and it was held in a morgage of $1,000. That's when I had to go off to work to raise money to pay that mortgage. My family never knowed how close they come to bein' without a home.

"The way I 'complished my property was this way: I first bought a small place that I later sold for $5,000. Then I borrowed $1,000 to go with that and put the whole $6,000 into a big six-horse farm. That was more farmin' than I could handle by myself, so I rented out part of it. For a few years I made money. Then the boll weevil got me and it got my renters too. They couldn't pay me and I couldn't pay off nobody I owed, so it was up to me to git out and work.

"I just left my family and went off to Indianapolis, Indiana, where I worked in a park at $3.00 a day. My next job there was in a boiler room and it paid $3.75 a day. Remember, all that time I had to pay my own 'spenses in that big city, keep up my family here, pay insurance and interest, as well as something on the principal of the mortgage, and then too I was trying to educate my chillun at that time.

"I never done much boardin' out when I was off from home at work. I'd just rent me a room as cheap as I could and buy what I et. When I could, I'd bile me a pot at night and eat on that as long as it would last. That was all right in winter, but things sp'iled too quick in summer for that, and then too in summer I didn't have no fire in the fireplace to bile pots on nohow. I never let my 'spenses run over four dollars a week, and I tried mighty hard to keep 'em down to where one day's work would cover my livin' cost for a week. I'd have the other five days' income for my family and to pay on the mortgage. Whenever I'd done spent as much as four dollars in a week, I just quit eatin' till the next week. I just couldn't see no sense in me payin' out five to six dollars a week for board like the other men that was off up there workin'. I lived like that for seven years.

"I ain't done no farmin' 'cept just on the land around the house here since I got back home from Indianapolis, but I'se raised as much as a bale and a half of cotton right around the house here some years. Other years I plants it all in corn. For the last two years I'se had to rent it all out, for I just haven't had the strength to raise even the corn, and ain't made one cent of money this year.

"We had six chillun; four of 'em's girls, and two's boys. They's all growed up and scattered out to other places. I never could git any of 'em interested in farmin'. I sent my girls through college. Susie here's a graduate, a registered nurse. She took her training in Atlanta.

"I tried to send our boys to college, but they wouldn't even finish high school. One of my sons didn't want to do nothin' but work around meat markets. They 'vanced him right along and when he died he was packin' meat in one of the biggest packin' houses in this country. My other son ain't never 'mounted to much. He just works around at anything he can git. He would-a made a good plowhand, but you know money's slow comin' in on the farm, and my boy don't like to wait on that. He wants his money soon and often.

"My chillun's educations ain't never done me no good, for they's all married and workin' for somebody else. I'se come to the place where I can't see that college education is no good to workin' people, be they white or be they colored. I really b'lieves they's better satisfied and works better without it. Common grammar-school education is plenty for them that's got to work.

"My ministry? Oh, I'se been a-preachin' the Gospel over thirty years now. It was while I was workin' in Rome, Georgia, that I felt the Lord had done weighted me down with the Gospel. I professed religion and was baptized in Silver Creek, near Rome. It wasn't more'n two years before I felt the actual call to preach, so I went on back to that old Baptist Church for my membership. How-some-ever, I'se never pastored no church in Clarke County. I'se pastored plenty of churches in Banks County, Georgia, and in Marion County, Indiana. While I was workin' in Indianapolis, I preached around at all the churches.

"I went and give myself bad luck here. I refused to accept when one church called me to be its pastor. Since that time I ain't suc-ceeded in gittin' a church to pastor in Clarke County. My hearin's done got so bad now, I don't seek no church to pastor no more, but I'll preach a sermon for any of 'em 'most any time. My member-ship's in Hills First Baptist Church, over in town, and that's where I attend preachin'.

"I worked every day when I was pastorin' churches. My mem-bers never wanted me to keep no other job, but just to preach for 'em and visit 'round 'mongst the disabled members. But I had to work out, 'cause I had a family to look out for and my chillun was in school. There was a debt on this here house, too, that had to be paid off. I just had to keep on the job every day and preach on Sunday.

"Takin' it all in all, you're only at a church long as you'n' the members agree on everything. Just let something come up in the church where the pastor don't see things just the way all his members wants him to, and right then they'll throw him out for sho, before he knows what's happenin'. I needed my daily wages too bad to depend on a church salary.

"Yes, I worked hard every day when I had a church to pastor, and it was mighty nice to have them wages comin' in, 'cause preachers don't git much pay. There was times now and then when I could git a few days on special jobs that paid extra good. . . . I don't never ask for the easiest jobs and the best pay. All I wants is to do my job so well that I'll leave my footprints in the sand at your door. That'll pay in the long run.

"It was 'bout seven years ago that I come back here to live. Right away I opened me up a little grocery store over on Broad Street. I done well [enough] with my cash sales that I tried to increase my earnings by givin' credick. I didn't last long after that.

"One Saturday night the police come in my store and told me they was goin' to search the place for liquor. I told 'em to go right ahead and search, for if there was whiskey in my store I had never knowed it. No, mam, they never found none. It was right funny though, when they come across a can of gasoline under the counter. They made sho they had the liquor, till they got it unstopped and smelt of the pure old gasoline. When they got through with their searchin' they said somebody had called 'em up and told 'em I was sellin' liquor and that if they'd make a search they'd find it. I told 'em right then that if anybody had liquor in my store I wanted it found for I didn't have no use for it myself and didn't want it around my place of business or my home either. No, mam, them policemen never come in my store again long as I run it.

"I had two calls for funerals lately. No, mam, it don't no ways bother me to preach funerals, for them's jobs the Lord sends, and I does the best I can. I'se got a strong tendency to sympathize with the family, and therefore I very strongly disapproves of these here long funeral services. They's too hard on the bereaved ones. Another thing I disapproves of too is the openin' of the casket at services in the home, the church, or the graveyard. The family has plenty of time to see the face of the dead before the services and lookin' at the corpse in public at them last services is too refreshin' on their minds. Then, too, there is a very strong tendency for the remains to spread germs. I'se knowed cases where folks got germs of the disease the corpse died of and that caused a spread of that kind of sickness that could-a been avoided by not openin' the coffin at the services. Did you ever attend one of our funerals?" John asked.

"Only once," I replied, "and I found it a very nice funeral service. It differed from the final rites for those of our own race in but two respects."

"What'd you see that was different?" John wanted to know.

"Well, for one thing the minister recited the scripture about 'Dust to dust, ashes to ashes,' at the church service. That is done as the casket is being lowered into the grave at our services. The second difference was that the casket was wheeled around before each member of the family for their last view of the dead."

"Who preached that service you was at?" John demanded.

"Some Atlanta man; I do not remember his name," I replied.

"Uh-huh! Just what I thought," John said. "That was this way. That preacher was from out-o'-town, and he knowed he didn't have no time to go to the graveyard. Most colored folks' graveyards is a long ways from the churches anyhow, so he just give 'em the graveyard service right along with the church service so there wouldn't be nothin' left for the undertakers to do 'ceppin' 'posit the casket in the grave. I'se knowed these out-o'-town brudders to ax another pastor to go with the family to the graveyard when they didn't have time to go with 'em theyselves.

"Now when they rolls that casket 'round to the family it's for a good reason—several good reasons. Maybe you ain't knowed that when our folks gits 'cited they just natchully falls out. When the family takes that last fond look at the beloved dead, their grief is so refreshed that they fall out. Sometimes they falls right into the casket and upsets it. I has knowed the corpse to roll right out on the floor in the 'citement and fallin' 'round. Now when the casket is rolled up before 'em, they can just set still and take the last look. It's so much easier on the family and on the undertaker too.

"I'se got this to say: you's done noticed well . I'se been to lots of funerals of my white friends. 'Course the white folks often has more money to spend on they funerals and they has finer flowers, but the customs is 'most the same.

"The marryin' business don't bring me in much money these days. Why, they ain't but two couples come to the house here for me to marry 'em this year. I'se been preachin' for fifty years, tryin' to serve my Lord and Master so I'll be ready when He calls for me to come up there with Him and I wants to leave a clean record behind me.

"Yes, mam, I'se been here a pow'ful long time, but"—he pointed to his thick white hair—"I ain't been here long enough to git bald-headed, and not long enough to git gray. I got white-headed when I was real young.

"I may look old to you, but I'se got a sister that's older'n me. Just 'cause she whipped me to make me mind her once when I was little, she still thinks I'se got to do just what she says. I tells her I'se a white-headed old man now, old enough to decide for myself, but that don't make no difference with her. She'll jump on me to make me mind her just as quick today as she done then. That whippin' she give me when I was little was about Old Miss—she was my mother's white mistress. Miss Maggie used to want me to recite for her company up at the big house. She had done larnt me all kinds of smarty little pieces to say and had done told my folks to dress me up clean and nice when she sont for me to come up there to show off recitin'. One time I got mean and contrary, and even said I won't goin', but when this sister of mine got through layin' on that strap I was mighty glad to go. . . . That's how I got so many of them old shinplasters. . . . White folks would give me a handful of 'em every time I recited. Shinplasters, you know, is them old pieces of paper money that didn't run no higher'n from ten to twer   -five cents.

"Playin' ball was the pleasure of my younger days, anu I sho don't no ways turn my head off now when I passes a ball game, not even if I is a preacher of the Gospel. But all the gatherin's I atten's now is at churches—mostly baptizin's and protracted meetin's—and, of course, I goes to all the church socials I can. Us preachers has to be careful 'bout where we goes and what we does. We's held up as shinin' lights for sinners to go by. One thing I sho regrets is that 'round in the towns and cities they's done quit havin' them good old August meetin's. August meetin's with us Baptists is like the old camp meetin's is with the Methodists. Mostly, the August meetin's that's held now is off out in the country. They ends up with a big baptizin' for them that the Lord in done weighted down with the Gospel. Them August meetin's is gatherin's that's enjoyable to attend.

"Education is a benefit to all the human races, but some of 'em needs it worse'n others. The thing that's been the greatest benefit to our race is insurance. I knows of more'n one instance where it provided a funeral where the corpse would-a had to lay out till somebody got out and raised the money to pay for the buryin'. Insurance is a great thing if we can just raise the little money it takes to keep it paid up.

"No, mam, I can't talk politics to you. Us preachers can't talk no kind of politics. That'll git a preacher in trouble with his congregation quicker'n 'most anything else, for you know nobody can't see the same way as all the others. Our folks don't go into politics as much as the white folks nohow, but when they does have a preference they's mighty strong in that belief."

John was silently rocking back and forth in his chair and gazing down the road. I knew he was tired and so I was about to say goodbye when he said: "Does you know where the old smallpox graveyard is?" I shook my head, and he continued, "It's on the other side of the East Athens Baptist Church. They buried the folks that died of the smallpox on the other side of the road, across from that church. There won't be no houses 'round about there then; it was all pine woods, and that's why it was counted a safe place to bury folks that died of smallpox. I'se cut wood and hauled it from that place many's the day, but I can't do it no more now. I'se just too no 'count for anything these days but to look after the chickens. I'se tryin' to raise a few chickens to sell so I can pay a little on my doctor bill. When you gits sick, it 'pears like you's just got to have the doctor, and it's sho a job to git him paid up.

"If it hadn't-a been for my [daughter] Susie here, I'd-a gone from my bed to the graveyard 'bout the first of this year. I had been livin' here by myself since my wife died five years ago. It didn't seem like home no more when I was all alone. Susie, she works in Atlanta, but when she heared I was sick, here she come and she's sho been good to me. She won't go off and leave me for nothin' or nobody. She will be blessed by our Lord and Master for bein' so good to take care of her old daddy.

"I ain't right well yit, and I'se got to stop and rest awhile now. Anyway, I'se done told you about all I can remember."

Grace McCune
Sarah H. Hall
John N. Booth

Tech 'Er Off, Charlie

JOHNSTON COUNTY, NORTH CAROLINA, 1939

"Son, . . . a catfish is a lot like a nigger.
As long as he is in his mudhole he is all right,
but when he gits out he is in for a passel o' trouble."

"Lawd have mercy, you done axed me a question whut's gonna take quite a spell to answer. But if you is got de gumption to put up wid de way I tell it, I'll do de bes' I can."

Uncle Charlie Holcomb rammed his worn hands under the bib of his faded blue overalls. The chill of evening and the smell of fresh-turned earth crept in through the open doorway of his two-room cabin. The wide pine floorboards were scrubbed the color of bleached bone, and a bright fire crackled in the whitewashed fireplace. Uncle Charlie sat in a corner where he could 'tend the cornpone that baked in the coals. A pensive frown creased his forehead as he hitched his cane-bottomed chair closer [to] the fire.

"We has always been tenement farmers and my pappy before me was a tenement farmer. Used to be, when I was a young man, I thought I could manage my business better and dat I was gonna be able to own a place o' my own someday, but dey was always sumpthin' come along and knocked de props from under my plans. My 'baccer was either et up by de worms, or it was de rust or de blight, or pore prices—always sumpthin' to keep me from makin' dat little pot I planned on. And den time de lan'lord had took his share and de cost o' de fertilizer and de 'vancements he had made, dey wan't but jist enought to carry on till de nex' crop.

"But Lawdie Lawd, dat was back when I was a high-minded young nigger and was full of git-up-and-git. Dey wan't nothin' in de world dat I didn't think I could do, and I didn't have no patience wid niggers what didn't look for nothin' but sundown and payday.

"I 'members good as yestiddy 'bout de place whar I was borned. It was a little pine-board shack 'bout like dis one, down in Sampson County, and it was set on de top of a red clay hill 'bout a quarter of a mile from de big road. De yard was swep' clean and hard as dis floor, and us chillun used to play dere from sunup till sundown wid de houn' dogs and whatever we could fine ter fool wid. Law me! We didn't hab no fancy toys or nothin' like de chillun does now, but we got along. We drawed lines on de groun' and played hippity-hop and games like dat. Shucks, we didn't need no toys. Dey was eight of us kids and dey was enough fuss and racket goin' on among us to keep from gettin' lonesome.

"My pappy shore was a powerful man, and he believed in hard work. He riz at four o'clock every mornin' and rousted us chillun out as soon as he got a fire goin'. My mammy would hab on a pot o' grits and a slab o' salt pork and it shore sot good on our little bellies. Our land was mighty pore and durin' de growin' season we'd be in de fiel' by sunup. We always slep' a little atter dinner, den we'd go back and work till sundown. Dat is, de ones dat was big 'nough to work would, and de rest would stay at home and play, or maybe chunk de fire under mammy's washpot.

"My gran'pappy lived wid us too, but he wasn't able to do much work. He had de miseries in his back and walked wid a stick. But he was right handy 'bout things like sloppin' de hogs and feedin' de chickens. I was his pet chile too, and he holp me out a lot in de little things a chile has to learn growin' up. I was a frail chile and wan't able to work in de fields like most chillun. And gran'pappy looked out for me. When dey was wormin' and toppin' to be done, he would take me to dig bait for him, and den we would go to de crick and ketch a mess o' catfish. He used to do a heap o' thinkin' while we was sottin' dar fishin'. I 'member once he caught a big, fat catfish and jist played wid him for a long time. He pointed to de fish and tol' me to watch him. Den he lifted de fish outen de water and dat fish kicked and thrashed sumpthin' turrible. Den he lowered de line and let de fish back in de water. When he did dat de fish jist swum around as easy as you please. Den gran'pappy pulled de fish out on de bank and we watched him thrash around till he died. When de fish was dead gran'pappy turned to me. 'Son,' he said, 'a catfish is a lot like a nigger. As long as he is in his mudhole he is all right, but when he gits out he is in for a passel o' trouble. You 'member dat, and you won't have no trouble wid folks when you grows up.' But I was jist a kid den, and I couldn't make much out of it. I let dat plumb slip my mind, and later on it shore caused me a heap o' grief.

"Gran'pappy knowed a lot 'bout 'baccer, and when de season for curin' come aroun' he would be de one to take care o' de firin' o' de 'baccer barn. We always did have a grand time durin' de curin', as we had ter stay wid de fire all de time 'til de 'baccer was done. Most o' de time some o' de neighbors would come over and bring a fiddle or a guitar and we would sing and dance and have de biggest kind o' time.

"I know how excited we all used to git when we started hangin' de 'baccer in de barn and gran'pappy would start layin' de wood for de fire. First he would put down some fat pine. Den he would lay some dry sticks on top o' dat, and last o' all he would put on some good sound hickory and white-oak sticks. It was always a great honor to light dat fire, and 'cause I was gran'pappy's pet he always let me do it. He would han' me a match and say, 'Tech 'er off, Charlie!'

"I was de las' chile to grow up and by dat time my mammy and pappy was gittin' pretty old. All de rest had either married or gone off to de public works, and I was de onliest one left to keep de ol' farm goin'. I never had been to school none to speak of, but I could read and write my name. All de time I kep' a-frettin' and a-hankerin' to git on a bigger farm and try to make sumpthin' outen myself. When de ol' folks died I lef' de place and moved over here to Johnston County and took a job on de public works. I saved me up a little money and married Dillie, and we took up dis place right whar we is now. Dat was over thirty year ago.

"Dis place was a lot bigger den dan it is now, but it don't take as much land for me now as when I was raisin' a family. I was full o' life den as a young bull, and meant to work hard and save my money and maybe buy de place later on. But like I done tol' you, dere was always sumpthin' dat come up to take all I had made. Back den dey wan't nothin' dat could disencourage me, and I kep' on a-tryin', and it wan't till my Willie was killed dat I lost de spirit.

"One time after I had sold all my 'baccer and de lan'lord took his share and de fertilizer money and de 'vancements out, it looked to me like I was gonna have a little left for myself. Den de warehouse man called me back and tol' me he had figgered wrong and dat I owed some more warehouse charges. I knowed it wa'n't right, and it made me so mad I jist hit him in de face as hard as I could. Den I kinda went crazy and might nigh beat him to death. I got twelve months on de roads for dat, and all de time I was away from home Dillie and de chillun had to try to make another crop, but 'course day couldn't do so good by deyselves and Mr. Crawford, dat's de lan'lord, had to carry 'em over. Hit took me three years to git him paid back.

"By dat time I knowed it wan't no use for me to try to ever make anything but jist a livin'. I was 'termined my oldest chile was gonna hab a chance in dis world, and I sent him all de way through high school. Willie was a mighty good boy and worked hard when he was at home.

"Atter he got outta high school he tol' me dat a man wid jist a high school eddycation couldn't git nowhere and dat he wanted to go to college. Me and Dillie talked it ober and we didn't see how we was a-gonna do it, but we let him go to de A & T College.* Will worked mighty hard and made good grades and worked out most o' his way. In de summer he would come home and he'p wid de 'baccer and we made some mighty good crops. Willie would take de 'baccer to market and go over de account, and he was pretty sharp and always come home wid money in his pocket.

"De last year Willie was in school he started gittin' fretful and sayin' dere wan't no future for a nigger in de 'baccer business, and dat he didn't want to come back to de farm. Dat hurt me, 'cause I had counted on Willie helpin' me, but I wanted him to do what he thought was best.

"When he graduated he was one o' de brightest boys in de class, but dat was when de trouble started. Willie knowed he had a good eddycation and didn't want to waste his time on no small job. But he couldn't find nothin' to do, and he finally come home and started settin' around and drinkin' and gittin' mean. I didn't know what was de matter wid him, and tried to reason wid him, but he wouldn' talk no sense wid me.

"Dat fall he took a load o' 'baccer to de warehouse, and when he come back he was all mad and sullen and I knowed he had been drinkin' again. All dat night he drunk and cussed sumpthin' turrible, and de nex' mornin' his eyes was all bloodshot and mean-lookin', and he had me scared. He said he was gonna take another load o' 'baccer to de warehouse, and I didn't want him to go, but he went anyway.

"'Long 'bout dinnertime one o' de neighbors come a-runnin'

---

*The Agricultural and Technical College of North Carolina, now the North Carolina Agricultural and Technical State University, Greensboro, N.C.

wid his eyes bulgin' clean out on his cheeks. He said dere had been a fight at de warehouse and dat Willie had been hurt.

"I got on my ol' grey mule and rode into town as fast as I could. When I got to de warehouse I seen a bunch o' men standin' around and den I seen my Willie layin' on de ground and a great puddle o' blood around his head. I knowed he was dead de minute I seed him. For a while I didn't know what to do. I looked around at de crowd and dey wan't a friendly face nowhar. Right den I knowed dey wan't no use to ax for no he'p and dat I was jist a pore nigger in trouble. I picked my Willie up in my arms and saw his head was all bashed in. Dey was tears runnin' down my cheeks and droppin' on his face and I couldn't he'p it. I found de wagon he had driv' inter town and laid him in dat. Den I tied my ol' mule on behind and driv' home. I never did ax nobody 'bout what happened to de 'baccer he took in.

"When I got home I washed Willie's head and dressed him in his best suit. Den I went out to let Dillie hab her cry. We buried him at de foot o' dat big pine at de left o' de well, and made some grass to grow on de grave. Dat's de mound you was lookin' at as you come up to de house.

"For a long time atter dat I couldn't seem to git goin', and dey was a big chunk in de botton o' my stummick dat jist wouldn't go away. I would go out at night and set under de pine by Willie's grave, and listen to de win' swishin' in de needles, and I'd do a lot o' thinkin'.

"I knowed Willie had got killed 'cause he'd been in a argiment wid somebody at de warehouse. Den I got to thinkin' 'bout what gran'pappy said 'bout de catfish, and I knowed dat was de trouble wid Willie. He had stepped outen his place when he got dat eddycation. If I'd kept him here on de farm he woulda been all right. Niggers has got to l'arn dat dey ain't like white folks, and never will be, and no amount o' eddycation can make 'em be, and dat when dey gits outen dere place dere is gonna be trouble.

"Lots o' times dere is young bucks dat gits fretful wid de way things is, and wants to cut loose and change, and when dey comes talkin' around me I jist takes 'em out and shows 'em Willie's grave. I been turrible hurt 'bout losin' my Willie, but it has give me a peace o' mind dat I couldn't a-got nowhar else. My other chillun has all moved off and has famblies o' dere own and dey don't hab much, but dey is happy.

"White man didn't Jim Crow de nigger—it was God Jim Crowed 'im, back yonder when Ham laughed at pore ol' Noah for gettin' drunk. Niggers is built for service, like a mule, and dey needn't 'spect nothin' else. Dey has got to l'arn to leave de thinkin' and de plannin' to de white folks. Niggers ain't smart 'nough to do de things de white folks does. Dey couldn't 'vent no radio, nor a meter for measurin' how many feet o' 'lectricity a man uses, nor a autymobile, or none o' de gadgets we has nowdays. Dat's for de white folks to do. A nigger's place is in de field and de road and de tunnel and de woods, wid a pick or shovel or ax or hoe or plow. God made a nigger like a mule to be close to nature and git his livin' by de sweat o' his brow like de Good Book says. And when a nigger is workin' and feelin' de strength o' his muscles and de good hot sun in his face he is happy. Long as he has plenty o' cornpone and pot likker to wash it down wid, he don't need nothin' else.

"I don't work much more like I used to. De chillun drap by now and den and he'p me wid de crops. I don't pay much 'tention to whether de prices for 'baccer is good or bad, 'cause I knows I always has 'nough to git by on. De lan'lord has been mighty good to me, and don't worry me in de least no more. I has my hog meat and plenty o' meal and collards in de summer, and Dillie always cans a little sumpthin' for de winter. Maybe I'se gittin' too ol' to care any more, but I knows de white folks takes pretty good care o' dere niggers, and I don't never worry 'bout whether my home is gonna be took by a mortgage or not. I has plenty to eat, 'cause my cravin's ain't very fancy, and I has plenty o' time to let my mind wander.

"Sometimes I git to dozin' and noddin' by de fire, and thinks back 'bout de time when I was a chile on my pappy's place. We didn't have nothin' much to wear, or much to eat, but we was happy. And I 'member how my gran'pappy used to pet me and take me fishin' wid him. Seems like when a feller thinks back he only 'members de good parts. De barn is always full o' yeller 'baccer, ready to be fired, and de kids all runnin' around whoppin' and hollerin' and somebody a-pickin' a banjo, and de air full o' de scent o' fryin' side-meat and cornpone. I can almos' see gran'-pappy down on his knees pullin' out a big fat splinter and handin' me a match and sayin', 'Tech 'er off, Charlie!' "

Author unknown

Roger T. Stevenson, Justice of the Peace

SEABOARD, NORTH CAROLINA, 1939

*Some wrote the Constitution, I reckon, as good as a lot
o' white men, but I'd find somethin' unsatisfactory, maybe an
i not dotted or a t not crossed, enough for me to disqualify 'em.*

" . . . I've quit farmin'. At seventy a man ain't fittin' to follow the
plow reg'lar. So I've retired. I rent out my little farm for what I can
get, which ain't much because my land's pore. All day long now I
don't do nothin' but keep the fires goin' and help out my old lady
with the odd jobs around the house. I miss farmin'; some days,
'specially as spring comes on, I get so restless I can't set still. I start
walkin' and just have to keep on walkin' till I'm wore out. With all
the children gone and my old lady feeble, I had to turn loose the
farm and stay around the house. In the daytime I set around Hicks's
store right smart, but when night comes I stay close to Mary. If you
want to see me at night you better come before seven, don't you'll
ketch me in bed. Mary's got high blood pressure, like most everybody else these days. No? Humph! Ain't no doctor goin' to take
my blood pressure unless they run me down to do it. . . .

"Forty-seven years I've lived with my old lady, and I told her the
other day I want to live with her forty-seven more. I was raised on
a farm at Midvale, and for a year after I got married I rented a little
farm there before I bought my place here on Butler Road. When me
and Mary got married, I didn't have but three dollars to my name,
which exactly paid for my license then. I borrowed fifteen dollars
from my daddy to buy me some chairs to set down in and a bed to
sleep on. I started with nothin' but credit, and I still got nothin'. So
I'm as well off as I ever was. . . .

" . . . My doctor and hospital bills has cost me more'n my home and farm would bring. When my son died of cancer twenty years ago, I spent $1,400 and then lost him. A few years ago I took a operation and later on another one, and was at the hospital seven weeks. My wife has to take medicine all time for her heart and blood pressure. All day I've been tryin' to catch a ride to Wells Ferry to get her some medicine.

"I reckon I'm a right smart politician. I been at it long enough. Governor Kitchin* appointed me magistrate twenty-five years or more ago, and when Richard was at the legislature the last time he had my term extended for another six years. Three years ago this spring, I aimed to run for the legislature. They need a man like me, a plain man right off'n the land, close to the laborin' class, the pore folks. I could tell 'em somethin' they ought to hear if they'd send me down there to Raleigh. The only reason I give up the idea was because one of the best friends I've got called me into his office and advised me not to run. He was for me all right, and if he had known a month sooner what I was plannin' he said he would o' helped me launch my candidacy. But all the precincts was done lined up then; I was just a month too late, and he didn't want me to get beat. His advice was for me to wait and run in the next primary. By last spring, though, Mary was so feeble I couldn't stand to go off and leave her. But the year I withdrawed I didn't support nary one of the men that run for the legislature. I had elected Williams to the last legislature, even though I knowed he wa'n't the type for public life. When he was tryin' to get elected the first time, he come and talked to me in the woods where I was workin'; but after I worked and helped get him elected he never had the courtesy to express no appreciation for what I had done—not that it made any difference, for I thought just as much of him, do today, as I ever did. During the session in Raleigh, he'd come over to Leesburg weekends when he was home and pass right by me on the court-house steps without even seein' me, much less stoppin' to shake hands. It was the same way with the other friends in the county that had elected him. He spent hours conferrin' with men that had done everything they could to beat him. In spite of all Richard had done to elect him, Williams never went a-nigh his office. I was convinced that he wa'n't the proper person to represent the county, that if he went the second time he might not know his wife! I told him frankly I wa'n't goin' to support him no more. I didn't support

*William W. Kitchin, governor of North Carolina, 1909–13.

Shorter, though, for he wa'n't the right man neither; I just didn't vote for no representative that year. Last spring I realized that Reams was a month too late announcing his candidacy, just like I had been, and knowed his fate a month before the primary and what was goin' to beat him.

"I can say this: this township has never gone against a candidate I supported! We have about 340 voters, with 700 in the whole township. For over thirty years I've conducted elections in the township, startin' back yonder in 1902. In 1900 I was a Red Shirt;* that was what they called us, though we didn't actually wear red shirts as they did in some sections. But the legislature had fixed it so we could disfranchise the nigger, and we aimed to tote our part in gettin' it done. Judge Farmer organized the county; they was about thirty-five of us around here that called ourselves Red Shirts. Up to 1900 the niggers had rushed in to register whether or no, and with control of the vote they had put in nigger officeholders all over the county. They wa'n't but one white family in the county that could get a office under the nigger rule of the time, and that was Dr. Hughes's. Dr. Hughes was so good to all the pore folks, goin' when they sent for him and not chargin' 'em a cent, that they'd give him anything he asked for. When the registration book was opened in 1900, the Red Shirts was ordered to get their rifles and shotguns and protect the registration from the niggers. When the word come to me, I remember I was in the field plowin'. I got my gun and hurried out to where the rest of the Red Shirts was assembled with shotguns.

"Word come that the federal authorities was comin' to protect the nigger vote; if they had, it would o' meant war. We wa'n't totin' shotguns just for show. Well, the upshot was not a nigger come nigh the registration book that day, from sunrise to sunset. Nigger rule was over!

"Two years after, when I first took hold o' registerin' voters, a right smart o' niggers come to register at first, claimin' they could meet the requirements. Some wrote the Constitution, I reckon, as good as a lot o' white men, but I'd find somethin' unsatisfactory, maybe an *i* not dotted or a *t* not crossed, enough for me to disqualify 'em. The law said 'satisfactory to the registrar.' A few could get by the grandfather clause,† for they was some free niggers be-

*A vigilante group that intimidated blacks.
†If a man's father or grandfather could have voted on 1 January 1867, he did not have to meet other voting requirements.

fore the Civil War, but they couldn't get by an undotted *i* or a uncrossed *t*. They wa'n't no Republicans in the South before the Civil War; the free niggers always voted like their old masters told 'em to—and 'twa'n't Republican! That's what the war was fought over, politics; they didn't care so much about freein' the slaves as they did the Republican party.

"A few years after we disfranchised the nigger, they was a great excitement down Butler Road slam to Allport. The niggers commenced to hold meetin's in the woods, and the report got out that they was fixin' to rise. You couldn't hardly travel the roads for niggers afoot, in carts, and on wagons, goin' to the woods. We found out about the meetin's through two white niggers who went to the woods along with the crowd—a nigger'll join anything, you know—and was voted out o' the meetin'. The leader, a colored feller by the name o' Henley from Allport, said these two was too white, that they didn't want no white blood in their organization. So the white niggers come to me and told me to warn the white folks to be on the lookout, for somethin' was up 'mongst the niggers; they also got their colored preacher to try to calm down his folks and persuade 'em out o' their plot to try to get back the vote. White folks down our way was mighty upset. Some gathered in neighbors' houses for protection. Henry Tyler and his boys set on their front porch all night long with their guns on their laps. It ruint Lambeth, it scared him so bad that for two years he was crazy. If you talk to him long enough now, you'll find out he ain't right. Me? I never lost a minute's sleep!

"Henley was arrested, but they couldn't seem to get enough evidence to convict him. The judge twisted the law around some way so Henley could be convicted of tryin' to interfere with the law, and he got five years in the pen. I never heard no more o' Henley round here. We found out it was a white scalawag* that stirred the niggers up.

"They ain't but two niggers that votes in this township now, and both of 'em's grandfathers was free prior to the Civil War. We've got no Republicans in our township, but they's some with Republican blood that I wouldn't trust no farther than I could lay my hand on, when it comes to votin'. They'll make out they're goin' to support our ticket and then sneak right around and vote Republican. The only thing that keeps the nigger from ownin' the county, with three or four of 'em to one white man, is that a nigger just

*Southern whites who were allied politically with blacks.

won't save. A nigger and a automobile is one of the dangerousest combinations in this country today; the road ain't safe long as he operates a automobile. Still, in another way it's the best for the white man to let the nigger spend his money for a car instead o' land. We're bound to keep the nigger down; it's all that saves us.

"Politics is the rottenest thing in the world. I ought to know, for I've been in it thirty years and over. Not meanin' to brag, I can say I've been honest and my hands is clean. I wouldn't twist a principle for no man. That's how come I got the influence I have in the county. The candidates come to me for advice and want me to get out and work for 'em, because they know I know practically everybody in the county—they ain't a man over forty I don't know—and can't nobody bring nothin' against my integrity. Not meanin' to brag now, my life counts much as my word; folks'll listen to a honest man. My methods ain't like some; I don't get out in the final heat of the campaign and hurrah and shout. By that time my work's all done. It's durin' the off season like this, when nobody's thinkin' politics much, that I do my workin', in a quiet homely way. I get votes pledged to my candidate—a man that won't stand by his pledge ain't worth his salt—and when the campaign gets hot I stay out'n the fight, knowin' the precincts is already lined up for my man.

"I don't make speeches; I could fix up somethin' so flowery it would make the hair rise on your head. But what's the use? It's the quiet reasonin', on the side, that counts. The only speech I ever made in my life was at a county convention, before the primary system come in, when Amos Foster was bein' opposed for county treasurer. I had to make a speech then. I rose in the courthouse and had my say. Mr. Foster was elected. I always said if any of Mr. Foster's boys ever wanted to run for office I'd be bound to give him my support. Much as I think o' Ab Sealey, I told him when Alec Foster was talkin' about runnin' for clerk o' court that'd mean I'd have to vote for Alec, good as his daddy was to me before he died. Ab said he didn't blame me.

"Yes, suh, I've voted Democrat all my life! My daddy rocked me in a Democratic cradle. Even though I didn't 'specially like Al Smith, I supported him for president.* We've seen since then that he didn't have the makin's of a president in him. Roosevelt did, I

*Alfred Smith, governor of New York, 1919–20, 1923–28, Democratic presidential nominee in 1928. Smith's Irish brogue, Catholicism, brown derby, and opposition to prohibition offended the white Anglo-Saxon Protestant South. He was the first

think; his aims is good even if his policies ain't carried out right in different localities. . . .

"Since I've been a justice of the peace, I've tried my best to keep peace. Some things I settle that I'm not really supposed to, but I jump jurisdiction whenever I can keep cases from goin' to court. Unless the charge forces things out of my hands, like carryin' deadly weapons or murder, I settle the difficulty without bindin' the parties over to court. Durin' my entire jurisdiction I've not had more than five or six white folks to come to trial; I can reason with 'em and get the contention settled without even a public hearin'; it's different with niggers, for they are fond of a lawsuit. Pore folks sometimes has to keep peace whether or no, because they don't have the money to get their warrant. In civil cases they've got to pay a fee before a warrant is issued, usually about four dollars; of course if any of this fee is left, they's a refund. In criminal cases the justice of the peace has to issue a warrant, fee or no fee. Sometimes lawyers don't want me to decide the case so they'll get two fees. Richard says I won't bind his men over to higher court if I have to put them in jail and sit on it. I do what I think's right, I don't care who the lawyer is. Usually when folks come to get me to issue a warrant I tell 'em to come back Saturday. By that time a lot of 'em cool off. If they still want the warrant, of course I give it to 'em. I've had lots of folks come back before Saturday and tell me to drop the warrant, for they've done made up with the disputant.

"Sometimes I have to try cases between two women, between men, and between a man and woman. Not long ago a nigger knocked his wife down and beat her up pretty bad with his gun. She got me to issue a warrant against him. When the case was tried, I put the nigger under such a heavy bond I knowed he couldn't pay it. Of course he had to go to jail. It wa'n't long before his wife come to me in the field and asked me to reduce the bond.

" 'What you want the bond reduced for?' I asked her.

" 'So I can pay my man out o' jail,' she said.

" 'What for? You want him to beat you up again?'

" 'He's promised not to, no more. Please reduce de bond, Mr. Stevenson.'

"And I did, to twenty-five dollars. She got her man out, and she ain't asked for no more warrants. But a white woman not long after that had me issue a warrant for her feller who had slapped her

---

Democrat after 1876 to lose the electoral votes of any Southern state. During the 1930s, he broke politically from Franklin Roosevelt.

down. On trial he claimed he pushed her and she done the fallin' herself. I fined him twenty dollars and costs. 'Twa'n't long before they was back together.

"Most times, my cases is disputes over boundary lines, fusses between men over women or women over men or somethin' as triflin', fights, thefts, or drinkin'. The other night a officer brought some drunk men to my house for trial. It was so cold I had to let 'em come in the hall to hear their case, and do you know they vomited on my floor! It was the first time the smell of whiskey had ever been in my house. No child o' mine has ever taken a drink or cursed a oath, not in my presence. I have drinked just to be sociable sometimes maybe, but I never got drunk and never drinked at home.

"Lots o' times I hold trials down here at Hicks's store. Folks like to hear cases, and the store is the most convenient public place close around here. When the womenfolks comes and parks their car near the store, I move outside or in the door so they can hear the trial. I open the case by askin' the parties if they're ready for trial. If they ain't, then I set a later date for the hearin'. If both sides is ready, we hear the evidence and either bind 'em over to higher court, put 'em in jail in default of the bond, or settle the difficulty right there. If it's a women's fuss, I sentence 'em sometimes to kiss and make up. I make the men shake hands.

"So far as Butler Road is concerned, we've got as good a set o' folks as you'll find anywhere. Never, since I've been a magistrate, has they been any difference, any fights, any drinkin' cases involvin' Butler Road white folks. Dr. Winter use to say that if everybody in the world was like the Butler Road folks, it would be a good place to live in. The road got its name from a family o' Butlers that use to live on it. Jameson's Old Tavern ain't got as good a record as some of our other neighborhoods in the township. They use to be a old tavern there where they had chicken fights and horse racin' and spreein'—tournaments they called 'em; my brother has been to 'em.

"Durin' my twenty-five years, I've had two murder cases for preliminary hearin's. I was eyewitness to one murder a long time ago, but the lawyers wouldn't let me get on the stand. It was a cold-blooded, premeditated murder all right. Ritter killed Parsons after a dispute over a boundary line, shot him down in his tracks, just like he aimed to do. But Ritter was freed; Ritter was a Mason. They was a Mason angle to another murder right close to our neighborhood later on. They've put the Rufus Johnson murder down as an unsolved mystery, but it could have been solved if the murderer had not been a Mason. Rufus went to feed his stock one mornin' before day, and when he didn't come back his wife went out to see what was to matter. There she saw blood splattered all over the barn door where it looked like somebody had busted a man's head open. The blood was traced on out of the lot, down the road, and finally Rufus's body was found lyin' by a branch between Five Forks and Oak Grove, his head under water. Now didn't nobody know about Rufus's habit o' carryin' money around his belt but one neighbor. The money was gone when the body was found. That neighbor was the busiest feller helpin' around you ever saw. Numbers and numbers of folks kept tellin' the neighbor— everybody suspected him from the start—not to touch the corpse, for they's a old superstition that if the murderer touches the body of his victim, the blood will pour from the wounds. I know the murderer was warned to look out for that. It was told that after the corpse was fixed up and laid out, the neighbor tended to the body like the undertaker had instructed and the wounds opened and the blood poured out. I don't believe in no such superstitious mess myself. Anyhow, detectives come and got so close behind the neighbor that the Masons hushed it up, and the detectives were sent out of the neighborhood. The neighbor was warned to leave the neighborhood, which he did, puttin' him up a nice house in town. He's dead, but he was the guilty man sure as you're born. It was a cryin' shame that murder went unpunished.

"So far as I know, they's never been but one hangin' and one lynchin' in the county since the Civil War. The lynchin' come about because of a white woman—a good old lady from the Oak Grove section—who was attacked along the road one day by a nigger. He was put in jail, but white citizens from all over the county gathered and made the sheriff surrender the prisoner so they could swing him up on a limb. We come mighty near havin' a serious situation on hand in the summer of 1917 when Hugh Harrison was killed by the Thorne nigger. If that nigger had been found, upset as everybody was, they'd have been a lynchin'. I always thought, to tell you the truth, that the nigger was lynched, things got quieted down so sudden.

"One thing the matter with the country . . is we got too many officers. We need one to about every three we've got. Of course we groan about high taxes, but they'll have to be still higher taxes if they keep addin' to the list of officers. Instead of one register of deeds, one clerk of court, one county superintendent, we got two now—one to do the work, and the other to draw the pay. You hear a lot o' complaint about the sales tax. What was it passed for? To pay the salaries of officeholders, that's what. I say it's the fairest and the unfairest tax in the world. If 'twa'n't for the sales tax, lot o' the salaried fellers wouldn't pay none, but I admit it's hard on the merchants. I say let 'em have five percent on their collections, to pay 'em for their bookkeepin'. I could tell 'em a lot o' things if they'd send me to Raleigh!

"Another thing the county needs is to put honest men in charge of the elections. They talk about election reform; we don't need no reform. The election laws and the election machinery is all right. The way to have honest elections is to put honest men at the polls, men who'd rather their arm was cut off than be a party to cheatin' and unprincipled tactics at the polls or anywhere else. We still got honest men. The election board is the trouble; the emphasis is put on gettin' poll holders that some of the bigwigs can handle. That's exactly what did happen in our last primary, and if prominent men hadn't been involved this county would o' been in the headlines. I can truthfully say they ain't never been no smell over elections in this county since I been at the polls. If the legislature abolishes the absentee ballot it will be the cruelest thing they ever done. It'll disfranchise men that has got to keep payin' taxes, that's got every right in God's world to vote, that can't in no fairness be denied the right of citizenship.

"The factions in the Democrat party in this county is one reason for the election disgrace last spring. The factions come about first over a school disagreement. The bone of contention all along has been the county superintendent—the sharpest politician in the county. One set of school officials who thought that County Superintendent Rivers ruled against them to build up another school got sore over the discrimination, as they saw it, and finally brought the fight in the open. Mr. Graven of Grover and Mr. Rivers had words and a little scrap on the courthouse square. Now Richard, a school official and a friend of the county superintendent, naturally took Mr. Rivers's part. This school and personal controversy got into politics and created two bitter factions. The primary heat has been pretty intense in our county and led to all sorts o' unpleasantness; it led last spring to the election mess, involving especially the Grover ballot box. I think the heads of the factions are gettin' closer together now, but—oh, politics is rotten, rotten! Last year I saw one feller vote twenty-five men for a Coca-Cola apiece!

"Marriages comes in my jurisdiction, and I do right much marryin', runaway couples mostly. One mad father followed up his runaway daughter and busted in on me after I had got the couple tied up good and on their way to his folks.

" 'Where's my daugher?' he said.

" 'God knows,' I said.

"The old feller seemed to be satisfied, though, soon as he found out his daughter was tied up, and went on back home. A couple seventy-one years old come not long ago, and I told 'em I tied 'em together so tight they couldn't get married no more if they lived seventy-one more years.

"Here last week a runaway couple come, scared to death her daddy would hear about the elopement and come in time to raise a fuss. She was visitin' in the neighborhood, and her feller—that wa'n't allowed to come to see her at her home—stole her and rushed here to me, sayin' they was in a hurry. I told him I could get in a hurry too; so I didn't even take time to get my book. I know the ceremony by heart anyhow if I can say it fast.

"They's one word in the part of the ceremony I put to the girl that I don't like. I don't believe in makin' the wife promise to obey unless you make the man promise too. They always ask me what I charge, and I tell 'em they ain't no charge, but usually folks pays me a dollar. As a rule the bridegroom slips the dollar in the license. One feller asked me to wait on him for the pay; so I married him on a credit and ain't never seen him since. After I told one couple what the groom usually give me, he pulled out fifteen cents, declarin' it was all he had, and the bride added fifteen cents which was all she had.

"Now and then they come to ask me how to go about gettin' a divorce. I wish it was in my jurisdiction to give 'em divorces. I tell 'em they need fifty dollars to start it, and then the lawyer will tell 'em how much more it'll take. That's where it stops in most cases that consult me, for fifty dollars is out of their reach, fifty dollars is between them and peace. So they just make up their minds to put up with each other best they can. I'd untie plenty of 'em if I could. When I see a pore wife worked to death and imposed on by a sorry man, with her little children hungry and naked and neglected, I wish I could buy her a divorce. That's another thing the country needs . . . and that's needed worse'n anything in God's world, for the sake of the pore folks! More divorces is what the country needs!"

Bernice Kelly Harris

Sam Sets It Down

No good times can come to the country
as long as there is so much discrimination practiced.

"At present I belong to the ranks of the unemployed. I have regular employment only four months of the annum, and sometimes that is just part-time." Sam T. Mayhew throws away the end of a fat cigar and settles back comfortably to be interviewed. The black expanse of face above hefty shoulders is interrupted by an impressive black mustache, which presents itself before the discontent in the big black eyes registers.

"The past year it was just part-time. We worked at the gin a few days the first of September and then were laid off till the middle, when the gin started running again. The gin shut down for the year on December 24, which gave me around 78 working days, 26 days to the month, for the year. I am paid $2 a day at the gin. So my income this year was 2 times 78—$156, I believe it is. I've got it all figured out and set down here in this little book. Now, to get an estimate of how much my family of seven has to live on, divide $156 by 12. I've figured it out; it's less than 50 cents a week, 7 and a fraction cents a day apiece for us, with everything we eat and wear coming out of the store. It's [wrong] . . . to say folks can't live that cheap; they can and do when they have to, such living as it is.

"Since February, I've been getting a little relief help from the government. Everything they've give since my first trip to Jackson I've set down in this little book; it starts out with 24 pounds of flour, 5 pounds of butter, 3 pounds of prunes and beans and ends up with 17 grapefruits and 3 pounds of butter, which is all they give me last week. I've figured up what the government has give me since February—counting flour at 75 cents, butter at 30 and so forth—and it comes to exactly $14.60. I've estimated that is just one-fourth of what we ought to have to live on, to eat. Several times I've asked for clothes the women make at the sewing room, but each time those have been denied.

"There's three grown folks and four children at my house, but what these children really ought to eat is more expensive than what we could manage on. I read considerably about the diet children ought to have—milk, butter, eggs, cereals, and fruits—but I can't stretch my income to provide it. I'm particular concerned into diets and meals, because at my house I have to do practically all the cooking since my wife has been physically and mentally incapacitated. My mother always taught her boys as well as girls to do every kind of work that came to hand, from cooking to washing, and it's well she did. The way I start the day is this: first, I make a fire in the stove, heat some lard in my frying pan, cut up an onion in the hot grease, then sift some flour and pepper and salt in the pan, and when the mixture is brown add a little water. This is the main dish for breakfast. Sometimes I stir up some egg bread with a spoon to serve with this onion gravy, sometimes biscuits.

"After breakfast the children get off to school and are gone till three-thirty in the afternoon. By time they get home, I try to have them a hot dish of dried peas or beans and some prunes or canned fruit if we have any. When there's meat, I season the beans with a little slice which I cut up into six pieces—I can't eat hog meat myself on account of high blood pressure—but when meat's out, I put a spoonful of lard in the pot for seasoning. Lunch? We don't have any lunch; two meals a day is all we have winter and summer. The children don't get very hungry, because they're used to it; sometimes when they see other children at school with candy and cakes, it's right hard on them. But they know I don't have so much as a nickel extra to give them to buy an apple or orange, and they don't complain.

"Sam Junior is in the eighth grade at school. He is the *Virginian-Pilot* paper boy and makes eighty cents a week, which only about takes care of his school supplies and book rentals. I don't know what Sam Junior wants to be yet; sometimes I think I ought to talk to him and help him decide. Then I'm afraid I won't be able to help him reach his achievement, which would make him more disappointed than if he had never planned anything. So, I'm just waiting, not saying yet what I'd like to see him do.

"I know what it is to be disappointed in a profession. I grew up with the ambition to be a bricklayer, a master brick mason, but circumstances over which I had no control eliminated me of it. I was born in 1890 to Sam and Mary Mayhew, both old slaves who had seen hard and cruel days during slavery. They reared me up in a true Christian home. At night Papa gathered us all around the fireplace and had each one to repeat a verse of Scripture and then the Lord's Prayer, as it's commonly called. Sometimes he led in prayer himself. He didn't have any worldly goods to bequeath to us, but he set us a good example of upright living. He acquired a little land but continued sharecropping for white people till rheumatism afflicted him. That little piece of land is still in the family, undivided, my sister living on it and paying the taxes. When I was just a boy in my teens, Dr. Stephenson employed me as a day laborer at eighty-five cents a day, a man's wages in 1906, but Doctor said I could do good as a man and ought to be paid according.

"In 1907 an opportunity was given for three colored boys from Northampton to go to A and M, now A and T, College in Greensboro, and I was one of the three selected. My father was unable to send me, though he provided what he could for clothes and books. My tuition was free, and I made my board working as janitor in a dormitory and firing a furnace for one of the professors. I had to enter the preparatory department since I had never been to school but four months in my life. In one nine months I was promoted to the freshman class, which I accomplished successfully, and was promoted to the sophomore. My plan was to take up bricklaying then, as lower classmen were not permitted to study a trade till after two years. That was when my father had to give up working on account of rheumatism, which necessitated me to come home and take charge of farming.

"In 1910, then, I sharecropped with Mr. Luke Jackson, but only for a year. The next fall I started working at the gin and planing mill here in Seaboard, and I've been connected with this gin for twenty-eight years. Back then I had an all-time job, ginning in the fall and sawing and planing the other months. My work at the gin has always been operating the gin, four eighties at present, and my employers call me an extra-good ginner. I know machinery and can detect any flaw as quick as anybody. Nobody in the state can turn out a better sample than I can. I watch the younger crowd, and if anything goes wrong I report it at once to my employer. All these years I've never had a promotion, except for a little raise in salary.

"One day—May 18, 1918, a date I'll never forget even if I didn't have it set down—when I climbed up on the planing mill to adjust some trouble with the machinery my foot slipped, and the blade of the mill cut my leg so bad it had to be amputated at the knee. My employers sent me to the hospital, paid my doctor bills, and provided me with a peg leg. But I was handicapped for life by this injury.

"The plane- and sawmill was discontinued in 1924, which threw me out of work eight months of the year except for just little catch-up jobs. By this time I had the expense of a family on me. Ella and I got married in 1914, and four children have [been] the result of this union, three girls and one boy. The house I now live in was where we first rented, moving from there to the Addie Leak's place, then across the railroad, and finally back here to our first home. Until the past few years, I had to pay rent, but since my work is only part-time now my employer has permitted me to live here without paying any rent. We have an acre or so which we try to have a garden on in the summer, but without a team available it's hard to cultivate vegetables worth anything. I've not been able to plow since 1918.

"Not only has my amputation been a great handicap, but also my wife's health has held me back. Not many years after we were married, she had to go to St. Phillip's in Richmond, where she ought to have taken an operation for goiter, but they thought she couldn't stand it. In a year's time, I had to take her to Goldsboro, for her mind completely collapsed; she'd take off her dress and run across the field unclothed, unless she was watched. After a year she came back home almost herself, but in twelve months she was mentally incapacitated worse than ever. After another stay in Goldsboro, she returned home almost normal and remained so until along in 1932; her health and mind both failed then. Two years ago we took her to Roanoke Rapids Hospital for a major operation, and she's been an invalid since. I told the doctors if they'd build her up so she could take the goiter operation the same time as the other, I felt that her mind might be restored. But they said she couldn't stand it, even with transfusions. Her mind is so bad now I can't trust her to do the cooking. If she starts a meal, I don't stop her, but stay close around to watch and help her. She's apt to use three times as much lard or salt as is needed, and then nobody knows what she might put in the food.

"So far as doing any work is concerned, she's worth next to nothing. She was always considered one of the best washers and ironers at all, and plenty of calls still come for her to do up the ladies' bridge covers and napkins, but she had to turn them down. All she does is the washing, no ironing, for Miss Alma, for which she receives around sixty cents a week. Sometimes she gets out the wash in a day's time; then again it takes her three days, depending on the state of her mind.

"My oldest children, Maud and Emma Bee, have been a disappointment to me. Maud married against my will and soon found out I was right about the fellow she married. His family were bootleggers, and Maud had to live in a whiskey joint, something she couldn't get used to. She was reared up in a Christian home. None of my children ever heard me curse an oath or saw me take a drink of whiskey. Always at the breakfast table I had the family altar, till my wife's health got so bad these late years; different ones read the Bible, and I offered prayer. Each Sunday, everything at my house went to Sunday School and church, and I tried to keep my children unspotted from the world. Maud left that bootlegger crowd and came back home. She's married ag'in now to a good man, and they're getting on all right.

"Emma Bee ran off and married Blossom Peoples, a trifling fellow I wouldn't allow her to go with. When I came home one day, she was dressed up, waiting for Blossom to come after her. My wife told me what was up, and I started for Emma Bee. She ran out the door toward Blossom's house fast as she could. I grabbed the shotgun and followed. I would have killed her if Blossom's folks had not got her into the house when they did, for I'd rather have seen her dead than married to Blossom. After the second child was born, Blossom ran away to New York, and that was the last of him so far as any support is concerned. Emma Bee and the two children had to come back to me to be taken care of. Until last summer she couldn't get any work, but for several months she cooked at Mr. Price's until they shut up their house this spring. Since then she has cooked a little in Jackson, but three weeks ago she got sick and had to give up her job. Her wages, $2.50 a week, never did us any good about household expenses, for Emma and her children were almost bare when she assumed a job, and it took all she could make to get clothes decent to work in and to dress the children. She helped me buy some wood; that was all.

"So that is our situation. Some years I have made around $200, but the total income for the seven of us this year was $156, plus the little change my family brings in and what my few catch-up jobs provide. On that we have to eat and clothe ourselves, pay for burial insurance at 60 cents a month—absolute necessities. I'd also put church dues in, but in 1918 when my amputation occurred the church cancelled my assessment indefinitely; all the men at Bethlehem-Seaboard Baptist Church are assessed $3 a year, but they've never said anything more about me paying. Of course when I have it, I give a free-will offering for a visiting minister or the various causes of our denomination. I consider food, clothes, insurance, doctors, and the Lord's work the absolute necessities of life; the rest has to wait. The last furniture I bought was ten years ago, and while it's beginning to look pretty bad it will have to do. There are using things in the kitchen that we need, but we need food to go in the pots we have worse than new pots.

"So far as recreation and good times, we have to make them for ourselves. The children play Chinese checkers and listen to Victrola music at night, while I read my *Virginian-Pilot* and the Bible or walk downtown to hear what the men are saying around the stores and filling stations. We never had a car to take trips on or go to shows; in the past we did take in the Florida Blossom and Silas Green shows at Weldon, though moving pictures were never available to us.

"I used to travel around considerably before our lodges became insolvent and were discontinued. I was a Knight of Gideon and an Odd Fellow and went as a delegate to meetings in Durham, Kinston, Goldsboro, High Point, and Winston-Salem. I got a glimpse of the mountains at Winston-Salem, but I've never done any seashoring. The lodges always called on me to do their writing; all the correspondence with brother Gideons fell on me.

"My chief interests are the church and school. Some white people here in town say they don't need a clock Sunday mornings; when they see me go on to church, they know it will soon be time for the last bell. I served as clerk of the church and Sunday School superintendent for several years and still make talks and offer prayer and assist in leading the singing and the business administration of the church.

"It was through my instrumentality that the colored people now have a high school here. I appeared before the county board of education and told them we had met the qualifications; there were twenty-five seventh-grade graduates, many of them unable to take up high-school work away from home. The chairman said we should have our high school, but the county superintendent procrastinated us and, I have reason to believe, worked against our cause. So, I began writing letter after letter to the state board relative to high-school instruction for our children here. These letters were all typed, and so more businesslike, and as forceful as I could make them. I got my typewriter through an advertisement in a paper, a secondhand Oliver. I ordered it from Chicago on the installment plan for thirty-three dollars. It came one afternoon, and by night I had learned to type well enough to write the company acknowledging receipt of the machine. In all the letters to the state department I used to quote Scripture, suiting the verse to the occasion. Reverend Seymour who preached the baccalaureate sermon here Sunday told the crowd that Dr. White and Mr. Elder said I prayed up a high school for Seaboard.

"The next thing I worked for was to get our high school accredited. In order to negotiate that through, we had to have one high-school graduate. So I got Junius Stith who had been to Garysburg three years to take his senior year in our school. Thus, two years after the high school was organized we had a graduate, and Seaboard became an accredited school.

"As the vice-president of the Parent-Teacher Association, I'm a member of the executive council and have attended a number of county meetings of the PTA. I think we've got a good man here as our principal. In fact, if Professor Fisher could silence his wife, I think he'd be a second Creecy, like the head of Creecy Institute in Rich Square. I've told Professor Fisher the same thing to his face, but Mrs. Fisher continues to rule the school. She's so unpunctual to her school duties that the other teachers resent it when they have to hew to the lines so strict and Mrs. Fisher does as she pleases. I'm afraid she's going to make him lose his job. I'd like to see a strong school built up here. Maybe it will help to do away with this superstition and ignorance that involves my race. The belief in conjuration—I've got no patience in the world with it.

"I've been voting some fifteen years, though my vote does little good here in this Democratic section. The first time I went to register was when Mr. Wilson was running for sheriff. Mr. Hamilton, the registrar, asked me to read and interpret a section of the Constitution. I had just started to do this when Mr. Wilson walked in. He told Mr. Hamilton that if the registrar was satisfied in his own mind that the applicant had the qualifications that entitled him to vote he need not require any constitutional interpretations—and to let me vote just so. I could meet the requirements all right. Since then I've never missed a primary or national election. For county offices I'm forced to vote for a Democrat, since no Republicans run, but I'd rather vote for a man I don't want than not to exercise my voting privilege.

"It's true I didn't think Landon would have made a good president. Neither do I think Roosevelt has. All the prosperity he has brought to the country has been legislated and is not real. Nothing he has ever started has been finished. My common way of expressing it is that we are in the middle of the ocean like a ship without an anchor. No good times can come to the country as long as there is so much discrimination practiced.

"I can't tell you my real feelings, but I think I can give you an idea of what I mean. Take me: I have applied for work at the welfare office, tried hard to get work. All they had for me, they said, came under the unskilled head. I tried one of these jobs— digging ditches for the sanitary department of the board of health. With my artificial limb, I simply couldn't compete with the other men who were digging ditches. So the inspector said he couldn't use me. It wasn't fair to the other men to pay me what they were getting; as hard as the work was for me, I couldn't take any less. So I didn't last long at that. Then I applied again for work, for something in the skilled labor line. I had seen men overseeing groups of workers, keeping their time, and so forth, and this I knew I could do as well as anybody. They told me that only white men had these jobs, that I would have to take something in the unskilled classification or none. I'm just as needy—needier I expect—as the white men, and I can do the job as well. Because of my color, I must ditch or work on the road, in spite of my college training and in spite of physical handicaps from amputation and high blood pressure— sometimes I worked at the gin last fall with a blood pressure of 190. That leaves me helpless, for in this agricultural area there are no jobs open to day labor that I am able to do for a whole day at the time. Besides, there are tenants to do all the odd work on the farms. I asked Mr. Lee the other day to let me come work out his garden for him; he said he had more men idle on his place than he could give work to. There's nothing for me except relief, and what's $14.60 for three months and—seventeen grapefruits? Seventeen grapefruits!

"The same thing is true of colored girls. Our high-school graduates need jobs just as much as the white girls. Go over yonder to the county office at the agriculture building. Not a single colored girl has a job there, when they could do the work as well and need it worse than the white girls. I don't think that discrimination is intended at Washington, but here in this county the colored race has no chance to get a job when it's a choice between color. I don't see much chance for our people to get anywhere when the color line instead of ability determines the opportunities to get ahead economically.

"In private industry it's the same thing. Twice there has been an opening for skilled labor at the gin, a job in the office weighing and tagging cotton. In spite of my twenty-eight years' service, always on time and always having the interest of the gin at heart, nothing was said about letting me weigh and tag cotton; the job was given to a young high-school graduate that didn't know half the business I do, that hasn't a typewriter. My employers are good to me, generally speaking; one of them is. Oh, well, the other one does let me stay in his house without paying any rent or taxes, yes. They do furnish me in the summertime when I couldn't get rations, yes; but they take it out of my salary in the fall. How do I get to Jackson to get the relief food? Well, one of my employers takes me, yes. How did I get back and forth to see my wife when she was in the hospital? My employer took me, yes. Do I ever work their gardens, cut their grass for the favors they show me? Yes, yes I do. Yes, they pay me for it of course. It's one of the catch-up jobs I have to depend on to help with our expenses. One of my employers is paralyzed, and the other is in a bad state of health, can't drive far. But they have something; I don't. When I get in a tight, I sit down and type them a note asking for money. Sometimes I get it, but more often I don't. The traveling men that come by the gin are right good to me, often sending me boxes of clothes and hats after I've handed them one of my typed notes. I wrote a well-to-do man in Norfolk the other day, but so far he has sent me nothing.

"No, I never thought about settling up North. There's no such hard distinction about color there, though. Four or five years ago, when I was trying without success to get the welfare to buy me a new artificial limb, I wrote to President Roosevelt asking him to interefere in my behalf, stating my circumstances and needs. In a short while here came a letter from the president, assuring me that the matter would be attended to through the proper agencies at once. I know it wasn't long before the welfare office at Jackson ordered me a new limb! My typewriter already had more than paid for itself—the limb was around $125—in what it has done for me personally and toward the advancement of education among our race, not to mention the pleasure it is to conduct business matters in a businesslike way."

Sam T. Mayhew rises. The interview is over. "Does your husband have any old underwear," he adds, "that you could give me?"

Bernice Kelly Harris

APPENDIXES
BIBLIOGRAPHICAL ESSAY

Appendixes

W. T. Couch, originator and director of the Southern life-history program of the Federal Writers' Project, provided field workers with a set of instructions and outlines for life histories. Those instructions, along with the outline initially used by the field workers, were reproduced in the Federal Writers' Project, *These Are Our Lives*, pages 417–21, and they appear below as Appendixes 1 and 2. Couch also issued another outline for a planned, but never completed, second volume of life histories, based on the lives of unemployed people. That outline appears below as Appendix 3.

APPENDIX 1

INSTRUCTIONS TO WRITERS

1. Materials are to be collected on tenant farmers and their families, farm owners and their families, cotton mill villagers and their families, persons and their families in service occupations in towns and cities, and persons and their families in miscellaneous occupations such as lumbering, mining, fishing, turpentining. Samples showing the nature of the materials to be collected are attached hereto.

2. The life histories may range from approximately two thousand words to ten or fifteen thousand words, depending upon the interest of the material.

3. An outline is attached hereto. This outline shows the nature of the subject matter which should be covered in the life history. However, it is not desired that each life history or story follow this outline in a rigid manner. The stories will not be useable if they are constructed on a rigid pattern. For instance, the writer may reverse the order of the outline, he may begin with any item which he considers of special importance in the case under consideration, he may follow the whole outline or limit himself to a part of it in any particular story. It is immaterial whether the stories are written in the first, second, or third person. Insofar as possible, the stories should be told in the words of the persons who are consulted. The effort should be made to get definite information. Avoid generalities such as "those who are industrious and ambitious can do well," "had not made

good use of opportunities"—wherever possible expand such wording to give detail, that is, exactly what industry and ambition might have done, or what the opportunities were that could have been used. In general avoid the expression of judgment. The writer will, of course, have to exercise judgment in determining the course of a conversation through which he gains information, but aside from this, he should keep his own opinions and feelings in the background as much as possible. For instance, if he sees people living under conditions which he thinks are terrible, he should be most careful not to express his opinion in any way and thus possibly affect the opinion of the person to whom he is talking. He must try to discover the real feeling of the person consulted and must record this feeling regardless of his own attitude toward it. Any story in which this principle is violated will be worthless.

4. Writers should not limit themselves to the types of stories shown in the samples. It is hoped that original modes of presenting the material will be developed. The criteria to be observed are those of accuracy, human interest, social importance, literary excellence. It may not be possible to combine all these in any one story. However, accuracy and literary excellence should be present in all. A story of some very exceptional family may be of great human interest but of minor social importance. The best stories will be those which combine all these elements. (By accuracy, it was explained in conferences, is meant simply write what you smell, see, hear. Writers cannot check on the accuracy of what is said. Get in the subject's own words what he has done, felt, thought. If the subject's head is filled with wrong notions, foolish thoughts, and misinformation, if this kind of material comes out in conversation, record it. Let the subject's mind speak for itself.)

5. While the majority of stories should be about families and should attempt to include information on all the points listed in the attached outline, it may be best in some instances to write about a section of a village or a community dealing with all the families in that section or community; or a story may be written about any one of the items in the outline, such as, for instance, the size of the family, the coming of children and the effect their coming has on the fortunes of the family. Any town, community, village, or open country from which a number of stories are secured should itself be described in a separate story.

6. Some topics of importance may come up which are not covered in the outline. It will be best to go ahead and treat such topics and not wait to ask for permission to deal with them. However, no state director should allow writers to abandon the outline and sample stories to such an extent as to change the nature of the work.

7. All the stories do not have to be solemn and packed with information. If an amusing incident reveals the attitude of a family towards some important problem, then this incident should be related.

8. The purpose of this work is to secure material which will give an accurate, honest, interesting, and fairly comprehensive view of the kind of

life that is lived by the majority of the people in the South. It is extremely important that families be fairly selected, that those which get along well or fairly well be selected for stories as well as those that make a less favorable impression. The subnormal, the normal, the above-normal, all should have stories written about them. As the work gets along, it will be necessary to expand it in order to include other important groups, but insofar as possible, a beginning should be made with the groups indicated above. In those parts of the South where cotton textile manufacturing is unimportant, and other industries dominate the scene, these other industries should be selected for treatment. For instance, in and around Birmingham, Alabama, both families in textile manufacturing and families working in coal and iron industries should be treated.

9. Each story should carry on the first page the date when the first version is written, the name of the writer and the name and address of the family written about. This information needs to be given for purposes of verification. Names will be changed in any material that is published.

10. It is hoped that out of this material four or five volumes will be secured which can be published under a series name such as LIFE IN THE SOUTH with individual names for each volume.

APPENDIX 2

*OUTLINE FOR LIFE HISTORIES**

  I. Family
      1. Size of family.
      2. Effect of family size upon financial status of family.
      3. Attitude toward large families.
      4. Attitude toward limitation of family.
      5. Occupational background of family.
      6. Pride in family, including ancestry.
 II. Education
      1. Number of years of school attendance.
      2. Causes of limited education.
      3. Attitudes toward education.
          a. Educational advantages desired for children.
          b. Whether worker believes school training is economic advantage.
          c. Evaluation of school system.
          d. Ambition, ideals. Idea of good life. Which comes first—owning home or owning car. Does family own car?
III. Income
      1. Comparison of present income with first weekly or annual income.

*Prepared by Ida Moore.

2. Actual needs to be covered by income.
3. Extent to which income covers actual needs.
4. Sense of relative values in expenditure of income.
5. What person consulted considers an adequate income.

IV. Attitudes Toward Occupation and Kind of Life
1. Pride or shame in work.
2. Influence of attitudes of others.
3. Basis of objections to or satisfaction with life.
4. Attitudes toward owners.
5. Advantages or disadvantages of present life in comparison with other types of life, e.g., working in mill compared with working on farm, life in town with life in country.

V. Politics
1. Extent of voting.
2. Degree of independence in casting ballot.
3. Preferences in choice of candidates.
4. Party consciousness.
5. Consciousness of changing trends in thought.

VI. Religion and Morals
1. Influence of religion on morals.
2. Attitudes toward various forms of amusements.
3. Relations to churches.
   a. Contributions.
   b. Attitude toward aid from churches.
   c. Attendance.

VII. Medical Needs
1. Money expended for hospital and doctor bill.
2. To what extent health has been protected through adequate medical care.
3. What effect work has had upon health.

VIII. Diet
1. Knowledge of balanced diet.
2. To what extent knowledge is applied.
3. To what extent it is possible to have balanced diet on wage earned.

IX. Miscellaneous Observations
1. Cleanliness and order of house; number of rooms.
2. Cleanliness of person.
3. Furnishings in house.
4. Sleeping accommodations.
5. Bathroom facilities.
6. Pride in possessions.

X. Use of Time
1. Annual routine, e.g., preparation of soils for planting—planting—cultivation—laying by—occupations and amusements

during interval between laying by and harvesting—harvesting—
settlement—moving.

2. Daily routine during the different periods indicated above.
3. Amusements, visiting, courting. Where do courting couples go?
Where do men spend their leisure hours?

APPENDIX 3

OUTLINE FOR LIFE HISTORIES

I. Conditions Surrounding Early Life
   1. Occupational background of family and economic status.
   2. Effect of family size on family's economic status.
   3. Pride in family, including ancestry.
II. Education and Preparation for Work
   1. Training in work habits in the home.
   2. Number of years in attendance at school.
   3. Vocational education in vocational schools, or vocational classes.
   4. Estimate of educational background.
III. Family Relationships
   1. Number of dependents:.wife, husband, children, parents, relatives.
   2. Advantages provided for family up to time of unemployment.
IV. Politics
   1. Extent of voting.
   2. Degree of independence in casting ballot.
   3. Preferences in choice of candidates.
   4. Party and attitude toward parties.
V. Religion and Morals
   1. Influence of religion on morals.
   2. Attitudes toward various forms of amusements.
   3. Relations with churches.
      a. Attendance.
      b. Contributions.
      c. Attitude toward receiving aid from churches.
VI. Medical Needs
   1. Money expended for hospital and doctors' bills.
   2. Ability to afford adequate medical care.
   3. Effect of work on health.
VII. Diet
   1. To what extent is there a knowledge of balanced diet? Is this knowledge applied?
   2. To what extent does income permit balanced diet?
VIII. Miscellaneous Observations
   1. Cleanliness of person.

    2. Cleanliness and order of house; number of rooms.
    3. Furnishings in house.
    4. Adequacy of sleeping accommodations.
    5. Bathroom facilities.
    6. Pride in possessions.

IX. Work History
    1. Years of employment.
    2. Types of work done.
    3. Rapidity of job turnover.
    4. Adequacy of income to cover needs.
    5. Satisfaction with types of jobs held.
    6. Evaluation of work experience.
    7. Reason for losing last job.
    8. Length of time unemployed.

X. Looking For a Job
    1. Method of looking for work.
       a. Getting leads from friends; last employer; former employers.
       b. Want ads.
    2. Number of jobs applied for.
    3. Amount of time actually spent looking for work.
    4. Persistency in search of work.
       a. Trips away from home locality.
       b. Applying for work where friends or others have said there was little or no possibility.
    5. Recollection of interviews between applicant and prospective employers.
    6. Was applicant offered any job which he did not accept?
    7. Effect of labor unions on applicant's search for work.
    8. Registration with State Employment Service.
       a. If not already registered, how soon after losing last job did subject register?
       b. Value of interviews to individual in morale; in extending scope of job possibilities; in addition to technical knowledge.
       c. Number of times subject visited employment office.
       d. Evaluation of service rendered.
    9. Efforts to secure WPA or other governmental work.
   10. Means of support while seeking employment.
       a. Eligibility for unemployment compensation.
       b. How much does expectation of unemployment compensation check affect desire to seek work?
       c. Help from relatives or friends.
       d. Appeal for direct relief.
       e. Borrowed money; mortgaged property, etc.
   11. Attitude of the individual toward his present condition.
   12. Outlook for the future.

Bibliographical Essay

The purpose of this bibliographical essay is to indicate the books and other materials that could be helpful to readers interested in learning more about the life histories, the Federal Writers' Project, Southern history, the 1930s, and oral history. This essay is suggestive, not exhaustive. The focus is on works that are central to the topic under discussion. The reader who wishes to go further than this will find that the works mentioned here provide a starting point.

Such As Us represents only a small sample of the many life histories collected. More of these life histories are in the Federal Writers' Project, *These Are Our Lives* (Chapel Hill: University of North Carolina Press, 1939). Interesting comparisons can be made between *Such As Us* and *These Are Our Lives*. Nevertheless, these two books constitute only a small sample of the life histories in various repositories. The majority of the unpublished life histories are in the Southern Historical Collection, University of North Carolina Library, Chapel Hill. The life histories in *Such As Us* are all in that collection, except for "Tobacco's in My Blood" and "Tech 'Er Off, Charlie." Those two life histories are in "People in Tobacco," an unpublished manuscript edited and partly written by Leonard Rapport. A copy of "People in Tobacco" is located in the Works Progress Administration papers in the Manuscripts Division of the Library of Congress. Small numbers of life histories are in the Alabama Department of History and Archives, Montgomery; the Louisiana Collection, the Louisiana State Library, Baton Rouge; the Oklahoma Historical Society, Oklahoma City; the P. K. Yonge Library of Florida History, University of Florida, Gainesville; and the Virginia State Library, Richmond.

The Writers' Project interviews with ex-slaves was related to, but separate from, the collection of life histories. While the two projects were separately conceived and administered, they shared a common goal. They both tried to let ordinary people become their own historians. Selections of ex-slave narratives with commentary on the materials and that program's history are available in B. A. Botkin, ed., *Lay My Burden Down: A Folk History of Slavery* (Chicago: University of Chicago Press, 1945); Charles L. Perdue, Jr., Thomas E. Barden, and Robert K. Philllps, eds., *Weevils in the*

Wheat: Interviews with Virginia Ex-Slaves (Charlottesville: University Press of Virginia, 1976); Norman R. Yetman, ed., *Life Under the "Peculiar Institution": Selections from the Slave Narrative Collection* (New York: Holt, Rinehart & Winston, 1970). George P. Rawick, ed., *The American Slave: A Composite Autobiography*, 19 vols. (Westport, Conn.: Greenwood Press, 1972–76), and *Weevils in the Wheat* contain almost all the known ex-slave narratives.

For a detailed historical survey and analysis of the life-history program, readers can consult Jerrold Hirsch, "Culture on Relief: The North Carolina Federal Writers' Project, 1935–43" (master's thesis, University of North Carolina, 1972), and the following unpublished papers: Jerrold Hirsch, "The FWP Southern Life Histories Program: Culture, Bureaucracy, and Relief," and Tom Terrill, "The FWP Southern Life Histories Program: Nature and Contents." These papers, originally presented at the Annual Meeting of the American Historical Association, December 1975, are available on request from the authors.

Readers who wish to pursue the program's history through the primary materials should examine the following collections: the Edwin August Bjorkman Papers; the Federal Writers' Project, Papers of the Regional Director, William Terry Couch; the Frank Porter Graham Personal Papers, and The University of North Carolina Press Papers, all in the Southern Historical Collection. In addition Records Group 69, Records of the Works Progress Administration, Federal Writers' Project, in the National Archives, Washington, D.C., are extremely important.

W. T. Couch's published views on Southern problems and needs are illuminating. His two review essays, "Reflections on the Southern Tradition," *South Atlantic Quarterly* 35 (1936):284–98, and "The Agrarian Romance," *South Atlantic Quarterly* 36 (1937):417–30, explain his differences with the work of the twelve Southerners who wrote *I'll Take My Stand: The South and the Agrarian Tradition* (New York: Harper & Brothers, 1930). Couch's "Landlord and Tenant," *Virginia Quarterly Review* 14 (1938):309–12, details his dissatisfaction with the view of Southern problems that Erskine Caldwell and Margaret Bourke-White offered in *You Have Seen Their Faces* (New York: Modern Age Books, 1937). Couch stated his own view of Southern problems on numerous occasions and in various forums, but perhaps nowhere as clearly as in the preface to the volume of essays he edited on *Culture in the South* (Chapel Hill: University of North Carolina Press, 1935). An understanding of Couch's perception of Southern needs and his attitudes to various proposed solutions helps explain the intellectual context in which he developed the life-history program.

Had there been no Federal Writers' Project, there would have been no Southern life-history program. The history of this experiment in the government's relationship to the arts and in creative ways of handling unemployment has only begun to receive critical examination, and much remains to be done. Several studies examine the genesis, growth, and demise of the Federal Writers' Project. Jerre Mangione's *The Dream and the Deal: The Federal Writers' Project, 1935–1943* (Boston: Little, Brown and Co., 1972) is a lively history and a loving tribute to the project. This study by the former national coordinating editor of the Writers' Project is rich in anecdotal material and shows extensive research. Two more formal studies are: Kathleen O'Connor McKinzie's "Writers on Relief, 1935–1942" (Ph.D. dissertation, Indiana University, 1970), which covers with ample documentation and detail areas that Mangione slides over, and Ronald Warren Taber's evaluation of the activities of the Writers' Project in one region, "The Federal Writers' Project in the Pacific Northwest: A Case Study" (Ph.D. dissertation, University of Washington, 1969). William F. McDonald has patched together in a haphazard and undigested fashion the unfinished work of the team of historians that the American Council of Learned Societies originally had hired to write a history of all the New Deal Arts Projects. McDonald's *Federal Relief Administration and the Arts: The Origins and Administrative History of the Arts Projects of the Works Progress Administration* (Columbus: Ohio State University Press, 1969) promises more than it delivers and must be used with caution. Monty Penkower's study, *The Federal Writers' Project: A Study in Government Patronage of the Arts* (Urbana: University of Illinois Press, 1977), offers an exhaustive examination of the organizational and administrative aspects of the Writers' Project. These studies taken together clarify the goals and organization of the Project, but they largely ignore the work of the Project.

The publications of the Writers' Project have not yet received the extended analysis they merit as a part of our cultural history. In his dissertation-in-progress, "Portrait of America: The Federal Writers' Project, 1935–1943," Jerrold Hirsch shifts the focus to the cultural and creative aspects of the Writers' Project. Tom Terrill is currently analyzing the portrayal of textile workers in the Southern life-history program.

The life histories are part of the evidence that the Writers' Project, in addition to providing economic relief, produced work of lasting value. They are a contribution to our understanding of Southern history, of American life during the Great Depression, and of the lives of anonymous Americans.

There are numerous works on Southern history that provide the larger context of events illuminated by these individual stories. The starting point in this area is C. Vann Woodward's *Origins of the New South, 1877–1913* and George B. Tindall's *The Emergence of the New South, 1913–1945*, vols. 9 and 10 of *A History of the South*, edited by Wendell Holmes Stephenson and E. Merton Coulter (Baton Rouge: Louisiana State University Press, 1948–1967). Still relevant are Rupert B. Vance's *Human Geography of the South: A Study in Regional Resources and Human Adequacy*, 2d ed. (Chapel Hill: University of North Carolina Press, 1935), and Howard Odum's *Southern Regions of the United States* (Chapel Hill: University of North Carolina Press, 1936). These two studies contain a wealth of information, and they illustrate the regional approach to Southern studies. This approach reached its zenith in the 1930s. It should be viewed in contrast to the Agrarian approach of *I'll Take My Stand*.

Although much has been written about Southern "problems"—economic, social, and racial—much of the cultural and social history of the region is still to be written. The lives of ordinary Southerners and their communities have been examined by sociologists and novelists, but too rarely by historians. The unpublished life histories await the historian who will use them as a source for the writing of Southern cultural, social, and labor history in the way that Eugene Genovese used the ex-slave narratives to write a cultural and social history of American slavery. The collection of essays in *Culture in the South* are still valuable as an introduction to Southern cultural and social history. And B. A. Botkin's *A Treasury of Southern Folklore* (New York: Crown Publishers, 1949) is full of evocative material, whether it all fits in the modern scholars' definition of folklore or not, and Botkin comments perceptively on Southern life and folkways. Recent works like Eugene Genovese's *Roll, Jordan, Roll: The World the Slaves Made* (New York: Pantheon Books, 1974) and Herbert G. Gutman's *The Black Family in Slavery and Freedom, 1750–1925* (New York: Pantheon Books, 1976) focus on slavery but have much to say about black culture in later periods. Lawrence Levine's *Black Culture and Black Consciousness: Afro-American Folk Thought from Slavery to Freedom* (New York: Oxford University Press, 1977) is an innovative study, using folklore to understand the black experience.

Many sociologists in the 1930s made detailed examinations of various aspects of Southern life. Hortense Powdermaker's *After Freedom: A Cultural Study in the Deep South* (New York: Viking Press, 1939) examines race relations in a small Southern town. Gunnar Myrdal et al., *An American Dilemma: The Negro Problem and Modern Democracy*, 2 vols. (New York: Harper & Brothers, 1944), is an outstanding and world-famous study that synthesizes the work of numerous scholars. Though it examines the "problem" from a national perspective, it has much to say about the South.

A plethora of studies was also published in the 1930s dealing with the textile industry and the farm-tenant system. Some of the better studies saw the cotton mills and cotton tenantry as a social as well as an economic system. Liston Pope's *Millhands and Preachers: A Study of Gastonia* (New Haven, Conn.: Yale University Press, 1942) examines the relationships between work, status, and religion in mill-village life. John R. Earle, Dean D. Knudsen, and Donald W. Shriver, Jr., *Spindles and Spires: A Re-Study of Religion and Social Change in Gastonia* (Atlanta: John Knox Press, 1976), reexamines and extends the questions Pope's study raised. Charles S. Johnson, Edwin R. Embree, and Will Alexander, *The Collapse of Cotton Tenancy: A Summary of Field Studies and Statistical Surveys, 1933–1935* (Chapel Hill: University of North Carolina Press, 1935), gained national attention for a serious problem. The theme of Arthur Raper's case study of tenant farming, *Preface to Peasantry: A Tale of Two Black Belt Counties* (Chapel Hill: University of North Carolina Press, 1936), is stated in the title. Margaret Hagood, *Mothers of the South: Portraiture of the White Tenant Farm Woman* (Chapel Hill: University of North Carolina Press, 1939), deals with women of the rural South. W. W. Norton & Co. has recently published an illustrated edition (1977) with an introduction by Anne F. Scott. New Deal agricultural policies intensified the plight of Southern tenant farmers. The Southern Tenant Farmers' Union protested policies that primarily benefited landlords. Donald H. Grubbs's *Cry from the Cotton: The Southern Tenant Farmers' Union and the New Deal* (Chapel Hill: University of North Carolina Press, 1971) is a detailed account of the union, a study of rural life in the Cotton Belt, and the New Deal agricultural program in the South.

Writers helped make the economic plight of the South a symbol of the nation's problems. Erskine Caldwell's novel of tenant farming, *Tobacco Road* (New York: Duell, Sloan and Pearce, 1932), and his novel about rural people in a mill village, *God's Little Acre* (New York: Grosset & Dunlap, 1933), combined the comic and the grotesque, sex and social protest, in a manner that aroused popular interest and attracted other writers to this material. In his review of *These Are Our Lives*, "Realities on Tobacco Road," in *Saturday Review of Literature*, 27 May 1939, Virginius Dabney argued, like many other Southerners, that Caldwell and writers like him presented a distorted picture of Southern life. Sylvia Jenkins Cook's *From Tobacco Road to Route 66: The Southern Poor White in Fiction* (Chapel Hill: University of North Carolina Press, 1976) tries to relate the poor white novels of the 1930s to an older Southern literary tradition of writings about poor whites. Like *These Are Our Lives*, James Agee's classic *Let Us Now Praise Famous Men: Three Tenant Families* (Boston: Houghton Mifflin Co., 1966) rejected the basic assumptions of much of the literature about poor Southerners. But unlike the Project Writers, Agee was preoccupied with the moral and aesthetic issues he felt he had to face in writing about the poor. Agee's preoccupations dominate the book, and the tenants rarely speak for themselves.

There is also a vast literature that tries to answer the question, What, if anything, makes Southerners, white and black, different from other Americans—climate, history, race relations? Those who want to pursue the question can start with Wilbur J. Cash, *The Mind of the South* (New York: Alfred A. Knopf, 1941), John Shelton Reed, *The Enduring South: Subcultural Persistence in Mass Society* (Lexington, Mass.: D. C. Heath & Company, 1972), and George B. Tindall, *The Ethnic Southerners* (Baton Rouge: Louisiana State University Press, 1976).

Readers who wish to place the life histories in the context of the 1930s can begin with the following works. The best survey of the New Deal is William E. Leuchtenburg's *Franklin D. Roosevelt and the New Deal, 1932–1940* (New York: Harper & Row, 1963). Paul Conkin's *The New Deal* (New

York: Thomas Y. Crowell Co., 1970) is a stimulating interpretative essay and commentary on the scholarship on the subject. Works dealing with the cultural and social history of the period are plentiful, but of varying merit. Dixon Wecter's *The Age of the Great Depression, 1929–1941* (New York: Macmillan Co., 1948) contains a wealth of material and offers some thoughtful observations. Caroline Bird's *The Invisible Scar* (New York: David McKay Co., 1966) probes the impact of poverty on attitudes and behavior. The articles collected in Bernard Sternsher, ed., *Hitting Home: The Great Depression in Town and Country* (Chicago: Quadrangle Books, 1970), analyze the impact of the depression in various parts of the nation.

Numerous anthologies offer the reader a chance to examine primary materials and a variety of views of the 1930s, some contemporary to the period and some based on historical study. Not only were the 1930s a period in which a poor tenant farmer lamented "Ain't Got No Screens," they were also the age of Amos and Andy, the Gashouse Gang, the Dust Bowl, the sit-down strikes, and the Spanish civil war. Two anthologies that offer a varied picture of life in America during the Great Depression are Daniel Aaron and Robert Bendiner, eds., *The Strenuous Decade: A Social and Intellectual Record of the Nineteen-Thirties* (Garden City, N.Y.: Doubleday & Co., Anchor Books, 1970), and Don Congdon, ed., *The Thirties: A Time to Remember* (New York: Simon and Schuster, 1962). Selections in Louis Filler, ed., *The Anxious Years: America in the Nineteen Thirties: A Collection of Contemporary Writing* (New York: G. P. Putnam's Sons, 1963), and Harvey Swados, ed., *The American Writer and the Great Depression* (Indianapolis: Bobbs-Merrill Co., 1966), show how writers viewed the depression.

The Federal Writers' Project and its various endeavors such as the American Guide Series and the life-history program reveal part of the impact of the depression on American culture and how Americans looked at their culture. Cultural historians have found in the popular and high culture of the 1930s an emphasis on cultural nationalism, the documentary approach to art and life, and an anthropological definition of culture. Important works in this area are Richard Pell's *Radical Visions and American Dreams: Culture and Social Thought in the Depression Years* (New York: Harper & Row, 1973), William Stott's *Documentary Expression in Thirties America* (New York: Oxford University Press, 1973), and Warren Sussman's "The Thirties" in Stanley Coben and Lorman Ratner, eds., *The Development of an American Culture* (Englewood Cliffs, N.J.: Prentice-Hall, 1970), pp. 179–218.

Finally, Studs Terkel's *Hard Times: An Oral History of the Great Depression* (New York: Pantheon Books, 1970) reveals some of what people remember about the depression—about what that experience has come to mean to the generation of Americans who lived through that period and what it has meant to their children. In a sense *Hard Times* can be read as a sequel to *Such As Us*, but the life-history program can also be seen as a precursor of *Hard Times*.

The life histories are an early example of oral history, though no one used that term in the 1930s. Like other examples of documentary art, they are democratic in approach. They dignify the ordinary. They attach importance to the common man's point of view. Culture, here, is no longer viewed as knowledge of the achievement of dead intellectuals and artists. And the recounting of an individual life history could be viewed as a worthwhile and creative contribution to the general culture. Such works as Theodore Rosengarten's *All God's Dangers: The Autobiography of Nate Shaw* (New York: Alfred A. Knopf, 1975) and Robert Coles's *Migrants, Sharecroppers, Mountaineers* (Boston: Little, Brown and Co., 1971) and *The South Goes North* (Boston: Little, Brown and Co., 1971) share in this tradition and contribute to our knowledge of Southern history.

Oral history can be used to reveal the history of individuals, communities, and events that would otherwise be forgotten. And it can radically alter views of history based primarily on the written records left by a small elite. A good example is Lawrence C. Goodwyn's "Populist Dreams and Negro Rights: East Texas as a Case Study," *American Historical Review* 76 (1971):1435–56. Methodological problems and research possibilities are discussed in Ronald Grele, "A Surmisable Variety: Interdisciplinarity and Oral Testimony," *American Quarterly* 27 (1975):275–95. Oral history conferences and the establishment of programs for collecting oral history have increased rapidly in recent years. To keep up with this field one should consult the *Oral History Newsletter* and Gary L. Shumway, comp., *Oral History in the United States: A Directory* (New York: New York Oral History Association, 1971). In the field of Southern history, the Southern Oral History Program at The University of North Carolina at Chapel Hill and the Oral History Program at Duke University do extensive interviewing and have important collections of transcribed interviews.

Index

A

Accidents, industrial, 139–41, 159, 191, 195, 202–3, 273; compensation for, 192–93, 196
Adultery, 176, 209, 213, 219–20, 225–26
Agrarians, xix
Agriculture. *See* Farming; Landlord (farm); New Deal, farm programs; Tenant farmers; Tobacco farming
Agricultural and Technical College of North Carolina, 257, 272
Alcohol, problems associated with, xvi, 59, 60, 62, 97, 98, 114, 151, 156, 226, 229, 232, 257, 266, 274. *See also* Violence
American Federation of Labor, 183
Anderson, Sherwood, xix
Athens Manufacturing Company, 147, 148
Atlanta, after the Civil War, 24
Auburn Polytechnic Institute, 131
Automobile, 56, 64, 65, 66, 91, 98, 146, 246

B

Beatty, "Tinker Dave," 14n
Black Draught (medicine for constipation), 79
Blacklisting, 186
Blacks, 103, 108–9, 207, 226, 233, 241, 254, 276; views of New Deal, xv; race relations in Big Ivy, Tennessee, 4; white views of, 14, 45–46, 48–49, 66, 74, 84, 106, 133–34, 232; views of whites, 25, 26, 27–28, 220, 224, 232; fear of whites, 27; discrimination against, 55, 120, 247, 277–78; view of race relations in heaven, 84–85; conflict with white landlords, 42, 55,

56–57, 80–85, 87–90; violence among, 208–9; disfranchised, 237, 240, 262–63; white supremacy over, 237–38; white violence toward, 257–58, 267; feelings of inferiority, 255–56, 258–59. *See also* Civil War; Discrimination; New Deal; Religion; Slavery; Slaves
Black Tongue (pellagra), 36
Bloomfield, R. L., 148, 149, 150, 152, 156
Boll weevil, 75, 77, 248. *See also* Farming
Botkin, Benjamin Albert, quoted, xvi
Brown v. *Board of Education*, xv, 241
Burial, 84, 154, 178, 225, 253, 258. *See also* Death; Funerals
Burial insurance, 91, 126
Burlington Mills (Burlington, North Carolina), 173

C

Caldwell, Erskine, xix, xxi
Calomel (a purgative), 110
Cardui calendar, 11
Childbirth, description of, 227. *See also* Family
Child labor, 131, 149, 150, 173, 206–7, 229, 244. *See also* Children
Child rearing, xvii, 95, 96, 105, 123; corporal punishment, 207, 222. *See also* Children
Children, 74, 86, 130, 182, 215, 226, 271, 273; parents' expectations for, xvi, 126, 131, 248, 257, 271, 274; parents' views of, xvii, 16–17, 51, 64, 91, 101, 131, 168, 185–86, 217; education of, 12, 25, 62–63, 73, 91–92, 126, 155, 177, 229, 244, 248–49, 257; care for parents, 34, 73, 153, 253; health of, 110. *See also* Child labor; Child rearing; Education; Family

Chowan College, 73
Church, 157, 161, 162, 169, 176, 189. *See also* Occupations, preacher; Religion
Civilian Conservation Corps, xiv, 114. *See also* New Deal
Civil rights movement, 241. *See also* Discrimination, racial
Civil War, 9, 12, 33, 150, 171, 267; battles of, 13, 14, 18, 33; prison experience, 14; ex-slave's experience of, 18; slaves celebrate end of, 19–21
Clothes, 32, 94, 126–27, 152, 155, 225, 231
Coal mining, 128–43; contracts in, 141; pillars in, 141; strike in, 142; price of coal, 142. *See also* Occupations
Colored Methodist Episcopal Church (Atlanta, Georgia), 24
Cone, Benjamin, 165
Cone, Caesar, 164, 165, 174, 177, 185
Cone, Herman, 161
Cone, Julius, 188
Cone, Moses, 164
Cone Mills (Greensboro, North Carolina), 157–89
Congress of Industrial Organizations, 201
"Conjure," 92–93. *See also* Superstition
Cotton, 4, 43, 75, 77; futures, 50, 51. *See also* Cotton mills
Cotton mills, xiii–xiv, 144–85; hiring whites only, xii, 119; wages in, xii–xiv, 147, 148, 149, 150, 151, 153, 154, 155, 175; paternalism in, xiv, 148–49, 175; unions, xiv, 163–64, 178, 182, 183, 184, 185, 187, 188–89; family work unit, 119, 147–48, 149; growth of, 119; post-World War I decline of, 120; stretch-out, 146, 178–79, 180, 181–82, 183; mechanization of, 147, 152, 154–55; child labor in, 149, 150, 173; strikes in, 149–50, 163, 165, 180–81; beamer, 150; spinner, 150; slasher, 150, 151; working conditions in, 155, 178–80; company-supported churches, 157, 161, 176, 189; farmers move to, 158, 160, 172–73; company welfare programs, 161, 173–74; card-rooms, 163; company stores, 164; battery fillers, 179; weave room, 178–80; blacklisting in, 186
Couch, William Terry, xviii, xix–xx, xxi
Courtship, 14–15, 26–27, 72, 81–82, 128–29, 211–12. *See also* Marriage

D

Death, 29, 34, 72, 83, 111, 129, 136, 153, 172, 215, 216, 225, 253. *See also* Funerals; Widowhood
Democratic party, 52, 112, 237, 264, 268, 276. *See also* Voting
Dialect, xxiii, xxvi (n. 20)
Diet, 32, 91, 103, 104, 105, 125, 126, 144, 174, 270, 271
Diphtheria, 36. *See also* Health problems
Discrimination, racial, xii, 55, 119, 120, 247, 277, 278. *See also* Jim Crow
Divorce, xvi, 269. *See also* Marriage
Doctor. *See* Health problems; Medical care
Duke University Hospital (Durham, North Carolina), 110

E

Education, 46–47, 52, 173, 191; level of, 97, 109, 131, 172, 173, 182, 221, 229, 244, 248–49, 257, 272; attitudes toward, 131, 159, 226, 249, 252, 257, 258; adult, 131–32, 138, 245; compulsory school law debated, 177; black high school, 275–76. *See also* Children, education of; Literacy; Religion; Sunday school; Slaves, education of
Entertainment, 4, 12, 32, 146, 275; play parties, 4, 12; court trial, 5, 266; market days, 5; movies, 93, 145; baseball, 155, 252; fishing, 106; hunting, 106; gambling, 208; shake-down dance, 228; Eagle Rock dance, 230

F

Family, xvi, 74, 147–48, 227; sex roles in, xvi, 96–98, 144–46, 233; description of ancestors, 3, 12, 33, 58, 61, 87–88, 92, 100, 109, 128, 131, 147–48, 150, 152, 171–72, 221, 222, 228–29, 243, 255–56, 271, 272; size of, 12, 31, 74, 86–87, 88, 177, 229; adopted children, 74, 103–4, 129, 130; illegitimate children, 74. *See also* Child rearing; Children; Cotton mills; Divorce; Education; Marriage; Widowhood
Farming, 41, 45, 103–15, 135–36, 137–38, 143, 244–45, 247, 248; migration from, xiv, 41, 119, 121; attitudes toward, 3, 61, 108, 109, 137–38, 143, 187, 260; declining prices, 43; crop diversification, 43, 75, 105, 137; future

of, 67, 77–78; compared to city life, 121, 124–25; compared to work in cotton mills, 160–62. *See also* Land; Landlord (farm); New Deal, farm programs; Tenant farmers; Tobacco farming

Federal Emergency Relief Administration, 138

Federal Writers' Project, xi, xviii, 238–39

Flood, 54–55

Forrest, Nathan Bedford, 14

Fox, George, 171

Funerals, 136–37, 250–51. *See also* Burial; Death

Furniture, 11, 54, 60, 61, 79, 87, 126, 170, 205. *See also* Housing

G

Gardening, 91, 146, 152, 174, 176, 273

Gardner, O. Max, 164

Ghosts (ha'nts), 30, 92

Gin and planing mill, 270, 272

Gorman, Francis J., 184

Grandfather clause, 262. *See also* Jim Crow; Voting

Great Depression, xiv, 119, 120, 165–66, 200

Greene, William, 183

Greensboro Daily News, 165n, 181

H

Harris, Bernice Kelly, xx, xxv (n. 12)

Harrison, Benjamin, 245

Health problems, 36, 64, 65, 72, 82–83, 86, 91, 101, 110, 111, 112, 149, 154, 158, 179, 180, 226, 260, 261, 273. *See also* Medical care

Hickory Grove Methodist Church (Pleasant Hill, North Carolina), 114

Hitler, Adolf, 52

Hoey, Clyde R., 164

Hog killing, 90–91, 104, 112–13

Hoover, Herbert, 165, 167

Housing, 51, 54, 55–56, 60, 79, 86, 122, 134, 143, 148, 157, 170, 178, 197, 205, 254. *See also* Furniture

Hunger, 175, 207

I

I'll Take My Stand: The South and the Agrarian Tradition, xix

Income, xii, 120, 187, 190, 200, 223, 274–75; in the South, xii, 120; of farmers, xiii, 64, 248; in cotton mills, xiii–xiv, 149, 150, 151, 153, 155, 161, 169; of tenant farmers, 41, 56, 66, 70, 73–74, 88–90; of hired farm labor, 41, 191, 244; of junk dealer, 49; of auctioneer, 52; of landlord, 65, 67–68, 70; of tobacco farmer, 102; in steam laundry, 124; of repairman, 125; of coal miner, 132–34, 138, 139, 141, 143; of preacher, 161, 169; in oil industry, 190, 191, 195, 197, 198, 199, 200, 201, 202; of logger, 206; of chimney sweep, 231; of mail carrier, 247; in boiler room, 248; in gin mill, 270; of day laborer, 272; of cook, 274; from washing people's clothes, 274. *See also* New Deal; Occupations; Relief

Insurance, 221, 252

Interviewers, xx–xxi, xxiv

J

Jews, xxii, 49

Jim Crow, 237, 258. *See also* Discrimination, racial; Voting

K

Kimball House (Atlanta, Georgia), 24

Kitchin, William, 261

Knights of Gideon (organization), 275

Knox Institute (Athens, Georgia), 244

Ku Klux Klan, 4. *See also* Blacks

L

Land: ownership of, 35, 64, 99, 109, 112, 114, 172, 248, 260, 272. *See also* Farming; Landlord (farm); New Deal; Tenant farmers

Landlord (farm), 41–42, 55, 56, 64–78, 256; view of tenants, 65–67, 68–71, 73, 77. *See also* Farming; Land; Tenant farmers

Landon, Alfred, 277

Lay My Burden Down, xviii

Lee, General Robert E., 33

Lewis, John L., 164

Lewis, Sinclair, xix

Literacy, 21, 33, 37, 46–47, 58, 127, 158, 221–22, 256. *See also* Education; Religion; Slaves, education of

Lynching, 267. *See also* Blacks

M

McDaniel, William, xxi

McGovern, George, 241

Main Street, xix

Marriage, 16, 33, 64, 100, 109, 173, 227, 244, 251, 256, 261, 268–69, 273; relationship described, xvi, 96–98; husband's view of, 72, 110–11, 215, 216, 232, 260; wife's view of, 83–84, 220–21, 226; wife-beating, 98, 215, 216, 228, 265–66; common law, 124. *See also* Divorce; Family; Widowhood

Masons (organization), 266–67

Medical care, 36, 91, 98, 110, 112, 191–92, 196, 253, 260, 261. *See also* Health problems; Root doctor

Mitchell, H. L., 43

Moore, Ida, xx

Morris Brown College (Atlanta, Georgia), 24

Mules, 45–53, 61, 108; blacks compared to, 45–46, 48–49; origins of, 46; price of, 48; judging of, 48–49

N

Negroes. *See* Blacks; Slavery; Slaves

New Deal, xiv, xv, xviii, 97, 220, 231, 237; relief programs, xiv, 5, 28, 37, 80, 114, 138; farm programs, xv, 43, 56, 70, 102, 112; landlord's view of, 70, 76, 77; labor laws, 187. *See also* Relief

Northampton County (North Carolina), discussion of politics and race in, 238–41

O

Occupations: preacher, 11–17, 157–69, 249–51; yardman, 25; domestic help, 25, 34, 83, 219–26, 232, 274; plasterer, 28; hired farm labor, 41, 191, 244; horse and mule trader, 45–53; junk dealer, 49–50; bank director, 50; liquor business, 50, 126; auctioneer, 52; tenant farmer, 58–63, 79–93, 272; mechanic, 59, 245; landlord, 64–78; tobacco farmer, 94–102, 254–59; housework, 96–97, 125, 144–46, 271; farmer, 103–15, 248; cotton mill worker, 109, 119, 147–56; oil rig builder, 119, 190–204; repairman, 121, 125; steam laundry worker, 124; coal mines, 128–43; blacksmith, 131; teacher, 132, 139; coal mine shift leader, 134; coal mine foreman, 138; coal mine loader, 138; coal mine superintendent, 142; cotton mill beamer, 150; cotton mill spinner, 150; cotton mill slasher, 150, 151; cotton

mill battery filler, 179; oil rig contractor, 191; oil crew pusher, 191, 198; carpenter, 194; oil driller, 195; oil foreman, 199; logger, 205–18; circus laborer, 207; chimney sweep, 227–33; railroad roundhouse worker, 228, 230; mail carrier, 245–47; boiler room worker, 248; justice of the peace, 265–66; gin mill worker, 270, 272; brick layer, 272; day laborer, 272

Odd Fellow (organization), 275

Odum, Howard, xviii

Old age, 3–5, 11–17, 28, 29, 30, 35, 36, 37, 83, 103, 110, 153, 252, 253

Osage Nation, 196, 197

P

Parent Teacher Association, 276

Parker's Chapel Baptist Church (Seaboard, North Carolina), 34

Peace Chapel (Pleasant Hill, North Carolina), 114

Peanut farming, 75. *See also* Farming

Pellagra (black tongue), 36

Pilgrim Glory (Hard Shell Baptist) Church (Big Ivy, Tennessee), 4

Politics, 112, 240, 252–53, 261, 262, 264. *See also* Voting

"Poor white," self-concept of, 61–62

Premarital sex, 74, 222, 229

Primitive Baptist Church (Union, Tennessee), 12

Proximity Mills (Greensboro, North Carolina), 173

Public Works Administration, 99. *See also* New Deal

Q

Quilting, 157

R

Ransom, General Matthew Whitaker, 33

Ransom, General Robert, Jr., 33

Reconstruction, 240, 245, 263

Red Shirts, 262

Relief, 5, 228; attitudes toward, xiv, 80, 113–14, 270–71; in cotton mills, 154; cotton mill church poundings, 161, 162, 169; discrimination in administration of, 277. *See also* New Deal

Religion, 19, 22–23, 52–53, 92, 115, 230; church attendance, 4, 14, 126–27, 222, 226; denominations described, 4, 16; belief in afterlife, 11–12, 21, 84–85,

114–15, 127; prayer, 13, 18, 21, 166, 175–76, 214, 222, 232, 274; salvation, 13, 15, 34–35, 208, 214–15, 217; call to preach, 16, 158; baptism, 16, 252; during slavery, 26, 32, 33; revival, 115, 252; Sunday school, 155, 156, 158, 274; tithing, 162; morality, 168–69, 214; sermon, 167–68. *See also* Church

Republican party, 4, 245, 263. *See also* Voting

Roosevelt, Franklin D., 28, 52, 80, 112, 165, 167, 237, 264–65, 277, 278

Root doctor (witch doctor), 22–24. *See also* Superstition

Russell, Daniel L., 240

S

Saint Mary's Church (Athens, Georgia), 155

Scalawag, 263

Shady Grove (Missionary Baptist) Church (Big Ivy, Tennessee), 4, 14

Slavery, 12, 243, 272; memory of compared with freedom, 31; overseer, 22, 31, 32, 150; patroller (paderoller), 32; white attitudes toward, 61, 171; folklore about, 165. *See also* Blacks; Slaves

Slaves: experience of Civil War, 18, 19, 21; attitude toward master, 18, 26–27; attitude toward mistress, 20, 31; education of, 21, 33; resisting system, 22; unity of, 22, 26; punishment of, 22, 32, 92; auction of, 25, runaway, 26; courtship among, 26–27; working in the great house, 31; anticipating the Civil War, 33. *See also* Blacks; Slavery

"Slinging pans," 221, 224, 225, 232

Smallpox, cemetery for victims of, 253. *See also* Burial; Death

Smith, Alfred E., 264–65n

Smith, Ellison D. "Cotton Ed," 237, 238

Southern Manufacturing Company (Athens, Georgia), 152, 153

Southern Tenant Farmers' Union, 41, 43, 56

Streetcars, 24–25

"Stretch-out." *See* Cotton mills

Strikes, 142, 149–50, 180–81, 188, 201. *See also* Coal mining; Cotton mills; Unionization

Sunday school, 155, 156, 158, 274. *See also* Religion

Superstition, 22–24, 30, 92–93

T

Tate, Allen, quoted, xxiv

Taxes, 75–76, 113, 267

Tenant farmers, 41, 42, 43, 54–57, 58–63, 64–65, 73–74, 79–93, 272; literature on, xix; wages of, 41, 69–70, 90; moving, 58, 59, 60, 70–71, 72, 80, 86; view of landlord, 42, 62, 80–81, 87–91; burn landlord's barn, 42, 82. *See also* Farming; Landlord (farm); New Deal; Tobacco farming

Tennessee Valley Authority, 4

Textorion, 184

These Are Our Lives, xi, xii, xviii, xx, xxii

Tobacco: loopers, 94; slide, 94; stringing, 94–95; sticks of, 95; trucks, 96; worming, 96; price of, 101. *See also* Tobacco farming

Tobacco farming, 94–102, 254–59; attitudes toward, 100, 102; future of, 102. *See also* Farming; Tobacco

Tobacco Road, xix, xxi

Turner, Nat, 29, 31, 32, 239

U

Unionization, efforts at: in cotton mills, xiv, 120, 163, 178, 182; in coal mines, 142; collective bargaining, 143; in oil industry, 202. *See also* Unions

Unions: attitudes toward, 187, 188–89, 202; accident prevention, 202, 203, 204. *See also* Unionization, efforts at

United Textile Workers, 184

University of North Carolina Press, xviii

V

Vance, Rupert, xviii

Violence: in fights, 17, 207–8, 210; against slaves, 22, 32, 92; feuds, 123; against children, 207, 222; in fight over a woman, 209; murder, 266–67; lynching, 267. *See also* Alcohol; Blacks; Marriage, wife-beating

Voting, 237, 262, 263, 268, 276. *See also* Blacks; Democratic party; Politics; Republican party

W

White Oak Baptist Church (Greensboro, North Carolina), 169

White Oak Mills (Greensboro, North Carolina), 165, 169, 173, 178

Widowhood, 34, 72, 84, 99, 103, 109, 129

Winesburg, Ohio, xix

Work, attitudes toward, 34, 97, 98, 131, 244

Works Progress Administration, xiv, xv, xviii, 97, 220, 231. *See also* New Deal; Relief

World War I, effect on cotton, 51

World War II, effect on the South, xi, xv

Y

Yankees, slaves' attitudes toward, 19–20, 27, 33. *See also* Slaves

You Have Seen Their Faces, xix

Younger generation, as described by older people, 4–5, 25, 35. *See also* Old age

Z

Zion Travelers Baptist Church (New Orleans, Louisiana), 219

Credits for Photographs

Farm Security Administration photograph by Dorothea Lange, from Howard W. Odum, Subregional Photographic Study 3167-B, Photograph no. 319. Courtesy of the Southern Historical Collection, University of North Carolina Library, Chapel Hill. /frontispiece

Photograph by Walker Evans, from Farm Security Administration Collection, LC-USF342-8056A. Courtesy of the Library of Congress, Washington, D.C. /p. 7

Farm Security Administration photograph by unknown photographer, from Howard W. Odum, Subregional Photographic Study 3167-B, Photograph no. 99. Courtesy of the Southern Historical Collection, University of North Carolina Library, Chapel Hill. /p. 39

Farm Security Administration photograph by Marion Post, from Howard W. Odum, Subregional Photographic Study 3167-B, Photograph no. 530. Courtesy of the Southern Historical Collection, University of North Carolina Library, Chapel Hill. /p. 117

Farm Security Administration photograph by Marion Post, from Howard W. Odum, Subregional Photographic Study 3167-B, Photograph no. 541. Courtesy of the Southern Historical Collection, University of North Carolina Library, Chapel Hill. /p. 235